The New Question Box

Answers for Today's Catholic

John J. Dietzen

The New Question Box

Answers for Today's Catholic

Nihil Obstat: Msgr. R. G. Peters
Imprimatur: ✝ Edward W. O'Rourke
            Bishop of Peoria
            June 30, 1981

The Nihil Obstat and the Imprimatur are official declarations that a book
or pamphlet is free of doctrinal or moral error. No implication is contained therein that those who have granted the Nihil Obstat and
Imprimatur agree with the contents, opinions or statements expressed.

Library of Congress Cataloging in Publication Data:

Dietzen, John J.
        The New Question Box
  A collection of writings from the author's syndicated column the
Question Box.
    Includes index.
    1. Catholic Church — Doctrinal and controversial works, Popular —
Miscellanea. I. Title.
BX1754.3.D52   230'.2   81-6785
ISBN O-940518-00-7   AACR2

Printed in the United States of America
First printing, July, 1981

Guildhall Publishers, Ltd.
Editorial Offices,
Box 325
Peoria, Illinois,
61651

PREFACE

Possibly few priests in the United States today are more aware of the spiritual and social issues that worry and wound Catholics in the 1980s than is Father John J. Dietzen, a parish pastor in Central Illinois, and author of the Question Box column carried in diocesan newspapers from coast to coast.

Syndicated by National Catholic News Service, Washington, D.C., the Question Box is read each week by millions of Catholics and other Christians, many of whom approach the author as a father-confessor, teacher, friendly counselor and guide, and who use him and his column as a sounding board for their views about the Catholic Church and society.

"The New Question Box" is a collection of five years of Father Dietzen's exchange, in print, with Catholics and other Christians of America — with readers who reveal anxieties, perplexities and frustrations, and who receive in return the information they seek, along with the gentle, sometimes strong, guidance and support of a caring priest.

Father Dietzen's background in the Catholic Press, parish work, and in family life programs in and outside of his diocese qualify him for his role as "pastor in print." A native of Danville, Illinois, he studied at St. Bede College, Peru, Illinois, and at St. Mary of the Lake Seminary in Mundelein, Illinois, before his ordination to the priesthood for the Diocese of Peoria in June, 1954. He holds a Master of Arts degree in English, and a Licentiate degree in Sacred Theology.

Father Dietzen's work as a priest includes 16 years as associate aditor of The Catholic Post, weekly newspaper of the Peoria diocese, and service to the Catholic Press Association as secretary and member of the board of directors. In the same period, he was responsible for the Family Life programs in his diocese, and gave pre-marriage, marriage and family life education programs in many cities. He also conducted seminars on marriage for the armed forces in Alaska, Japan and the Philippine Islands, and gave retreats to high school students, men and women and married couples in many parts of the country.

In 1973, Father Dietzen elected to re-enter parish work full time and was given charge of St. Mark's Church, Peoria, a position he still enjoys. He has a background in radio broadcasting, and has been a popular radio guest on topic shows in central Illinois, often appearing with clergy of other denominations in debates on timely subjects.

Father Dietzen began writing The Question Box column for The Catholic Post in 1975; it proved popular and was soon accepted by National Catholic News Service for nationwide distribution.

Not unexpectedly, the feature draws heavy mail from many parts of the country, and the author responds to his scattered "parish" of correspondents with the same sincerity and compassion he shares with the families of St. Mark's. Because readers have asked for his columns in book form, and because many letter writers ask questions he has answered previously and is unable to devote column space to again, this compilation of "The New Question Box" is appropriately timed.

Since this book contains nearly 500 questions and answers on a wide variety of subjects, any attempt at classification was necessarily rudimentary, and readers will find some topics treated in more than one chapter, but in every case from a viewpoint corresponding to the chapter theme. There is a detailed index.

"The New Question Box" — subtitled "Answers for Today's Catholic" — is offered by its publisher with the certainty that readers will find in it information both enlightening and entertaining, and that they will discover and welcome the comfort, security, and peace of heart and mind that a knowledge of their faith, and the answers to their questions, can bring.

Guildhall,
1981

INTRODUCTION

We Catholics, along with the rest of Christianity and the human race, have become so accustomed to changes during the past generation that we're tempted to forget what brought them about and what they are meant to accomplish. Looking back, I think most of us would agree that some serious re-thinking of who we are, and what we are about, was more than called for by the history of our time. The racism which has ravaged so many predominantly Christian nations (South Africa, Germany, and the United States, to mention only three) stands as but one of numerous messages to leaders and other members of the churches that something radical has been missing in the Christian's understanding of the relationship between the Gospel and life.

The experiences of World War II played a great role in those changes. Perhaps it was in the conversations, writings, and witness of martyrs like Protestant theologian Dietrich Bonhoeffer and Franciscan Father Maximilian Kolbe, both of whom died in the concentration camps of that war, that the long-germinating seeds of reform began to mature. At least it was in the experience of those years that one of the first lessons of a pilgrim and wounded church was learned: Numbers are no criterion of the quality of a Christian community.

Many more lessons followed this one, all of which to some degree affect the character and purpose of this book. Some further explanation of one in particular will be helpful. Whatever one's opinion of current directions in theology and Catholic teaching, one essential element of those directions is quite clear: The church places far more confidence in the judgment and faith of its members, indeed of all mankind, than it appeared to even a generation ago. The reasons for this are complex. Some of them result from the evident difficulty the teaching church experiences in being unified and clear about numerous areas of human moral activity, a difficulty it would have vehemently disclaimed not more than fifty years ago. In addition, whether one speaks of Scripture studies, interpretation and development of doctrine, professional ethics, the sacraments, or conjugal morality, the church has, far more than we sometimes realize, integrated into its life much that is good and useful from the insights of what has been called the "personalist revolution" of our time, insights which inspire a new respect for our human knowing, willing, and experiencing, as well as for our life of faith, our relationship to the Mystery of God.

While both of these — our human and participated Divine life — exist and interweave in all of us personally, they each deserve proper respect and integrity, a fact which has for too long gathered dust in the corner of Catholic and general Christian thinking. The "church," whatever meaning the individual Christian gave to that word, was to produce black-and-white, clear-cut answers on demand about any important human question — particularly questions about moral life.

During the last few generations, the Catholic Church has discovered through painful experience that such a view of the relationship between the church and its individual members is more than a little dangerous. As with all mysteries where two seemingly contradictory truths coexist, we must respect both truths and learn to live with, and profit from, the tensions between them. In a way similar, if only faintly analogous, to the humanity and divinity of Jesus, our life of grace coexists with our human activities of thinking, loving and planning; one cannot be melded into or absorbed by the other without crippling both our humanity and the Divine life which suffuses it. (The same mistake is frequently made, with even more disastrous results, in confusing the human and Divine elements of the church itself, when its human activities, signs, and procedures are too facilely and universally identified as acts of God himself.)

This broadening experience of a new dimension in its own life is nudging the church, often grudgingly, sometimes imperceptibly, but nevertheless relentlessly, to exciting new discoveries about itself, discoveries vastly enlarging its appreciation of the breadth and depth of the presence of the Holy Spirit in the People of God.

"The New Question Box" will, I hope, make a trustful, light-hearted enjoyment of the Catholic faith a little more available to the average Catholic in his or her daily living. It is therefore written from a pastoral viewpoint. Many large questions facing the church today are not dealt with at all (they will have to wait, perhaps, for a future volume). And none are discussed in a manner that could remotely be called exhaustive. One might best look on the work as a handbook of basic information and, where necessary, historical background needed by Christian, particularly Catholic, men and women in responding to some questions of conscience, belief and practice of their faith.

It does not mean to be a theological treatise, nor does it make a particular point of declaring for one side of controversy over another. It is intended to assist and encourage a frame of mind in which the Catholic Christian can function with fidelity to the teachings of the church and to his God-given intelligence, common sense and faith, and with confidence that any risks are taken in the shadow of the enduring love of a faithful God.

Lastly, my profound gratitude to those whose professional competence and generosity contributed to the preparation of "The New Question Box" and to the thousands of correspondents and many friends whose questions, insights and criticisms have made this book — and the column — possible. They, their crosses and their hopes, will always have a special place in my heart and in my prayers.

John J. Dietzen
July, 1981

TABLE OF CONTENTS

Chapter V: Right or Wrong?   133

Formation of conscience — age for serious sin — moral decision-making — pre-marital sex — living together — sterilization — hunger strikes — conscientious objection — cloning — abortion — Natural Family Planning — fast and abstinence — birth control — euthanasia — right to die — capital punishment — sin — scrupulosity — gossip — obscenity — Sunday rest — Catholic Social Doctrine — Masonic Order — dreams — Rosicrucians — Ku Klux Klan — healing by television ministry — masturbation — trans-sexual surgery — alcohol.

Chapter VI: Marriage and Family   179

Marriage vows — purposes of marriage — permanence — church regulations — marriage as sacrament — banns — preparation for marriage — divorce — remarriage after divorce — ministry to divorced — Beginning Experience — divorced in parish life — divorced and sacraments — rash judgment about remarried — annulments — responsibility of parents — interfaith marriage — promises in interfaith marriage — infidelity — Catholic marriage in Protestant church — birth control — onanism — alcoholism — illegitimacy.

Chapter VII: The Church   233

The People of God — "one, true Church" — magisterium — changes in the church — ecumenical councils — Roman Rota — priests — women in the church — Religious — permanent deacons — popes — Christian communities — infallibility — theologians — Baltimore Catechism — liturgy movement — dogma and theology — celibacy.

Chapter VIII: Ecumenism   277

"Roman Catholic" — interfaith Communion — Catholic participation in Protestant services — Protestant participation in Catholic services — women's ordination — World Council of Churches — interfaith marriage — use of Catholic churches.

Chapter IX: Death and Burial   299

Fear of eternity — cremation — anatomical gifts — limbo — funeral services for non-Catholics — funeral Masses — burial sites.

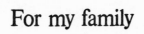

For my family

The Bible

Church and Sacred Scripture

A priest we know has said some things recently I would like to understand better. He said the church existed before the Bible, at least before the New Testament. I realize this is true. But today, he added, we can do without the Bible, but we cannot do without the church. This is more than my understanding of our faith can absorb. Could you tell me in more detail what he meant?

As you say, the church certainly existed before the New Testament was completed. Many Christians were born, lived and died before the last book of the Bible was even written somewhere at least 60 or 70 years after Jesus died. The Bible was not solidified in its present combination of books until centuries later.

The statement that the church could do without the Bible is, in my view, at least ambiguous. In a way, of course, he is right. Theoretically the church could do without the sacraments of baptism, penance, holy orders and possibly even the Eucharist. Who are we to say that the church could not have been formed in a variety of other ways than Jesus actually arranged?

The church which really exists, however, is unthinkable without all of these elements, and it is just as unthinkable without the Bible. Surely, the living community of faith with its leaders (particularly the pope and other bishops) will be the living carrier of the message and life of Christ to the world until the end of time. There is one sense, then, in which this living family of Christ will always be the final interpreter of the biblical word of God. It is equally true, however, that Scripture enshrines the teachings of the Lord and of the apostles with a special clarity and universality, so that it will be for all time the norm against which the church measures all its actions and its faith.

Whatever we propose as "might have been," the real church would soon be lost without Scripture. This is why the church has always venerated the Bible just as she venerates the body of Christ. "From the table of both the word of God and of the body of Christ she unceasingly receives and offers to the faithful the bread of life, especially in the sacred liturgy" (Dogmatic Constitution on Divine Revelation of Vatican II). The council document goes on to say that "all the preaching of the church must be nourished and ruled by sacred Scripture."

With this view of Scripture, it is impossible to understand how the church could get along without it. As that same constitution of the Vatican Council says, "It is clear that sacred tradition, sacred Scripture and the teaching authority of the church, in accord with God's most wise design, are so linked and joined together that one cannot stand without the others. All together and each in its own way under the action of the one Holy Spirit contribute effectively to the salvation of souls." (No. 10)

Biblical Literary Forms

I am sick and tired of hearing that the Bible is full of allegories and parables. If the word of God does not suit your 20th-century ungodly lay and scientific concept of the world and of God, don't snipple here and there to your liking. Don't you believe the Bible is the word of God?

I'm sorry you are sick and tired of hearing it, but the plain fact is that much of the Bible is made up of allegories and parables — and poetry, fictional short stories, speeches, fables, and numerous other forms of literature.

You are, of course, free to believe what you wish about the Bible, even take it as word-for-word history if you can figure out how to do that. But the church's teaching is clear: The "truth" the Bible expresses is to be found in the meaning that the sacred writers intended when they wrote that particular part of Scripture. And to arrive at that truth, one must investigate whether that writer was producing straight history, a fable with a moral lesson involved, poetry, or another kind of writing. Only then do we discover most accurately what God is saying to us.

I like the example of George Washington and the cherry tree. The "truth" of that story is not in the facts of the plot, but in what it says about George. Should a scientist some day prove there never was a cherry tree at Mount Vernon, our answer would be, "so what?" The story is not about a cherry tree, but about the honesty, integrity and nobility of the character of our first president. Furthermore, the man who thinks it is a tale about cherry trees and horticulture will miss the whole point.

Similarly, the man who thinks, for example, that the story of Jonah is mainly about man-swallowing whales and storms at sea will miss the real "truth" of the story which the author intended — that God's love for mankind is universal, and the many other revelations which that book so enchantingly unfolds. In that particular instance, it makes not one whit of difference whether the whale carried our hero around for three days, or whether there even was a Jonah in the first place.

As Vatican Council II teaches, it is in all these ways, including some sections of straight history, "that the books of Scripture must be acknowledged as teaching solidly, faithfully and without error that truth which God wanted put into the sacred writings for the sake of our salvation" (Constitution on Divine Revelation, paragraph 11).

The acceptance and proper understanding of the written word of God is naturally of primary importance to Catholics. If you're really interested in what the church teaches on the subject, read the "Constitution on Revelation" which I just quoted, or the encyclical "Divino Afflante Spiritu" of Pope Pius XII (1943). Any priest should be able to help you find at least one of these.

Bible Only For Experts?

You mentioned that in reading the Bible it is important that we have some idea of what the writer intended when he wrote a particular book, and how the people understood it then. How can an ordinary person be expected to know all this? Shouldn't we read the Bible unless we do know these things?

Reading the Bible in a spirit of prayer and faith in God's word is always good and fruitful. In fact, someone who approaches Scripture with this attitude will reap far more benefits than one who has a lot of technical knowledge about the Bible, but no faith.

However, at least a little information about the background of the Bible and its books can make the reading of Scripture more beneficial and prevent much confusion and misunderstanding. Very little of the Bible is "straight" history as we think of it. Most of it is poetry, parables, personal or community reflections on memorable events, legal documents, visions or other manifestations of what were interpreted as God's reactions to human happenings, prophecies veiled in extremely mystical symbols — and even efforts by ancient theologians to put together in a cohesive way this whole series of revelations and experiences.

Since, in addition, all of what is now in the Bible was handed down by writing or word of mouth during a period of thousands of years, it's obviously an advantage to know, for example, what *kind* of writing each book was meant to be, and even to know some of the historical circumstances of the time. A parallel might be a 1935 newspaper being read today by an older man and a high school freshman. The paper would be far more intelligible and significant to the man who experienced those years than to the 14-year-old who knows only the words he sees on the paper.

The Living Bible

I was given a "Living Bible" by a Protestant friend for Christmas. I know she gave it as a gift between two Christians, not trying to convert me.

I liked it because she said I should feel free to underline or mark words that moved me or had special meanings. So I did. Is this wrong? Is it wrong for me, as a Catholic, to be reading the "Living Bible." I'm in my teens.

The Bible was a thoughtful gift from your friend. You can, of course, read it. You might keep in mind a couple of thoughts as you do so, however.

Most Bibles printed under Protestant auspices omit several Old Testament books or parts of books that are in the Catholic Bible. Also good Catholic Bibles such as most editions of the latest translation published under the title "New American Bible" usually include numerous notes and background material which Protestant editions traditionally shy away from.

More importantly, you surely noticed that the "Living Bible" identifies itself in the opening pages as a paraphrase of Scripture. This means that instead of trying to give a faithful, modern translation of the actual biblical texts, the authors worked at giving the meaning of the text, even if that meant skipping, filling in, or otherwise shifting thoughts and words.

The "Living Bible" is a beautiful and helpful book. But as its preface admits, there are dangers as well as values in paraphrases: "A paraphrase is guided not only by the translator's skill in simplifying, but also by the clarity of his understanding of what the author meant, and by his theology."

Don't Fear Scripture

A group of us talked of starting a study club, at least during Lent, at which time we would study the Bible. Our plan was to read one of the Gospels or other books, especially the New Testament, discuss what it means and try to apply it to our lives.

A couple of the people involved didn't think we lay people should do something like this by ourselves. They say that without a priest we probably would get into heresy. The rest of us don't agree. What do you think?

I think your plan sounds most worthwhile and sincerely hope you will follow through. The combination of discussion on the meaning of Scripture, with some attempt at seeing how the word of God applies to our lives today, should make your meetings valuable to everyone who takes part.

I suggest that you use some text of Scripture that will assist you with basic background and explanatory notes. Several excellent booklets are in print for this purpose to assist groups such as yours. Some treat each book of the Old and New Testament separately. Others, for example, the fine monthly publication of Paulist Press, "Sharing the Word," are designed around the Scripture readings for the following Sunday's liturgy.

The St. Joseph edition of the New American Bible, for example, would probably enrich your discussions considerably because of the extensive helpful information it contains.

As for the concern of some of your group, you might remind them that heresies in the history of the church are generally started by priests and bishops, not by lay people. So don't let that fear stop you. Good luck!

Age of the Human Race

Last week's newspaper had a story about some people finding human skeletons that are supposed to be over three million years old. I don't know that much about the Bible, but a friend and I were discussing the article and she said that, according to the Bible, the whole world is only about 6,000 years old. I'm sure we don't believe that. At least I don't. But what can you say to someone like that? Is there any reason we can't believe that the human race is three million years old?

You raise a lot of big questions. Answers will vary greatly depending on one's understanding of the Scriptures, of religion, of God — and even of science.

There is absolutely nothing in our Catholic faith that would prevent us from accepting any age for the human race. The Bible was never meant by God to be a course in archeology, paleontology, or even of history, in our usual understanding of that word. It is a story of God's saving plan for mankind, wounded and crippled by his own selfishness and pride, and how that plan unfolded. It is a book of faith, not of technical information.

This goes especially for the first 11 chapters of Genesis, which "covers" the whole history of the world up to God's call of Abraham as the father of the Hebrew people somewhere around 1800 B.C. The great Jewish theologians who put those stories together (creation, the flood, etc.) several centuries before Christ, had many ancient myths and legends to go on, but basically they knew even less about the details of the origin of the world than we do.

This bothered them not in the least. Their purpose, under the inspiration of God, was to make believers, not scientists, out of their people.

There's no reason at all you cannot believe men and women were strolling the earth three million years ago — if you're satisfied with the scientific evidence.

To the other part of your question: If someone insists that every fact, figure, name and event in holy Scripture is technically, scientifically, and historically accurate, don't waste your time arguing about such things as the age of man. You're simply on different wave-lengths about the meaning of biblical truth.

Armageddon

A member of another religion mentioned to us about a battle of Armageddon, which is supposed to happen at the end of the world. She said it is in the Bible, but didn't explain any further except that they believe it will be a terrible conflict to separate the good people from the bad. Do you know what she was talking about?

The book of Revelation (chapter 16) speaks of a battle in the last stages of the world involving the devils and the kings of the world — "the great day of battle of God, the sovereign Lord." This event is to occur at a place called Armageddon.

As with so many parts of this highly symbolic book of visions, it is not easy to place what is said in any kind of clear historical or geographic context. The usual interpretation is that the word comes from the Hebrew "har Mageddo," or "mount of Mageddo." Mageddo was an ancient fortress-city of Palestine, overlooking the main pass through the Carmel mountain range. Thus it occupied a key position along the primary military and commercial route between Egypt and the rich countries of the Fertile Crescent.

Mageddo was captured and recaptured numerous times in its long history, and became somewhat synonymous with a battlefield. For this reason, it would be a likely symbol for the "ultimate conflict" between God and his friends, and the followers of the devil.

Were There Magi?

At Christmas time, a priest speaking on television said maybe there were no Magi who came to the crib of Christ. This story is in the Gospel. What does the church say about our belief in the Three Kings? Is it possible that the story did not really happen?

You've certainly asked a mouthful in a few words.

First, we're not speaking here about anything which is part of our required belief as Catholics or Christians. Particularly does it not involve any belief in "three kings." The Gospel of Matthew, the only one that tells this story, does not call them kings, nor does it say how many there were. Eastern Catholics, for example, traditionally speak of 12 kings, not three.

The answer to your question involves many technicalities of biblical interpretation referring to the literary form, or style of writing, used in this Gospel. We are fairly certain, from careful study of the Gospel and other documents written about the same time, that Matthew contains several examples of what is called "haggadic midrash" — that is, stories that are used to spin out and clarify the meaning of a particular event or teaching.

Such stories were intended to convey as clearly as possible the truth of the mystery being considered. They were not meant by their author to be taken literally, in our sense of the word, and were quite common among Jews as effective teaching tools.

One may believe that the story of the Magi happened exactly as it is described in the Gospel, or that it is partly made up but based on some actual journey of Magi to Jerusalem about the time of the birth of Jesus, or even that the story is legendary and intended to call attention to the fulfillment of the prophecies referred to by Matthew.

Any of these understandings is compatible with the Catholic understanding of the meaning and divine inspiration of the Bible.

The "Unforgivable" Sin

In the Gospel of St. Matthew (12,31), Jesus speaks of a sin "against the Holy Spirit," which will never be forgiven in this world or in the next. What is this unforgivable sin?

This passage has always caused discussion among Christians because it seems to contradict the numerous times Jesus clearly teaches that as long as a sinner is alive, there is hope for return to God if he only repents. In fact, the church has officially and formally taught precisely this at least since the year 251, when it condemned a heresy called Novatianism. According to this anti-Catholic teaching, anyone who renounced the Christian faith in time of persecution could never come back. The church rejected this, saying that repentance is always possible.

St. Augustine, St. Thomas Aquinas and many others believed that by the "sin against the Holy Spirit" Jesus meant the sin of final unrepentance, which is the refusal to repent of one's rejection of God through a serious sin, even at the moment of death. This probably is still the most common view, since it is a total, final rejection of all the helps the Holy Spirit offers us to turn away from evil and toward God.

Perhaps another way of saying the same thing is that anyone who deliberately and maliciously refuses the helps which the Holy Spirit gives to keep us from sin in the first place sins against the Holy Spirit. As St. Thomas says, many gifts of the Spirit are meant to help us avoid sin in our lives. The gift of hope keeps us from despair. The gift of fear of the Lord keeps us from presuming in the wrong way on God's mercy and love, and so on.

All these gifts, he tells us, are effects of the Holy Spirit within us. When we refuse to hope, when we refuse to acknowledge the majesty and power of God in our lives, we, in effect, tell the Holy Spirit we don't need him, and we're in deep trouble. Repentance is impossible because, when we're in that frame of mind, there cannot be even enough humility for us to admit that we have sinned and need repentance at all.

Whatever the meaning of this Gospel passage may be, the one all-essential truth to remember is that, if we have sinned, God our Father is always there with open arms to receive us back to him, and the Holy Spirit is always ready to help us go there.

"Testing Kidneys"

In a Bible discussion group, we came across a passage that spoke of God "testing kidneys." What is the meaning of this strange phrase?

Among ancient peoples, the kidneys were often considered the seat of a person's deepest affections and intentions. They were frequently combined in this meaning with the heart, which we still refer to as the center of feelings of love, hatred and goodness.

This is also the reason that kidneys, or kidney fat, were among the choice parts of an animal that the Jews were commanded to sacrifice to God in the book of Leviticus.

The more common traditional word in English Bibles for this part of the body is reins — coming from the Latin word for kidneys, "renes." More modern translations generally give us the meaning rather than the exact word. In the seventh psalm, for example, God is described as Searcher of the mind (or soul) and heart, rather than the kidneys and the heart.

Slavery in the Bible?

Is it true that the Bible accepts the idea of slavery? St. Paul has been quoted that Christians should submit to slavery, and not try to change things, as if he were really in favor of it.

Not everything that we see people doing in sacred Scripture, even very holy people, represents the highest ideal of human activity.

The Old and New Testaments unfold the gradual understanding by men of the full implications of God's Word as he reveals it to us. Obviously, this understanding even now has a long way to go.

It is true that early Christians were a lot more tolerant of slavery and other social evils than we would be. Perhaps it is better to say that they accepted it as a fact of life that could not change quickly, and they tried to live with it, being as faithful to the ideals of Christ as they could.

Speaking of St. Paul, perhaps his brief Letter to Philemon is the best example we have of Paul's spirit on the matter. He returned Philemon's runaway slave, Onesimus, to Philemon, even though the slave wanted to stay with Paul as his companion. Paul insists in the letter that he doesn't wish to force Philemon's generosity by keeping Onesimus without the owner's permission. But Paul strongly hints, or warns, that slave or not, Onesimus and Philemon were of equal value in God's eyes — a fact which the slave owner had better keep well in mind in deciding what to do about the matter.

In other words, Paul seems to insist on the Christian ideal, without attempting in one swoop to upset an entrenched social structure.

Evidence exists, by the way, that Philemon did return his slave to Paul. Onesimus is often identified as the later bishop of Ephesus, who was well known to many early Christians.

Why Keep the Commandments?

If a person has to keep the Ten Commandments to get to heaven, why did Jesus Christ die on the cross and shed his blood for us?

Romans (3:24) says we are "justified freely by his grace through the redemption that is in Christ Jesus." Isn't it by the blood of the Lord, and not by the observance of the law, that we are forgiven our sins and have eternal life?

You're right. We do not keep the law of God and Jesus Christ in order to "buy" God's love and our sharing in his life. These are free, totally unmerited gifts.

Jesus does tell us, however, what we must do because we are his disciples, part of his family. Several times he corrected his followers when they tried to act, or even prompt him to act, against that lifestyle. (See, for example, Matthew 7:21, 19:17 and chapter 25, and John 9:21.)

In other words, there are certain ways we Christians do things. And Jesus tells us we must operate our lives freely according to that way, or we just won't fit into the kingdom.

The Dead Sea Scrolls

It has been many years since the discovery of the Dead Sea Scrolls. I have heard people ask why they have not yet been fully translated.

Some think the reason the work is so slow is that the higher-ups are afraid people will lose their religion if everything is learned about

them. I want to be the first to deny it. True religion needs to be afraid of nothing. Why the delay?

The delay in the translation and publication of the Dead Sea Scrolls is due entirely to the unimaginable technical difficulties involved in that work.

First of all, the discovery of the scrolls extended over several years. In some instances, more years of political controversy took place over who owned the documents and who had the right to attempt the scientific work which would follow their discovery.

Many years of work were frequently required simply to unroll the documents without destroying them or without making illegible the writing they contained. More years were needed to decipher the documents and translate them and finally match them with parallel documents and archeological discoveries. Much scientific work on the scrolls, in fact, remains to be done even today.

The contents of the Dead Sea Scrolls have been nothing but a thrill to Scripture experts and other scholars whose scientific fields are affected by the discoveries. The scrolls certainly raise some intriguing and challenging questions, but they have revealed nothing which is a threat in any way to our Christian faith.

Call Priests "Father"?

Some Protestant friends have told me many times that one of the things we Catholics do wrong is to call our priests "Father." This is against the teaching of the Bible, according to them. How do we explain what we do, since it does say in Matthew 23,9, "Call no one your father on earth, for one is your father in heaven."

The practice of using the title "Father" is not new. It goes back to the earliest centuries of Christianity, and has been in use ever since, though the name is traditionally applied more commonly to monks than to secular priests. Protestants abandoned its use gradually after the Reformation.

The reasons for calling the priest "Father" are simple and very natural. He is the usual minister of those sacraments that, in the name of Christ and his church, give us the new birth and life of grace — baptism, the Eucharist, penance and so on. By his continuing care, instruction, and support, he nurtures the life of God which we share as Christians in a manner parallel to the role of our natural fathers.

For this reason St. Paul does not hesitate to call himself the father of his Christian converts. "Although you may have 10 thousand others to teach you about Christ," he told the Corinthians, "remember that you have only me as your father." (1 Cor. 4,15 — Living Bible translation)

He also twice calls Timothy his son, because he had brought Timothy's family to the faith of Christ. (Phil. 2,22 and 1 Tim. 1,2)

Understood literally, this section of the Gospel of Matthew would mean we were forbidden to call our natural fathers by that name, or to call our instructors teachers. The whole context makes clear that Jesus was not hung up on the word father or teacher, but that he condemned the practice of some leaders in heaping titles on themselves out of pride and self-importance. As one of the most respected Protestant biblical commentaries remarks, "If one takes this command literally, the titles 'doctor' and 'professor,' as well as 'rabbi' and 'father' are forbidden to Christians in addressing their leaders." (Interpreter's Bible; volume seven, on the Gospel of St. Matthew)

Does Israel Belong to Jews?

In connection with the present fights between the Jews and the Arabs, the claim has been made by the Jews that the land of that area belongs to them. They say God gave it to them. Do you agree? How could they claim such a thing?

In the Old Testament, as God formed Abraham and his descendants into his "Chosen People," he is believed to have particularly destined them for the territory which we now know as the state of Israel. The cohesiveness they would develop in relation to this land would be an important part of the many ways God would develop the theological and social conditions necessary to prepare for the coming, and for the work, of Jesus.

Some (most?) Jewish people feel this Divine plan still gives a foundation for their claim to the land. My conviction, and, I believe, the position of any official statements by the Catholic Church, is that the Old Testament theological claim has little or no relevance to the present situation. Settlement of the problem must be on the same basis of political and social justice as might lead to the solution of any other such dispute — and that would include consideration of the history involved during the past 2,000 years as well as in the time before Christ.

Our Father Reworded?

A column in a Catholic paper suggested that we change the wording of the Our Father. Isn't the way Christ said it (Matthew 6:9-13) good enough?

If a Catholic in confession were given a penance of five Our Fathers, and it was said in this new way, would that fulfill the penance? I thought surely our pope would have a comment on that.

I'm afraid you are under several misconceptions concerning the Our Father. First of all, no one knows for sure what exact words Our Lord used when he gave us what we Christians commonly call the Lord's Prayer. Jesus did not speak English. What we have are translations from the Aramaic that Jesus used, or even translations of translations.

Since any good translation from one language to another involves a translation not merely of words but of ideas, the exact wording of something like the Our Father might differ greatly according to who is doing the translating. The various English editions of the Scriptures do differ greatly from each other.

As it is, the form of the Lord's Prayer we Catholics are accustomed to is different from the one you refer to in the Gospel of Matthew — and even more different from the form given in the Gospel of Luke (Luke 11:2-4).

So we don't really know which words Jesus used. He may have used different words at different times. We do know the ideas he was trying to express, and that's the important thing.

While I haven't seen the column you refer to, I'm guessing that it had something to do with the suggestions that English-speaking Christians come up with a form of the Lord's Prayer they can all agree on. We've all had the experience at funerals, weddings or other occasions, when Protestants and Catholics tumble over each other in attempting to join in something as simple and basic as the Our Father. It's embarrassing at the least.

Leaders of all Christian churches acknowledge the desirability of a common text, but it's easier said than done. Since all Christians know the Lord's Prayer if they know anything, emotional and devotional ties to the words they are accustomed to are very strong.

To answer your second question, a different translation or form of the Our Father would certainly fulfill one's penance for confession.

Gift of Tongues

What is the gift of tongues? Do you believe in it? What do you think of the Pentecostal Movement, where people are supposed have the gift of tongues?

The gift of tongues is one of the special manifestations of the presence of the Holy Spirit in an individual or group by which the individual (or group) speaks in a language that no one present could understand without a corresponding gift for "translation." It was not uncommon even in the early days of the Christian Church; St. Paul treats the subject at some length in 1 Corinthians, chapter 14.

There is some dispute whether the gift of tongues, as experienced then and apparently in a number of instances today, is a miraculous ability to speak a foreign language (which could have some missionary symbolism), or an ecstatic expression of syllables totally meaningless to anyone except another person similarly inspired to "interpret" the tongues. Maybe it is a combination of both — or even two separate gifts entirely.

There is no question that speaking in tongues may be a special gift by which the Holy Spirit makes his presence and power evident in a group. One difficulty, of course, as St. Paul points out, is that self-deception is quite easy. An individual, or others, may believe he is speaking in tongues when the vocal expressions result only from a hyper-emotional state. The test of genuinity, according to Paul, is whether the experiences increase faith, serve a constructive purpose, and bring peace to the group rather than confusion.

Participation in charismatic (sometimes called Pentecostal) prayer activities seems to have helped many to a better life of faith and close-ness to God. Supposedly, the gift of tongues has been experienced in some (relatively few?) charismatic meetings, but it is by no means essential or common to them.

Jesus' Birth on Dec. 25?

One night our study club realized that no one knows exactly when Jesus was born. How did we come to celebrate Dec. 25 as the anniversary of his birth? Do we know what year he was born?

Strange as it seems, we have no idea of the date of Christ's birth. The Gospels are absolutely no help on that. From information given especially in the Gospel of Luke, scholars generally believe that Christ was born between the years 8 and 6 B.C. Though our present calendar was supposedly based on the year of Christ's birth as the year one, the science of historical scholarship was not sophisticated enough for them to come to as precise a determination as we are capable of, thus the difference of six or eight years.

Numerous theories have been put forward through the last 2,000 years to explain Dec. 25 as Christmas Day. The most likely one, however, the one most generally accepted by scholars now, is that the birth of Christ was assigned to the date of the winter solstice. This date is Dec. 21 in our calendar, but was Dec. 25 in the Julian calendar which predated our own, and Jan. 6 in the Egyptian calendar. This latter date is still followed by some Eastern-Rite Christian churches.

The solstice, when days begin to lengthen in the northern hemisphere, was referred to by pagans as the "Birthday of the Uncon-quered Sun." During the third century, the Emperor Aurelian pro-claimed Dec. 25 as a special day dedicated to the sun-god, whose cult was very strong in Rome at that time. Even before this time, Christian writers already had begun to refer to Jesus as the Sun of Justice. It seemed quite logical, therefore, that as Christianity began to dominate the religious scene in the Roman Empire, the date of the "new-born sun" should be chosen as the birthdate of Christ.

Apparently, it bothers some people that the date for Christmas has its roots in a pagan feast. Be that as it may, it's the best explanation we have for the choice of Dec. 25 to celebrate the birth of Jesus.

The End of the World

When will the world end? Does the church teach anything about it?

The thousands of false predictions which have excited the world at one time or another ought to convince us, even if nothing else does, that God hasn't let us in on his plans for the date of the end of the world.

Whether it is 100 or 100,000 years away, we don't know. The Bible, at best, only speaks of situations which will be present before the end of the world. Even then, it is usually hard to discover what the Scripture writers really mean.

However, those who parade around with signs declaring "The end is near" do have a point. Neither Scripture nor the church is concerned with satisfying our idle curiosity, but rather with reminding us that the day we leave this earth, not the day it burns up, is the end of the world for you and me.

Writings Found by Archeologists

Several years ago I read that Jewish archeologists discovered evidence of writings related to Jesus dating from the first century. These were to be released later, but I've heard nothing on the subject since. Have you any knowledge of what these might be?

During the past few decades, archeologists have discovered numerous writings apparently dating from around the time of Our Lord. To my knowledge, however, none of them deal in any explicit way with Jesus and his life, unless they are documents already familiar to historians.

Throughout Christian history, considerable attention and respect was naturally afforded anything that would enlighten us about Christ. Full texts of many documents have been handed down, even though the original, or even a very early, manuscript had never been found. Certain modern discoveries seem to give us parts of some of these documents, but contain nothing specifically about Jesus that we did not already know.

Some texts of the Dead Sea Scrolls, discovered after World War II in the southern part of the Holy Land, speak of a Teacher of Righteousness. Certain scholars conjectured at first that this teacher might be Jesus, or at least a man closely connected with him. Experts now agree that this is not so. The Teacher of Righteousness, whoever he was, died some decades before Our Lord, and apparently had no more connection with him than any of the other holy men living in first century B.C. Palestine.

The Millenium

What is the meaning of the passage in the book of the Apocalypse that says the reign of Christ will be 1,000 years? Does this mean anything at all to us, or does it really mean that his reign in the world is 1,000 years?

One is bound to be hopelessly confused about the book of Revelation if he forgets that this is a book of visions and extremely complicated, and often totally mystifying, symbols. Several groups, some quite large, in the history of Christianity took that passage (Revelations, chapter 20) quite literally. They believed in an actual millenium (from Latin "mille anni," 1,000 years) during which Jesus would reign, and then take the saved into heaven after the final defeat of the devil.

Among ancient people large numbers were frequently symbols of an unmeasurable, infinite time. Perhaps the idea of a final 1,000 years is based on a non-biblical book called the "Secrets of Enoch," in which the world is described as 7,000 years old — with the present time being the final 1,000 years.

With few exceptions, millenarists became rare after the first thousand years came and went after Christ, and it became evident that there must be another meaning to the passage.

Treat Others Like Outcasts?

My family had quite a discussion on the meaning of the Gospel one Sunday. What is the interpretation of the passage where Jesus speaks about attempting to correct our "brother" by ourselves, or with a few others, or finally by the church itself. If he doesn't listen, we are told to treat him like a "Gentile or a tax collector."

This passage occurs in a section of St. Matthew's Gospel in which Jesus describes several aspects of his Kingdom as embodied in the church, that is, in the assembly of his people on earth. Gentiles were non-Jews, and therefore heathens as far as the Jews were concerned. Tax collectors, and especially publicans, were in those days considered (often rightly) as sinners, extortioners and traitors. Both groups were held in contempt as outcasts, people to be avoided.

The seemingly harsh words of Our Lord must be understood in relation to what immediately follows. Jesus says that when two or three are gathered in his name, he is there, and will grant whatever they ask. Part of his point is that the spirit of charity, prayer, and trust in him should hopefully prevent any conflict from reaching the point of division which it might reach if approached with only a cold, legalistic attitude.

Another factor in understanding the passage, forgiveness, comes up in the very next verse. Peter asks Jesus if one must forgive his brother up to seven times, which Peter obviously considered as excessively generous. Jesus replied that our forgiving, without demanding undue retribution or revenge, must be unending, at least if that's the way we want God to treat us.

Payment for Our Sins

On a recent Sunday, part of the Bible reading at Mass included the words "Not according to our sin does he deal with us, nor does he requite us according to our crimes."

I cannot understand these words. I thought that we must answer for our sins even though they are forgiven.

You refer to the responsorial psalm (103) for the eighth "ordinary Sunday of the year." The theme of this Mass is that God has committed himself to us with a permanent, inviolable covenant. His dealings are on the basis of that loving loyalty toward us, not on the basis of what we deserve by our sins — or even what we "merit" by our repentance.

The point of the psalm is simply that, from our side, and from our own resources were we left entirely to ourselves, we have no claim on his healing and forgiveness. It is solely his good will and faithfulness to his promises that moves us back toward him, and reunites us with him after we have failed.

Anything to Do in Heaven?

This may be a childish question. If it is ignore it.

If we are to live in heaven always and forever, wouldn't it get awfully boring? If there is no work and no play, what would we do? Just hang around? I'd really like to know.

You're not the only one. This profound, frustrating question has intrigued Catholic and other Christian theologians for centuries.

The final truth is we just don't know. Scripture and other Christian traditions tell us a number of things about life after death, but they do not fill in many details. We know first of all that we will rise to a new life. We also know that this being which will exist in eternity will be ourself — each of us with full consciousness of our identity from before death and with our full human nature, body and soul.

Furthermore, from the evidence of Jesus after his own resurrection, we know that this human nature will be dramatically different; our mental and physical capacities will go far beyond our experience in this life.

One thing is sure. Confronted with the unveiled infinite reality of God, with all the potential of creative love that is — in our limited human way of speaking — barely scratched by all the creation we know, and with the highly elevated spiritual and physical powers we will have to know and love that divine nature, I really don't think we'll have a problem of boredom.

We can only walk so close to that great reality of heaven before we are confronted with the simple fact that we are dealing here with a mystery hidden deeply in the heart of God. No theologian has ever gotten far beyond St. Paul's declaration, "Eye has not seen, ear has not heard, nor has it entered into the heart of man what God has prepared for those who love him."

I suppose we just have to trust in God that Paul knew what he was talking about.

Did Jesus Have Long Hair?

Most, if not all, of the pictures and statues purporting to portray Jesus have long hair. But doesn't I Cor. 11:14 make that seem improbable? ("Nature itself (teaches) you that it is dishonorable for a man to wear his hair long, while the long hair of a woman is her glory.") St. Paul had an interest in both Jesus and hair lengths, and was associated with men who were associated with Jesus.

If any useful argument whatsoever about hair length is possible, one that tries to settle the question by using the Bible is futile.

The significance and acceptability of length of hair is entirely a matter of time, place, and culture. Ancient Egyptians, for example, except slaves and peasants, wore shorter hair, and men were clean shaven. Custom in the Near East, on the other hand, including the land of the Jews, dictated longer hair and beards — through Old Testament and into New Testament times.

Victors in battle commonly cut the hair of defeated leaders as a sign of dishonor. (See 2 Sam. 10:4) Short hair and beards could also be a sign of mourning.

In Corinthians, Paul was writing to a group of Christians in a notoriously dissolute city, for years a key city in the Roman Empire and one whose culture was basically Roman. Roman men wore their hair short, while the women — except perhaps for sacred (pagan temple) or run-of-the-mill prostitutes — wore theirs longer. It is understandable, therefore, that Paul urged Christians to follow the "natural" custom in their area. He applied his own religious interpretations to that custom.

Reconciled Before Communion

A Sunday Gospel says, "If your brother has anything against you, leave your gift at the altar and first go and be reconciled with your brother." Does this mean that if a person has truly offended another person and has not apologized in any manner, he must first be reconciled before going to Holy Communion?

This passage is one of many in Scripture which makes clear that our relations with those around us hold a primary place above our actions and prayers of worship. There is no question that we tend to minimize the impact and importance of that truth, which is probably why Jesus stresses it as he does, especially in this part of the Sermon on the Mount. (Matthew 5 to 7)

For one thing, our public actions of worship, especially the Mass, are signs of our shared brotherhood as children of the Father, and as brothers and sisters of Jesus. Deliberate hurt, or arousing anger in our brother, makes that act of worship a lie unless it is repaired beforehand by some effort at reconciliation.

Furthermore, we know that our relations with our family, friends and acquaintances constitute the only real barometer of our friendship with God himself. Jesus tells us this in so many words, as does St. John, when he says that the way we know we have "passed from death to life" is that we love our brothers. (1 John 3)

Obviously, the degree of necessity for this reconciliation before Communion will vary with circumstances. But the urgency of the principle Jesus gives is quite clear.

Composition of the New Testament

To settle an argument, how long did it take to write the New Testament?

If you're talking about the actual writing and putting together of the books of the New Testament as they are in our Bible, the earliest was the first letter to the Thessalonians, written around the year 50 or 51, about 20 years after Jesus' death.

The Gospel of Mark, the earliest of the four Gospels, dates from perhaps the year 65, though all the Gospels made use of documents, liturgical rites, and other traditions which existed in the Christian communities before that date.

The last books were probably the three letters of St. John and the Book of Revelations, all of which were probably written sometime between the years 90 and 100, or 105.

Thus, the basic composition of all the books covered a period of somewhere around 50 years.

Did Jesus Despair on the Cross?

In the Gospel of St. Matthew, Chapter 27, Jesus cries out on the cross, "Eli, Eli lama sabachtani" — that is, "My God, My God, why have you forsaken me?" In what language did Jesus speak? Is it possible he said rather, "My God, where are you?" The Jesus I know would never say he was forsaken, since he loved and trusted his Father throughout his life.

This passage has puzzled Christians for centuries. At least two points may be helpful in understanding it.

There is no doubt that Jesus did suffer much of our common human experience of desolation, grief, aloneness, and possibly even bafflement, at the time of his Passion. It was an agonizing torture so severe that it caused a bloody sweat and brought him close to a feeling of almost total dereliction. We say "close" because in the cry itself is the expression of profound faith in the midst of all the pain — "My God, My God!"

Second, this exclamation of our Lord has long been seen as possibly a wrenching prayer using Psalm 22, one of the graphic passages in the Old Testament which in an uncanny manner parallels the suffering of Jesus on the cross. The words we are considering are the opening words of that psalm. The same psalm is quoted just a few verses before this passage of Matthew (verse 43), and the following verses about Jesus' thirst recall the later words of that same psalm, "My throat is dried up like baked clay, my tongue cleaves to my jaws...they have pierced my hands and my feet."

If it is true that Psalm 22 was involved in this cry, as many Christian writers and biblical scholars believe, the words become one of the most powerful acts of faith, love and victory ever uttered by Our Lord.

Loophole in Post-Flood Contract?

The Bible says the rainbow is a sign that the Lord will not flood the earth again. Could that also mean, technically, that it won't rain 40 days or more so crops won't grow that year and hard times, if not

death, will follow? People have abortions, mercy kill, rob, steal, lie, and escape punishment on a technicality of the law. Would God take this wording about rain and use it for some reason?

If I understand you correctly, it seems you're asking: Did God word the covenant after the flood very carefully, leaving himself a loophole through which he could thrash us properly if he ever decided to do so again?

First of all, the question fails to recognize the largely symbolic nature of the story of the flood and its aftermath. What actual disasters lie behind these chapters of Genesis we probably will never know.

We do know that the main reason for the story is to bring out certain important truths about man and his relationship with God, and one of those truths is surely not that God is a combination accountant and FBI agent waiting to tan our hides on a technicality. Seeing natural disasters as "acts of Divine vengeance" has no place in true Christian theology. God does not go about seeking ways to punish us. He has enough trouble trying to get us out of, and heal, the messes we make for ourselves.

Which Day is the Sabbath?

We commonly refer to the Sabbath as the seventh day of the week. The Bible does not say this. It does say many times that the Sabbath is the seventh day after six days of work.

There is a big difference in these two sevens. The seventh day of a calendar week is one set date each week, but the seventh day after the beginning of the first day of work can be any day of the week.

The Bible does not speak of any consecutive seven-day cycles up to the time of the Israelites' first Sabbath. Therefore, we know that before this time, there was no standard weekly calendar used such as the one in use at Christ's time.

Though God commanded a Sabbath rest day, he did not necessarily mean the seventh day. Thus, Sunday-keeping saints have not gone to hell for not keeping Saturday.

You may be right. I'm not sure how practical your suggestion is, however. No matter how theoretically correct you are, I don't believe the argument will carry much weight with people who believe we must observe the Sabbath on Saturday.

I believe you would find it difficult to discover evidence that observance of a seven-day week came after the Jewish regulation of rest on the seventh day. Long before the observance of the Sabbath rest was an established regulation among the Hebrews, a seven-day week was not all uncommon in several Near Eastern cultures, including that of the Jews. Apparently this resulted from the division of the lunar month (28 days) into four sections, though other cultures, such as the Greeks and Romans, divided the lunar month into three sections of roughly 10 days each.

It is entirely possible that the Hebrew tradition of six days work and one day rest developed out of the context of the seven-day week, the last day of which would be a day of recuperation from labor. In other words, the history of the Sabbath may be a fascinating study, but it doesn't offer much ammunition against Sabbatarians (those who insist on Saturday as the holy day). Our reasons for observing Sunday as the Christian holy day arise from entirely different sources.

John's Baptism

On the Feast of the Immaculate Conception, a question arose concerning baptism. We are told the Blessed Mother was born without the stain of original sin. Furthermore, our Lord was like us in every human way except sin. If baptism removes the stain of original sin, why did John the Baptist baptize Jesus who was born without sin? Was it just to set an example?

I'm sure you realize that the baptism of John, with which Jesus was baptized, was not our rite of baptism, a Christian sacrament that was instituted after our Lord's baptism in the Jordan.

John's baptism was one of the numerous ritual purifying washings practiced not only among the Jews but in many other non-Christian religions. The word "baptism," in fact, simply means a washing, coming from a Greek word for dipping or immersing. None of these baptisms, including John's, was believed to accomplish anything sacramental in our sense of the term. They constituted merely a symbol of some change of heart or of purification which the individual himself accomplished by his own intentions, and which he proclaimed by being baptized.

Thus, John the Baptist told the people that his baptism was to signify that they repented of the wrongs they had done, and were determined to amend their lives. He also clearly proclaimed that his baptism of water was significantly different from the baptism of Christ, which would be accomplished by the Holy Spirit. (Mt. 3:11)

Understanding John's baptism this way, it is easy to see why Jesus not only accepted, but insisted on receiving, such a baptism. As the savior, our Lord was in a real sense taking on himself the sins of all mankind to atone for them and reunite mankind in friendship with the heavenly Father.

This salvation would, of course, reach its climax in his death and resurrection, but it was symbolized and prepared for in many ways, including his acceptance of John's baptismal reminder that men and women are separated from God by their sinfulness, and desperately need someone to heal that alienation.

As the Baptist himself proclaimed, it was precisely because he was the Lamb of God, who would bear and take away the sins of the world, that Jesus came to John to be baptized. (John 1:29)

Jesus' Brothers and Sisters?

A non-Catholic friend is attending a series of talks on the Bible. She reports that in this class she is told that the Blessed Virgin Mary had other children born to her after Jesus.
I went to a Catholic school and never heard of this. Is it true?

Students of the Bible, including today the vast majority of Protestant scholars, agree that neither the books of the New Testament nor other early Christian writing offer any substantial evidence that Mary had other children besides Jesus. It is impossible to deal with all traditional arguments to the contrary, but none of them, when examined carefully, offer basis for a claim that Jesus had brothers and sisters.

The extreme care that the writers of the Gospels of Matthew and Luke take to insist that the conception of Jesus was accomplished by a special intervention of God certainly indicates a Gospel bias in favor of the virginity of Mary — a bias which would be overcome only by some pretty strong evidence.

Perhaps the text most commonly brought forth to claim that Mary had other children is Matthew 2,47, which speaks of some of the disciples as "brothers" of Jesus. This apparent problem dissolves when one realizes that the Jews of Jesus' time had one word that covered all kinds of kinships, from brother or sister to distant cousins. When this particular Aramaic word ("aha") is used to designate the relationship of some individuals to Jesus, it requires quite a stretch of meaning to conclude that they are his brothers and sisters in our sense of those words.

Because the perpetual virginity of Mary was commonly taught by the great teachers in the church from the very earliest decades after Christ, the church has long held that Mary was a virgin also after the birth of Christ. She therefore bore no other children after Our Lord.

Why Didn't Jesus Cure More People?

Why didn't more people request cures of Christ who apparently never refused such requests? It seems to me that the path to his temporary home would have been thronged with people who heard of this miraculous healer.
Blind people, crippled, all sufferers have some faith that someone,

somewhere, can cure them. Apparently Christ never failed to cure those who approached him. A really successful healer in San Francisco would crowd the town very quickly. Why were there any sick left in Israel?

As you might suspect, you are not the first to be puzzled by this question. Through all the centuries since Christ, Christians have noted and meditated on the fact that if Jesus cured one person, he could have cured everyone.

Furthermore, since his powers of healing were not limited to time and space, he theoretically could have cured everyone in the world and put an end to all human suffering.

The fact that he did not eliminate all pain and evil from our human condition certainly cannot be attributed to his lack of power, or to his lack of compassion and love. He overwhelmingly showed both of these, most of all by his own suffering, death on the cross, and resurrection.

It seems clear, then, that the healing miracles of Jesus had other larger purposes beyond the relief of pain. For one thing, Jesus saw his healing actions (and other physical miracles such as giving back life to those who had died) as signs of his supreme power over all evil.

To him they were witnesses to the fact that neither physical suffering nor the worst of human sinfulness could ever be larger than the power of good, the power he embodied as God. On occasion he makes this connection quite explicitly, as in the healing of the paralyzed man in Luke, Chapter 6.

Another conclusion Christians have drawn from Jesus' approach to human suffering is that he did not come to take it away, but rather to give it meaning — or at least to help his people understand that there is a need for it. It is as if he said:

"If I don't take away all your suffering, it is not because I cannot do so, or because I do not love you enough. Buried deep inside the nature of mankind, and inside the human heart, there is the mystery that fulfillment — perfection — comes from the passage through death to life. The best I can do is tell you this, show you that it applies even to me, and then ask you to follow me and trust me."

If this answer does not sound as final and perfect as you would like, we must remember that we are dealing here with one of the oldest questions human beings have wrestled with: Where does evil (physical and moral) come from, and why is it here? Among the many reasons for Christ's miracles, one is that they were his way of helping us deal with this question. If he could not give us a perfectly satisfying answer, he at least helps us to see that in the mystery of God's providence there is an answer, an answer that is revealed, if only dimly, most of all in his own death and resurrection and in our following of him in this paschal mystery.

When Is Christ With Me?

Please explain to me the remark of Christ, "Wherever two or more are gathered in my name, I am there." Why wouldn't he be with me when I am alone?

I suggest you read the whole 18th chapter of the Gospel of Matthew from which your quote comes. In a series of parables and admonitions, we find strong reminders of Jesus' plan that his followers should not be hordes of isolated individuals somehow faithful to him, but rather an assembly, a "church" of people mutually interdependent and helpful. This community of believers was to constitute their home, the place they went for assistance, support, and even for the forgiveness of their sins (18, 18).

The intent of our Lord's remark is obviously not that one should never pray alone. He himself often went off by himself to speak with the Father. Rather, the saying affirms that a special and powerful presence of Jesus, as Savior, occurs when even a few of his family of believers gather together in prayer. That group becomes, as it were, a "little church," or perhaps better, they represent — and in some unique way share in — the power of the whole church at prayer.

Were Adam and Eve Real?

My son came home from high school the other day and said his teacher told them Adam and Eve never existed. This goes down to the fundamentals of our faith, doesn't it? Did they, or didn't they? If there were two people who started the human race, how do we explain the different races — Chinese, Negro, etc.?

We don't know (and probably never will) whether or not there were two original human beings from which all the rest of us descended. And if there were, we surely do not know their names.

One thing is certain: We will never find out from the Bible. Holy Scripture simply was not written to pass on to us such details of anthropology as this. Whether there were two "first parents" or 200, or exactly where they came from, has little to do with the spiritual and theological intent of the biblical story of Adam and Eve — which was put together in the form we have it only a few hundred years before Christ.

Rather, that story, which we find in the first chapters of Genesis, is meant to convey to us some of the most important truths of our faith — that the world, including the human family, owes its existence to the one true God; that this world, as it came from God, was good, and was meant for mankind's happiness; that whatever misfortunes there are on earth come from man's own stubbornness and sinfulness; that even in the beginning, God had a plan to eventually save man from his sinfulness, and so on.

I don't know why this should be so "fundamental" for your faith. The great facts about God and our relation with him are the real message of Holy Scripture. As for the rest, scientists generally agree that any certainty about such things that happened way back in the dawn of history, tens or hundreds of thousands of years ago, is well nigh impossible.

The position of the church on this subject was made clear in the encyclical "Humani Generis" of Pope Pius XII (1950). In it, the Holy Father insisted that the theory that there were more than two "first parents" of the human race should not be taught as an established fact. And that's where the matter stands.

Concerning the origin of the races, neither the Bible nor Christian revelation gives us much to go on. Some of the more fundamentalist Christians profess to see hints in the Scripture about how some of the races started. But the church's position, once again, is that this type of question must be answered by the sciences of anthropology and paleontology, not by theologians or Scripture scholars.

Many Adams, Many Eves?

You say we may accept the possibility that there were more than one Adam and Eve who originated the human race. I have no big problem with this, but do have two questions. How do you explain scriptural references such as St. Paul's remark, "Through one man (Adam) sin entered the world" (Romans 5,12)?

And isn't it true that many church councils, such as the infallible Council of Trent, and several church documents refer to Adam as "the first man?"

One critical point to remember in considering both your questions is that neither Scripture nor the council you mention were addressing themselves at all to the question of polygenism (that is, whether there were many first parents). Therefore, one must be careful in claiming they answered a question that, up to that time, had never even been approached seriously, if at all.

To your first point, preachers and other orators quite commonly use the device of referring to well-known historical characters to make a point, with absolutely no intention of declaring judgment on the actual existence of these characters. When a priest in a homily, for example, refers to the Prodigal Son or the Good Samaritan, he is not professing a belief that these particular individuals of Jesus' parables ever really existed. They fit the point to be made, and that's all their mention really means.

Jesus did this, St. Paul did it, and conciliar decrees and other official church documents do the same. As mentioned above, these documents were not directly concerned with polygenism. But if reference to the scriptural story of creation helped explain or support their teaching, they rightly had no hesitation in using it.

In "Humani Generis" Pope Pius XII explained some doctrinal and scriptural problems with polygenism (some of which have been resolved in the last 30 years, incidentally), and says that no Catholic should hold that opinion (polygenism) as a fact, since "it is not apparent" how this opinion is compatible with certain Catholic beliefs.

"Humani Generis" labels the belief in more than one Adam and Eve a conjectural opinion. It does not call that opinion erroneous or heretical.

By the way, there is no such thing as an "infallible council." A particular truth may be taught infallibly. But the fact that some truths are taught solemnly in a conciliar or papal document doesn't mean that everything is, even if it's in the same sentence.

Feast of Adam and Eve?

In some older missals, the Feast of Adam and Eve was listed for Dec. 24. This seemed so right and appropriate. In the present liturgy, does this feast remain? If so, when?

Through the centuries Adam and Eve have understandably had a prominent place in much of the church's liturgy and prayer during Advent. However, none of the official martyrologies (lists of saints) that I know of ever numbered them among the saints, or assigned a date for their feast.

Adam or Dinosaurs?

I am confused about creation. When I was little I was told that reptiles and dinosaurs came first. Recently I read that Adam and Eve came first. Can you tell me the answer?

Yours is a scientific question, not a religious one. But I am confident that scientists would be unanimous in asserting that prehistoric creatures such as we call dinosaurs predated the entry of mankind on the earthly scene. Whether they did or not, however, is totally irrelevant to our faith; such questions are not at all addressed by the Bible or other Christian sources of revelation.

Jesus and His Father

I have a Scriptural question. In the Gospel of Mark (13:32) Jesus says something I do not understand about his relationship to the Father. We know Jesus and the Father are one with the Holy Spirit.

Yet Jesus says that no man and no angel, not even the Son (meaning apparently himself) knows the hour of the passing of heaven and earth. How could Jesus say something like that?

We find numerous remarks like this in the Gospel which seem to be incompatible with the fact that Jesus is the second person of the Trinity and therefore shares in all the knowledge of God.

No full answer is possible since we are dealing here with the mystery of the Trinity itself and of the Incarnation. Two general directions of answers, however, are possible.

First, Jesus could be speaking here solely in the context of his human nature, which is limited, as is all human knowledge and understanding. How human limits coexist with divine omnipotence and infinity is, of course, the mystery of the Incarnation.

Another explanation can be that Jesus is speaking not so much of his own personal relationship with the Father, but rather of his mission to reveal to mankind all the truths regarding God that would contribute to the development of our relationship with him here and in eternity. This may be one reason why such seeming contradictions appear often in the Gospel of John, which was written rather late, and therefore is able to reflect much more the Christ who is the Risen Lord and head of the church, as distinct from the Jesus who walked the earth with the apostles. In fulfilling his mission as Lord and Savior, Jesus knows much which he cannot tell us — not because of some unworthy jealousy on the part of God, but simply because we could not grasp such knowledge or use it creatively even if it were given to us.

Jesus certainly made clear that he considered it part of his own responsibility to determine how much of what he knows of the Father he should make known to us.

Did Jesus Learn?

I read recently some ideas that I think strange.

I wonder if it is right to say "Jesus learned obedience through suffering." Wasn't he born obedient? When the devil tempted him on the mountain for 40 days, wasn't he being tried for weakness? It seems to me that our Blessed Lord died giving glory to God his Father, who is our Father. Jesus didn't have to learn obedience; he was God!

The quote you give did not originate with a modern writer. It is straight out of the letter to the Hebrews in the New Testament. It is, in fact, only one of many statements in that letter and elsewhere in the Bible which stress a truth many Catholics have a hard time believing — that Jesus was really, truly human, with all that implies in body and spirit.

From my own experience, it seems that the denial of the humanity of Jesus is easily one of the most serious errors of faith in our day. For historical reasons dating back several thousand years, we have so concentrated on the fact that he is God that we have greatly underplayed the truth that "He is like us in everything except that he did not sin." (Hebrews)

The remarks in Scripture about Jesus growing, learning, suffering, crying, struggling with weakness and fear, and so on, were as vital to the early Christians as they are to us. These Christians realized, as we should also, that our belief that Jesus is truly human is just as important as our belief that he is God. If either were not true, his saving life, death, and resurrection would be only an empty gesture. If, for example, Jesus is only God and not man, it might prove God's benevolence toward us, but we would not be the saved people we believe we are. Jesus could only accomplish salvation, as we believe in it, by being fully and actually one of us.

St. Luke's Gospel tells us that Jesus grew in wisdom and overall manliness in the sight of God and man. As Hebrews puts it, Jesus is able to be the compassionate and effective priest he is because he once shared our weakness, and was himself "made perfect" and "learned obedience" through the things he suffered.

The quote you give simply repeats, therefore, what the Bible says about Jesus' humanity, a most important truth if we are to appreciate properly the mystery of the Incarnation and his role as our Savior. All passages about Jesus going through the same processes of development and struggle as the rest of mankind (as long as we eliminate any moral weakness or sin) simply reflect this essential element of our faith. We not only can believe it, we must believe it, if we are to be faithful to our Christian traditions.

We do not, of course, ignore the obvious problem of how these human conditions coexist in a person who is God. How can God learn, or be puzzled, or tired? For that matter, how can God be born, have his diapers changed, be hungry, and die? This is the heart of the mystery of the Incarnation — that Jesus, our Savior, is both God and man. We cannot allow ourselves to resolve that mystery by denying it.

Who Were Joseph's Parents?

We know the parents of the Blessed Virgin Mary were named Joachim and Anna. Have we ever learned the names of the parents of St. Joseph?

Outside of Scripture, Christian tradition gives us no information at all about the parents of St. Joseph.

In fact the Bible itself is no help. Two different fathers are listed for St. Joseph in the Gospels. In Matthew (1:16), the father of Joseph appears with the name Jacob. In Luke (3:23), Joseph is said to be the son of Heli. However, neither genealogy intends to give a complete line of descent. Matthew obviously wanted to emphasize Jesus' descent from King David and Abraham; Luke's concern is Jesus' human descent from Adam.

In either case we cannot tell how close the relationship was between one of these two "fathers" and Joseph. One may have been his real father. More likely they were both ancestors a little further back.

About Joseph's mother, not even Scripture gives a hint.

Mary's Surprise Pregnancy

I'm still confused about that part of the Bible concerning the birth of Christ. It deals with the problem Joseph had when he found out that Mary was with child. Apparently it was perfectly all right with everyone that Mary was going to have a baby before she was even married. It seemed to be no problem for St. Joseph either after he found out it was somehow God's doing.

Were unwed mothers that common in those days, too?

The explanation really isn't all that complicated. You've certainly heard that in ancient times (in fact, up to the present day in some places), marriage consent was given not only by the bride and groom, but by the families involved. This promise of marriage often took place at a formal, though not necessarily elaborate, ceremony. Sometime after this consent came the actual nuptials — when the groom officially took the bride into his home.

Jewish custom at the time when Joseph and Mary were married seems to have followed something like this procedure. First came the betrothal, which included the consent of all concerned and the giving of the dowry to the groom by the bride's parents. Later came the marriage celebration, with the marriage feast Jesus later referred to often in his teachings and to which he compared the Kingdom of God.

Bride and groom might be together as husband and wife immediately after the betrothal, or wait until after the nuptial ceremony. St. Luke and St. Matthew seem to say that it was during the period between these two events that Mary became pregnant with Jesus. It would not have been at all unusual.

Who Wrote the Gospels?

During a sermon on the radio, a Protestant minister said that the Gospel of John was not written by the apostle John the Divine, and that Catholics and Protestants agree on this. Don't we have to believe that the New Testament was written by the apostles? If not by them, then who did write the Gospels?

It has long been known by Scripture authorities of all Christian faiths that several books of the New Testament were not actually written by the persons traditionally thought to be their authors. The Gospels of Matthew and John are almost certainly two New Testament books of this nature.

There's nothing surprising here. In ancient times a literary work commonly bore the name of the person out of whose teaching the work was formed, even if the man himself did not write it — or perhaps was no longer even alive. The book would still be recognized (and even named) as the teaching of that particular "master" or famous person, though developed, edited, and expanded upon by others perhaps over a period of many years.

This, of course, has no bearing on whether or not the books of the Bible were inspired. The church has never made doctrinal declarations about the authors of the books which make up the Bible.

Noah and the Ark

During my young years I thought that everyone and everything perished during the great flood except Noah and his family and animals (two of each). His family and the animals survived because he took them with him on the ark. Now my granddaughter, who taught Bible school at her Catholic Church, tells me the story of the great flood and Noah was only a myth, or words to that effect.

We cannot read stories of the Bible, especially those which go back tens or hundreds of thousands of years into prehistory, as if they were written by modern scientists or historians. Just as Jesus used parables (which are fictions to convey a truth he wanted to teach), other parts of the Bible can do the same.

We must remember that the Bible does not pretend to be a technical textbook of archeology or geology. It is a faith-book in which God's intention is to reveal his love for us and our response of love to him, and how those loves and relationships have developed.

Except for those Christian groups who are biblical literalists (meaning that they accept every part of the Bible as literally true, as if they were scientific and historical documents in our modern sense of the word) almost no one today would, for example, view the story of Noah and the Ark as literally and historically accurate.

This by no means says that the story is not true. The truth of the story is not in whether or not the details are accurate, but rather in the knowledge it reveals to us of God's power, man's capacity for both good and evil, God's desire to forgive and save us, and so on. Sometimes, in fact, when we concentrate too much on the technical details of stories like Noah, we tend to miss the real message which God is telling us if we listen in the right way.

A point you mention in your question is one proof that the Noah story was never intended to give intricate details. You note that Noah took two of each animal into the ark with him. This is true according to one part of the flood story (Genesis 7, 8-9). Later on, however, we are told there were seven pairs of clean animals taken into the ark (Genesis 7, 25). This seeming contradiction obviously posed no difficulty for the writer who finally put the story together as we have it, because his purpose was not to count animals or days of rain. Under the inspiration of the Holy Spirit, he had a far more profound message than that.

Did Abraham Commit Adultery?

I don't understand the story in the Bible about Abraham. He had a wife, Sarah, but he also had a son (Ishmael) by a slave girl before the son of his real wife. Now, wasn't Abraham committing adultery?

If you check the book of Genesis (chapter 16), you'll note that the slave girl, Hagar, was actually Abraham's concubine. In the Old Testament, however, a concubine was more than simply a mistress in our sense of the word. She was an actual wife, but of some lower status than the wife (or wives) who enjoyed the full legal status of wife.

The possession of concubines seems to have constituted a kind of transition practice between polygamy (having more than one wife), which was quite common in the ancient world, and monogamy (one wife). No one seems very sure of the exact difference between a wife and a concubine. Probably much depended on the particular time and culture. But having children by concubines was considered completely proper and legal.

The practice continued for centuries after Abraham, who lived about 1600 B.C. In fact, among the Jews as well as other ancient cultures (and in some localities even into modern times) the best barometer of a man's wealth was the number of concubines in his harem. About 925 B.C., a major indication that King Solomon was the richest man in the world was that he had 700 wives and 300 concubines — which has got to be some kind of record! (see I Kings, chapter 11)

Jewish Dietary Laws

I read in the Catholic Bible that pork meat is not supposed to be eaten. How about bacon and grease from it? Or don't these laws apply to us? It seems to me that if it is in the Bible it should still be a rule.

The dietary laws of the Jews of the Old Testament were established for a complicated combination of religious, health and cultural reasons. In many ways they paralleled similar regulations observed by the pagan cultures around them. Christians, including Catholics, are in no way obliged to follow them.

It is true that Jesus respected these regulations most of the time in his life, but that is because he was a Jew living in a Jewish culture and dealing almost exclusively with fellow Jews. At the same time, he frequently showed that he considered himself above those laws and was able to change them if he wished.

Not only did he refuse to bind his future followers to such regulations, he insisted that they are obligated to follow an entirely new kind of law, and that they would be identified by things other than what they eat and drink.

Isaias and the Virgin Birth

I have been told that there is no support in the Old Testament for our belief that Jesus was conceived and born of a virgin. However, we were taught in the past that the passage from Isaias 7 refers to Christ and Mary when it says, "The Virgin shall be with child, and bear a son." Can we or can't we use that to help prove the virgin birth?

It is true that the church often uses this text of the prophet Isaias in connection with the virginal conception and birth of Jesus. As so much of this magnificent biblical book (really the "book" of Isaias is at least two books) Isaias 7:14 gives us rich insights into the significance of the coming of the Savior.

However, several things prevent these words from being a "proof" of the virginal conception of Jesus.

First, the original Hebrew of Isaias, written about 600 years before Christ, does not say virgin, but young girl — "almah." When it was translated into Greek a few hundred years later, the Greek word "parthenos" was chosen — which usually does mean virgin. It was this Greek translation, for instance, which was quoted in the Gospel according to Matthew, in the story of the infancy of Jesus (Mt. 1:23).

Because the prophet did not actually use the word virgin, most modern translations working from the original texts use the words maiden, or young woman, in this passage. The New American Bible, which you quote, does say "virgin," but a footnote explains the confusion over the exact meaning of the sentence.

Furthermore, there remains real uncertainty whether Isaias himself intended these words as a prophetic reference to the coming Messiah. He may have meant them to refer to specific persons he was dealing with politically at that time in his life. At any rate, the text apparently was not understood by anyone in reference to the Messiah, or to virginal conception, until its use by St. Matthew.

Why Are Things Unclean?

The more I read the book of Leviticus the more confused I become. Why are perfectly normal functions and things considered unclean? Where did all these strange laws about food, lepers, death, and so on originate?

According to Jewish law, contact with four categories of things rendered an individual unclean, that is, unfit to participate in any worship. These four categories include leprosy, dead bodies, certain foods that were labeled unclean, and sexual functions. Nearly anything that had to do with sexual intercourse, whether sinful or lawful, was considered unclean.

This uncleanness was not necessarily something spiritual, and generally had nothing to do with holiness. In fact, usually it could be taken away by simply washing oneself. But the system was severely adhered to among the Jews. We learn from the Gospels that at least some groups of Jews, such as the Pharisees, insisted on the most rigid observance of all such laws, a position for which they are frequently attacked by Jesus.

No one has ever been able to give a satisfactory explanation of the origin of these Hebraic regulations. It seems clear that they relate somehow to similar laws observed by pagan cults among whom the Jews lived, but every explanation suggested appears to have as many arguments against it as for it.

Jesus' primary objection to the whole system centered on its focus on externals. As he said, it isn't what a man eats or what he touches that really counts, it's what is in his heart and what comes out of that heart that determines how good a person he is.

Protestant Bible

I heard a preacher on the radio refer to the Protestant Bible and the Catholic Bible. I thought there was no such distinction any more, and even that there is a Bible that both Protestants and Catholics can use. Do we have a Catholic Bible now?

Those names can be confusing, partially because they can mean several things. For a long time, for instance, Catholic and Protestant Bibles differed on translations of many passages. Today the science of biblical textual studies is so advanced that one can hardly have a Catholic Scripture any more than he could have a Catholic appendectomy.

Too, Protestant Bibles traditionally avoid interpretive footnotes, based on a conviction of private interpretation into which explanatory notes should not intrude.

The major difference remains today: Certain books are left out of Protestant editions of Scripture which are included in Catholic Bibles.

For historical reasons, these are called deuterocanonical ("second canon") or apocryphal ("hidden") books, and include the books of Tobias, Judith, Baruch, First and Second Maccabees, Ben Sirach (Ecclesiasticus), Wisdom, and parts of Daniel and Esther.

Though these books have not been considered part of Scripture by most non-Catholic churches since the Reformation, they are included in many modern Protestant Bibles in a separate section because of their inspirational and historical significance.

Saints

Book of Saints?

In the church's celebration of feasts of the saints, is there an ABC rotation of feasts as there is for the Sunday Scripture readings? Is there an up-to-date book of saints similar to one I have which is almost 50 years old? Does it relate to our present calendar?

The reason for asking probably will not interest many readers but it is important to me. For some time I have been attempting meditation using a saint each day, and then linking that person's life with the way Christ might have lived in him. Up to now the attempt is feeble, but it has been fruitful for me.

Your question might not be nearly as uninteresting to other Catholics as you seem to believe. I am often deeply impressed by the number of people who are seriously and sincerely attempting to develop and enrich their life of prayer.

The variety of ways through which they do this is also impressive, and yours is not that unusual.

In the recent revision of the church calendar (which takes place every few hundred years just to eliminate a lot of confusion that develops with the addition of new saints), several dates were changed. There is no rotation of these observances from year to year. Each saint's feast is celebrated each year, unless, of course, that feast is superseded by a Sunday or other more solemn feast.

A few books describing the lives of the saints according to the present church calendar are now available. The classic in this field, however, remains Butler's "Lives of the Saints." The four-volume set covering the entire year is relatively expensive but well worth saving up for. It presents information not only on the major saint of each day (the one whose name appears on Catholic calendars) but on many other perhaps lesser known but equally inspiring holy men and women whose feast falls on the same date. The set may be ordered through almost any book store.

I hope you persevere in your worthwhile effort.

Non-Catholic Saints?

You seem to refer to the saints by including them among some of our "fellow Christians." Isn't it true, however, that the Catholic church does not recognize non-Catholic saints?

First of all, other Catholics are our "fellow Christians" also. That phrase does not automatically refer to Protestants.

If you mean does the Catholic Church acknowledge the presence of holiness in other Christian churches, and in the members of those churches, the answer is by all means yes.

In at least one instance, the Catholic Church has actually canonized (officially declared as a saint) a non-Roman Catholic Christian. This occurred a few years ago in the canonization of a group of African young men who were murdered for their faith late in the last century. They are known as the Martyrs of Uganda, and one of their number was an Anglican.

With perhaps one exception, the Roman Catholic Church is the only Western Christian church which has any custom such as canonization. Thus, there are no Protestant "saints" in that more formal or official sense.

Praying to the Saints

I am not a Roman Catholic. I've never received a sufficient explanation why Catholics pray to the saints and give them so much tribute. I believe that Jesus Christ is the one Mediator between God and man.

This special relationship with the saints cannot be understood without recalling a fact that the New Testament is full of: All of those who believe in Jesus, who acknowledge him as their Savior and live according to his teachings, form a special, very close family — whether they are living, or are already dead and "with" God, as St. Paul puts it. As Paul also said many times, all true Christians are in some way saints in that they share in the sanctity and love of the Father, along with and in Jesus, with whom they are united by ties of loyalty and love.

The people we usually call "saints," however, are individuals whom the church, their fellow Christians, acknowledge as having lived the Christian life in an especially holy way, and who thereby give great praise to God and an unusual witness to their fellow men. When we pray to them, we do it simply to be glad with them and ask them to add to our prayers their own intercessions to Jesus, and through him to the Heavenly Father, for whom they have proven their love.

One Protestant lady with whom I was speaking about this recently put it perfectly: "Then it's really just asking these holy people to talk to

God with us, and for us, for the things we need! That's beautiful, because it's just what we do with people who are close and dear to us here on earth." The pope couldn't have said it better.

Perhaps much of the problem is in the phrase "pray to," which had a much broader meaning in the past. In present English usage, it more often implies the kind of adoration and relationship that belongs uniquely to God. It is particularly important, therefore, to understand precisely what is meant by "praying to" the saints.

Mary Magdalene

A recent article on the saints dealt with Mary Magdalene. It has me confused.

I attended Catholic schools through college and never was informed that Mary Magdalene was the sister of Martha and of Lazarus, who was raised from the dead. Could you tell me on what authority it is concluded that they are one and the same?

Even though biblical evidence is heavy in the other direction, a tradition in the Latin Church honors as one person three women in the Bible — the sinful woman in Luke (chapter 7), Mary of Bethany — the sister of Lazarus, and Mary Magdalene, who, among other mentions of her in the New Testament, experienced the vision of Jesus in the garden after the resurrection.

The Latin Church, unlike the Greek Church, honors all three women together under the title of St. Mary Magdalene on July 22.

Most, if not all, Scripture scholars today agree with the Greek tradition. The Gospels are speaking of three distinct women. Far too many discrepancies appear between them in the Gospels to allow an identification of Mary Magdalene with Mary of Bethany.

Why Catholics Have Statues

What light can you throw on why Catholics have statues in their churches and most Protestant churches do not?

Images of Jesus and the saints have been used, as you probably know, for decorational and devotional purposes since the very beginning of Christianity. Today, only the most grossly uninformed person gives any credence to the old accusation that Catholics worship these statues or pictures.

Several hundred years ago, the Council of Trent explained the practice perfectly: "The images of Christ, the Virgin Mother of God, and of the other saints are kept and honored in churches not because it is believed that there is any divinity or power in these images, or that anything may be asked of them, or any faith be put in them. The honor shown to them is really being given to the persons whom they represent. Through these images which we kiss, and before which we bow with bared heads, we worship Christ, and not the saints whose likenesses they display."

Even many Catholics do not realize that, since such pictures and statues become intimately connected with what people believe about God and his revelation, the church is very careful about what images are allowed for public veneration. All such pictures or sculptures must be approved by the bishop or other proper authority.

The reasons most Protestant denominations do not allow images in their churches are varied. One is that, early in the Protestant Reformation there was much misunderstanding about the meaning of honoring images of Jesus and the saints, and "no statues" became one of the symbols of protest against the church of Rome.

Perhaps a more significant reason is that many early Protestant leaders, especially of the Calvinist and other Puritan traditions, were extremely austere and considered any sort of display, color, or emotion, such as might be encouraged by statues and pictures, totally out of place in religious worship.

Is St. Patrick Still A Saint?

An argument arose in our group when we were talking about St. Patrick's Day as to whether or not St. Patrick is still considered a saint. Some say they read that he is no longer considered as such by the Catholic Church, but the rest of us say that is impossible.

In the past few years a good deal of confused comment has appeared in the press in connection with St. Patrick's Day celebrations, so it's understandable that your group is confused, too. Several years ago, following extensive scientific reasearch in the catacombs and other ancient locations, Catholic Church officials acknowledged serious doubts about the existence of certain early "saints," at least with the names traditionally given them. The mistakes came from misinterpreting inscriptions on tombs, misreading old documents, and so on.

St. Patrick was not one of these. He is among another group of saints whose feast days were dropped from the universal church calendar for automatic observance by Latin-Rite Catholics everywhere. Many saints' feasts were eliminated this way, or otherwise de-emphasized, in order that more liturgical attention might be given the seasonal celebrations of the mysteries of Our Lord — Christmas, Lent, Holy Week, Easter and others.

Though not in the general church calendar, however, these feasts can still be celebrated in countries and localities which desire to do so — as St. Patrick's Day is in most parts of the United States on March 17.

Ironworkers Patron?

Some of us would like to know the patron saint for ironworkers, if there is one, for a forthcoming celebration. When is his feast day?

The most commonly accepted patron of metal workers is Saint Eligius, bishop of Noyon in France. He learned the metal working trade from his father, and became one of the most skilled in his art in Europe during the early Middle Ages.

For years he held the position of official artisan for King Clotaire of France. Many of his works still exist. He was also noted for his remarkable honesty, and his concern for the poor who were always seen around his home. His feast is Dec. 1, the date of his death, in the year 660.

St. Catherine of Mt. Sinai

A news story during the Israeli-Arab war mentioned Mount Sinai and referred to a Christian Saint Catherine who is supposed to be buried there. My name is Catherine, and I never heard anything about her before. Was the story true?

You are referring to an early Christian woman, perhaps a martyr, Saint Catherine of Alexandria, who supposedly died about the year 300.

Almost nothing is known about her. Two accounts exist. One is a story of her birth as a princess, and her mystical union with Christ in prayer. The other describes her martyrdom in Alexandria (after she converted to Christianity as the wife of the Emperor), and the transfer of her body by angels to Mount Sinai. Neither of these accounts seems to contain much that is certain.

When some Eastern monks founded a monastery on Mt. Sinai centuries later, the veneration of St. Catherine grew, and since the 900s has been widespread.

A number of other saints named Catherine existed about whose lives and holiness much more is definitely known. A good example is Saint Catherine of Siena, a woman very influential in the history of the church during the 1300s.

Private Revelations — Fatima

Our local newspaper and some recent books have included information about Fatima, the appearance of the Blessed Mother, and the miracles that were supposed to have happened there. The church I attend tells people that the first Saturday devotion (receiving Communion on the first Saturday of each month, which Mary was sup-

posed to have requested at Fatima for world peace) is only a private devotion.

What is the church's teaching about Fatima, and whatever became of the letter that was to be opened in 1960?

First, a few words about private revelations are in order.

God can speak to us in thousands of different ways. Giving special messages to individual men or women to pass on to the rest of us is one of them. In fact, the prophets of the Old Testament and hundreds of Christians since then have filled precisely that role.

The church has enormous respect for the role of prophets. It realizes, however, that individuals can easily fool themselves into thinking that God is giving them private messages in support of their own prejudices. From the evidence of my own mail, I can testify that there is hardly a weird idea possible in the field of religion that someone doesn't believe God has told him to preach.

Some private revelations (Lourdes is perhaps the most famous) the church has officially approved. Some, such as the alleged appearances of Our Lady at Necedah, Wis., in the 1950s, it has officially rejected. About many of them it has said nothing one way or the other.

When the church approves such messages, all it says is that there is nothing in them contrary to Catholic faith or morals, and that following the suggestions in these messages can be helpful in our efforts toward holiness. It is essential to remember that the church never imposes a special belief, or practices contained in these revelations, as obligations for all Catholics. The Mass and sacraments, the teachings of the Gospel, and universally accepted traditional practices of our faith are basic for everyone. Apart from them, no one is obliged to accept or follow anything in private revelation, though a proper respect for the fact that God can speak to us this way is proper for us, as it is for the whole church.

Now about Fatima. Church officials, including popes, have many times indicated acceptance of the fact that the mother of Jesus appeared to the three shepherd children at Fatima, Portugal, during 1917, urging prayer and penance by all Christians for world peace. Surely many people in the decades since then have been inspired to these spiritual good works by the message of Fatima.

Again, however, no Catholic is obliged in any way by the church to special practices, devotions or prayers suggested at Fatima, except insofar as they are already contained in the responsibilities we have as Catholic Christians. In that sense, Fatima, and everything connected with it is private revelation.

The letter you speak of was reputedly passed down by one of the shepherd children to be opened in 1960. Rumor had it that the letter threatened that if mankind did not return to God by that year, the sword of God's vengeance would descend upon us.

What happened to the letter, if it ever existed? One wag suggested a few years ago that Pope John lost it. Whatever the answer may be, the church has never put much stock in that kind of view of a vengeful God, poised above us in his wrath, and ready to clobber us properly if we don't shape up. Our sins have enough evil consequences on their own without outside help.

Any Poor Catholic Saints?

Can a poor Roman Catholic have a chance to become a canonized saint? Such people do not belong to church societies, do not do much volunteer work, do not attend fairs and luncheons because they cannot afford it, and often don't come in contact with the pastor. All a poor Catholic can do is attend Mass on Sundays and holy days, practice the teachings of the church, raise his children to know their faith, and do small kind deeds the best way he can.

So is the Catholic Church fair in picking out canonized saints? God shows no such partiality.

Probably the most striking and happy note about your letter is that you seriously consider becoming a saint. Great for you. You mention the "only" things a poor person can do. Those aren't so insignificant as you seem to believe. Follow through on them and you can't miss.

You have a couple of misconceptions, however, about canonized saints. One is that there are no poor people among them. The list of poor saints is so huge one wouldn't know where to begin.

It is true that most canonized saints, particularly in the last several hundred years, have been members of religious orders, or people of some prominence in the church. That is partly because the process of canonization is so long and so complex, that a fairly large number of people have to be interested in the project, and able to carry it through many years for a successful canonization procedure. It is not all that rare, though, for a relatively unknown man or woman, lay person or Religious, to be officially declared a saint.

More importantly, in canonizing saints the church in no way says these are the only holy people, or even the most holy people, in the world. It is entirely likely that among the saintliest persons are thousands or millions who were completely unknown to all but a few family members and friends, but whose faith and love and closeness to God will shine brilliantly throughout eternity.

When the church canonizes anyone, she doesn't declare that this man or woman was the holiest on earth. She simply says that the individual led a Christian life of sufficient and evident heroism that we can be sure that person is in heaven, and that we on earth might in many ways use that saint's life as a model for our own.

So maybe you will never have a church built in your honor. Don't let that bother you. To paraphrase an old saying, some of my best friends are uncanonized saints.

St. Gerard

My husband and I wanted a child badly and someone gave us a prayer to St. Gerard to say for this intention. Who was he, and why is he supposed to be a "patron" for people like us?

St. Gerard Majella was an Italian lay brother and mystic who died at the age of 29 in 1755. After a childhood filled with an unusual share of mental and physical hardships, and after being rejected by the Capuchin monks because of ill health, he was finally accepted in the Redemptorist novitiate as "a useless lay brother."

So many miracles were attributed to him that even in his lifetime he became known as the wonderworker. Then, and after his death, a number of these miracles involved situations which caused him to become the special patron of couples who seemed to be unable to have children. His feast is Oct. 16.

Visions at Garabandal

What is the church's position on the apparitions of the Blessed Virgin at Garabandal? I know the church treats these things in a low-key way, but a film I saw on this subject moved me deeply and I'd like to learn more about it.

Garabandal is another of those shrines at which, after extensive investigation by competent religious and scientific authorities, claims of some supernatural activity have proven groundless.

In March 1967, Bishop Vicente Montis of Santander, Spain, (Garabandal is located in this diocese) reported the following after his own investigation: "There have been no apparitions of the Blessed Virgin, of Michael the Archangel, or of any other celestial person; there have been no messages. All of the reported happenings in that area have a natural explanation."

In spite of the bishop's findings, local devotees continued their activities. The following year, the succeeding bishop of Santander upheld the decision of Bishop Montis, insisting that priests and lay people refrain from visiting a chapel built at Garabandal "in rebellious resistance to the findings of the church" concerning the so-called apparitions. These statements remain the official position of the church regarding Garabandal.

Fatima Named After Mohammedan?

Is it true that the town of Fatima, where the Blessed Virgin Mary appeared several times, is named after a Mohammedan? I was told this is a sign of the future conversion of the Mohammedans to Christ.

The prophet Mohammed, who lived about 600 years after Our Lord, had a daughter named Fatima. Centuries later, after hundreds of years of Moslem occupation of southern Europe, one of the last Moslem officials in the area of Portugal (which now includes Fatima) also had a daughter by that name. She married a Catholic, and became a Catholic herself. Supposedly, her husband named the town after her.

Some have seen a sort of symbol in the appearances of Mary at Fatima of eventual better relations between Mohammedans and Christians. Interestingly, Moslems have a great devotion to Mary as the mother of Jesus, whom they consider a prophet. They even believe in her Immaculate Conception, and in the virgin birth of Jesus. After the death of his daughter, Fatima, Mohammed wrote these words to her: "You will be the most blessed lady of all women in Paradise, after Mary."

Luther a Saint?

I heard recently that the Catholic Church is thinking of canonizing Martin Luther! How is it possible for the church to make a saint out of someone who lived like he did, and who caused such a terrible break from the Catholic Church?

I hardly know where to start this one. First, it may ease your mind to know that, rumors to the contrary, no one, Catholic or Protestant, is pushing to get Martin Luther canonized, to my knowledge.

A bit of explanation why these rumors have even arisen may help respond to the rest of your question. Sources and methods available to modern history scholars have brought about a major re-evaluation of Luther, and of the whole period that began the Protestant Reformation. One fact clear today, for example, is how drastically the harsh, bitter spirit of debate during the early decades of the Reformation affected the accusations and recriminations of both sides. These writings formed the major basis of what Catholics said about Luther (and Lutherans), and what Lutherans said about Catholics, almost up to our own generation.

Among facts widely acknowledged by historians are that much of what has been written about Luther's personal life is unfounded, and that many of his "heretical" teachings (about faith and the Eucharist, for example) are most compatible with Catholic doctrine when they are understood as he understood them, not as some of his early opponents interpreted them.

In addition, the most authoritative historians on the Council of Trent (which started the year before Luther died, and lasted 18 years) tend strongly to the belief that the reforms of that council would never have happened had it not been for the movement set in motion by Luther and some other early reformers. Pope Paul had several times said we all have much to repent in the tragic separation between Catholics and Protestants. He referred, in part, to the fact that the church was in many ways in a sorry condition at that time. A sweeping reform was long overdue, but even the heroic efforts of courageous Catholic reformers like St. Bernardine and St. Catherine of Siena had achieved only limited and local results. Something like Luther and his movement was probably inevitable to make the renewal happen.

This is, of course, not to defend everything Luther did and taught. It does, however, put his life, and what he "caused," in a considerably more charitable light. Lutherans themselves do not, I believe, admire him as a saint, nor as the perfect ideal of a Christian, but as a man who reacted with courage and intelligence to a personal and Christian crisis.

Immaculate Conception

I realize we have Scripture and tradition as a basis for our beliefs. But when someone not of our faith asks for proof of the Immaculate Conception of the Blessed Virgin Mary from the Bible, what should be our answer?

There is no proof, in the ordinary sense of the word, of the Immaculate Conception in the Bible. But this is not strange; every Christian believes quite a number of things which, even if he does not realize it, cannot be proven from the Bible.

There are some texts from Scripture, however, that may strongly suggest or imply a belief by the earliest Christians in the Immaculate Conception of Mary — that is, that she was sinless, by the saving grace of Jesus, from the time of her conception in the womb of her mother. Certain passages in the first part of St. Luke's Gospel concerning her and her relation to Jesus clearly indicate a conviction of the first Christians that she was an exceptionally holy person who shared in a particularly intimate and total way in the victory of Our Lord over sin, perhaps even to being totally free from any stain of moral imperfection or offense. But these texts are not what one could call proofs.

The more detailed theological implications of Mary's holiness and of her sharing in the work of Jesus as Savior (such as the Immaculate Conception), while hinted at in Scripture, were only gradually clarified and understood by the church through the centuries.

Mother of God?

Several weeks ago, two Jehovah Witnesses came to my door. Normally I just tell them I'm Catholic and am not interested. This time was different, since one of the women recognized me as a school friend.

One of them asked why we refer to Mary as the mother of God in the Hail Mary, since she is known as the mother of Jesus. I didn't know the answer, but told her it was worth checking into.

Yes, I would agree it's worth checking into! In fact, I would hope that most Catholics could give the answer.

We believe Jesus is God, the Second Person of the Blessed Trinity, who came to this earth and became man. Jesus is God (and man); Mary is his mother; therefore, we believe Mary is the mother of God.

Since Jehovah Witnesses do not believe in the Trinity, and in fact reject that doctrine as a pagan superstition, there is no way they could believe that Jesus is God. Obviously, then, there's no way they could accept the belief that Mary is the mother of God.

Who Is Mary?

I trust you will be willing to answer a question from a Protestant who is greatly puzzled by the reference to Mary as the mother of God. God is the Creator, without beginning or end. Mary was born of earthly parents. Then why do Catholics call her the mother of God?

You are not alone in being puzzled. The same question is frequently asked by other non-Catholic Christians. The answer begins with different beliefs about Jesus himself. According to our Catholic belief, Jesus is truly and completely both God and man. God the Son, the second person of the Trinity, came to this earth and took on a human nature. In doing this, he did not stop being God, of course, but he became also perfectly human. As the Letter to the Hebrews puts it, he is "like us in everything except that he did not sin."

Many Protestant churches believe that Jesus is Lord and Savior, that he is "God's Son," and that he is an exceptionally holy man. But they do not believe that he was (we should say is) truly God. This difference in belief about Jesus will have obvious results in our beliefs about his mother.

When Catholics speak of Mary as the mother of God, they do not mean that she was God's parent from eternity, but that she was the mother of Jesus when he came to earth. Since Jesus was God from the first moment of his coming in the womb of Mary, she is correctly called God's — that is Jesus' — mother.

Mary has been referred to with this title, by the way, from the earliest centuries of the church. That title for her was, in fact, jealously safeguarded by Christians not primarily to honor her, but to be sure that the church preserved its proper belief about Jesus himself being the Incarnate God.

Serious questioning of the title "Mother of God" as applied to Mary only began when certain Christian groups denied the divinity of Jesus (that is, that he is both God and man) after the time of the Protestant Reformation.

Is Mary Divine?

Your answer concerning Mary as the mother of God said that early Christians referred to Mary not primarily to honor her but to honor Jesus. If this is true, how can the church urge that we pray to Mary, as the pope recently did when he recommended prayer to her for an increase in vocations to the priesthood and religious life. Isn't it true that Catholics pray to Mary? I don't believe there is any place in the Bible that says that she is divine.

We do not believe Mary is divine. She is a human being who needed the saving graces of her Son just as we do. We pray to her in much the same way as we pray to the other saints, or for that matter, in much the same way we "pray" to any other people when we ask them to pray for us. We simply follow a basic human and Christian instinct that there is a bond between us that even transcends death.

You will notice that the prayers to our Blessed Mother, as our prayers to the other saints, always ask her to use her own words of prayer to her Son, or to the Father, or to the Holy Spirit, and these always end with our common formula for prayer: "Through Jesus Christ our Lord."

As long as we keep this perspective (and our Catholic tradition certainly does), the prayer and honor that we give to Mary can be nothing but a source of joy and pleasure to her Son. Beginning with the Gospels themselves, she has never been in any competition with him, nor has he been with her.

Where Was Mary Born?

On a trip to Greece we were taken to an island where the Blessed Mother was said to have been born. If this is true, how did she come to Bethlehem and Nazareth?

To the best of our knowledge, Mary was born in Jerusalem. While there may be some doubt about that, I know of no tradition that places her birth in the area you indicate.

Perhaps you're thinking of the ancient city of Ephesus which, according to some traditions, was the home of John the Evangelist in his later years. Since Jesus shortly before his death on the cross gave Mary into John's care, this tradition could also place Mary's final days in Ephesus. It is more commonly believed, however, that she spent her last years in or around Jerusalem and died there.

Mary's Death?

I was surprised at your answer concerning the place of Mary's birth and death. You said she probably died in the vicinity of Jerusalem.

I thought we believed that Mary did not die, but was taken up into heaven by God in the Assumption. Do we believe that Mary died or don't we?

Catholic doctrine says nothing one way or the other about Mary's death. Christian writers through the centuries have debated both sides of this question. It has, however, nothing to do with the doctrine of the Assumption.

When Pope Pius XII defined the doctrine of the Assumption in 1950, he deliberately avoided any attempt at settling the controversy. He simply said that "at the end of her earthly life" (the official Latin text reads "expleto terrestris vitae cursu"), Mary was taken body and soul into heaven by God.

The most common belief is that Mary died just as everyone else has, including Jesus. But there is no official church teaching on the subject.

Assumption of Mary

The doctrine of the Assumption of the Blessed Virgin Mary has been a real problem for me to accept since I see our Blessed Mother as a human being like myself. She was blessed by God, but completely human.

If she was more than human, where then would Jesus receive his human nature? We know that he was totally God and totally man.

You certainly have a fine grasp of the basic theology concerning Mary and Jesus. She is completely human as we are; she is not some sort of "demi-god" that would place her somewhere between God and man.

The doctrine of the Assumption in no way detracts from that total humanity. It simply says that after she finished her life on this earth she was taken body and soul to heaven. This does not imply that she was not totally human, any more than our own final resurrection will mean that we are not fully human.

Mary and the Rosary

I have a special devotion to Mary and try to say my Rosary daily. I have heard that there is now a new "Rosary" with five mysteries instead of 15. Is this true? And if it is, which one should we use?

My attention has been called a few times recently to a different form of the Rosary, combining the major events in the life of Jesus and Mary into five mysteries instead of the traditional 15. I know nothing more about it, however.

One is free, of course, to use any meditative themes in such devotions, if they help one to pray better. The 15 mysteries of the Rosary have a special place in Catholic prayer and tradition because they confront us with the key events in the story of our salvation.

The Eucharist

Mass on Sabbath Day?

A few weeks ago, I saw a reference to the obligation of hearing Mass on Sunday, tying it to the commandment to keep holy the Sabbath Day. Is this really a law that not even the pope could change?

The commandment to "keep holy the Sabbath day" could never be interpreted as a commandment referring to Sunday Mass. For one thing, the Mass was still many centuries in the future when Moses received the Ten Commandments. For another, the Sabbath day — from the Hebrew verb "sabat," rest — was Saturday, the seventh day of the week, not Sunday.

Christians have, of course, celebrated Sunday as the Lord's Day from the earliest centuries; but the obligation to attend Mass on Sunday, as we know it, is comparatively recent. That obligation, as it now exists in church law, could be removed or modified by the church itself.

"Far Out" Liturgies?

I've heard several times about so-called "far out" liturgies. What are these "far out" Masses?

Obviously the phrase isn't a technical one and doesn't appear in any official church documents. So it might mean a lot of things.

For some people, a Mass with guitar music, or with a lady lector or Communion minister, is far out. A large group of Catholics still believe that our new English Mass is itself far out, if not downright heretical, and that the Holy Father has betrayed the church by allowing it.

More commonly, however, "far out" means a liturgy that violates serious regulations of the church concerning the Mass and the sacraments. Church authorities — ultimately, the bishop of each diocese —

have the responsibility of seeing to it that a spirit of decency, dignity, and reverence is preserved in all official worship. This doesn't mean that they can arbitrarily impose their own likes and dislikes on everyone else. Nor can they in justice refuse to permit perfectly legitimate varieties in the liturgy, not recognizing that genuine differences in personality, background, and age, ought naturally to be reflected in the way people worship.

It does mean, however, that all — priests, especially — have the responsibility to observe those basic regulations by which the church attempts to keep ceremonies of the worship of God from becoming cheap, tawdry, and sometimes offensive displays.

For example, certain rules exist concerning the dress of the priest and the place for the offering of the Mass. They are intended to be observed in all but the most grave circumstances. Therefore, to offer the Holy Sacrifice in shirt sleeves around the kitchen table would certainly be unlawful, would seem to demonstrate some lack of community consciousness and concern — and by almost every definition would be "far out."

Sunday Mass Where?

Our family has attended Mass quite regularly outside our own parish. Someone recently told me this was against the church's regulations. We know what we must do if we want our children to grow up with a love and appreciation for the Mass and their faith. But out of curiosity, is there any church law on this subject?

The only actual church regulation on this subject is the present (1918) Code of Canon Law. It says (Canon 467) that the Catholic faithful should be "exhorted to participate in divine worship and hear the word of God in their own parish churches frequently, insofar as this is convenient or practicable."

Children Won't Go To Mass

My teen-age children think I'm wrong in forcing them to go to Mass on Sundays. They are 14 and 16, but they say they "don't get anything out of it." We battle every Sunday. Can you help me put the record straight? What can I do?

What record? It's all in your question, and it sounds awfully frustrating and unhappy for both you and your children.

Looking at it only from your direction right now, it's critically important for parents and any others responsible for growing children to keep clearly in mind what they are aiming at, long range, in their religious training.

I'm sure your primary goal is to help your children toward a mature, living faith and trust in God, and a feeling of reverence for the place of the Eucharist in the community of Catholics that will be with them in their adult lives. Your purpose is not simply to be able to congratulate yourself after 20 years that you've been able to get them through those church doors every Sunday morning.

Clearly, the understanding of the Mass and the community of faith that should ideally exist between parents and children have broken down seriously in your home. If, when your children are in their mid and upper teens, you are still forcing and battling over something as central to Catholic life and worship as the Mass, I think you'd have to agree there isn't much likelihood that they are building a faith they will love and be proud of later on.

There is still time for you to reconsider seriously what you really want to achieve in your children in the matter of religion. This may involve asking yourself some pretty brutal questions such as: What does your own faith mean to you, and why are you so concerned that your children share it? Why do you go to Mass yourself?

If you're to be any support and guide to your children, make yourself be very specific in your answers. Perhaps a conversation with a priest or a teacher who deals regularly with teen-age children would help you. It's too bad this wasn't done more thoughtfully before — like 10 or 15 years ago.

More on Teen-agers and the Mass

Dear Readers:

My response to the mother who wrote saying that she had a battle every Sunday morning with her teen-age children about going to Mass must have hit many tender nerves. Here's a sampling of readers' reactions:

From Texas: You are wrong in saying something has seriously broken down in a home when teen-age children have to be battled and forced to go to Mass. Catholic education must share in the fact that, of our eight children, only one still practices her religion. You're as frustrated as we are.

From Illinois: Your answer is typical of the parish administrator who can't be bothered with pastoring, who doesn't inquire into the possibility that the "turned-off" teen-ager may be his fault.

From Arizona: I'm not too sure you believe in the laws of the church or the first of the Ten Commandments. I was terribly mixed up, but a true and old-time priest friend told me: Just remember the things the good nuns taught you.

From Florida: I don't know what ivory tower you've been living

in. Children who went to church with enthusiasm in their earlier years seem to undergo a personality change in adolescence. "As the twig is bent by the peer group, so the tree shall grow."

From Ohio: In a good Catholic high school my daughter was taught she did not have to go to church every Sunday. Where have you been? Don't you know what they are teaching these days? Many parents are having the same problem, and it starts at school, not at home!

My only further response to these and others who wrote is that it is useless, and usually grossly inaccurate, to assign blame for the religious floundering of young people today. The parent asked what she could do about the problem, not what churches or schools could do. I tried to answer her.

Home, church and school are closely interrelated, and normally reflect each other. I still believe, however, that the home is the major factor in what a person becomes as an adult — which may be quite different, incidentally, from what he is as a teen-ager.

As for what is being taught in schools, have you ever gone straight to the teacher involved and asked what exactly is being said and taught? I have, several times. It can be a helpful and sometimes enlightening experience.

Finally, I'd like to pass on what one reader claims would have been the "correct answer" to the question. I disagree with some of it, especially the first sentence, which he himself contradicts at the end. But it makes many good points. Here it is:

"Until large numbers of priests learn to make their liturgies the meaningful and beautiful services they can and should be, there is nothing you can do. Your best efforts are nullified by the lifeless, sterile and cold liturgical services conducted by so many of our priests. You might try searching in your area for a parish where the priest does something more than go through a ritualistic ceremony which not even he seems to believe in.

"So many priests make no effort to turn the child on. Although they are the celebrants, they refuse to treat the Mass as a celebration. They resent and often refuse to offer the sign of peace. They think love is a dirty word when used by one person to another, and are horrified by the idea of a kiss in the sacred confines of the church.

"CCD classes are devoted to catechism-like teachings by rote, with no attempt to understand what their students need and want. They are satisfied with reports to the bishop which show that they do, in fact, have a Mass and CCD schedule. After that, in the words of one priest in our diocese: If they don't come, the hell with them.

"These comments do not apply to all; they do apply very often.

Keep trying. In the meantime, don't blame yourself. Do your best to inculcate Christian values in your children; continue to love them, encourage them and pray.

"Because of God's gift of free will, they cannot be forced to be practicing Catholics. Continue to give good example. Let them know that you yourself are aware of their problem, but are trying, through the Mass and sacraments, to stay close to God and his church."

"Dry Mass?"

A liturgy book we are studying refers to a "dry Mass." What is this?

The "dry Mass" was a devotional ceremony which was for several hundred years observed on special occasions in parishes and monasteries. If a priest officiated, he might be fully vested as for Mass, though the prayers usually excluded everything between the bringing of the gifts and the Communion.

In ways, this practice resembled some current para-liturgical ceremonies. The wake service for the dead, for example, is patterned after the Liturgy of the Word at Mass and is, in that sense, similar to some of the "dry Mass" liturgies.

Retarded at Mass?

Often when I attend our parish Mass, a group of retarded teenagers is present with a person in charge. Why do these poor people have to attend Mass? Surely they do not understand what is going on and are not interested in being at church.

Do they have the obligation to attend Sunday Mass?

In my opinion you vastly underestimate the ability of many mentally handicapped people to understand and participate in the liturgy, or other activities for that matter.

A group from our local association for retarded citizens regularly attends Mass in our parish. In addition, I frequently celebrate Mass myself with a number of mentally and physically handicapped children and adults. My experience is that, while their intellectual grasp might not equal that of others, their joy, their awareness of the presence and love of God, and their simple human warmth are unmistakable.

True, much of this results from the unusual degree of tenderness and care given them by their parents and family, and from the love of the many remarkable people who volunteer to help them. But it's real nonetheless.

Such children probably would be excused from Sunday Mass. By no means does it follow, however, that they cannot receive much from, and offer much to, those who celebrate the Eucharist with them.

Hear or Read Scripture?

Our parish has booklets for people to use at Mass. Until recently, our booklets had the readings from the Bible that are read in Sunday Mass. Now they do not.

Our pastor said they were not supposed to be in the booklets any more. Can you tell me why? It has been a big help to be able to read the Scripture passages while the priest is reading them.

For those of us who were raised with the notion that the ideal was to use a missal and follow the priest at Mass, it certainly is puzzling when we're told we should not be reading at Mass, even the readings from the Bible.

The main reason for our puzzlement is that we have forgotten that *hearing* the Word of God is a liturgical act, an act of public worship. When the Mass was in Latin, meaningful hearing of the Word was, of course, impossible. So, after English translations of the Mass became permissible around the beginning of this century, we fell back on following what the priest was saying by reading the English version.

When the lector (reader or priest) proclaims the Word of God at the celebration of Mass, he performs an act of worship; and we perform an act of worship with him by *listening* attentively and prayerfully to that Word. Thus, the church's directives discourage whenever possible the printing of the Scripture texts in Mass booklets.

Obviously, this doesn't mean that private reading of Scripture is unimportant or discouraged. It's simply that the solemn proclaiming of the Word during Mass is not the place for it.

In fairness, I believe two things should be provided before the Scripture texts are taken out of the hands of the worshipers. First, the church ought to have a decent and adequate public address system. Second, the lectors should be trained to read the Scriptures clearly and intelligently so they can be easily understood. Until these two qualifications are met, it's probably better to have the printed texts in hand. But even then, we should try to wean ourselves away from reading to listening whenever we can.

Particles of the Eucharist

Isn't there danger of desecrating the Host from particles falling on the lips, hands, clothing, pews, or floor after Communion? What should one do about such fears?

It is Catholic doctrine that Jesus Christ is present in the Holy Eucharist as long as the reasonable appearance of bread and wine is there. The traditional theological phrase is that Christ is present "under the species of bread and wine." The Latin word "species" means "that which can be seen," or "that which makes manifest."

Thus, when the "species" of bread or wine are no longer there, as for example in almost microscopic crumbs, the Body of Christ is no longer present. The church wants us to deal with the sacraments with the eyes of faith, but also in a common sense, human manner. Don't worry about tiny particles that "may" have fallen and adhered to clothing or fingers. This kind of scrupulosity is unnecessary, and actually distracts from the attitude of love and devotion that should surround our reception of the Eucharist.

Unconsecrated Chalice at Mass?

Recently a priest offered Mass in the home of a friend. The friend wanted the priest to use a cup that belongs to their family as a chalice, but the priest refused. He explained he could use only a consecrated chalice. I thought this rule had been changed. Has it?

There are some changes in the rules about chalices, but the priest was correct. Only blessed chalices should be used for offering the Eucharistic Sacrifice. The reasons for this are clear; anything used this intimately in the Eucharist should be reverently cared for and not be put to common use.

It is true that now chalices probably become "blessed" simply by being used for the offering of the Eucharist. But once they are so used, they should remain set apart for that purpose thereafter (see the "Rite for the Dedication of a Church and Altar," 1977).

If the occasion arises again, and if the cup meets the necessary qualifications, perhaps your friends would be willing to give the vessel to the priest or to the parish church to be used as a chalice.

Who Banned the Tridentine Mass?

I have been told that the documents of the Second Vatican Council never intended to outlaw the traditional Latin Mass, and that Pope Paul had never revoked the Mass as set by Pope Pius V.

Exactly who, or what assembly, officially banned the traditional ("Tridentine") Mass for Roman Catholic parishes? Did it originate with the American bishops?

The Roman Missal approved by Pope Pius V in 1570 was officially revoked and replaced with the new Rite of the Mass by Pope Paul on April 3, 1969.

The Vatican Council's job was not to construct new rituals for the Mass and the sacraments. It laid down the principles and theology which were to guide the church in the years following as this work was done.

In his Apostolic Constitution of 1969, Pope Paul VI pointed out that the Roman Missal approved in 1570 was one of the admirable results of the Council of Trent, and served the church well for four centuries.

Since then, he continued, a liturgical renewal developed among Christians that recent popes have seen as a sign of God's providence and of the saving action of the Holy Spirit.

After reviewing the developments and work before and after the Second Vatican Council, Pope Paul officially gave the force of law to the new Roman Missal, and expressed the hope that it would "be received by the faithful as a help and witness to the common unity of all." He then explicitly stated (as is common in documents like this) that the new regulations for the Mass supersede and replace previous regulations issued by popes or anyone else.

Thus, if Latin Masses are desirable for some reason in a parish, they are allowed, but they must be according to the revised rite as approved by the Holy Father.

Chalice

Is it true that the chalice at Mass doesn't have to be gold or gold plated any more?

Until recently, the rule was that at least the inside of chalices, and other vessels used to hold the consecrated wine and hosts at Mass, had to be gold plated.

According to present regulations, such sacred vessels should be of some material which would be considered locally as having some value and appropriate for sacred use. Ebony or other hard woods are mentioned as examples of appropriate material.

Incidentally, the regulations as to the shape of the vessels are broader also. It is required only that they have a form that is in keeping with the local culture and with their purpose in the liturgy.

Sacred Vessels

During the past weekend I attended Mass at the parish church of my son and his family.

Toward the end of Mass, instead of washing the chalice and dish himself, the priest let the servers take the chalice to the side table where the servers washed them.

This is a new one on me. Isn't the priest the only one who is to wash the sacred vessels any more?

The General Instruction of the Roman Missal states: "After Communion the acolyte helps the priest and deacon to wash the vessels and arrange them. If there is no deacon, the acolyte takes the vessels to the side table where he washes them and arranges them" — meaning, of course, one who has been officially installed in the ministry of acolyte. The same applies, incidentally, to special ministers of the Eucharist who have been designated to distribute Communion.

In anything dealing with the handling of the Eucharist, the church always presupposes that such individuals are mature, responsible adults, who have been properly instructed and trained for this responsibility. It is entirely inappropriate, therefore, to allow regular Mass servers to purify the sacred vessels as part of their responsibilities.

Can Women Give Communion?

I was in a church for Sunday Mass and saw a woman helping to distribute Communion. Since when is this allowed?

At least since April 30, 1969, and in some places in the world before that. On that date, the Vatican instruction entitled "Fidei Custos" provided for the authorization by the local bishop of certain individuals to help distribute Communion in parishes or other institutions where the priest for some reason needs such help.

Frankly, I'm surprised you have only recently encountered the practice. The qualifications for such ministers of Communion are that they be "mature Christian persons of excellent character, who take their faith seriously and live a Christian life." There is no requirement as to sex.

Can Women Be Lectors?

Is it true that women are now allowed to be lectors (readers) at Mass? If so, why are there so many churches where only men have this privilege? We are in a small parish and have some women lectors. Visitors from other places, however, sometimes tell us that they do not like the idea, and that only men are allowed in the sanctuary.

According to present liturgical regulations, except for functions reserved to priests and deacons, women have almost the same right to liturgical ministry as do men. This includes leading the singing, directing liturgical participation, acting as commentator, reading Scripture, and serving as extraordinary ministers of the Eucharist. One exception is actual assistance at the altar as a server.

By decree of the Congregation on Divine Worship, only those qualifications may be required of women as are required of men —

worthiness of life, and so on. The same decree also requires that when women do read the Scripture, they do so where the other readings are proclaimed, so that a single place is reserved for all biblical readings. In other words, it is no longer stipulated, as it once was, that women remain outside the sanctuary. Whatever a woman does, she should do in the most appropriate place.

The American bishops emphasized the same thing in a 1971 statement on the liturgy: "In the liturgical celebration, as in other facets of the church's life, there should be no discrimination or apparent discrimination against women."

The exercise of the ministry of reader by women is provided for in the present Order of the Mass (1969), the Instruction of the Congregation for Divine Worship of 1970, and the above-mentioned liturgical instructions issued by the American Bishops' Committee on the Liturgy of 1971 — among numerous other documents.

A Question on Holy Communion

I cannot understand why Catholics do not always receive Holy Communion from the chalice, in addition to the Host. Why is the blood of Christ not as important as his body, when he gave both at his supper and said we should have both to have eternal life?

I'm a convert to the Catholic faith and trying hard to understand some of these things.

Speaking strictly and theologically, we receive the whole living, risen Jesus Christ whenever we receive Holy Communion, whether we receive that Communion under the form of bread by itself, wine by itself, or both together. I'm sure you realize that Jesus is not somehow divided up in the Eucharist, with half of him under the form of bread and the other half under the form of wine. The words "eating" and "drinking" express two ways we can make our eucharistic communion with him; but we receive Jesus, whole and entire, either way.

On the other hand, Communion under both species is much more than a mere liturgical frill. This manner of receiving Communion sacramentally expresses the reality of the eucharistic meal with far greater richness than Communion under one species alone.

The General Instruction to the Roman Missal puts it very well: "The sign of Communion is more complete when given under both kinds — bread and wine — since in that form the sign of the eucharistic meal appears more clearly. The intention of Christ that the new and eternal covenant be ratified in his blood is better expressed, as is the relation of the eucharistic banquet to the heavenly banquet...The faithful should be urged to drink from the cup, for this brings out the sign of the eucharistic meal more fully." (240 and 241)

Thus, it is good to take advantage of any opportunity to receive under both species. Just keep in mind that when we receive only the bread, or only the cup, we are "eating his body and drinking his blood" since we receive the living, risen Lord.

Mass Intentions

I have visited many different parishes in our state in which the name of the deceased person for whom a Mass is being offered is not mentioned. In fact, in our area this practice has been eliminated almost completely. Is it just that priests do not want to bother, or is there another reason that the Mass intention is not indicated at the Mass itself?

I can think of two reasons. First, most priests today try to reduce announcements during Mass to a minimum. Since the special intentions for daily Masses are usually in the parish bulletin, everyone at church already has access to this information.

If a particular name is to be designated, the appropriate place would be in the Prayer of the Faithful or possibly in the Eucharistic Prayer at the commemoration of the dead.

Second, there is a greater realization today than in the past that all celebrations of the Eucharist are for the entire church, universal and local. This fact is emphasized frequently by the very prayers of the Mass themselves.

Even though the phrase is used in some pious prayers, there is no such thing as "an abandoned soul." Every offering of the Holy Sacrifice has the same intention as the first offering of that sacrifice by Jesus on Calvary and in the resurrection: the salvation of the world.

The practice of having special intentions for the offering of the Eucharist has a long, honorable and continuing tradition in the church. We continue that tradition today by our "special Mass intentions."

That fact, however, should not lead us to forget that the intention of Christ and the church in every offering of the Mass is much larger than any specific personal intentions of our own.

Easter Duty

Is the obligation of the Easter duty (going to confession and Communion between the first Sunday of Lent and Trinity Sunday) still in effect? We hardly ever hear it in church any more. What happened to that very strict ruling?

The obligation of annual Communion during the Easter time still exists. The obligation for the sacrament of penance during that period, however, is still as it always has been, binding only if it is necessary for an individual to be able to receive the Eucharist.

You may understand why we do not hear much about it any more if we recall that the obligation of yearly Communion began in a period of great decline in the practice of receiving the Eucharist. By the 12th and 13th centuries, when this regulation was first mentioned for the whole church, even priests and Sisters of many strict religious orders considered Communion five or six times a year as more than enough. Laymen might go years without the Eucharist.

It took centuries for that to change. Actually it was not until Pope Pius X early in this century decreed early and frequent Communion that the shift to even monthly Communion gradually became accepted and widespread. Today, practically everyone who considers himself a practicing Catholic already receives far more than once a year — which is the reason not much is said about the Easter duty any more.

The 1918 Code of Canon Law states that all who have reached the age of reason should receive the sacrament of penance at least once a year (Canon 906). In establishing the law, however, the church did not intend to impose a new obligation for confession, but simply to prescribe a time within which mortal sins should be confessed. Therefore, the law does not apply to anyone who is not aware of an unconfessed mortal sin.

It bears repeating, though, that this law deals with the minimum required. By no means does it recommend receiving the sacrament of penance only once a year, or only when one is conscious of serious sin. The healing, forgiving and strengthening powers of this sacrament are such that it should be, in some way, a regular part of our spiritual lives as Catholics.

When A Priest Has A Cold

You or some responsible person should give a good answer to a problem I have observed during my 64 years in the Catholic faith. The priest arrived late for 6 a.m. Mass. It was obvious from the beginning that he had a bad cold. He handled and rehandled his handkerchief to the point where sanitation was gone. It would be better if the priest held a platter at Communion time and each person took the Host.

The situation you describe may seem trivial but I know it bothers many people. Most priests are sensitive to it, and attempt to safeguard the dignity and propriety of their ministry at the altar in spite of any such illness they might have.

It's easy to exaggerate the problem, but if anyone had a helpful suggestion for me in such circumstances, I'd be grateful for their saying so. Your pastor would probably feel the same if a number of people in your parish are bothered by this as much as you are. Letting people take the Host directly from the Communion plate is not a proper way to distribute Communion; but, when necessary, he might ask another eucharistic minister to distribute for him.

Fast Before Communion?

What exactly is the present rule for the fast before Holy Communion? I receive different answers, especially concerning the sick. Are the rules the same for the entire world?

At the end of the third session of the Second Vatican Council in 1964, Pope Paul considerably simplified the eucharistic fast. According to this 1964 decree, persons should fast from food and liquids, including alcoholic liquids, for one hour before receiving Communion (not, therefore, one hour before the Mass at which they receive).

Water does not break the fast, and may be taken anytime. The same goes for medicine.

The reason for this regulation is simply to aid in preparing oneself spiritually and mentally for participating in the offering of the Eucharist at Mass, and for receiving it in Communion.

Basically, this regulation applies to the whole church, though there are some variations in different parts of the world.

Lay Eucharistic Ministers

Dear Readers:

I received a letter from a lady who said that if she had to receive Communion from a lay person she would not receive at all. Return mail, much of it more than a little emotional, proved two things: that the church of the past 75 years or so succeeded remarkably in instilling practices aimed at reverence for the Holy Eucharist, and that this very success has created enormous confusion, and plain error, in the beliefs of many Catholics.

The following excerpts represent recurrent themes in the protests mailed to me, and my responses.

From Missouri: You mention that the church has excellent historical, theological and liturgical reasons for allowing lay persons to distribute Communion. Whatever that means, if they exist in the 1980s, they also existed in the 1920s and 1930s, if Jesus is really present in the Eucharist. If touching the Host in the 1930s was such a serious matter, why can everybody handle it now?

In all the responses, this was the most common error — confusing belief in the real presence of Jesus in the Eucharist with practices or regulations which often governed our attitude toward it. I, too, was raised with the strong admonition that to touch the Host, or even the chalice unnecessarily, was a serious sin.

What we did not realize was that these policies (insofar as they were "rules" at all) were only church rules, and were in fact observed only in certain parts of the world even at that time.

Therefore, the church could change them, as it changed the Lenten fast and Friday abstinence.

From Delaware: I will not go to Communion to a lay person. He's no better than I, so why can't I give Holy Communion to myself?

You are able to give Communion to yourself, if you choose to receive Communion in your hand. However, a eucharistic minister — priest, deacon, or lay person — will still distribute it to you.

From Florida: All the reverence we had for the Host is gone. It seems to be only a piece of bread. Is the church drifting back to the days of Martin Luther?

The church introduced the current eucharistic practices for the very reason that it senses a need to safeguard truths about the Eucharist that have been lost in recent generations. When it allows a layman or woman to give Communion, as it did for centuries in the past, the church in no way implies a lessening of its belief in, or its reverence for, the eucharistic presence of Our Lord.

Martin Luther, incidentally, believed firmly in the real presence of Jesus in the Eucharist until he died.

From Iowa: These two fantastic fingers of the priest were the next thing to God. And now anyone can give Communion? No way!

As gently as I can, I have to say this understanding of the priesthood borders on superstition. A priest is not ordained, nor are his hands (not two fingers) anointed with oil, to qualify him to give Communion, but to designate and empower him to preside at the celebration of the Eucharist — or offer Mass, if you will — with his Catholic Christians.

May People Drink from Chalice?

Are priests permitted to let the people go around the altar for Mass, and then to take Communion from the chalice after receiving the Host? This goes on at our church at daily Mass, but not on Sunday.

Not only is it permitted, but receiving Communion under both forms, bread and wine, is recommended by the church whenever it is practical to do so.

Both practices you mention help in their own way to express externally the union with Our Lord and with each other, as his brothers and sisters, which he accomplishes through our sharing in the Eucharistic Sacrifice and meal. Obviously, being around the altar together is impossible with the larger crowds at Sunday Mass, but it can be, and is, most appropriate with smaller groups such as might be present in most parishes on weekdays. The experience of many proves that sharing in the Eucharist this way, at least on occasion, can contribute much toward a deeper awareness of the meaning of the Mass and how it affects our relationships with each other.

The same may be said for drinking from the chalice as well as eating the Host. While one receives Our Lord in either way by itself, receiving under both forms more perfectly signifies our response to Jesus' command to eat his flesh and drink his blood, and our prayerful desire for the gifts he promised to those who do so.

Daughter Doesn't Like Wine

Our five-year-old daughter doesn't like to receive Communion under both species. She doesn't like the taste when she drinks from the chalice, or even when the Host is dipped into the wine. Would it be offensive to ask the priest to use another kind of wine?

First, good for you for having a five-year-old who goes to Holy Communion. We presume, of course, that she knows what she is doing. Certainly most five and six-year-olds, especially those in good Catholic homes, have the capacity to understand all the eucharistic theology the church requires of them for receiving this sacrament.

As for the wine, she's not alone. It can bother adults, too, including some priests. There may, in fact, be medical reasons involved, such as diabetes, which could prompt an individual not to want even the small amount of wine received at Communion.

It's surely all right to mention it to the priest if you wish. Communion under both species is optional even when it is offered at a particular Mass. Your child should know that she may pass up drinking from the chalice and still receive the entire sacrament, the living body and blood of Christ.

Communion Under Both Species Necessary?

Several Protestant friends have asked me a question I can't answer. At the Last Supper, Jesus commands us to take and eat his body and drink his blood. Why don't we do that? Please don't tell me that's changing; it doesn't explain why it was not done up to now. And don't tell me it's not practical or convenient. If this is

what Jesus wanted, who are to we to say it's too time-consuming?

Your question is a good one, and frankly I'm not sure there is an answer that will satisfy your friends. As usual, however, a little history on the subject puts it into better perspective.

For most of the history of the church (about 12 centuries), Communion under both species was standard at Mass. Much theological and spiritual significance was placed on the symbolism of receiving the Lord in Communion under the form of both bread and wine.

Even during this time, however, all the way back to the earliest years, Christians clearly understood that one did not have to receive both forms in order to truly receive the living Lord. Never was there some sort of gross supposition that in the bread one received the dry body of Christ, which later became alive with the blood when one drank from the chalice.

Communion under one species was, therefore, not at all unusual from the beginning. The Eucharist would be taken to the sick at home, for example, under the form of bread alone, and no one doubted that the individual received the whole sacrament. Infants or young children, and the sick who could not swallow food, were given Communion only in the form of wine.

Around the 12th century, a few groups began to claim that one did not truly receive the Eucharist unless one received the form of both bread and wine, a trend which prompted the church to look more favorably on Communion under one species. Later on, as some Protestants began to push the idea that the whole Christ is not present under only one species, the church increased its emphasis on the ancient truth: Anyone who receives only the form of bread or wine receives the living Christ in Communion.

For this reason, church law eventually went so far as to forbid the people to receive from the chalice at Mass. Thus, the practice of receiving only the Host became common not to deny that both species was the ideal, but simply to make clear the rejection of the error that demanded both species.

Today, of course, the danger of that doctrinal error is long past, so the church has resumed its insistence that receiving under both species is the ideal, symbolically whole way to receive the Eucharist. The point appears numerous times in official liturgical documents. It appears at least twice, for example, in the General Instruction of the Roman Missal which says the people "should be urged" to take part in Communion under both forms, "which brings out the sign of the eucharistic meal more fully."

The major instruction on the liturgy of September, 1970, repeats that Communion under both kinds "is the more perfect expression of the people's participation in the Eucharist."

From all this at least two points seem clear. First, anyone who says we must both eat the bread and drink from the cup in order to truly receive the Eucharist contradicts the belief and practice of Christians from the beginning.

Second, anyone who believes that Communion by bread alone is the normal way of Catholics, and that Communion also from the chalice is merely a dispensable liturgical frill, is out of touch with the long eucharistic tradition of the church, not to speak of present liturgical directives.

For us Catholics (and one would hope for all Christians), it comes down to this: Jesus, living in his church, is the best interpreter of those teachings and commands assigned to him in the Gospels.

First Communion Before Confession?

My grandchildren attend a parish in our city where children cannot go to confession until after they receive first Communion. I think that is wrong. How can the teachers and priests there do that?

I have come to believe just about anything is possible, but I seriously doubt that any parish follows a policy that forbids first penance before first Communion. It would be extremely difficult to defend such a position.

Recent documents from Vatican congregations remind us that "When he arrives at the age of discretion, the child has the right, in the church, to receive both sacraments (penance and Eucharist.)" There should be no "general rule" anywhere requiring reception of Holy Communion before the first reception of the sacrament of penance. (On First Confession and First Communion, from the Congregations for the Sacraments and Divine Worship, and for the Clergy, March 31, 1977.)

This means that as a child reaches the age of reason, he has a right as a Catholic to be instructed at his own level about the sacrament of forgiveness by his parents and teachers, and he has the right to an opportunity to receive this sacrament.

Perhaps that parish, as many or most other parishes, provides assistance to children and parents to prepare for both penance and the Eucharist, and then urges parents to present their children when they are ready for either one. In other words, in those parishes children are not *required* to receive the sacrament of penance before first Communion.

Children do have a right to receive the Eucharist as soon as they are aware of the basic doctrines and have a desire to receive. There's the famous story of Pope St. Pius X (called "the Pope of the Eucharist") who offered Mass one day for a group of pilgrims. While giving Communion, he came to a six-year-old boy whose parents said, "Holy Father, he is not yet old enough to receive." The pope turned to the boy, held up the Host, and said, "Who is this?" The child answered, "That is Jesus."

"He knows enough," said the pope, and gave the boy his first Communion.

Thus, just as any other Catholics who are not conscious of a mortal sin, children should not be maneuvered or forced into going to confession as a *condition* for first Communion.

Many customs developed concerning the sequence of these two sacraments during recent centuries, especially in light of the practice of very infrequent Communion in the time of the Jansenistic heresies and after. Many Catholics still alive remember when even outstanding members of the Faith received Communion two or three times a year, and confession automatically preceded Communion every time. Naturally, first Communion would be no exception.

As the congregations indicate, children have a right to both penance and the Eucharist, and this right must be honored in accord with solid traditional doctrine of the church concerning these sacraments.

Communion Twice a Day?

On a recent Sunday, I saw someone receive Holy Communion at two Masses. Was this wrong, or does she have some sort of special permission or privilege to receive more than once?

The answer to both your questions is no. It is not wrong, and one needs no special permission to receive Holy Communion more than once a day.

For several years, church regulations have clearly not only allowed, but actually encouraged, receiving Communion each time one attends Mass, even if it is more than once a day. The reason is simple: Sharing in the Eucharist at the Communion table is an essential part of the Mass, and if one is participating in the liturgy, he or she should normally follow that principle.

Thus, the church points out numerous occasions when Communion might be received more than once a day — such as weddings, funerals, and Masses for special gatherings, or when baptism or one of the other sacraments is administered. In practice, the rule is simple: If one is at an extra Mass it is likely to be for one of these reasons, and one may receive the Eucharist.

Communion more than once on the same day is forbidden when a person attends successive liturgies simply to multiply Masses and Communions. To act on the principle that if one Communion is good, three or six must be better, borders on superstition and betrays ignorance of what the Eucharistic Liturgy is all about.

How Often to Receive Communion?

A recent homily in our parish left several of us perplexed. The priest emphasized that we should not go to Communion each time we go to Mass. We should not go to Communion sometimes, he said, so that others who do not go will feel more comfortable. Also, we should not give our children the example of going each time; they should also see us not go.

To be honest, these statements hurt us deeply since we go to Communion often and hope our children will want to go also. To us, not going to Communion is like going to a banquet and then not partaking in the best part. I hope you can clear this up for us.

Like you, I find it hard to understand those kinds of statements, assuming, of course, that you are reflecting accurately what the priest said.

It is true that some priests (and lay people) feel for some reason that many Catholics go to Communion today when they should not. I have, in fact, heard similar ideas expressed by some of my priest friends in Europe. After remarking on the difference between their Sunday Masses, at which perhaps half the people receive Communion, and our own, where almost everyone receives, they revealed their suspicion that if American Catholics were as spiritually honest as they should be, fewer of them would be going to Communion so often.

I am fully aware that the consciences of some Catholics have become dulled to the point that they see no conflict between seriously sinful lives and receiving Holy Communion. But I fail to understand how anyone might claim that half, a quarter, or even five percent of our people are walking around in mortal sin. It seems to me this would involve, among other things, some very rash judgments.

Another explanation is possible. There is still more than a little touch of Jansenism loose in the Catholic Church. Jansenism, a heresy quite strong in Europe and America into our own century, taught that few people are worthy to receive Communion more than once or twice a year. That attitude deeply infected Catholic spirituality, and traces of it remain to this day.

Fortunately for all of us, none of whom would ever be worthy to receive under such severe restrictions, the church has long since rejected Jansenism as a distortion of the function of the Holy Eucharist in our lives. Put simply, this sacrament is meant to be food and strength for our pilgrim journey in this life; it is not offered as a reward for a holy and sinless life.

I'm with you. Parents, priests and teachers must help children develop a healthy and delicate conscience about sin and its relationship to the Eucharist. But we must also help them understand that the Eucharist cannot be simply an occasional or incidental element in either the Mass or in their own lives.

We have no doctrinal or psychological basis for assuming that deliberately refraining from receiving Holy Communion will help us effectively fill either of these responsibilities.

Is Creed Necessary?

A young priest who has been in our area for about five years never says the Profession of Faith, neither the Apostles' nor the Nicene Creed. I have asked him why he does not do this, even on Sunday, and he says the Creed is reserved for special occasions. However, it is not used even on Christmas or Easter.

As a Catholic I feel I have not fulfilled my Sunday obligation if I have not attended a complete Mass. Could you please explain the policy concerning the Creed.

The presence of a Creed does not determine the validity of one's participation in the Eucharist. The praying of the Profession of Faith is not an essential part of the Mass on Sunday or any other time.

The official instructions for the Mass, however, provide that the Creed be recited by the priest and people at least on all Sundays and special feasts. There is no liturgical basis whatsoever for neglecting that part of the Mass on a regular basis.

It is certainly permissible for good pastoral reasons to omit the Creed, or the Gloria, on occasion. The church has excellent reasons for placing it as somewhat of a climax, a summation of the Liturgy of the Word. The Creed or some other proper profession of faith — for example, the renewal of the baptismal promises — should normally be a part of every Sunday Eucharist.

What Begins Mass?

In addition to the Entrance Song at Mass, should the celebrant make the Sign of the Cross? I was told by one of our priests that the Entrance Song started the Mass, therefore there is no need to start Mass again with the Sign of the Cross.

Also, is the Alleluia sung before the reading of the Gospel?

In a way, your priest is correct. The Entrance Song, when one is used, is the beginning of the liturgy.

It does not follow, however, that the Sign of the Cross should be omitted. This solemn and simple action by which the power and presence of the Trinity are invoked is not necessarily the "beginning" of the celebration. It should always precede the Penitential Rite and the Liturgy of the Word.

The Alleluia verse before the Gospel is not required, though it should certainly be used on Sundays and other special occasions. The Alleluia verse should always be sung, never recited.

Aged and Sunday Mass

I am 81 years old and was told by a priest that I was excused from Sunday Mass if I didn't feel up to going.

Also, someone told me I never had to go to confession, and I could receive the sacraments. Is this true?

At your age, you certainly are excused if you do not feel comfortable going on any particular Sunday. In fact, if you cannot go without danger of getting sick, or serious danger of perhaps falling and hurting yourself, you are completely excused from Sunday Mass.

Your priest was right. God does not want you endangering yourself to attend Mass. Keep up your prayers and go to Mass when you can. That is sufficient.

The only time one must receive the sacrament of penance before Communion is when he or she is conscious of a deliberate mortal sin. I am sure it is all right for you to go to Communion whenever you have the opportunity, even if you do not get to confession.

If you are unable to go to Mass for a few Sundays, or even longer, please call a priest in your parish and ask him to bring you Communion. Many parishes also have special ministers of the Eucharist who might bring Communion to your home each Sunday. If the priest himself comes sometime, perhaps you could use that opportunity to receive the sacrament of penance.

Holy Day Masses

When a holy day of obligation falls on a Monday, are vigil Masses for that holy day permitted on Sunday? May a person go to Mass twice on Sunday — once for the Sunday, and once for the holy day?

Masses are permitted on the evening before the holy day regardless of the day of the week, if, of course, the bishop has approved such Masses for that diocese.

The character and discipline of our observance of holy days of obligation certainly leaves much to be desired liturgically, particularly when the holy day falls on Saturday or Monday.

The complications over which Mass to attend for which obligation can become almost ludicrously legalistic. According to current church legislation, however, it is possible to do as you say — attend Mass on Sunday morning for your Sunday obligation, and in the evening for the holy day of obligation.

One might also attend the evening Mass on Sunday for the Sunday obligation, and attend Mass the following day for the holy day.

It is certainly more appropriate to attend these respective Masses with the appropriate readings and prayers (Sunday Mass for Sunday, and holy day Mass for the holy day), but this is not actually required for fulfilling the obligation for either Sunday or holy day Masses.

As I mentioned, the bishop of each diocese determines whether there will be evening Masses in anticipation of Sunday and holy days, and at what time those Masses may be offered.

All Men — or, All People?

Today I attended the liturgy at a local parish and was surprised to hear the priest use the words "for all people" instead of "for many" or "for all men" in the words at the consecration of the wine.
Is this permissible, and by what authority?

In a nutshell, the answer is that normally no priest has any authority to introduce these kinds of personal revisions into the Eucharistic Prayer of the Mass. A little background is necessary, however, to put this response into perspective.

In recent years, many have protested what they consider to be sexist terminologies in the prayers of Mass and other liturgies. In response, the International Commission on English in the Liturgy (ICEL), composed of liturgical and language experts from the English-speaking countries, has prepared a text eliminating terms that may appear to signify only males when the intent is to include all human beings. Any change, however, must be accepted by the bishops of a particular country and then be approved also by the Vatican.

One recommended change is in fact already approved. As of November, 1981, at least in the United States, the Eucharistic Prayer officially reads "for all" instead of "for all men."

Note that only changes of some words are proposed even in the revised ICEL text. No one has even suggested approval of spontaneous changes in the Eucharistic Prayers by the presiding priest.

In other words, changes like the ones you heard should not be introduced by priests. The faith and theology embodied in the Eucharistic Prayers are too sacred and too vital in the church's life to be subject to the personal inclinations of each priest as he offers the Eucharist.

This principle, stressed often by the Holy Father and other church leaders, was repeated under Pope John Paul II: "Only the Eucharistic Prayers included in the Roman Missal or those that the Apostolic See has by law admitted, in the manner and within the limits laid down by the Holy See, are to be used."

"To modify the Eucharistic Prayers approved by the church or to adopt others privately composed is a most serious abuse."

("Inaestimabile Donum," Instruction on Certain Norms Concerning Worship of the Eucharistic Mystery, issued by the Congregation for the Sacraments and Divine Worship, May 23, 1980)

Hats for Women?

Our ladies study club wants to ask: Why do women no longer cover their heads at Mass, and wear slacks, shorts and pants suits? Did Pope Paul VI say we no longer have to wear a head covering? Or Pope John Paul II? If not, why don't the pastors take a stand on this and speak out?

It seems to me that any normal adult Christian woman will have enough sense of style and propriety to answer for herself whether or not she should wear a hat in church.

The remarks in the Bible, and some later church rules about women covering their heads, are related to specific cultures and social traditions and do not necessarily apply everywhere all the time. To expect answers to these kinds of questions from the pope — or from one's pastor, for that matter — is to misunderstand the real function of the church's leaders as guides for our lives as Christians and Catholics. Some things one should be able and willing to do without direct word from the pope.

I suspect, and hope, the Holy Father and the rest of the church have more important things to worry about.

Eucharistic Para-liturgies

This summer I attended a charismatic meeting and liturgy at a retreat house in our diocese. The basket of hosts was passed around. One lady in our group was not Catholic so I passed the basket to a Catholic. Another Catholic lady took the basket and handed it to the non-Catholic, who took it and received it at Communion time. She also drank the wine from the chalice.

Has the church given its approval for this? Also, may Catholics receive Communion at non-Catholic services? Some of my friends have told me that they do.

According to your description of the ceremony, I wonder if perhaps this was not a celebration of the Eucharist but rather what is called a para-liturgical service. Such a service is not an actual liturgy in the official Catholic sense, though it may have many similarities to the Eucharist.

I have been present several times at a "sharing of the bread and wine" ceremony which is obviously intended to recall the Last Supper, but which everyone present understands is not a real Mass.

If the ceremony you attended was an actual Eucharistic Liturgy, there were a lot of serious problems about it. First of all, a non-Catholic member of the group unquestionably should not receive the Eucharist under these circumstances. If the priest in charge knows it is being done, he should kindly but clearly explain the Catholic teaching and policy about Communion of non-Catholic Christians at a Catholic Mass.

I also have serious concerns about the whole liturgy you describe, again assuming it was a valid eucharistic ceremony. The bread should, under no circumstances, be "passed around" as you describe it either before or after the Eucharistic Prayer. Communion should be distributed by the priest or other eucharistic minister in the proper way for the symbolism for the Eucharist to be fulfilled.

The same goes for drinking from the cup.

Catholics should not receive Communion at an official eucharistic or "Last Supper" liturgy in a Protestant church. Again, however, sharing the bread and wine at a para-liturgical devotional ceremony with people of other faiths is certainly permitted.

Obviously at least a few people in the ceremony you attended were confused. Whoever is in charge of such a ceremony should make clear to everyone, for the sake of their own consciences, the precise nature of that ceremony.

Sunday Mass Age Limit?

Is there a regulation stating that persons over the age of 59 are not obligated to hear Mass on Sundays and holy days? A friend of mine contends that there is.

Many older people may be so handicapped or otherwise unable to get to Mass that they would often, or perhaps most of the time, be excused from Mass. The obligation to participate in Mass on Sundays is a serious church law, but anyone is excused on a given Sunday for serious reason.

There is, however, no age limit on the Sunday Mass regulation for a Catholic, once that individual has reached the age of reason.

Watching TV Mass

If I cannot get to Mass on Sunday because of sickness, what am I obliged to do to make up for it? A friend said she thought I have an obligation to at least watch the Mass broadcast in our city on television on Sunday morning.

When one is excused from Sunday Mass because of sickness or any other reason, he is not strictly obliged to any substitute prayers or devotions. Naturally, one may wish to unite oneself with the worship which his fellow Catholics are offering to God that day at the Eucharistic Sacrifice. This might be through reflection on the Scripture readings of the day, the other prayers of the Mass, or even by watching and uniting oneself as much as possible with the Eucharist via a tele-vised Mass.

Any of these are purely a matter of personal preference, however. One is not obligated to any of them.

Why Are Masses Different?

It used to be that we could attend Mass at any church and it was the same at all of them. Now it's different at all of them. Why? Also, why don't they all use the same books so as to be uniform?

Part of the answer to your question becomes evident if we recall a little history about the Mass.

During the first 15 centuries of the church's life, the Mass was not the same in all the churches. Especially in the first several centuries, the celebration of the Eucharist was just that — a celebration. Actions, words, music and whole atmosphere of the Mass were different according to who was there, the condition and circumstances of their lives, and so on.

For a variety of reasons, the Mass gradually ceased being an event that the people participated in as members of the Body of the Risen Christ. It became rather a sacred ceremony, carried out by the priest, that the rest of the people were simply required to *watch* reverently.

By the time of the Council of Trent in the 1500s, much of the early history of the Mass which we are aware of today had been completely lost. The bishops at that council, however, were faced with numerous attacks against the Mass and the Eucharist from leaders of the new Protestant Reformation. They understandably responded to these attacks by taking one form of the Mass — the form used in Rome at that time — and declaring it the *only* form of the Mass allowed in the Western Church. Every action and prayer was spelled out in minute detail. No options were offered. No variations were permitted.

Long before the Second Vatican Council, church leaders were aware that this kind of frozen liturgy was blocking the growth of real liturgical prayer and worship, and that something had to be done to loosen things up. The purpose wasn't variety for variety's sake. It was to ena-ble people of different ages and times and temperaments and circum-stances to make the Mass a genuine, living worship-celebration of their Christian life.

The variations you speak of are now specifically allowed and sug-gested in the official instructions on the Mass. Numerous options for Scripture readings are offered. Several prayers or exhortations are accompanied with the notation that the priest should "use these, or similar words." Wide leeway is given in such things as music and actions. The sign of peace, for instance, is to be given "according to local custom."

When you're present for a Mass that is different than you're used to, why not relax, try to get into the spirit of it, and share in it as well as you can? A little giving in, and trying to share what others are feeling could be a real act of charity toward those around you as well as to yourself.

Why Strike Your Breast?

Why do some Catholics strike their breast at the "Lamb of God" part of the Mass? What does this signify? Should it still be done?

Striking one's breast with the hand or even with a stone is an ancient symbol of repentance and sorrow.

The reason seems to be that since the heart is considered in our culture the focal point of feelings, striking the heart signifies that we are "broken-hearted" about what has been done. In fact, our word "contrition" comes from the Latin phrase "contritus corde," which literally means "crushed in the heart" or "broken-hearted."

Striking the breast as a symbol of our need for God's forgiveness can still be a significant sacramental action, but it is not required at Mass.

Doxology or Amen?

I travel a lot and would like to know which is right: Should the people say the "through him, with him" prayer with the priest at the end of the Eucharistic Prayer, or not? In some places they do, and in others they do not.

The prayer you speak of, which is known as the Doxology — literally "prayer of praise" — at the end of the Eucharistic Prayer of the Mass should not be said by the attending people, but only by the priest. The people's part is the solemn response, "Amen," which should normally be sung, or at least recited fully and solemnly by all present.

While it is considered avante garde to say the entire Doxology together, the practice rather betrays an unfortunate ignorance of the majestic significance of the great prayer "Amen." This word goes back centuries, even to the prayer of the Jewish people in the pre-Christian era. It means: "All this is true, we believe it." In other words, it is a profound and reverent affirmation of all that was just said and done. As such, it is a magnificent conclusion to the Eucharistic Prayer by all present who share in the offering of that Eucharist.

In the book of Revelations (Rev. 3,14), Jesus himself is called "the

Amen, the faithful witness" of the Father, the one who reflects and affirms perfectly all the Father wishes to be and to say to mankind.

Considering the half-hearted, timid manner with which most congregations respond with this great "Amen" at Mass, whether it is sung or recited, it is understandable that many feel the whole Doxology should be said by everyone just to keep that entire solemn moment from falling flat. But that is not the way it should be.

Mass in a Private Home?

If Communion can be brought to a sick person, why can't Mass be offered for them at home, too? My father is confined to a wheelchair except when he goes to the doctor. Would it be possible for a priest to have Mass in his home sometime? It would mean very much to him and to the rest of us.

More than once during recent years, the church has indicated that bishops may allow Masses outside of churches or chapels — in homes, for example. One of the many different circumstances in which such Masses are explicitly approved is the gathering of family and friends in the homes of the sick or aged who cannot otherwise participate in the Eucharistic Celebration.

Some rather obvious regulations are indicated for such celebrations to preserve the propriety, serenity, and sacred character of the Mass. (See the Instruction for Masses for Special Gatherings, May 15, 1969.)

Home Masses for the sick, and for other gatherings and events, are not uncommon in our country. In most dioceses, Mass may be offered in homes at the discretion of the pastor of the family in whose home the Mass is to be celebrated. I suggest you ask your pastor or other priest you know about a Mass in your father's home.

Dipping the Host in Wine

Why do some priests dip the Host in the chalice before giving Communion to the people? Couldn't this cause a problem for an alcoholic?

Dipping the host into the chalice is one of three ways we can receive Holy Communion under both species — that is, under the form of bread and wine.

The church permits (and in some circumstances recommends) receiving of both the bread and wine since that way of receiving the Eucharist more perfectly symbolizes the fact that we share in the *whole* Christ at Communion, and thus fulfill his words, "He who eats my body and drinks my blood has everlasting life." Strictly speaking, of course, we receive the whole, living Christ even if we are given the Host only.

The manner of giving Communion you speak of, dipping the Host in the chalice, is called "intinction." Some parishes give Communion this way at all daily Masses.

Another quite common way is for those who receive the Host to then drink from the chalice. According to a third, and extremely rare, form of receiving under both species, each person receives the Host as usual, and then drinks the wine through a straw. For some reason, this procedure has been used in the past at certain Masses celebrated by the Holy Father.

The slight amount of wine may present a problem for some alcoholics, as well as for some diabetics. If such a person notices that the priest is giving Communion by intinction, he or she may simply indicate to the priest that he should not dip the Host in the chalice before the Host is given.

If Communion under both species is being given in the second manner, one may always easily bypass the chalice.

Married Before A Judge

My Catholic nephew married a divorced woman and therefore was not married in the church. His wife was married to a Catholic the first time by a judge.

The situation has disturbed my sister immensely. Since she is getting old, she would like to see her son back to the practice of his faith, and able to receive the sacraments.

My nephew and his wife go to Mass every Sunday, but it hurts her, too, that he cannot receive Communion. I'm puzzled why some people who seem to be in the same situation can go to Communion and others cannot.

Your letter left out many details essential for a complete answer. But one detail you do give is very important and should be followed up on if you are sure it is true.

You say that the wife's first husband was Catholic, and they were married before a justice of the peace. If that is true, the chance is good that her first marriage was not valid in the eyes of the church, for the simple reason that a Catholic must normally be married before a priest to be validly married.

Are you sure the priest in the parish knows this background? Assuming this was the only marriage the woman had entered before she married your nephew, or that there are no other significant elements in the situation of which you are perhaps unaware, your nephew and his wife might well be able to have the marriage validated in the Catholic Church and he could return to the sacraments.

If they haven't done so already, please encourage them to discuss the situation thoroughly with a priest.

Wedding Mass for Sunday

My fiancee and I are setting the time for our wedding Mass. When would be the earliest time we could set our Mass on Saturday in order that our guests could also fulfill their Sunday obligation?

In my parish no nuptial Masses are set after 2:30 p.m., and our priest does not consider that late enough to fulfill the Sunday obligation. According to my fiancee's parish priest, that time would be permitted for fulfilling our guests' obligations. What is the church rule on this?

The bishop of each diocese (not the individual parish priest) determines whether Saturday Masses anticipating the Sunday will be permitted in that diocese, and if so, what time those Masses may begin. So no general rule can be cited for the whole church, or even for the country, except that such Masses must be in the late afternoon or evening.

In some dioceses, anticipation Masses for Sunday may not begin before 4 p.m. The bishop of your diocese (in Ohio) has said they may begin at 3 p.m. So your parish priest is right in saying that a 2:30 p.m. wedding Mass would not fulfill the Sunday obligation for people attending that wedding at your church. The rule is the bishop's, however, not the pastor's.

You do not say whether your fiancee is from the same diocese. If she is, the same rule would apply. If she is from another diocese, it is possible that a different time is in effect there.

Sunday Mass Useless?

I have several friends, both Catholic and non-Catholic, who think weekly Mass is useless. One of them says it is better to go to Mass three or four times a year, when he really gets something out of it, than to go every Sunday just because it's the law. I guess I don't agree with it, but I don't know why. Doesn't that attitude really make sense?

That attitude would make good sense if the Mass were just another of several optional prayer services. It doesn't make sense, however, if one understands the focal position that the Eucharistic Sacrifice and sacrament hold in the life and actions of a Christian.

We might start with the fact that the requirement of weekly sharing in the Eucharist (or, if you prefer, "going to Mass every Sunday") isn't something new. Way back in the early years of Christianity, centuries before there were any "church laws" in our sense of the term, participation in the Sunday Eucharist every week was expected, in some ways more urgently than it is today. We have documents that reflect early Christian policy if one of their number deliberately failed to be present for the Eucharist for two or three weeks running; they were considered as no longer members of the church, no longer Christian!

If this appears severe, it obviously means that they believed something about the Mass that we have lost through the centuries. For them, it wasn't a matter of committing a "mortal sin" by disobeying a law about Sunday Mass. It was simply a conviction that one could not really understand and believe what the Mass is all about, and then fail to be there for even a few weeks.

Today, the church is trying hard to help us reclaim that conviction — that the sacrifice and table of the Eucharist, sharing in the offering of Christ to the Father, and receiving together his body and blood in Communion, is the *key* and indispensable way Jesus intends to unite men and women with himself and form them into his family until the end of the world.

In other words, Mass is where, above all, we learn the spirit and message of Jesus. Through reflection on the words of Scripture, and through the language and actions of the liturgy of the Eucharist, it is where we continually identify ourselves as his members, acknowledge who are our brothers and sisters because of him, and assure each other of our mutual encouragement and support. In that larger sense, even in a church with 500 persons, the presence or absence of one really affects everyone — including the individual himself.

If this way of speaking about the Mass sounds strange, it is unfortunate. Perhaps it is one of the prices we have paid for coming to see missing Mass on Sunday as a mortal sin because it is against a law of the church. The fact is that, even if there were no such law, presence at the Sunday Eucharist would still be "required" simply because one is a member of the family of Christ, simply because one is a Christian.

Communion After Remarriage

If even non-Catholics can go to Communion sometimes in our church, why is it that divorced people cannot? We are members of the church, we believe in the Eucharist, and we're trying to do what's right. It hurts very much not to be able to receive the Eucharist, and we need it maybe more than the others do.

I hope you are aware that simply being divorced is no obstacle to Holy Communion. I assume from your letter that you are remarried; but if you are not, there is nothing preventing your reception of Communion if the usual other conditions are fulfilled.

If one is divorced and remarried, it becomes an entirely different problem.

By present church law, it is true, divorced and remarried Catholics are unable to receive the Eucharist. Without getting too complicated, it must be noted that the church is seriously concerned about moving toward a more understanding and open stance in relation to such Catholics. It recognizes the difficulty and delicacy of the effort to accomplish this without compromising its belief in the permanence of marriage, as well as its convictions about the Eucharist being a sign of unity and faith which has at least to some degree been broken by the individual's remarriage in contradiction to the laws of the church.

It seems to me we are experiencing an increasing awareness of the need to recognize that at least many divorced and remarried Catholics are, in the present circumstances of their lives, still members of the church who spend themselves generously for their spouses and their children. They are doing all they are morally capable of doing to live as good Catholic Christians.

The American bishops acknowledged the urgency of this question, and the possibility of its being resolved, when they requested the removal of excommunication for divorced and remarried Catholics. The church cannot recognize the second marriage as valid, they said, nor does their move concerning excommunication "of itself" (an important phrase) permit remarried Catholics to receive Communion. This "most difficult question — return to full eucharistic Communion — can be resolved," explained the bishops, "only in a limited number of instances, depending on particular circumstances."

Clearly, much more reflection on the subject can be expected. In the meantime, I suggest you take the bishops' advice to remarried Catholics: "Take the next step by approaching parish priests and diocesan tribunals to see whether their return to full eucharistic Communion is possible."

(Quotes are from the statement of the American bishops when they petitioned the pope in May, 1977, to rescind the excommunication of divorced and remarried Catholics which had been in force in the United States since 1884.)

Some Missed Opportunities

I am 78 years old and was married to a Catholic who passed away some years ago. I then married a non-Catholic. After 36 years of marriage, he died seven months ago. I have gone to church all these years. Now I want to know how I can get back to receive Communion.

Judging from the information you give, there is no obstacle whatsoever to your living a full Catholic life, including reception of the sacraments.

In fact, unless you have left something important out, there's no reason you could not have received the sacraments during all these years. I assume, of course, that you were married in the Catholic Church after the death of your first husband, and that there was no other obstacle to the sacraments for you.

If you have not done so already, I urge you to go to a priest, explain the situation, and ask him to help you set your mind at rest. It seems you have worried and lost many opportunities for the sacraments unnecessarily for too many years already.

Shopping for Saturday Mass?

Does a Saturday Mass which doesn't have the Sunday liturgy — such as a wedding, funeral, or jubilee Mass — still fulfill the Sunday obligation? There seems to be a difference of opinion on this.

I hate the thought of "shopping around"; it certainly seems to negate the spirit of the Mass. But that's what I feel like I'm doing when I must check with the priest first to see if the Mass "counts" or not. This problem also came up in the last Easter Vigil.

You're really asking three questions, so let's take them one at a time.

1. The Instruction of the Vatican on Eucharistic Worship of May 25, 1967, which provides for anticipating the Sunday Mass obligation on Saturday evening, says that when a parish Mass is scheduled on Saturday for that purpose, the liturgy for the Sunday should be celebrated. It does not, however, make the actual Sunday liturgy a *condition* for fulfilling the Sunday obligation. Thus, a Catholic could fulfill that obligation, if he intends to do so, regardless of which Mass is offered — presuming, as you said, that it is within the required time period for your diocese.

This is similar to a Mass on Sunday itself. We all know that even if one attends a wedding, anniversary Mass, or special parish feast day Mass on Sunday, he still fulfills the obligation to attend Mass. There is no indication that the church intended to make the Saturday evening privilege more strict.

However, each bishop, as the chief liturgist in his diocese, has the responsibility for establishing specific regulations for that diocese, including setting the time when Saturday Masses in anticipation of Sunday may begin.

2. How about the "shopping around?" Differences of opinion are possible on Saturday Mass as on many other subjects. If you come to a decision in good conscience, however — perhaps on the advice of a priest whom you consider competent — that is sufficient wherever you go. Whether a Mass "counts" or not does not depend on the opinion of the parish priest who offers it.

3. All of the above is irrelevant to the situation on Holy Saturday. The Mass at the Easter Vigil is liturgically *the* Easter Mass even more than the one the following morning.

Jesus' Words at Mass?

The words of consecration in our "new" Mass are different than they were in my English missal in the old Mass. How can this be? Isn't the Consecration supposed to contain the words that Christ used at the Last Supper?

Jesus obviously never spoke English, so any words we have can be only a translation, an effort to put the meaning of what he said into another language.

If you look at the Gospels, and at St. Paul's description of the Last Supper in the Letter to the Corinthians, you will find that even they differ in the words they ascribe to Jesus in the institution of the Eucharist. The reason is that the exact words of Jesus were not that important to the writers of the Gospel, who probably reflected the words used in the Eucharistic Liturgy at the time and place that particular part of the New Testament was written.

It's the same today. In the Eucharistic Prayer, which, as the name implies, is essentially a prayer of thanksgiving and remembrance, the important thing is that the words give the meaning that Jesus intended, as this meaning is handed down to us in Scripture.

Saturday Mass Limited?

I have heard that a Catholic may fulfill his Sunday Mass obligation on Saturday evening only if he cannot get to Mass on Sunday morning. Is this true? If so, it's news to me.

It's news to me, too. The Vatican's Instruction on Eucharistic Worship which deals with this privilege places no such restrictions on one's right to fulfill the Sunday obligation on Saturday evening.

Saturday Masses Elsewhere?

My wife and I both belong to a church and a diocese which do not have a Saturday night Mass.

When someone from our parish attends a Saturday night Mass in another diocese, and comes home Sunday, is he obligated to attend Sunday Mass in his own church to fulfill his own Sunday duty?

As I'm sure your pastor would agree, the laws of the church on this matter are very clear. If you are a visitor in another diocese, the laws of that diocese regarding such things as Sunday Mass apply to you.

Therefore attendance at a Saturday evening Mass in that diocese would fulfill any obligation for the Sunday Eucharist that you have. You would not be required to attend another Mass the following day.

I must confess that I am extremely uncomfortable answering your question this way. Our weekly celebration of the Eucharist is such a beautiful and important thing in our lives as Catholic Christians that it is a shame to have to reduce it to such details of obligation as this.

The purpose of the church in allowing the fulfillment of this responsibility in a Saturday evening liturgy was to provide a broader opportunity for observance of the Lord's Day. Such a regulation certainly makes sense, especially in light of the church's celebration of Easter itself (after all, each Sunday according to Christian tradition, is a "little Easter") which is anticipated by evening Masses on Holy Saturday.

Thus, a solid Christian tradition lies behind the opportunities given by the church for uniting the hours of Saturday evening to the celebration and observance of the Lord's Day.

Sabbath Changed to Sunday?

Why was the Sabbath changed from Saturday to Sunday, and is there a chance it might be changed back someday? The Seventh Day Adventists are passing out pamphlets dealing with this subject, and they are so convincing that I've decided to go to Saturday evening Mass until this is explained.

The very early Christians changed the "Sabbath" day to Sunday for a variety of reasons. First, the fact that the resurrection of Jesus is recorded in Scripture as occurring on the first day of the week certainly had much to do with the fact that this seemed the most appropriate day to celebrate the Eucharist to commemorate that event. The first Christians also made a point of changing their days of observance (including fast days) from those prescribed by Jewish law to emphasize their departure from traditions and customs of the people of Israel.

When the Seventh Day Adventist Church was formed about the middle of the last century, the four men and one woman who became its nucleus were somehow convinced that Saturday, not Sunday, should still be the "holy day" of the week. It is one of the lesser ways the teachings of that church depart from general Christian tradition. There's no reason whatsoever to suspect this Sunday tradition will ever change.

Sunday Mass Still Obligatory?

I've heard in recent years that one need not go to Mass on Sunday unless it is "meaningful." Attending Mass is only a matter of

"substantive" obedience, it is said. If you're not getting out of it what you think you should, don't go, and don't worry about it.

A short time ago, however, I read again that we may miss Mass only for a serious reason. Has that teaching changed? I'm a convert, so I don't know a lot of things.

Attendance at the Sunday Eucharist is a serious obligation for Catholics for reasons that far transcend the fact that it is a church law. This obligation binds us unless we are excused from it for a proportionately serious reason.

What, precisely, such a reason would be must be determined ultimately by the individual himself in the light of his overall respect for and observance of this obligation. "Substantive" obedience to the Sunday Eucharist regulation simply means that when one is otherwise faithful to that responsibility, he need not worry or feel guilty when, on occasion, something — a vacation, unusually exhausting work, and so on — makes it exceptionally difficult or inconvenient to get to Mass.

The question of attending Mass only when one "gets something out of it" is another matter. Contrary to what certain psychological experts seem to tell us, there is nothing wrong at some point in our lives in doing something because someone says we must. It is an essential part of our maturing process to act in certain matters simply because someone important to us (parent, teacher, priest, church) says, "It's good for you. Do it." We all go through this. It's one of the steps we take toward making values our own — or, if you wish, doing a thing because "I get something out of it."

Surely there's something spiritually incomplete in a 30 or 50-year-old Catholic who hasn't long ago passed the point where he goes to Mass only because the church says he must. His problem isn't, however, that he once went for that reason. Every child or teen-ager has gone or will go to church for that reason somewhere along the line. The mature adult's tragedy is that he was never helped to grow beyond it, a description which sadly fits too many Catholics today.

"The Spirit, the Lord"

In the Creed at Mass, why do we say we believe in "the Spirit, the Lord?" What is the significance of this, since that title is always reserved for Christ? Are there other creeds or liturgical books where the Spirit is called Lord?

In the church's tradition, the title "Lord" (in Greek, "Kyrios") does most often refer to Jesus, but not always. Christ enjoys that title most appropriately as the God-Man, the unique mediator between God and creation, and therefore Lord of the world.

The title has also been used for the Holy Spirit, however, since he shares in the divine nature of the Father and Son, and therefore in all the prerogatives and attributes they have as God.

The church in the East (Constantinople), with its heavily Spirit-oriented mysticism, speaks of the Spirit as Kyrios more than does the West (Rome), and usually relates this title to the Third Person's work as Giver and Generator of life. Some early Eastern forms of the Apostles' Creed, as well as the Creed of Nicaea we use at Mass, illustrate this tradition.

The reference to the Holy Spirit as Lord was not in the original Creed of the Council of Nicaea; it was added by the Council of Constantinople half a century later.

Are Latin Masses Allowed?

Will you please explain the present ruling of the church concerning Latin Masses? Some priests have told us they are not allowed. A group in a nearby city, however, advertises that they have "the old Latin Mass" every Sunday.

If Latin Masses are possible, why don't more churches have them?

According to present regulations for the celebration of the Eucharist, the language of the Mass should normally be that of the people who are attending, in other words, the local vernacular tongue.

For a good reason, and if a sufficient number of people request it, a Mass may be celebrated in Latin, but it must be according to the new rite for the Eucharist established by Pope Paul VI in 1969.

Certain groups of Catholics who refuse to accept the authority of our recent popes in these matters insist on attending Mass only in Latin and in what they call the "old rite" — by which they mean the so-called Tridentine Rite approved by Pope Pius V in the 16th century. This rite was in effect until the liturgical reform after Vatican Council II.

These public celebrations of the Eucharist using the Tridentine format are forbidden today. Any priests or lay people who promote such ceremonies are acting in direct disobedience to their bishops and to the pope, who have the responsibility to guide and direct the church in its official public worship.

Why don't more churches have Latin Masses using the new eucharistic rite? The answer is simply that the majority of Catholic people just do not seem to be enthused about the idea.

During recent years, numerous parishes have decided to schedule a regular Latin Mass at the request of some Catholics who express a nostalgia about the way things used to be. At first, memories of beautiful Latin chants, hymns and high Masses may attract a fair number of

Catholics. In a short time, however, nostalgia wears thin and the people realize that their appreciation of the Mass and the importance of their personal participation has changed and grown considerably since the old days. The limitations of a Eucharistic Liturgy in a foreign language, even in the new rite, appear quite clearly and the Latin Mass experiment is abandoned.

I'm among those who profoundly miss many moving aspects of our liturgical heritage which we are gradually losing (at least for a time) because of our change from the Latin language to the vernacular. The opportunities for a common worship with our fellow Catholics from other countries when the occasions arise, as they do more frequently now than formerly, is another reason for keeping in touch with our Latin liturgical traditions.

I firmly believe, however, that the instincts which guided the bishops at the Vatican Council and which have guided church authorities in liturgical reforms since then are unassailable. Any foreign language, including Latin, simply cannot today be a vehicle for the primary purpose of the Eucharist as the church sees it: to offer the fullest worship to our Heavenly Father and to be the primary expression of our unity with Our Lord, and through him, with each other as his church.

Latin Mass or Latin Music?

In your comments about the traditional Latin Mass, you state that if Latin Masses are desirable for some reason in a parish, they are allowed. You did not give a specific reason. It seems to me that there is a definite reason. The reason is that the church insists on the use of Latin.

The Vatican II Constitution on the Liturgy says, "Steps should be taken so that the faithful may also be able to say or to sing together in Latin those parts of the Ordinary of the Mass which pertain to them." (Para. 54)

In 1964, the Instruction of the Sacred Congregation of Rites states: "Pastors of souls should carefully see to it that the faithful also know how to pray or sing together in the Latin language those parts of the Ordinary of the Mass which pertain to them." (Para. 59)

In 1974, Pope Paul again reminded us of the wishes of the church that the faithful be able to pray together in Latin, therefore, the use of Latin is required as a matter of obedience. It is not a matter of preference.

First of all, the question and comments dealt with the Latin Mass, not the use of Latin in some of the sung parts and responses at Mass to which you refer. There is quite a difference.

You do have a point, however, in that the church is interested in keeping some acquaintance and contact with the Latin language as part of our liturgical heritage. Because of the high mobility of people between countries and continents, for example, liturgies which join Catholics of many nations and languages are more and more common. Anyone who has shared in such international ceremonies, and heard or shared in the common singing of major parts of the Mass in Latin, will appreciate how enriching and enlarging a liturgical experience such as this can be.

I do think that some of this heritage has been neglected during the past 15 years or so, not because of deliberate neglect, but simply because of the exhausting amounts of time and energy necessary to understand and establish the major reforms in liturgical ceremonies, most of which presuppose the extensive use of the local language, at least for a long time.

As time goes on, I believe some of the customs of which you speak will be revived in the spirit of the new and deeper understanding of the meaning of our liturgy achieved since Vatican II. In fact, such is happening already in many places both in our country and abroad.

Multi-Cultural Liturgies

I have read that the church is allowing awfully strange customs at Mass in foreign countries — Hindu ceremonies in India, tribal dances in Africa, and even ancestor worship in China. I know things are changing, but will the Mass be the same from one place to another at all any more?

The Mass will always be the same in its essentials — the renewal of the offering which Jesus made to the Father on Calvary, and the Communion of his body and blood as the sign and source of the one Body of Christ. In other words, it will always be a sacrifice, and a sacred meal.

Apart from these essentials, however, eucharistic worship will depend on the culture, customs, language and temperaments of the people who offer it.

Certain historical circumstances have caused most of us to think of the Mass as unchanging and "universal" in the wrong sense. Enormous and irreparable damage has been done to the cause of the church because of small-mindedness and short-sightedness in this matter. A few hundred years ago, for example, an imaginative missionary effort that might have brought all of China into Christianity collapsed because officials in Rome insisted on such things as that all Masses be in Latin, that priests must wear Western-style dress and vestments, and so on.

This attitude, long in disrepute, was officially put down by Pope Pius XII. When the church attempts to call a people to a better way of life under the inspiration of the Christian religion, he said in one of his encyclicals, "she does not act like one who recklessly cuts down and uproots a thriving forest. She grafts good stock upon the wood so that it may bear even better fruit." The policy of using anything in local cultures, even religious customs, that can conceivably be meshed with Christian beliefs is now well established.

Chinese, incidentally, do not "worship" ancestors. They have traditionally a remarkable reverence and honor for them. A misunderstanding of this custom has been another costly mistake for the church.

Pius V's Mass Trampled?

Would you please explain why the Latin (Tridentine) Mass of Pope St. Pius V was not translated into English or other native tongues, rather than trample it underfoot? I understand, and know there was a curse also, that no one could ever change the Mass. If they did they would suffer the curse.

At the Second Vatican Council, the bishops of the world laid down the rules for the revision of the Mass. These requirements are found in the Constitution on the Sacred Liturgy, "Sacrosanctum Concilium."

The revised missal, they said, should be drawn up so that both texts and rites "express more clearly the holy things they signify"; that the several parts of the Mass should be clear as to their nature and purpose, and how they are connected together; that the active participation of the faithful be more easily accomplished; that the "treasure of the Bible be opened up more lavishly so that richer fare may be provided for the faithful at the table of God's word"; and that a rite for concelebration by many priests be incorporated into the new missal.

In other words, just as Pius V saw the need for action in his day, Paul VI, along with the rest of the bishops, felt strongly that the so-called Tridentine Mass lacked too many of these elements to serve well the liturgical and spiritual renewal of modern Catholics.

It is more than a little sad, and a testimony to the shallowness of faith of many Catholics, that the eucharistic altar, the great sign of Catholic unity, should become the stage for belligerence and even rejection of the authority of Jesus in the person of the Holy Father and others who have the responsibility of guidance in the church. The fact that some can even speak of a "curse" for revising the Mass is further evidence that their understanding of the Mass is one step above superstition. It also proves they know nothing of the history of the church or of the liturgy.

When Pius V issued his edition of the Roman Missal, he pleaded that it be an instrument of liturgical unity and a witness to purity of worship in the church. Paul VI did the same when he issued the current one after Vatican II. The "legitimate variations and adaptions" allowed for in the new rite were themselves a basis for hope, he said, that the revisions "will be received by the faithful as a help and witness to the common unity of all."

Every sincere Catholic will do everything possible to make that happen.

Black-Power Sign of Peace?

We recently saw children using the black-power sign at Mass. Is that permitted?

I presume you refer to that part of the Mass known as the Sign of Peace. In the instructions concerning ceremonies of Mass, the church is very broad on what this "sign" should be. It says only that some expression or symbol of peace should be exchanged in accord with the custom of the place.

The idea behind the sign of peace is obvious. Since the receiving of the Body of Christ in Holy Communion is *the* great sacramental sign of unity in Christ among all those who share it, it is appropriate that those who are soon to share this Eucharist should express in some way their awareness of what they profess in receiving it. Even though they may not be warm friends, or even acquaintances, their common love and friendship with Jesus, and their awareness of the fact that they are brothers and sisters of Jesus, is a deep and personal reality that deserves acknowledgement.

While some may not like the black-power sign and what they think it signifies (indeed, many don't like the "peace sign" either) among black people and whites who are sympathetic to their concerns, the black-power sign usually symbolizes a spirit that is well within this Christian context — brotherhood, willingness to stand and be counted, and a common concern for justice to blacks.

Any attitude of belligerence or animosity is, of course, clearly out of place at the Sign of Peace.

Women Give Communion

At early weekday Masses in our parish, when there is no deacon present, a laywoman holds the chalice for those who wish to receive Communion under both forms. Is this permissible? Legal?

It sounds as if you have some fine liturgical practices in your parish. You are lucky.

It is entirely proper for a laywoman to minister the chalice to people receiving Communion, provided, of course, that she is a properly commissioned special minister of the Eucharist. Lay eucharistic ministers distribute Communion either under the form of bread or wine, and it is completely legal.

Bow or Genuflect?

A couple of times recently, I have seen people — in one case, a priest — bow toward the altar and the Blessed Sacrament instead of genuflecting. Can you tell me why they do this? Shouldn't we genuflect if we really believe in the presence of Jesus in the Blessed Sacrament?

Genuflection — bending one or both knees as an act of reverence — happens to be the act of reverence Catholics of our time and country are most accustomed to, but a profound and devout bow can be just as reverent. Until perhaps 300 years ago, bowing was the common way of showing reverence to the Eucharist, or to the crucifix. It was considered quite proper, in fact, for young girls to curtsey to the Blessed Sacrament.

Our practice of genuflection derives mainly from practices of imperial Rome and the later courts of Europe. Bowing is still used in preference to genuflecting by some religious orders, and is the practice almost exclusively in the Eastern churches.

Regardless of time or country, of course, some appropriate sign of reverence to Our Lord in the Eucharist is required from the nature of man's relationship to God.

Theological Pulpit Language

We've been going a lot to a church where the priest gives some marvelous and helpful sermons. The only problem is that he uses some big words I don't understand, and I think I am a pretty well educated Catholic. What do "eschatological" and "parousia" mean?

I had to straighten out your spelling; those words are not exactly a part of everyday vocabulary, but I believe these are the words you meant.

"Eschatological," or eschatology, comes from the Greek word "eschata," which means the latest, or final, things. In sermons, it would refer to what theology usually calls "the last things" — death, judgment, hell, heaven, and most especially as all these relate to the second coming of Jesus at the end of time.

"Parousia" is another biblical Greek word which means "presence" or "coming." The church uses it to denote both the continued presence of the Risen Savior in his people and in this world now, and his second coming at the end of time. It is usually a combination of the two, with emphasis on the second coming, that is intended when the word is used today.

Eschatology and parousia are common words in theology. But priests, like physicians and lawyers, often forget that most of their technical jargon is, excuse the expression, Greek to the rest of us.

Communion in the Hand

I was taught in a Catholic school that the priest's hands and his right thumb and forefinger were especially blessed for handling the Body of Christ and dispensing Communion. If this is so, how can nuns and lay people be allowed to give Communion?

I am still not sure about the idea of receiving the Body of Christ in my hands. It seems to me it should be placed on one's tongue. Can you clear this up? I don't necessarily dislike it. I just don't understand.

Contrary to what many Catholics report they were taught, it was never true that the priest's thumb and finger were anointed in order that he might "handle the Body of Christ." The symbolism of placing oil on a person, whether at baptism, confirmation, or ordination, is not intended as a particular sanctification of that part of the body. It signifies that the entire person is consecrated and dedicated to an exalted position as a member of the family of Christ.

Jesus himself is said to be anointed by the Father; in fact, that is the meaning of the word "Christ" — one who has been christened or anointed to a role and mission of particular dignity.

Certainly a focal part of that mission for the ordained priest is to preside at the Eucharistic Liturgy and make possible for the rest of the Christian people, and celebrate with them, the unbloody renewal of the death and resurrection of Our Lord. The anointing, however, is not directly related to giving Communion any more than it is to the forgiveness of sins, or any other priestly function. This point is particularly clear from the fact that for 1,200 years or so, it was common for any Christian to give Communion to any other Christian. People took Communion in their hands at Mass, gave it to each other, and even took the Eucharist home to family or friends who could not be present at Mass.

Within the past few centuries, in an effort to counteract certain heresies which denied the real presence of Jesus in the Eucharist, the church gradually built up the detailed prohibitions we learned about not touching the Host. When I was small (in the 1930s), we were taught that it was seriously sinful to touch not only the Host itself, but even the chalice, paten, or ciborium in which the Host and consecrated wine were contained.

We now know, however, that such prohibitions did not reflect (as we then assumed) what the church had "always" done, and that they involved nothing essential to Catholic doctrine or practice.

You are never, of course, forced to receive Communion in your hand if you do not wish to do so. There's always the option to receive either way. Frankly it seems to me that the hand is no less holy than the tongue. The incredible fact is that Jesus gives us his body and blood as our spiritual food and drink in the first place. From that viewpoint, at least, to make a big deal out of which part of our body touches the Host first appears to me to be supremely ridiculous.

Mary, on Communion in the Hand

I have read all the explanations for receiving Communion in the hand, but I am still troubled by the message given by Our Lady at St. Damiano, Italy. In her appearance there she said, among other condemnations of what is going on in the church, "The Holy Eucharist is trampled underfoot! My children take the Holy Eucharist in their hands! My Son, Jesus! Sacrilege upon sacrilege."

Pope Paul was aware of these messages and he still gave his permission. What is your reaction?

My first reaction is that either Mary's memory is awfully poor or her indignation is awfully late. Christians were receiving the Eucharist in their hands for 800 or 900 years after Christ, and it didn't seem to bother her at all.

I intend no irreverence to Our Lady because I don't believe any of this nonsense came from her in the first place. Obviously, as you say, Pope Paul didn't either.

I can easily believe that some poor soul who is emotionally upset by what the bishops and popes are doing believes herself to be the chosen messenger of God to tell the leaders of the church how wrong they are. This isn't the first time for such an occurrence, however, and through the centuries the church has learned that there are ways of discerning with some assurance whether the voice is that of the Lord (or Mary) or of a well-intentioned person with some psychological instability.

For better or worse, with rare exceptions that Jesus generally makes unmistakably clear, he has left the governing of his people to the prayerful, intelligent good judgment of those he places as servant-leaders in his church, the church to which he promised his presence and guidance. Such revelations to private persons may be helpful to individual Christians, and occasionally to the whole church; but faith in them, or submission to their "demands" is never required of anyone, pope or layman.

Communion Before Mass

Do the new rules of the church forbid the priest to give out Communion before Mass on weekdays?

I go to weekday Mass frequently and see many parishioners leave before Communion. Sometimes they stay for Communion but leave right afterward. I hate to see them miss Communion.

For a long time, including the time many of us were growing up, most Catholics had largely lost awareness of the intimate connection between Holy Communion and the Mass. At best they were considered as two separable events. The important thing was to receive Communion; missing the rest of the Mass seemed not all that significant.

This attitude is a gross distortion of the meaning of the Eucharist, and the church is trying hard to correct it. The proper time to distribute and receive Communion is at the appropriate place in the Mass, and this should be the normal procedure in every parish.

When an individual cannot receive Communion at Mass, however, whether because of age or illness or for other reasons, yet wishes to receive Communion, the priest should see to it that the person has the opportunity.

The practice instituted by a parish will depend much on the local community, how many churches and other Masses are available, and so on. In our parish, for example, during Lent we schedule three Masses each day, plus an early morning Communion service for those who cannot come to Mass.

If an individual simply cannot be present for Mass and receive Communion at that time, he should explain the situation to his parish priest. In such circumstances, church regulations present no obstacle for a priest to give Communion outside of Mass.

Communion From the Cup

As a parish priest I see conflicting practices concerning Communion under both species. I've seen the chalice left on the altar; each person came, picked up the chalice and drank from it. At other times, Communion ministers have given the chalice to the people.

Do you know if both of these practices are correct? What is the rule?

The chalice should never be left on the altar for each individual communicant to pick up and drink. The theology and entire symbolism of the Communion rite require that the Eucharist be "ministered" to the individual communicants.

Regulations on giving Communion are clear on this. It is no more correct to receive Communion from the chalice this way than it would be to receive the Bread by just picking it up from the ciborium on the altar.

The church is so conscious of the need for ministering the Eucharist that it provides an emergency procedure when not enough ministers are present at a particular Mass. When sufficient eucharistic ministers are lacking for some reason, the priest may "appoint a suitable person who in case of genuine necessity would distribute Communion for a specific occasion." ("Immensae Caritatis," 1973, instruction of the Sacred Congregation for Divine Worship.) A brief commissioning ceremony for that particular situation is given in the same document.

Just as the minister of the Host holds the Host and says, "The Body of Christ," the minister of the chalice presents the cup to the communicant and says, "The Blood of Christ." The communicant answers, "Amen."

How Communion in the Hand Happened

Why did the American bishops set such a bad example for American Catholics by voting for Communion in the hand in 1978?

At the pope's Mass at St. Mary Major on New Year's Day, the same year, there was no Communion in the hand. Don't the American bishops follow the example set by Christ's highest representative on earth?

The rule of the church is that if two-thirds of the bishops of a nation vote to do so, they may request permission from the Holy Father for the option of Communion in the hand in their country.

Italy's bishops have not asked for or received permission for Communion in the hand. Thus, when the pope, as Bishop of Rome, declines to give Communion in the hand, he is not necessarily attempting to set an example for anyone, including other bishops. He is simply observing the law which is at present in effect for all Italian dioceses.

Bishops in the United States (and 60 or 70 other countries) have asked for and received permission from the pope for the option of receiving the Eucharist in the hand.

Communion in the Hand in Rome?

I read with interest your answer that Communion in the hand is not allowed in Rome. A few years ago, I made a pilgrimage to Rome

with the retarded and handicapped. We celebrated Mass in the North American College, in St. Peter's Basilica and in St. Paul's Outside-the-Walls.

If Communion in the hand is forbidden in Rome, somebody should tell the priests who are distributing Communion, or else a lot of good priests will be going to hell. Only a pure-bred ostrich could say that this practice is forbidden in Rome.

I didn't say it wasn't done in Rome. I said the bishops of Italy had not approved it.

If "good priests" are going to hell for giving Communion in the hand, legally or not, there isn't much hope for any of us. I'm counting on God having a better set of priorities than that.

Communion in the Hand a Fraud?

A booklet entitled "On Communion in the Hand and Similar Frauds" has opened up a can of worms in our church. We were invited to take a copy or not as we so desired.

How authentic is it? Or is this propaganda?

I have noticed that the above publication does not carry the official approval of the church (nihil obstat or imprimatur).

I'm not familiar with the publication. If, as I suspect, the title accurately reflects the theme of the book, it's clear why it had to be printed without approval of any bishop. It rejects the teaching of the church, and a practice officially approved by the pope and the bishops of most of the Catholic world, including the United States.

Can Infants Receive Communion?

Our new Catholic neighbors have several children, teen-agers and up.

Their mother told me the other day that all their children received First Communion when they were infants, before they came to this country. How is this possible?

If her children did indeed receive Holy Communion as infants, I suspect that this family is a member of one of the Eastern-Rite Catholic Churches, a suspicion which is strengthened by the fact that you say they came from another country. For many centuries, in fact up until about the year 1200, babies were given Holy Communion immediately after baptism, at which time they were also confirmed. In other words, the three sacraments of initiation — baptism, confirmation, and the Eucharist — were commonly ministered all at one time. Certain Eastern churches continue that custom.

When you have a chance, check with your neighbor. If her husband belongs to an Eastern Rite, so do all the children, in which case they would receive their Christian initiation according to that rite.

Kiss of Peace

How and why did the practice of the Kiss of Peace or shaking hands at Mass originate? Do you think Our Lord shook hands with the apostles when he said, "My peace I leave with you, my peace I give you?"

How can this practice be avoided by those who find it obnoxious?

The Kiss of Peace is among the oldest rites connected with the Mass. At least five times, the New Testament speaks of Christians greeting each other with a "holy kiss" or a "kiss of love." It is probable that already this ceremony was part of the liturgy. We know for sure that by around the year 150, the kiss as an expression of unity and peace among Christians constituted a regular part of the Eucharistic Liturgy.

For centuries the Pax (Peace) as it was called was exchanged by everyone at Mass. Toward the late Middle Ages, the practice began to be observed only by the attending clergy, and other signs (embraces and so on) often substituted for an actual kiss. This continued until our present time when the kiss, or sign, of peace is once again prescribed in some manner for all the faithful. The church's official Order of Mass states that just before the breaking of the bread in anticipation of Communion, "all exchange the sign of peace and love, according to local custom."

Thus, in spite of your misgivings and suspicions, the sign of peace has deep roots as a fitting external expression of the Christian meaning of the Mass and Holy Communion. In the beginning, the rite took place early in the Mass, but soon found its way to the time around Communion, the sacrament which we still refer to as "the sign of unity and the bond of love."

If we really believe that in receiving the Eucharist we share the table and the meal which Jesus provided to express and build our family unity as his brothers and sisters (and therefore as brothers and sisters of each other), doesn't it seem rather bizarre that anyone would consider it obnoxious to reach out and touch another in a gesture of charity and unity just before going up the aisle with him to receive the body of the Lord?

The church's long adherence to the Kiss of Peace as a significant element of the Mass might reasonably suggest that anyone who finds that part of the Mass annoying lacks something fundamental in his understanding of what the Eucharist is all about.

Finds Handshake Painful

Concerning your answers about being rebuffed at the Sign of Peace, has any priest considered the many thousands of people who have arthritis or other ailments of the hands? I have a severe disease and have had two fingers amputated, and a possible third later on. It can be very painful for many of us, and if it's a man with a hearty handshake it can hurt for a couple of hours. We may look healthy, but if we look down when the priest announces the Sign of Peace, this could be the reason.

Your point is a good one we might all keep in mind. Everyone should be alert and thoughtful of this possibility. In these instances the individual can express the sign of peace with a smile or a word.

Permission for the Sign of Peace

In several churches pastors do not permit any sign of peace whatsoever, except when a visiting priest has not been warned. How does this fit in with submission to authority and the concept of community that, as I understand it, is the reason for the sign of peace?

If one takes the liturgical instruction book literally, there is no specific gesture required for the sign of peace. The official guide for the ceremonies at Mass state that after the celebrant has said, "The peace of the Lord be with you always," and the people have responded, "And also with you," the priest "may add: Let us offer each other the sign of peace. All exchange the sign of peace and love, according to local custom."

However, this is not the whole answer to your question. A statement on the Sign of Peace by the United States Bishops' Committee on the Liturgy notes that "the re-introduction of the kiss of peace within the Mass was not perhaps preceded by sufficient catechesis covering its history, significance and use." We still suffer from this lack of understanding, which affects both priests and laity. It is not helped at all by the tragic decline in appreciation of the place of symbol in liturgical ceremonies, a decline which has occurred for many reasons over the past few hundred years.

Many priests and lay people are still suspicious of any close personal interaction with another at Mass. They feel safe with words, but not with actions which might give expression to those words. So they are not comfortable with this exchanging of a sign, or kiss, of peace, even though it is simply an effort to express externally what will happen a few minutes later when those same people will share in eating the body of Christ.

While not absolutely commanded, therefore, the Sign of Peace is more than an incidental or optional part of the Eucharist. These words from the bishops' statement may help to explain why:

"The liturgical renewal has recognized the value of the assembly and its right to participate actively in the liturgy. The (Vatican II) Constitution on the Liturgy, in indicating the various forms of the real presence of Christ, emphasized his presence in the assembly itself.

"In view of this providential re-evaluation of the liturgical assembly, it is proper that...it is clearly stated that, at the invitation addressed to the faithful, all exchange the sign of peace according to local custom. It is not a peace that moves out from the altar, a clericalized peace, but a community peace exchanged among those in whose midst is the real presence of Christ the Lord."

Does Water Break Communion Fast?

We were always taught that we should fast before Communion. Now we have a priest who keeps a glass of water on the altar, and he drinks from it a dozen times during Mass. This is bothering me and a lot of other people.

I thought surely every Catholic knew by now that water, taken anytime, doesn't break the Communion fast. Your pastor obviously has some affliction that requires him to drink water often. Why don't you ask him?

When Host Is Dropped

Does the Catholic Church still have the dry sink where the dropped Host was put directly into the ground? It seems now the priest picks it up and keeps on going.

I remember going anywhere in the United States and the Mass was the same. Now you don't know from one Sunday to another. One time the priest comes from the back of the church, the next from the sacristy. Is this what the church calls keeping up with the times?

It was never suggested, or even proper, for a Host to be disposed of in the sacrarium, which is the proper name for the sink you speak of. Many churches have such a place, leading directly into the ground, to dispose of holy water, for example, which should not be poured into the common sewer.

The consecrated Bread and Wine, however, are never treated that way, as long as the appearance of bread or wine is still present. If the priest does not feel comfortable distributing a Host to someone after it has fallen to the floor, he may keep it and consume it himself later.

The rest of your concerns are further evidence that, for many people, the biggest problems with the "new church" are not doctrine or even moral teaching, but practices that they have become comfortable and familiar with. That isn't all bad, of course, because many of our happy memories and emotions are connected to those practices.

It helps, however, to keep an open mind about them, and try to understand why some things today are done differently than we recall. You mention, for example, the priest often coming to the altar from the back of church. This form of entrance, if it is done well, adds much dignity to the Mass. It emphasizes the solemnity of what is about to begin, and it places proper importance on the various roles that will be played by ministers in the procession — the reader of the Word of God, for instance. It also provides a better framework for the song which should normally open the liturgy.

I can only urge you to try to participate in your heart, as well as in your actions, in what is happening. It will be good for your faith as well as your nerves.

Peace Sign Obnoxious?

Some time ago your column included a question on how the practice of shaking hands at the Sign of Peace can be avoided "by those who find it obnoxious."

You didn't answer the question. Some of us do find it obnoxious to submit to that gesture. Our dislike has nothing to do with understanding or not understanding the Eucharist. If the Sign of Peace is so deeply rooted in the liturgy, why did not the American church discover it before 1965?

I can only strongly disagree with you. Dislike and rejection of that part of the Mass unquestionably has a good deal to do with understanding or not understanding the Eucharist.

One may question, as many do, whether a handshake or a hug is the most appropriate sign of friendship and love in our country. (What would we put in its place?) But that some appropriate external expression of affection and unity is proper sometime during the Mass cannot be denied by anyone who understands that the Eucharist is the sign of the bond that unites us as followers of Christ.

I don't presume to judge anyone's conscience on this or any other subject. Many of us, after all, grew up in a climate that saw the Mass solely as a prayer, totally personal between the individual and God. We do not easily move beyond such training.

The fact is, however, that such a view of the Mass is, at best, grossly incomplete. It was precisely to help us broaden our understanding of the Eucharist in our Catholic lives that the church introduced (or reintroduced) elements of our Eucharistic Liturgy which remind us that the Eucharist is first and above all a community worship — the worship of people who are together precisely because they are brothers and sisters of Jesus Christ, and therefore of each other.

A handshake, an embrace, or a kiss, may not be the best possible sign of peace. Imperfect as these actions may be, however, they carry a message that we need to understand if we are to celebrate the Eucharist together as Christ intended it to be celebrated.

What Is Spiritual Communion?

What exactly is a spiritual Communion? I am a convert, and an older Catholic tells me that we receive the same graces from this as from actually going to Communion. Is this true?

A spiritual Communion is a conscious, serious internal act of desire to receive Holy Communion, or more specifically, to have the union with Our Lord that normally accompanies the proper reception of this sacrament. It can, of course, be made in one's own words or thoughts, and those who prayerfully desire Communion with Jesus in this way enjoy the blessings and helps of the sacrament itself.

One hears less about spiritual Communion today because of the comparative frequency with which the Eucharist is actually received at Mass. Spiritual reception of Communion began to be quite common 800 or 900 years ago when Holy Communion was received rarely, perhaps only a few times during one's lifetime. Older people still alive today can remember when the majority of Catholics received Communion once or twice a year. In this kind of atmosphere, formal spiritual Communions could naturally play a much larger role in one's spiritual life.

Such Communion "by desire" is still good, of course. But much of its spiritual significance is absorbed today by the richer understanding of the sacrifice of the Eucharist, and its proper influence in our daily prayer and work.

Sin or Sins?

I have noticed in the Gloria of the Mass it says "You take away the *sin* of the world." But in the Lamb of God it reads, "You take away the *sins* of the world." Why the difference?

The variation in the wording is deliberate; the words mean two different things. "Sins" refer to the actual offenses committed against God or our fellow man that are contrary to the law of love of God and neighbor that we are bound to follow.

"Sin" denotes more generally the "sinfulness" in the world — the disharmony, alienation and selfishness, and other tendencies under which human beings live and from which sinful actions and many other evils come. Jesus came as Redeemer not only to forgive sins, but even more fundamentally to heal that sinfulness, to rebuild the harmony within ourselves and our neighbor and God. This redeeming restoration of order and love is what we acknowledge in the Gloria.

Sacraments

How Many Sacraments?

A few of us Catholics are in a discussion group with some Protestant couples. A question came up recently about the sacraments. Where do we get seven sacraments? If Christ instituted them, why do the Protestants recognize only two?

There was no actual enumeration of seven sacraments until more than 1,000 years after Jesus' resurrection. During those centuries, however, the Christian church recognized that among all the religious ceremonies, some rites carried with them in a special way a contact with Christ and his life, and were connected with times in the lives of Christians — birth, life, growth, worship, forgiveness, sickness and death.

As early as the year 200, the theologian Tertullian wrote about the special goodness of those marriages which the church blesses and seals and which the heavenly Father ratifies.

Around 1150, another noted theologian, Peter Lombard, researched all this Christian experience and came up with a list of seven sacraments in what approached our "scientific" sense of the word. This list was accepted by St. Thomas and other theologians. There really was no serious disagreement about it until the Protestant Reformation nearly 400 years later. Interestingly, while the Western (Latin) and Eastern churches fought violently over many matters of faith, this is one thing they agreed on.

The reasons most Protestant churches acknowledge only two sacraments (baptism and the Eucharist) are complicated. Mainly it is because these two are (even in our Catholic doctrine) the focal sacraments of the Christian life and because they are more obviously founded on explicit texts of the Gospels. However, it might be noted that some Protestant communities do increasingly provide rites for other sacraments. Some Lutherans, for example, celebrate a rite for confession, and Anglicans for the anointing of the sick.

The list of seven sacraments was defined as a matter of Catholic faith by the Councils of Florence in 1439, and Trent in 1547.

Qualifications for Baptism Sponsors

I have several questions referring to Catholic baptism. Must there always be two Catholic adults to act as godparents, or is one Catholic adult and one non-Catholic sufficient? Or is either one required to be a Catholic? Is there any age requirement?

How can a priest from one parish tell me one thing and a priest from another say something different? Isn't the purpose of god-parents to assure a Catholic education if something happens to the parents?

The rules of the church in these matters are very clear. At least one Catholic sponsor is required at a Catholic baptism.

According to the Rite of Baptism, the requirements for a single sponsor are mainly that the sponsor:

1. be mature enough to take the responsibility to testify to the faith of an adult convert, or to profess with the parents the church's faith when a child is being baptized;

2. be able to help the parents as necessary to bring up the child as a good Christian;

3. have received the sacraments of baptism, confirmation, and the Eucharist; and

4. be a member of the Catholic Church.

No specific age is required for the sponsor.

If there is only one sponsor, that sponsor may be a man or woman, regardless of the sex of the person baptized. If there are two sponsors, church law still urges that they be a man and woman unless there's an exceptional reason to have both of the same sex.

When only one Catholic sponsor is assigned, a baptized non-Catholic Christian may stand in place of the second sponsor. However, this non-Catholic is not a godparent in the canonical sense of the word; he or she is officially referred to as a "Christian witness" to the baptism.

Since all the above is explicit Catholic policy around the world, you shouldn't be receiving conflicting information from priests. Perhaps some of them are not familiar with church regulations on the subject, particularly in the Introduction to the Rite of Baptism itself and in the Directory for Ecumenical Matters of May 14, 1967.

Though parents do hold the primary obligation for the religious upbringing of their children, baptismal sponsors are by no means without their own responsibilities unless the parents die. The baptism ceremony, in fact, directly asks the godparents if they are willing to help the parents in their duties as mother and father. This help may be given in various ways: by moral support to the parents, by staying close to their godchild in showing interest in his spiritual development, by perhaps a small gift on the anniversary of birth or baptism, and so on.

The Introduction to the Rite of Baptism beautifully states that the godparent is added spiritually to the immediate family of the one to be baptized, and represents Mother Church. As occasion offers, he will be ready to help the parents bring up their child to profess the faith, and to show this by living it.

Should Priest Delay Baptism?

During the last few years I've heard of priests hesitating, or even refusing, to baptize children. Recently my nephew told me that when he and his wife took their first child to the priest for baptism, the priest gave them a hard time. He told them he would have to talk to them a few times about their own practice of the faith before he would baptize the baby.

I don't know what my nephew will do, but I do know that other parishes do not hold up baptisms like this. Isn't there a church law that says children are to be baptized as soon as possible after birth? Does the priest have any right to postpone baptism this way just because the parents don't go to Mass as often as they should?

The heart of your question and of the priest's approach with your nephew lies in the last phrase of your last question. Whenever a Catholic couple (or the Catholic partner in an interfaith marriage) is seriously deficient in the practice of religion, the parish priest has not only a right but an obligation to delay the baptism of their child until he can help the parents straighten out their own faith.

True, current canon law directs that children should be baptized as early as possible after birth. The law assumes, however, that the parents are practicing Catholics prepared by their teaching and example to bring their children up as good active Catholic men and women.

There is, however, another canon which provides that when parents are not practicing and active Catholics, baptism of their children should be delayed until the parents can guarantee that their children will be properly raised as Catholics. While the church intended this law primarily for mission countries, the principle applies everywhere.

The Introduction to the new Rite of Baptism emphasizes the point. At least twice during the ceremony, Catholic parents openly proclaim that they accept and believe the faith in which that child is being baptized, and that they are willing to give the example and teaching necessary for that child to be raised in the faith, and so on. Under any normal circumstances, this promise cannot be made by supposedly Catholic parents unless they themselves are faithful to the practice of their faith, and are not simply bringing that child for baptism out of a sense of family tradition or a vague feeling that "it's the right thing to do" — which is often true today with parents who do not go to Mass regularly or otherwise are weak in their beliefs, or are not very faithful in practicing what they say they believe.

Obviously the church is concerned that parents not be placed in the position of making a profession of faith that they do not honestly and fully believe. Thus, the parish priest is directed to work with the parents who are not yet ready to profess that faith completely and to assume the responsibility of educating their children in the faith, and then to decide upon the right time for the baptism.

I realize that such regulations may startle many Catholics. But being realistic, we are in a situation different from the one we were in when the church instituted the practice of almost automatic baptism of children of baptized Catholic parents. Frankly, in this, as in numerous other aspects of our faith, the church today is trying to pull us (both clergy and laity) away from viewing the priest as simply the administrator of a religious club, who is there to respond and satisfy religious needs, as it were, on demand.

Anyone who knows the history of the church of the past two or three hundred years is aware that by automatic baptisms, first Communions, and so on, whole populations of people were left at an almost primitive level of Catholic faith. One generation of baptized non-practicing Catholic parents followed another. Few, if any, were required to deal honestly with their own need for God, and to open themselves to the possibility of growth to anything like a full Christian Catholic life. As someone put it well, a church which never says "no" to parents who are seriously deficient in their belief and practice of their faith will never allow them to become deeply believing parents.

I believe your nephew and his wife are fortunate to have a priest who is trying to help them question seriously who and what they are as Christians, and to be certain in their own hearts that the baptism of their child will be what it was meant to be, a genuine recommitment of all their family to their Catholic faith.

Baptism and Parents' Faith

How can you be so stupid? In spite of what you say, no priest has any right to refuse or delay to baptize a baby any time.

Whatever happened to original sin? How can you condemn a baby for something it didn't do?

No priest better ever hesitate to baptize a grandchild of mine just because his parents don't go to Mass the way they should, or I'll give him a piece of my mind.

I must admit a number of people wrote protesting what I said in that column, but you have an unusually delicate way of expressing the point.

To answer the question implied by your letter, there has been a change in the church's attitude toward baptism of children. The assumption that parents are practicing Catholics, and that the child is actually being baptized into a genuine Christian community which includes the child's family, is no longer possible. It is too often contradicted by the facts.

Baptism of a child (or an adult) is not an individual matter between the person and God. It is an action of the whole Christian community welcoming that child as part of a family that belongs to that Christian community, and it is the child professing its belief (through its parents and godparents) in that community, and wishing to become a part of it.

This is not something incidental to baptism; it is essential to it. Admittedly it is an aspect of baptism that was not stressed in the past because it didn't need to be. Today the situation is quite different. A highly respected canon lawyer made the point succinctly a few years ago at a meeting of the Canon Law Society of America. Speaking of the right to baptism (and the other sacraments of initiation, the Eucharist and confirmation), he said, "Surely human beings have a right to enter that community and participate in it. But they have no right to enter it to destroy it. The community itself has the right of self-preservation and growth. It has the right to be what God intends it to be. And this right of the community conditions the right of individuals to enter it." In other words, before an individual is baptized, the parish — and the whole Christian community — has a right to know that the commitments made in that ceremony are honest.

This is not only for the good of the community, but also for the good of the child. You may have forgotten that in baptism the individual baptized makes some awesome promises to participate as a full active member of the Christian community as he grows in that community. It is totally unfair for parents to commit a child to that kind of responsibility when they have no intention of properly assisting that child to grow in that community and enable it to fulfill those promises honestly and sincerely in later years. Parents who do not practice their faith have no right to make commitments on the part of the child that they are not willing to help that child fulfill. It's basically as simple and as direct as that.

We still believe in original sin, but the baby is in no way being condemned for something it didn't do. The church has never taught that unbaptized children or adults will lose their soul, or will even be through no fault of their own deprived of the presence of God in eternity. We know that Jesus commands baptism for his followers and that this is the normal way for entry into the kingdom. God never assured us, however, that he has revealed all his plans to us, or that he does not have ways of bringing his life and grace to human beings in other ways than through baptism. Certainly the church has never taught, for example, that unbaptized pagans who possibly never even heard of God or of Jesus are automatically deprived of eternal salvation. It has, on the contrary, always taught that God has ways which man does not know, and these are his own secrets to reveal or not as he wishes.

He gives his church the responsibility of directing its own life in a way that will help that community to remain faithful to what he commands, and to the lifestyle that he has revealed, including procedures for administering and receiving the sacraments.

The shift in the church's perspective is solidly established in our present legislation and policies concerning the sacraments. In addition to numerous references to this policy in the Introduction to the Rite of Baptism itself, the Congregation for the Doctrine of the Faith (June, 1970) insisted that a well-founded hope for a Christian education of a child must be present or the child should not be baptized.

In other words, the church is making every effort to lead us to a richer and fuller understanding of the church as the family of Christ, and how all of her activities, most especially the sacraments, must reflect that vision.

Parents' Responsibility at Baptism

Your answer about possible hesitation to baptize babies has me really disturbed.

I have a grandson a year old who has not been baptized, but my hands are tied. The infant's father, my son, has become one of the hordes who have ceased attending Mass.

He's in a mixed marriage but there's no interference from his wife. He was educated in Catholic schools through college. I feel a condition such as this needs deep consideration before a decision to delay baptism of the baby. It could mean complete severance from the church. Why don't you consider this?

I certainly do consider it, and any priest who has to deal with this kind of situation considers it very carefully. Receiving people into the church, whether infants or adults, is one of the greatest joys of the priesthood. We do not lightly pass up that opportunity.

We do have, however, an obligation to the Christian Catholic community and to the parents of children who are presented for baptism. We must not perpetuate a lukewarm or non-existent connection with the church by supposedly Catholic people simply because they want a baptismal ceremony.

Somewhere along the line, parents of children must decide where they stand with God and with their religion. We do them no service by pretending that being half in and half out is no problem as long as they come around to the church for big moments in their lives.

I, and other parish priests, do not simply refuse to baptize people. We spend many hours and sometimes weeks working with parents, trying to help them to come to a decision about whether they can honestly present their children for baptism and commit themselves to the kind of life that will be necesssary if their children are to be raised as Christians and Catholics.

Frankly, from my experience, I believe the likelihood of greater severance from the church is most remote. By our working with parents in this way, many parents have come to realize that they must stop playing games with their faith and with God and lay their life on the line as Catholics and Christians. Others have not come to this conclusion yet, but I have known no one who has ended up more separated from the church than they were before.

Understanding, and the proper kind of encouragement, incidentally, from grandparents and friends can be a great assist to fathers and mothers who are contemplating the baptism of their children, and prompt the kind of personal commitment this ceremony will demand from them.

Orthodox Godparent

A friend of mine who is Russian Orthodox was recently godmother for her Catholic friend's baby. Is this permissible?

As I explained earlier, in place of a second Catholic baptismal sponsor, a Christian of a Protestant denomination who may be a relative or friend of the family may serve as a Christian witness of the baptism with a Catholic sponsor. A Catholic, incidentally, can do the same for a member of a Protestant denomination. In both cases, of course, the responsibility for the Christian education of the person baptized belongs to the godparent who is a member of the church in which the person is baptized.

An even closer participation is permitted when the person to be baptized is a member of one of the separated Eastern churches, which would include the Russian Orthodox. A member of one of these churches may be godparent, together with a Catholic godparent, at the baptism of a Catholic infant or adult.

Your friend therefore acted quite properly in being godparent at the baptism, at least according to the regulations of our church. In all such instances the individuals involved from other faiths should be sure that their action is not contrary to the regulations of their own church as well.

Protestant Godparents?

My husband and I recently had our second child. We are both Catholic; he is a convert of four years. Our problem is we have no Catholic friends. And because our marriage was a mixed one, there are few family members to choose from.

Why can't my husband's brother and his wife stand as godparents? They are practicing Presbyterians and good Christians, which is what I feel it is all about, right?

I explained earlier why our church requires that at least one sponsor at baptism be Catholic.

You may be missing something in your search for a Catholic godparent. You say this is your second child. Are you aware you can have the same sponsor for this child as for your first?

Also, the Catholic sponsor need not be present at the baptism. If one of your family or friends lives at a distance and is willing to be godparent, he or she may be represented at the ceremony by proxy. This proxy need not be Catholic.

Parents out of Church

My son was in the seminary for 10 years. He left the seminary and married a non-Catholic divorced woman who had two children, and they had two sons of their own.

My son is willing to have his sons baptized, but won't raise them as Catholics, and he doesn't go to Mass even on Easter and Christmas.

I am wondering if it would be all right to have the children baptized in some other religion. That way they would at least be Christians.

A child should not be baptized into any Christian community unless at least one of his parents is committed to that faith and intends to raise and educate the child in that religion. Merely having children baptized does not make them Christian unless they are entering a Christian community (their family and a larger Christian comunity) that will nurture that Christian faith and make it a reality in their lives as they grow.

From your letter it seems obvious that your son and his wife do not consider themselves Catholic. In fact, unless you have omitted something important, it doesn't seem that they have any religion at all. Arranging for the children to go through a baptism ceremony will not solve either their parents' problems or their own.

Is Infant Baptism Wrong?

Our newspaper had a short article about baptism. Apparently there is a new ceremony for baptizing adult converts. But the article quoted some Catholic authority that infant baptism is wrong, and that we shouldn't do it any more. Is this true? Surely we aren't going to stop baptizing babies now!

There is a beautiful new rite for initiating an adult into the Christian faith which includes, of course, the sacrament of baptism.

I have read quotes of the remarks probably referred to in your letter concerning this new rite. The introduction to the ceremony indicates that this rite is the norm for all initiations into the church. One noted liturgical scholar has, it seems, interpreted this to mean that anything except adult baptism is abnormal. According to the quote I have seen, he said, "The normative nature of adult initiation means that departures from the norm, while necessary for serious reasons, are always abnormal. Hence, indiscriminate infant baptism, while common, is abnormal and should be stopped."

Infant baptism of the children of Christian parents has been a practice of the church almost since its beginning. The psychological and spiritual community of the family as Christian people was recognized very early. Even though the child was too young to believe on his own, his parents knew they were a "new creation."

Their Christianity was not an incidental frosting on their personality. They believed, as St. Paul said, that for them, "To live is Christ." It was only natural, therefore, that their child share from its earliest days in their faith and love — and their baptism.

Not only has the church embraced this practice through the centuries. The discoveries of modern psychology concerning the deep spiritual and religious involvements between parents and children seem only to strengthen the wisdom and validity of that tradition.

If, then, our author means to say that the practice of infant baptism in itself is abnormal, I believe he must yet bring forward a good deal of evidence and argument if he expects to make his case.

If, however, by "indiscriminate infant baptism" he simply means that we should not pour the baptismal waters over everyone that comes along, I can only agree with him. But I don't know many priests who do that.

Child of Non-Catholic Widow

Our son joined the Army Medical Corps, and while in the service married a non-Catholic girl from South Carolina. A child was con-

ceived and was born eight months after our son died.

Around Christmas time, I asked his wife if she would have the baby girl baptized. She said, "What is that?" After I explained, she said her parents had recently joined a Protestant church and there were no Catholics in their area of the state. But she consented for us to have the baby baptized.

Our parish priest then told me the mother would have to promise to raise the child Catholic before he could perform the ceremony. As a CCD teacher, I teach that when you are baptized you become a child of God. An innocent baby receives all these graces, and I believe this rule should not apply in these certain circumstances.

The priest said he believes as I do, but has to obey the rules. Please give your views on this.

Apart from a danger of imminent death, no child should ever be baptized in the circumstances you mention. At least three weighty considerations are involved.

First, the baptism would place serious religious obligations on the mother which she is at present apparently unwilling and almost certainly unable to fulfill. Several times the baptismal rite emphasizes that the parents (and godparents) must realize their duty to raise the child in the faith and church in which that child is being baptized, and they profess that they intend to fulfill that responsibility. Not being Catholic herself, and isolated from any significant support from Catholics, she is right in being reluctant. It would be totally unfair to place that burden on her.

Second, the sacrament of baptism does bring with it many precious gifts of identity with Jesus and his Mystical Body on earth. Our concern over the importance of baptism, even for infants, is most legitimate. However, the Catholic Church does not teach, and never has taught, that God's love and life and promise of saving grace are denied to the unbaptized.

To the contrary, as Vatican II noted, we believe that the Father's providential care and Christ's redeeming love are at work in all men. Baptism is important in Our Lord's plan for us, but we mustn't panic if someone is not baptized.

Finally, baptism might place the child in some jeopardy later on because of her relationship to many church laws. For example, with no chance of being raised Catholic, even the validity of a future marriage (according to Catholic marriage legislation) may be in doubt, through no fault of her own, if she is baptized a Catholic in the present circumstances.

Baptism is a great and powerful sacrament. But it isn't magic; the church's guidelines for it are intended to keep it in proper perspective. The priest was right in his advice to you.

Must Child Wait for Baptism?

We have a dear friend, a boy nine years old. His parents do not want him baptized until he is old enough to decide for himself if he wants to be a Catholic.

If he were baptized by a Catholic priest, would he automatically become a Catholic? I always thought this didn't happen until after instruction, confession, and first Communion.

When a child is born and baptized into a Catholic community (whether baptized by his parents, a priest, or someone else), that child is considered a Catholic, though, of course, he may repudiate that faith and that church later in his life.

If, as you say, the boy's parents do not intend to raise him Catholic, much the same answer would have to be given here as in the previous question.

Change Son's Godparents?

Is it possible to change our son's godparents? They do not go to church and do not practice their Catholic religion. We have found someone we would rather have than them. Our son is two years old.

There is no way you can change the official godparents, who receive that role permanently at the time of baptism.

If godparents fail to live up to the responsibilities they accepted at that time, as the ones for your son seem to have failed, you might ask someone you do trust and feel good about to look after the spiritual well-being of your child, especially if something happens to you.

Your situation emphasizes once again the care that should be taken in selecting godparents, particularly for children.

Parents Are Sponsors?

I attended a confirmation ceremony and it looked as if some parents were sponsors for their own children. Is this always allowed, or is special permission needed?

A parent needs no special permission to be sponsor at confirmation. The only requirements are those stated for any sponsor. In effect, that simply means that the individual is mature enough to fulfill this role (no specific age is given), and that he or she belongs to the Catholic Church and has received the three sacraments of initiation, baptism, confirmation and the Eucharist.

Are Godparents Obsolete?

Recently, I was godmother for a relative's baby. I was disappointed at the baptismal ceremony. As godmother I had no part or say while the baby was being baptized. The mother and father held the infant and stood in the center while the godparents were standing beside them.

I don't see why godparents have to be chosen since they are not doing their traditional part.

Apparently you have not had an opportunity to attend a baptism for a good many years. Throughout the renewed ceremony for baptism, the primary responsibility of the parents in the training and education of their children is emphasized far more strongly than in the older rite.

As you indicate, the parents now hold the child and they make the primary promises for the Catholic upbringing of the child who is baptized. Don't you agree that this is precisely the way it should be?

It may be true that, in the ceremony itself, godparents take a less active role, though there are several actions and promises that involve them personally. Their primary function always has been, and still is, to support and assist the parents in every way possible as the child grows toward full Christian manhood or womanhood.

If anything, a thoughtful and faithful godparent means more to parents than ever before. Heaven knows, mothers and fathers today need all the help they can get in giving example, support and guidance to their children in the critical years of development. Godparents who take their responsibilities seriously are badly needed by both parents and children.

Maybe you did not get to hold the baby at baptism. I hope you remain conscientious about the much bigger responsibility that is still there.

Can Only A Bishop Confirm?

I read with interest your answers to questions in our paper. Born and raised a Protestant, I desired for a long time to be a Catholic, and converted in 1976.

The priest in the parish gave me instructions for about six weeks, and then administered the rite of confirmation. Since that time, some close Catholic friends have wondered whether a priest can give confirmation, or can only the bishop do this? Now I am not sure if I am truly a Catholic. Am I?

No need to worry. If you followed the instructions and procedures your priest suggested, you are a full-fledged member of the Catholic faith.

Until a few years ago, the sacrament of confirmation was ordinarily administered only by a bishop. Now, however, a parish priest may administer this sacrament in several circumstances, one of which is the reception of an adult convert into the church. After the baptism (or after the profession of faith if the person is already baptized,) the rite of reception into the church calls for the priest to minister confirmation to the new Catholic.

This proper procedure seems to be what happened in your case.

Confirmation Sponsor

I have heard that it is now possible for the same person who was sponsor at baptism also to be sponsor at confirmation. Is this correct? Also, does the confirmation sponsor have to be a Catholic?

According to the revised regulations concerning confirmation, it is not only permissible but desirable that the godparent at baptism also be the sponsor at confirmation, if he or she is present for the ceremony. The reason is obvious. The responsibility assumed by the sponsor at confirmation is the same as that of the sponsor at baptism, that is, to help the candidate for the sacrament to live up to his baptismal promises, under the influence of the Holy Spirit. Having the same sponsor on both occasions emphasizes this responsibility more effectively.

There may, however, be a different sponsor for confirmation. In fact, this function may be filled by the parents of the candidate.

Included among the qualifications for the sponsor are that he be spiritually qualified, that he be sufficiently mature to undertake the responsibility involved, and that he be a Catholic who has already received the three sacraments of baptism, confirmation and the Eucharist.

Confirmation Name Needed?

Our daughter will be confirmed soon, and nothing has been said about a confirmation name. Is it still proper to have a special name at that time?

It is no longer required to have a confirmation name different from the one given at baptism. The use of the person's baptismal name is allowed at confirmation, since this better expresses the close relationship between these two sacraments, both of which are part of the process of Christian initiation and commitment.

Candidates may choose a new name for confirmation if they wish. I'm sure this will be explained in your parish.

Problem of Conversion

I am married to a Catholic man and gradually have come to realize I would like very much to be a Catholic also.

My problem is that before I knew my husband I had an abortion. I realize this is against the teaching of the Catholic Church. If I become a Catholic, would I have to admit in confession that this is in my past? I hope I would not even have to bring it up in confession.

Please do not let this fear deter you from entering the Catholic Church. Many factors will make this problem much smaller, in fact, than it may look to you right now.

First of all, only serious sins, which the individual knew were serious sins at the time they were committed, must be mentioned in confession. From your letter it would appear that you perhaps did not realize the enormity of the sin of abortion when you were younger.

In addition, as you learn more about the Catholic faith, and specifically more about the sacrament of penance, I believe you will find that the fears which seem so huge right now will pretty much fade away. The options open to you about where you go to confession and to whom, the strictest kind of secrecy which binds every priest when he ministers this sacrament, and above all, the healing and forgiveness that comes to us from Jesus and his church, will in the end make things much easier than you could now imagine.

Penance: Prayer or Action?

The last time I went to confession, the priest gave me a penance to do something which I won't explain here. I asked him what prayers I should say, and he told me my penance was "the action, not the words." Can you explain this?

It's quite simple. The "penance" requested in the sacrament of penance is intended not only to make up for our sins, but to help us remedy the weaknesses that cause our sins, and to commit ourselves to a new life. Sometimes the priest may feel that some action — like an act of kindness — will serve that purpose better than "three Our Fathers and three Hail Marys."

The church encourages such penances. In the document outlining the revised ceremony for this sacrament, (Rite of Penance, paragraph 18) we are told that the satisfaction or penance imposed should "correspond to the seriousness and the nature of the sins confessed, to the extent possible. This satisfaction may be suitably performed by prayer, by self-denial, especially by service of neighbor and works of mercy through which the social aspect of sin and its forgiveness may be expressed."

You're lucky to have gone to a priest who tried to help you receive the greatest benefit from the sacrament of penance in this thoughtful and creative way.

Can A Priest Hear Confessions Everywhere?

A priest-friend of our family told us recently that he could not hear confessions in our church without permission from the bishop. (He is from a neighboring state.)

We didn't have an opportunity to ask him to explain, but that sounds unbelievable. Doesn't a priest have the right to hear confessions anywhere?

No, he doesn't. Apart from an emergency, a priest cannot administer the sacrament of penance (or perform certain other public functions, such as preach or witness marriages) without permission from the bishop of that diocese.

The reason such delegation or permission (technically called "faculties") is necessary, is that the bishop is the one responsible for the liturgy in his diocese. Priests have authority to exercise their public ministerial functions only from their bishop. The same goes for priests who happen to be in a diocese other than their own.

Generally, bishops give the pastor of each parish the power to give such delegations to visiting priests.

Only Sins Are Confessed

There is this young married couple, married in church, and one was born and raised Catholic. They both love children and plan to have a family as soon as they feel they are mature enough and their personal circumstances permit.

They have been using the rhythm method, but because of the limited period of "safety," they use an artificial method of birth control also. They do not believe in their hearts that this is wrong, but feel they should express their love for one another at other times than just during a short period.

Their problem is that they do not feel like going to confession and confessing this, as they do not feel they are sinning. Must someone go to confession in a case like this? I'm afraid they are seriously considering leaving the church for another if this is so.

Your letter raises a number of points about which I suspect this couple might need enlightened rethinking, not the least of which is your expression of their reasons for delaying a family; of course, you don't give their ages.

I'll limit myself, however, to answering your direct question. No one is ever required to confess anything that he or she honestly feels is no sin. In fact, when an individual is convinced that what has been done is morally permissible or good, it normally should *not* be mentioned in confession; it might only confuse the priest concerning the penitent's state of conscience.

In forming one's conscience on any serious moral question, the guidance of the church on that particular subject — here, birth control — and on the whole process of reaching practical conclusions in our own conscience, must have a significant influence for Catholic Christians. But when one receives the sacrament of penance, it is for the forgiveness of *sins* — that is, actions which an individual is convinced in his own conscience are wrong, but which he goes ahead and does anyway.

Presuming that you reflect this couple's dilemma correctly, they seem to have one of two problems. Perhaps they do not understand confession properly. Or they might not be quite as sure as they say they are that their course of action is right for them, and they feel uneasy enough about it that they feel they should confess it.

Confession Once A Year?

In response to a question about the Easter duty, you tell us "The obligation of confession during the Easter season is still as it always has been, binding only if it is necessary for an individual to be able to receive the Eucharist."

I refer you to the church canon: "If anyone denies that each one of Christ's faithful of both sexes is bound to confess once a year according to the regulation of the great Lateran Council...let him be anathema."

How do you explain your answer in the light of this statement?

The best — in fact, the only — way for us to discover the proper meaning of a moral or doctrinal statement of the church is to examine what the church itself meant to say at the time, and how it interprets that statement.

So here, in spite of the seeming absolute command of yearly confession, the fact is that, in its sacramental practice and regulations, the church has always, at least as far as I can determine, meant this to apply only where a mortal sin had to be confessed. The context of the Council of Trent's canon, and even more the context of the Fourth Lateran Council statement to which you refer, support this interpretation. Moral theologians, old and new, agree almost without exception.

If you wish a specific example close to home, refer to the Baltimore Catechism No. 3, which was for decades before Vatican II the most official and authoritative expression of beliefs and practices of American Catholics. Question 293 asks: "What is meant by the commandment to confess our sins at least once a year?" The answer: "By the commandment to confess our sins at least once a year is meant that we are strictly obliged to make a good confession within the year, if we have mortal sin to confess."

I trust you realize this is not what the church recommends; it is simply the bare minimum required. If one is in the state of mortal sin, he must receive the sacrament of penance within the year. Of course, if one is guilty of serious sin, he would need to go to confession simply to fulfill the other annual sacramental obligation, to receive the Eucharist sometime during the Easter time.

Any Catholic who understands how the sacrament of penance heals us in our sinfulness and other weaknesses, and how it strengthens and reconciles us to God and to our fellow members of the church, will normally receive this more than once a year, mortal sin or not.

Confessionals Should Go?

I think the time has come for the confessional box to go, and I'm convinced thousands agree with me! You can hear what is being said on the other side, and even in the back seat of the church. It's very embarrassing.

I wish there would be more group confessions at Mass. Where do they have these?

The problems you mention are not yours alone. Many churches now have confessional rooms (also sometimes called reconciliation or penance rooms) rather than, or in addition to, the traditional booths. This not only provides more privacy, but allows a face-to-face relationship with the priest which many find helpful. A completely private confession with a "screen" is also possible in these rooms; it's up to the penitent how he wishes to do it.

To receive the sacrament of penance at group penance services, at least private confession of sins is normally required, though all the other ceremonies and prayers for the sacrament may be public. You would have to watch the parish bulletins for these occasions, or call a parish to obtain the information.

Incidentally, you will do the priest in question a favor if you tell him about the overhearing problem. He's probably unaware of it.

Penance Without Serious Sin

What does one do when he is sent from the confessional and told not to come back until he has committed a mortal sin? Does that mean we should never go to confession? I know a number of elderly

people who are facing this problem. I would like to receive this sacrament more often but I'm confused.

About the only advice I can give to you is to do as the priest says; don't go back — to him — for such a confession. Go to another priest — and there are many of them — who do not have such a rigid view of the nature and purpose of the sacrament of penance.

A confession of this nature is usually called a "confession of devotion," that is, only venial sins or previously forgiven sins are told to the priest. Such confessions have been and still are strongly encouraged by the church. The Introduction to the new Rite of Penance stresses the value of "confession of devotion" as having its own kind of healing power. "Those who through daily weakness fall into venial sin draw strength from a repeated celebration of penance to gain the full freedom of the children of God," says this document. Frequent and careful celebration of this sacrament, it continues, "is not a mere ritual repetition or psychological exercise, but a serious striving to perfect the grace of Baptism so that, as we bear in our bodies the death of Jesus Christ, his life may be seen in us ever more clearly." (Paragraph 7)

In other words the sacrament of penance is not only for the forgiveness of sins, but for many other spiritual benefits — the growth of purity of heart, a living spirit of sorrow and humility before God, an increased openness of our hearts to the healing power of God for sins of the past, a more intimate sharing in the saving power of the sufferings of Christ, and so on.

As one of the decrees of Vatican Council II puts it, this sacrament "greatly fosters the necessary turning of the heart toward the love of the Father of mercies."

Naturally, we must never allow such confessions to become mechanical or superficial, or without a true spirit of sorrow. Also, we shouldn't forget that sins can be forgiven in many other ways — prayer, penance, good works, and especially in the Eucharistic Sacrifice, which should always remain the center of our spiritual lives. I'm happy, however, that you see more to the sacrament of penance than simply taking away sins. One of the insights that the church has gained more clearly is that this sacrament has as one of its major effects a strengthening of our minds and hearts and wills in developing the virtues that can make our lives more Christian, and in helping us deal with the sinfulness of selfishness, pride, greed and the other things which are the source of our actual sins.

I suggest that when you receive the sacrament of penance, you focus attention more on these weaknesses and tendencies toward sinfulness, rather than simply on the actions that you think might be sinful, whether venial or mortal. The forgiving and healing love of God are present in a unique way in the sacrament and I'm glad you are concerned about using it well.

Is Ex-Priest Bound By Seal?

If you tell a serious sin to a priest in confession, and he leaves the priesthood, could he repeat it to someone? I need to know this.

No. A priest is bound by the seal of confession for life. Even those men who leave the priesthood consider this one of their most sacred obligations, always.

Penance After Mortal Sin?

Is it really necessary to go to confession before receiving Communion if one has committed a mortal sin?

Yes. If someone is certain that he has offended God that seriously, he should receive the sacrament of penance before going to Communion, except for emergency situations.

It is true, of course, that such a person reestablishes his or her friendship with God before confession by turning back to him in honest sorrow for the wrong that was done. But going to confession in a case like this is not an empty, superfluous formality.

Any sin, especially more serious sin, injures our relationship not only with God but with our fellow man — and most of all, with our fellow Christians. It may be that the sin involved others directly. At least indirectly, our loss of holiness, our self-centeredness in the sin, and the crippling of our generosity in prayer and other good things we do for others, all in some way affect the human "family" we belong to. It is only fair and just, then, that we first confess our sin, and receive the "public" forgiveness for it from the priest, who acts in the name of Our Lord and all his people in the sacrament of penance.

After that, the sharing of the Eucharist in Holy Communion, which is the sign of our mutual friendship with Christ and with each other, makes more genuine sense.

General and Open Confessions

What exactly are the "general and open confessions" some churches have today? Are they new? From what I've heard, I think they would be a wonderful and moving spiritual help if we could have them every month. How could we find out where these take place?

I believe you are speaking of what is more properly called a communal penance service. And it is becoming more popular all the time in many parts of the country.

Basically, a communal penance service is a simple ceremony shared by a group of people and consisting of Scripture readings, songs, prayers, reflections and perhaps a homily on some aspect of God's forgiving love and our conversion to him — and possibly, private confession of one's sins to a priest.

Such a service does not necessarily include the reception of the sacrament of penance, but can be the setting in which that sacrament is received. Group penance ceremonies have become more popular recently with the growing realization that sin is not only a matter between oneself and God, but that it somehow affects the entire Christian family of which one is a part. The covenant between God and his people is in some manner injured when one does wrong, even when the wrong committed seems to be quite private. So it is most proper — in fact, necessary — that sorrow and forgiveness express the fact that one is reconciled not only to God, but to one's fellow man and fellow Christians.

For centuries, Christians were much more aware of these "family" ties with other Christians than we are, so common penance services are not new. In fact, private confession as we know it was unheard of for hundreds of years after Jesus died, and only became a common thing in the church after perhaps 1,000 years.

So there's no misunderstanding, it should be noted that public announcement of one's hidden personal sins is not part of any penance ceremony.

Call the parishes in your area for time and places of communal penance services.

Priest Confessors

Why not have mass confessions now? If anyone can give out Communion, anyone can forgive sins.

Ordination to the priesthood is not, and has never been, a requirement for distributing Communion. It is required in order that one be the church's minister of the sacrament of penance.

Generic Confession

While my mother and I were discussing the new confession rite, she told me that in her parish, during a communal penitential rite, people come up in groups, kneel down before the priest one at a time, and he gives them absolution. They do not mention their sins, and the same penance is given to everyone.

I'm not saying this is completely wrong. But it could have disadvantages as well. It gives people an "easy way out" of confessing serious sins if they do not have to tell the priest. It does bring people

back to confession who maybe haven't gone in years. People are even coming from other towns to that church. Your thoughts on this will be appreciated.

Your letter brings up some interesting facts about the sacrament of penance which may be of increasing significance in communal penance services.

The kind of confession you mention is called a generic confession. The penitent simply says he has sinned, without indicating the kind of sin or the number. Such a confession is perfectly legitimate at any time, if one is not confessing serious, mortal sins, whether at a communal penance service or not.

This indication of having sinned, and that one is sorry, need not be made in words. It could be in action — such as your example of kneeling before the priest, which in the context of the penance service obviously means, "Father, I have sinned, and I am sorry." In at least one parish to my knowledge, each penitent who wishes to receive the sacrament of penance at a communal service, comes and puts his or her hands in the hands of the priest, who then says the words of absolution for each individual.

This method of confessing has some obvious defects, along with equally obvious and attractive advantages. Most of all, it limits drastically the helpful and healing interaction that should occur between the priest and penitent in the new Rite of Penance. But such generic confessions are perfectly legitimate any time venial sins are involved.

Generic confession of mortal sins is permissible only in a special emergency situation. These sins should be mentioned later when the first opportunity for private confession presents itself.

As long as these distinctions are somehow made clear, the practice you describe has much to recommend it. Obviously, a lot of people find something in it quite attractive.

Generic Confession For Me?

You said that a generic confession, in which specific sins were not mentioned, should be made only in an emergency if serious (mortal) sins are involved. Many years ago, a priest chaplain in a mental hospital where I was hospitalized told me that for the rest of my life, I should confess only by saying I am sorry for all my sins as God sees them, and that I should go to Communion whenever I go to Mass.

Do you think that advice still holds for me?

It surely does still hold for you. The response I gave concerning generic confession dealt with the regular norms for the sacrament of penance. Priests are trained, at least in the basics, to discern and help people to deal with special types of personal difficulties relating to this sacrament. The priest who gave you this advice surely did it on solid information he perceived in dealing with your problem. The best and right thing for you to do is to continue to follow that advice.

Why Penance Services?

Should we go to confession to gain sanctifying grace, which we were taught we gain from this sacrament, or does the penance service replace going to confession? Our catechism never mentioned penance services.

A communal penance service, which had fallen into disuse in the church long before our catechisms were written, is an increasingly popular rite. It is simply a ceremony in which a group of Catholics (or other Christians) confess their sinfulness before God and each other, reflect on the meaning of their sins with the help of Scripture and meditation, and ask forgiveness for any offenses committed against God and their fellow man.

From the catechism you mention, you will remember that prayer and contrition of this kind can forgive sins. However, this does not mean that such a service (without sacramental absolution) replaces the sacrament of penance, which is a very special way of meeting a forgiving God in a spirit of sorrow for our sins, and a desire of reconciliation with him. Certain healing, forgiving and sanctifying graces are the fruit of this sacrament, which makes it different and unique among all penance rites.

The sacrament of penance is often included within the kinds of common penance services you speak of, but such is not necessarily the case.

Penance Service and Sacrament

One parish in our area announced that the communal penance service would "take care of" anyone who desires to receive the sacrament of penance. How do you explain that?

A communal penance service, the second method provided for in the new Rite of Penance, usually includes the opportunity for private confession of one's sins for those who wish to do so, and private absolution. The other requirements for the sacrament of penance can easily be included in the "communal" part of the ceremony.

The announcement you quote probably indicated that the communal service would provide this opportunity.

Hearing Problem in Confession

I cannot hear well and have problems with confession. I never know what my penance is; I just leave and say what I always did for years, and add a few more prayers to be sure. I don't know if I'm doing the right thing or not. I only go to confession a few times a year on account of this, and it really upsets me.

It is useless to confide in my parish priest. I am hardly able to understand him when he is standing next to me. This applies to all the priests I go to, even when there are special hearing aids in the confessional. How can I get some help soon?

Priests are always willing to give special assistance to those who cannot hear well in the usual confessional arrangement. Today, when face-to-face confessions are much more available, no one who can hear at all need be deprived of an opportunity to hear and be heard satisfactorily in the sacrament of penance.

In the meantime, continue your present practice about your penance. What you are doing is quite proper and sufficient.

Children Resist Confession?

Perhaps you can advise me on a problem I'm having with my daughter. She received first Communion about two years ago, and made her first confession about one and a half years later. Although she receives Communion regularly, she resists confession. I have not made a big issue of it.

Must I force her to go if she resists, or should I let it slide for a while?

Yours is a widespread problem these days. We should not be surprised, first of all, at your daughter's confusion since most adult Catholics are still trying to discover just where this sacrament fits into their lives.

No one, not even a parent, should force another to receive any sacrament. That can do no real good either spiritually or psychologically. On the other hand, you should not "let it slide for a while." I think there is a middle way.

Helping your daughter by your own words and actions to understand a few essential things about sin and the sacrament of penance is important. One crucial truth forgotten by many who say confession is useless unless one has committed a mortal sin, is that all sin, even slighter sin, is an offense not only against God, but against all the church. It weakens and diminishes the holiness of all by lessening one's own holiness and spiritual goodness in it.

When I sin, I injure the body of Christ, and to the degree of my sin, distort the image of Christ existing in all my brothers and sisters. I become part of a sinful church. To be whole, to be honest again, I need not only the "private" telling of my sin to God, I need the church, through its priest, in that living encounter of confession and forgiveness, to say to me: "We forgive you. In the shadow of the cross of Christ, let's all undergo a change of heart and try to be again the sign of his loving presence to each other and to the world that we were meant to be."

There are other ways in which our daily faults are forgiven apart from confession — through prayer, good works for others, the Eucharist, and so on. Even most of these, however, relate closely to our ties to our fellow Catholics. But the special encounter with God's forgiving and healing love in the sacrament of penance brings him directly into the everyday realities of our guilt, our need for cleansing from sin, and our identity with the death and resurrection of Jesus in a way nothing else does.

These tremendous realities must be thought through and made our own if we expect them to become real to our children. I suggest you use one of the many good books on confession geared for younger people and available from a Catholic bookstore or through a Catholic catalog you could borrow from your pastor.

I am truly happy you want to help your child become more comfortable with the sacrament of forgiveness. One of the great priests and theologians of our time, Jesuit Father Karl Rahner, spoke once of how many Protestant leaders today recognize the need of regular confession of our sins. He added, "With this situation facing us, would it not be very strange if we began to neglect frequent confession out of carelessness and a desire for comfort in the spiritual life?"

With thoughtful parents like you, maybe that is changing.

What Is Perfect Contrition?

What is an act of perfect contrition? Does it take away mortal sin?

The theological terms, perfect and imperfect contrition, have had differing and sometimes controversial meanings over the past several hundred years. Since the Council of Trent in the 16th century, however, the difference has been placed mainly in the motive of our sorrow for sin. Perfect contrition is sorrow over offenses primarily because of our love for God and for Jesus Christ, and because those sins violated that love. Imperfect contrition, on the other hand, looks more toward ourselves — that our sins are shameful in themselves and cause us to deserve punishment for them.

Obviously, the difference between the two makes more sense in theory than it does in practice. Even imperfect contrition arises from the help of God's grace and has behind it basic elements of faith, hope and love. Otherwise the shame over breaking God's law and the fear of punishment or separation from him would not be there in the first place.

In both cases the sorrow arises, at least in some degree, out of the virtue of charity, and both include a firm turning away from any serious offense against God.

Either of these kinds of contrition is sufficient for receiving the sacrament of penance. Understanding the distinction between them in the above traditional manner, however, it is usually understood that perfect contrition is required after a mortal sin in order to re-attain the sharing of divine life that we call sanctifying grace. The Baltimore Catechism puts it succinctly: "A person in mortal sin can regain the state of grace before receiving the sacrament of penance by making an act of perfect contrition with the sincere purpose of going to confession."

All the prayers which we call "acts of contrition" reflect sentiments which clearly fall into the category of perfect contrition. They may speak of fear of punishment, but the predominant feelings are those of faith, and the awareness of having betrayed the trust of a loving God by acting against his wishes and commands.

Can't Remember My Sins

It sure is hard to remember all your sins when you go to confession. When you can't remember them all, how do you tell them to your priest?
I am nine years old and in fourth grade.

First of all, I congratulate you on your interest in the sacrament of penance, and your desire to receive that wonderful sacrament in the right way.

It is always important to remember something I'm sure you already know. This sacrament not only forgives sins, it strengthens us to live good Christian and Catholic lives. The grace which Jesus gives when we go to confession, therefore, helps us to remember, and to want to direct our lives along the lines that Jesus tells us.

One consequence of this is that we should not bother ourselves too much in trying to remember in detail all the sinful or partially sinful actions that we have done. With your attitude there are surely no serious sins in your life. It's more important that you aim at trying to grow in your trust in God, and your love in a practical way for God and for those around you — your family, your friends, and, of course, yourself.

I mention these items only to emphasize that the first thing Our

Lord wants from us is to be comfortable and happy in our meetings with his forgiving love in the sacrament of penance. Beyond that you need to read up on this and other elements of your faith. Your knowledge in these subjects should grow along with your knowledge of other things as you move toward adulthood.

If your public library has no books that will help you at your level of faith and understanding, I suggest you go to a nearby Catholic bookstore, if one is near where you live, or ask your parish priest for one or two catalogs from Catholic publishers. For not too much money, you will find two or three publications that will assist in your understanding and use of this and the other sacraments.

Can Foreigner Go To Confession?

A Catholic friend of mine is from a foreign country and does not speak English. She wants to go to Communion, but is hesitant because she cannot go to confession.

Is it all right for her to receive the Eucharist without confession, or what should she do?

Your friend's situation is not uncommon. Many people from foreign countries stay here for longer visits with family, or take up residence permanently without being able to carry on a conversation in our language.

It is quite possible for an individual like this to receive the sacrament of penance. Confession of sins must be made in some way, but there are other ways than by speech when that is impossible. While specific details may not be expressed so easily in other manners, the penitents can, for example, indicate which obligations or commandments have been violated and by other signs express in some general way their sorrow for their sins and their acknowledgement of having done things for which they wish the forgiveness of God.

Please help your friend to talk with a priest. Most priests have had experience with this kind of situation. Perhaps with a little help from an interpreter, they can easily arrange a comfortable and perfectly satisfactory way for her to go to confession.

Confession How Often?

Our parish has a big confession twice a year with several priests hearing in all corners of the church.

After watching others, I think my sins may be rather childish. We go to Mass every day, so our sins are mostly small ones — missing prayers once a week, talking about my neighbors, and things like that.

Someone told me simply to say that I have sinned against charity

and am sorry for all the sins of my life. Maybe you could help make it simpler.

It seems to me your priests have already helped you greatly in simplifying your use of the sacrament of penance. Communal penance services combine prayers and reflections together as a group, with private confession of sins and private absolution. This you mention as your present parish practice.

Reception of the sacrament of penance twice a year for someone like yourself is certainly reasonable. Either way of confessing that you mention is fine, though I think it is more helpful, and more to the point, to focus attention on our sinfulness, the sources of our sins like greed, pride, selfishness and so on, than on the sinful actions that result from those "capital" sins.

I think you're on the right track, and I hope you continue to find the sacrament of penance as helpful for you as it seems to be now.

Excused From Confession?

Is it possible to be excused from confession if you are 75 years old? And with a speaking and hearing problem? The sin I have trouble with is against purity. I've been told everything by at least seven priests — from "If you waste the seed you are a murderer" to (in a very loud voice) "You do that when you're drunk."

I never married because I thought it was unfair for an alcoholic to marry. I know now that was a larger mistake than our New Orleans Superdome.

I think a major part of your problem is just too many priests. Priests may very legitimately deal with your problem differently, but it's important that you pick one you can talk to, trust him, and be at peace following the guidance he gives you. Drifting from one confessor to another usually brings nothing but more confusion.

As a non-resident of New Orleans (though I confess I have on occasion wished I were), I'm not about to involve myself in the superdome controversy. I will say only that, whatever mistakes have been made, they are using it. Which is what you must do now with your life — use it! God willing, you have a good number of years ahead of you. I hope you find peace and enjoy them.

Communion After Sin

Is birth control a sin that must be confessed before one can receive Communion, or can one receive, and confess it at the next confession?

One of the main requirements for receiving Holy Communion is that the individual not be aware of any unrepented serious offense against God, or in other words that he be in the "state of grace." This simply means that he be in a state of mind and soul that fits into what Holy Communion signifies — a closeness to God, a desire for a deeper union with him, and a willingness to accept God's healing for the effects of whatever wrong he has done.

This includes going to confession before Communion. But in fact a person returns to God's friendship after a serious sin before he actually confesses it — through a genuine Act of Contrition and a renewed acceptance of God's love which is offered to us when we turn back to him. Therefore, for a serious enough reason, one may receive Communion before confession after a mortal sin. The sin should be confessed, however, at the next opportunity.

A sin that might be committed in the category you mention is no different in this regard than any other deliberate refusal to obey what one sees as God's law.

Communion Before Confession

I blame the priests for much of our loss of morals. When you give the opinion that it is okay to go to Communion after a genuine Act of Contrition, and that one need not confess a sin against birth control until the next confession, there is something very wrong with the Catholic Church.

If you look again at the answer given, you will note it says that "for a serious enough reason" a Catholic may receive Communion before confession after a mortal sin. Apart from being traditional Catholic theology, this is also the official law of the Catholic Church concerning the reception of Holy Communion.

Canon 856 of the Code of Canon Law says that confession should precede Communion after a mortal sin, *unless* there is some urgent necessity (what type of necessity required is not further spelled out), and there is no appropriate opportunity to go to confession. (The Latin is "si urgeat necessitas ac copia confessarii illi desit.") As indicated before, this implies true sorrow, "perfect contrition," for whatever sin was committed, and the intention of confessing the sin at the next opportunity.

If your point is that a mortal sin which might be committed in the area of birth control is so horrendous that it does not fall under these basic rules for any other serious sin, you would find it difficult to support your opinion. I do not agree with it.

Absolution Over the Radio?

During a blizzard near our town, four men died — they froze to

death. One was talking on a CB radio to a lady, but due to the blowing snow, couldn't tell where he was. If he could have talked with a priest on the radio and asked for absolution, would the priest have been able to give it?

No. The sacraments are always actions of Jesus in his church acting through human beings — the minister of the sacrament involved — and through the outward sign of word and action that makes the sacramental encounter. For this, personal presence is required between the minister of the sacrament and the one receiving it. Just as a priest could not be ordained or a baby baptized over the radio or the telephone, so one cannot receive the sacrament of penance that way either.

This does not mean, of course, that a person in the situation you mention is spiritually abandoned. His spirit of faith and trust in God, his sorrow for sin, and his desire for the Eucharist and the sacrament of penance can bring him the forgiveness of his sins, and the other helps from God that these sacraments are intended to provide in such a time of need.

Confession to Laymen?

A booklet on confession says that lay people used to hear confessions in the Catholic Church. The book has an imprimatur, but I bet someone that this was never done. Who is right?

Strange as it seems, confession to laymen, or to monks or others who were not priests, was quite common for many centuries in both the Western (Latin Rite) and Eastern Churches. During the early centuries, deacons and certain laymen were sometimes acknowledged to have this function in the church, even to absolve sin, though persons with serious sins had to confess them to the bishop for public penance.

In the Middle Ages, it seems to have been rather common that people turned to monks (most of whom were not ordained at that time) for counsel, confession and absolution. Even later, in the 12th and 13th centuries, some of the great theologians still taught that one could confess to laymen for forgiveness not only of small but even of more grave sins.

Was this confession and absolution considered to be what we now know as the sacrament of penance? It's hard to say, because the technical theology of this sacrament developed in detail rather late, mainly after the 12th and 13th centuries. For a long time, theologians disagreed on the point. St. Thomas Aquinas, for example, seemed to say in some of his writings that confession of mortal and venial sins to laymen had some sacramental value. Others said such a confession was useless from the sacramental viewpoint.

At any rate, as theology developed, confession became more and more limited to the priest or the bishop. One ecumenical council said that confession should be made to "his own" priest at least once a year. Much later, the Council of Trent finally decreed that only confession to a bishop or priest fulfills the requirements for the sacrament of penance.

Self-Confession?

What is your opinion of self-confession? I have heard of some priests saying you can confess to yourself as long as you don't feel you've committed a mortal sin.

A priest I know tells us we are the ones to judge whether we are worthy of Communion or not — not someone else.

I've never heard the expression "self-confession." From the rest of your question, I assume you mean: Can we have sins forgiven without confessing them in the sacrament of penance? The answer to that is definitely yes. The church teaches that any sins which do not completely destroy our friendship with God and the basic direction of our lives toward him, in other words, sins which are not "mortal," can be forgiven many ways — by prayers of contrition, good works, penitential rites such as those at the beginning of Mass, Holy Communion, and so on.

Concerning your second point, the individual involved is the only one who can possibly make the final judgment about his own worthiness to receive the Eucharist in Communion. The Gospels and the teaching of the church should certainly be a major factor in the formation of our conscience, and of our evaluation of our actions. But the Council of Trent simply reflected traditional Christian practice when it said that, to be worthy to receive Communion, one should not be *conscious,* or *aware,* of any unforgiven serious sin.

Anointing of the Sick

I recently attended a church ceremony in which a friend of mine received what we used to call Extreme Unction. Several people received the sacrament, including some who were young and didn't look sick at all.

Isn't it necessary to be "in danger of death" to have this sacrament? And what is the proper name for it? I've heard it called several things.

This sacrament for the sick is one that has undergone significant development during the past 25 years. The Constitution on the Liturgy of Vatican Council II recognized this development when it said, "Extreme unction, which may more properly be called the Anointing of the Sick (its official name today), is a sacrament not only for those who are in danger of death."

Thus, the sacrament is for the sick, but by no means only for the dying. In a scriptural passage which forms one of the main bases for the anointing of the sick, St. James says: "Is anyone sick among you? Let him ask for the elders of the church. They will pray over him, and anoint him in the Name of the Lord." (James 5,14)

According to our new rite for anointing of the sick, then, an individual need not be in danger of death, but "dangerously ill" either from sickness or advanced age. In other words, older people are considered eligible for the sacrament simply because of the general infirmities of old age, even if they are suffering from no serious specific disease. Moreover, the illness need not be physical. Guidelines on this sacrament issued by the American bishops note, "Sickness is more than a medical phenomenon. Sickness is a crisis situation in the life of a Christian as regards his salvation, his life with Christ in the community of the church." Anointing of the sick may be administered, then, to people suffering from various kinds of spiritual or emotional crises.

The official directions concerning this sacrament mention several specific circumstances in which people should be anointed. — such as old age, before serious surgery, and sick children.

All this simply means that there could be many explanations for the situation you encountered. People no longer need to be dying, or even look sick, to receive the sacrament of the anointing of the sick.

Anointing and Viaticum

I appreciate your answer explaining the present understanding of the anointing of the sick.

A question was prompted by a priest's remark recently that this sacrament is not the sacrament of the dying. Does this mean that one who is dying should not receive this sacrament? I can hardly believe that. What did the priest mean?

One who is dying can and should most certainly receive the sacrament of the anointing of the sick. Such an individual needs all the spiritual and physical benefits this sacrament can give.

The priest might have meant two things. First, he perhaps was making the point that the sacrament of the anointing of the sick is not only for the dying, or those who are in danger of imminent death, as some formerly believed. As I explained, it is only necessary that the individual be "dangerously ill," even though there may be no real danger of death.

He might also have meant that the real sacrament of the dying is not the anointing of the sick, but rather the Eucharist, which is also perfectly correct. Christian tradition, in fact, gives a special name to Communion when it is received by the dying. We call it "Viaticum" — literally, something which is to be with us and help us "on the journey" through death into eternity.

We should, therefore, be certain that our friends or relatives have every opportunity to receive Communion whenever possible as they approach death.

Can Lay People Administer Anointing?

I understand that a lay person can baptize and administer last rites when a priest cannot be located.

If this is true, can you please explain the procedure to me so that I will be prepared in the future?

In emergency situations a lay person can administer the sacrament of baptism. When this occurs, the simplest elements of the rite are used. Water is poured over the person and the words are said, "I baptise you in the name of the Father and of the Son and of the Holy Spirit."

No person should be baptized, however, unless we have reason to believe that he would want to be baptized if it were possible to express that desire consciously. Even children or infants should not normally be baptized unless one knows that the parents would not object.

If by last rites you mean the sacrament of the anointing of the sick, only a priest can administer this sacrament. Obviously, however, any lay person may, and should, assist someone who is seriously injured, or ill and possibly dying, by helping the individual to pray with acts of faith and hope and love of God. This should be done, in fact, even when one is simply visiting another who is seriously ill. Sometimes hearing another person pray can be extremely consoling to a seriously sick person who does not have the physical or mental strength to accompany that prayer.

I'm happy you are trying to prepare yourself for this kind of opportunity.

Right or Wrong?

What Is Right, Wrong?

I always thought that when we have to decide whether something is right or wrong, we are supposed to follow our own conscience. However, I mentioned this in a group recently, and the priest said it was not true. According to him, we are obliged to follow the teaching of those in authority, especially in the church. Who is right?

Possibly much of your confusion arises from the fact that the word "conscience" can mean many different things.

You are correct in believing that our personal moral decisions must be made on the basis of what we ourselves honestly believe is right. Whatever another may say or do, God holds us responsible for our moral actions, and that responsibility cannot be shifted to someone else. We must reach our decision, and then trustingly be able to stand before God and say, "I may be wrong, but to the best of my ability, I sincerely believe this is what I should do."

What the priest possibly was attempting to tell you was that an honest conscience is not, as many people today appear to believe, a kind of blind instinct or spontaneous feeling. This could come more from selfishness or cowardice than from any good motive.

The church has spoken explicitly on this subject often in recent decades. The bishops at Vatican Council II summarized it well in their Declaration on Religious Freedom: "Every man has the duty, and therefore the right, to seek the truth in religious matters in order that he may with prudence form for himself right and true judgments of conscience...In all his activity a man is bound to follow his conscience faithfully...He is not to be forced to act in a manner contrary to his conscience. Nor, on the other hand, is he to be restrained from acting in accord with his conscience, especially in religious matters." (nos. 2 and 3)

A genuine Christian conscience is the product of persevering effort in charity, faith, maturity, reflection, prudence and prayer. It involves giving proper weight in these reflections to what our common sense tells us, to the principles given to us by Our Lord in the Gospels, and to the insights and teachings presented for the guidance of our Christian lives by those who have responsibility as teachers in the church.

All of this is required in developing a sincere and adult Christian conscience, which is the kind of conscience we have an obligation and right to form and follow.

Age for "Serious" Sin?

We are trying as best we can to help our oldest child prepare for his first confession. We haven't received much help. We would really like to know how to help all our children form a good conscience without seeing sin where there isn't any — or at least not anything serious.

If you can help us with this question, it will put some things in focus for us. At what age do you think a child is responsible enough to realize he is committing a mortal sin?

First, you deserve a lot of credit for approaching this task with your child so thoughtfully, and for asking some right and extremely important questions. A correct perspective on this matter can help not only children but most of us adults, too.

No one is guilty of any sin, of course, unless he realizes what he is doing. So what you are really asking is: At what age is a child able to commit a mortal sin?

In practice the answer will differ enormously from person to person. Even theoretically, it might vary widely depending, for example, on exactly what kind of moral perception and spiritual growth is psychologically possible at a given age. But a few things can surely be said. (Note that what follows refers to mortal sin; we are not concerned here with lesser, or venial, sins.)

A mortal sin is, as you know, any action by which a person consciously and with full deliberation and determination turns his whole self away from the friendship and love of God. It contains genuine undertones of eternal commitment because, in itself, the decision is total and permanent, even though repentance and conversion may come later.

Now, such a decision demands considerable grasp of one's personal worth and identity, an awareness of one's control over the deepest directions of his loves and commitments, and a fairly profound spiritual perceptiveness. In other words, one must be able to give himself consciously, deeply and fully to God before it can make sense to say he can refuse to give himself to God in committing such a serious sin.

We are talking, then, about something which surely surpasses the moral capability of a normal 7 or 8-year-old. We do not allow even a 12-year-old to marry, or to make religious vows. We know he or she is insufficiently developed both psychologically and spiritually for that kind of love, or that kind of radical decision on the direction of his or her life.

This tells us much about the answer to your question. Since a child cannot reject (in a serious sin) a love and commitment he has not yet been able to make in the first place, something like the same development and age seems necessary before a person can commit a mortal sin. We are probably talking about somewhere in the middle or late teens, or maybe later.

Naturally, one's understanding of mortal sin affects the answer, too. If we insist, for example, that a child can commit a mortal sin at the age of 12 or 14, with all of that age's mental, spiritual and psychological gropings, then it seems we are making mortal sin something considerably less than the catechism and good theology tells us it is. We also threaten to establish a child's whole religious relationship on a rather superficial basis, as if love and friendship with God were something that a person can pop in and out of several times a month.

Threaten With Sin?

You have described earlier the conditions for a mortal sin. You said that the psychological requirements for mortal sin are normally probably not present until the middle or late teens, and maybe even later than that.

Isn't this just encouraging children to sin?

Isn't a threat that they may sin the thing that often helps them act right? Don't you think if children learn this they would just use it as an out for doing something that is wrong?

If I understand your question correctly (and I'm afraid I do) it reflects an attitude toward sin and conscience that should be unthinkable, but which has been all too prevalent in much of our past religious education.

First, and most important, we have no right to lie to children to make them behave. Particularly we have no right to thus play God, and say, in effect: "Even if they haven't committed a serious sin, it's better that they think they have. It will train them to do what is right."

This attitude is, or at least has been, not uncommon among some well-meaning religion teachers. It is, however, a gross injustice to both God and to the individual we're dealing with, and can do irreparable damage to a young person's understanding of his relationship with God.

Of course, if by some mental gymnasics a young person does reflect so fully and completely on the meaning of a serious sin that he consciously figures it is an "out" for him, it would be a good sign he knows what he is doing. The point I made in the previous answer was that until some considerable maturity is attained, a young person psychologically and spiritually cannot adequately comprehend the radical commitments and rejections involved in a mortal sin.

Moral Decision-making

If the church can't or won't say what is a sin, can we ask if there really is any sin? It would seem that everyone, including Hitler, could rationalize their doings.

I am not really sure what connection you are attempting to make between the church's statements and the existence of sin.

Unfortunately, there is, no doubt, such a thing as sin. The church can and does make absolute statements about sin. However, maybe our expectations of what exactly the church can or should say about God's laws are wrong.

Above all, we cannot think of "the church" as a sort of answer machine for every question about life and morality. The church is a living community of people struggling and working at every point through history to understand and respond to God's laws — especially the primary law of Christ to love God above all, and to love our neighbor as ourselves. The bishops and pope have the primary teaching responsibility through the charism of their office, but they, too, are part of this pilgrim church. History has always taught, as it does now, that the black and white answers some people seem to demand are often not possible, or at least that such answers are not at all evident.

Second, we must remember that what we call God's laws often deal with matters of "natural law" — that is, those laws or principles of action that people must follow in order to be truly human, to provide for the right kind of physical, emotional, intellectual and spiritual growth that will make them more perfectly alive and whole as human beings. Among these would be, for example, the principles underlying the Ten Commandments.

The church, again mainly through its college of bishops and the Holy Father, guides us in applying these principles to our daily lives. In carrying out such guidance the church is faced with an ever-changing array of social, scientific, economic, political and psychological realities — all of which in some way affect what is the truly "human" or moral way to act in specific instances.

Our traditional moral principles tell us that circumstances which partially determine what is morally right or wrong change not only from one part of the world or one culture to another. They also change from one time to another.

The classic (but by no means only) example concerns accepting interest on invested money. For centuries the church taught repeatedly that this was seriously wrong because the custom seemed to threaten the economic stability of families and society. One ecumenical council (the Council of Vienne) decreed that anyone who taught that taking interest was not a sin should be punished in the same way as a heretic.

That position gradually changed, of course, as the requirements and nature of large economic systems became evident. The change occurred, however, only at the cost of long confusion and disagreement among bishops, theologians, priests and others about the legitimacy of the practice.

Christ promised us all the guidance we will need to make good, sincere moral decisions. We would do well to remember that promise, and remember that, even in the midst of what seems like confusion, Jesus always keeps that promise. If occasionally there is more gray area than we find comfortable or desirable, perhaps that is his way of telling us to be a little more self-reliant and a little more open to his grace and to the fact that we still have a lot to learn — all of us.

Finally, a key word in your question is "rationalize." One rationalizes morally when he knows what he wants to do, knows his motives are doubtful if not downright evil, and yet fishes around for some phony justification to delude himself and others. This is pure dishonesty right from scratch, and has nothing to do with genuine moral decision-making.

Is Pre-Marital Sex Wrong?

I am a Catholic, dating a Protestant girl. We are in our 20s and considering marriage in the future, maybe in two years.

I have never had an affair with anyone, but is it wrong to have sexual relations with the one you intend to marry?

I have never felt this way about anyone before. My girl says she loves me very much and would like to marry some day. We have talked of having sexual relations, but I'm really confused. I do want to marry her, but I also want to do what is right.

We need an answer that will help us both. I know one of your answers may be that if you love each other enough you will both wait. We both want to be sure.

Catholic moral teaching remains, and is likely to remain, that sexual relations before marriage are wrong. Within the limits of our space here, I can mention only a few, but I believe very important, thoughts that may help.

First, you must realize that your desire for sexual union with the girl you love is not only normal, it is the way you ought to feel about her. Any man or woman who plans to marry and doesn't strongly want sexual intimacy with his or her partner is in trouble. They need either a medical examination or psychiatric counseling — or a serious re-examination of their choice of partner.

Such a desire is, however, no basis, all by itself, for judging whether sexual intercourse is morally right or wrong for you. As all Catholic-Christian moral doctrine, this teaching of the church was not pulled out of thin air. The church simply confirms by its own insight and belief what is common human experience — complete sexual intimacy between people who are not married is hurtful in serious ways that are usually not even dreamed of beforehand. And it is therefore sinful.

The total giving of themselves that sexual intercourse involves implies an acceptance of responsibility and permanent, committed trust of another that you are simply not able at this point to profess honestly. No matter what you say you mean to each other, you do not have the assured and promised commitment to one another that marriage, and only marriage, brings with it.

The vows you one day profess (if you marry each other, and that's still a big "if") will not be a mere legal formality to make official what was already there before. As your family and friends and church will witness by their presence, the promises you make on that day will make your relationship for the first time more than just a private arrangement between the two of you. Only then will you have established the kind of permanent, public responsibility to and for each other that makes sexual intercourse an honest, truthful expression of what you are together.

Contrary to what one regularly hears today, there is no evidence whatsoever that sexual intimacy before marriage increases the chances for a happy union after the wedding. If anything, the contrary is true, for some very practical reasons.

Many of the joys, adventures and excitement of sexual experience and fun can easily (much more easily than you might believe) become old hat. There may possibly even accompany this experience at least some sense of guilt. Sexual intimacy can thus become seriously blunted in its potential for helping couples in working patiently and tenderly through the tensions, uncertainties and new responsibilities of the first years of marriage.

Sexual intimacy also tends to become almost obsessive, especially when divorced from other needs and responsibilities which accompany normal daily married life. Once sex is begun, it can become a kind of hovering presence for a young man and woman. When they meet for a date, they know how the evening will end. All ingenuity in finding and learning other ways of having fun together, in communicating their hopes and concerns and ideals, even in exploring how they can make some gift of themselves to others who need them — all this easily becomes crowded out and ignored. Sex is always available, and it requires little in the way of thought, personal effort or unselfishness.

Your ideals and your love for each other are obviously deep. I hope you will keep them that way and always think through your moral decisions in this light. The payoff in happiness and peace of mind will be worth whatever it costs.

Living Together Before Marriage

I have accepted most of the changes in the Catholic Church and feel they were for the betterment of all concerned.

However, something has recently occurred in our church which is beyond comprehension. A Catholic young lady and a Catholic man, living together for at least the last eight months, finally decided to marry. Banns were published in the church bulletin, and they were married in a Catholic church on Saturday evening with all the church's matrimonial services. They lived together up to the time of the services.

Is living together before marriage now acceptable? Please explain if this is a customary procedure.

Living together before marriage is definitely not acceptable in Christian morality. It is a hurtful, sinful situation, regardless of how the couple involved may view it at the moment.

On the other hand, a man and woman have a right to marry, and Catholics have a right to a Catholic marriage ceremony. I believe, however, that the solemnity and public character of that marriage rite must be determined by balancing the rights of the rest of the Catholic community — the right not to have the marriage ceremony subjected to ridicule and reduced to meaningless gesture; the right not to have themselves and their children exposed to a scandalous flaunting of a shameful situation, and so on.

After some sad experiences as a pastor, I still don't think I would allow a public, solemn marriage ceremony for a couple living together at the time of the marriage.

I, and maybe your fellow readers, would appreciate any insights and practical suggestions we might receive for handling this kind of situation.

Engaged Couple Shares Bedroom

When a couple is engaged, one set of parents of the couple see no wrong in the couple moving into the boy's bedroom. The other

parents believe this is seriously immoral. In this case, doesn't the parish priest have the obligation to tell the couple and the condoning parents that it is wrong, and to help guide them back into the Christian lifestyle — instead of condoning it?

I understand your hurt, disappointment and frustration over what this young couple is doing. In addition to being wrong, this kind of arrangement makes difficult, if not impossible, the real joy and mutual support that the discoveries of living together can bring when accompanied by that special commitment and covenant as husband and wife.

The trust and faithfulness these discoveries help build in the context of marriage pay rich dividends in future years. You want this, of course, in the fullest degree possible for your son or daughter.

You wonder what you can do. At this point, not very much, at least in the light of the few details you have given. Obviously, no parents have any obligation to condone or allow such an arrangement in their home. Nor should they.

As for the other parents' feelings, or the priest's, have you discussed this with them? And I mean personally! Much misinformation and misunderstanding in situations like this result from second or third-hand sources, however reliable you think they should be.

Talk to all the individuals involved. Don't be ashamed of your position or hesitate to enforce it. At the same time, make your love and care for these young people as clear as you can. Remember, God is their judge, not you.

Scripture and Sterilization

Is there any Scriptural text in either the Old or New Testament which directly or indirectly condemns sterilization of a man or a woman as a means of birth control?

We could never expect to find a text in Scripture directly condemning such an operation. When the Bible was written, and for centuries afterwards, sterilization procedures of the kind you ask about were not even dreamed of.

Indirectly, both the Old and New Testaments have much to say, and Catholic theology on the subject draws heavily from these teachings. You are surely aware that the Bible insists numerous times that human life, including one's own, is primarily a gift of God and in his hands, not ours. As St. Paul puts is, "None of us lives as his own master and none of us dies as his own master. While we live we are responsible to the Lord, and when we die we die as his servants. Both in life and death we are the Lord's." (Romans 5, 7-8)

This clearly means more than that we cannot kill ourselves or others. We must respect the limits of our rights over the members of our bodies, and the functions of our life as well — proportionate, of course, to how intimately a particular part of our body is related to the wholeness of our person and our life.

Rarely, if ever, may we look to Scripture for answers to specific cases involving modern technology of any kind. Bioethics, for example, presents us today with baskets full of moral questions which the writers of the books of Scripture could not have imagined. That does not mean, however, that the Bible does not have some very critical things to say on the subject.

Hunger Strike

In light of the hunger strikes among prisoners in Northern Ireland, I would like to know the church's position on this type of protest. Would someone who starved himself to death for a cause be considered a suicide? Or is it considered that only a fanatic would do such a thing, and therefore he would be buried in the church as having been temporarily insane?

The speed and manner with which one deliberately destroys his or her own life does not change the morality of the action. Killing oneself by refusing to eat is certainly suicide.

In practice, the church gives anyone who has committed suicide the benefit of the doubt and (as it should, of course) leaves the judgment to God. In some ways this policy makes even more sense in the cases you mentioned, since the individual's ability to make clear judgments fails rapidly, especially in the later stages of starvation.

On Conscientious Objection

In connection with the new U.S. draft registration recently, our study club has enjoyed some lively discussions on conscientious objection. Can you tell us what the church's attitude is on this now? Mainly we want to know if Catholics who are conscientious objectors have any support or approval from Catholic teaching. Is there anything we could read to bring us up-to-date on the subject?

Conscientious objection of the nature you are discussing may be universal (against all wars), or selective (against a particular kind of war, such as nuclear conflict or a particular war itself, as, for example, the war in Vietnam).

Through the history of Christianity right up to the present, Catholic teaching has acknowledged the possibility that individuals or groups might find universal or selective conscientious objection to a war a demand of their conscience as Christians. This is the explicit position of the universal church and of the U.S. bishops today.

The International Synod of Bishops meeting in Rome in 1971 declared: "It is absolutely necessary that international conflicts should not be settled by war, but that other methods better befitting human nature should be found. Let a strategy of non-violence be fostered also and let conscientious objection be recognized and regulated by law in each nation."

Later that same year, the U.S. bishops issued a declaration on the same subject. "In the light of the Gospel and from an analysis of the church's teaching on conscience," they said, "it is clear that a Catholic can be a conscientious objector to war in general or to a particular war 'because of religious training and belief.' "

A few excellent places to find the church's present position concerning war and related questions would be Pope John XXIII's encyclical, "Peace on Earth," the major statements of Vatican II on war, especially in the "Constitution on the Church in the Modern World," (no. 80); the address of Pope Paul VI to the United nations in 1965, and the pastoral letter, "Human Life in Our Day," of the U.S. Catholic bishops in 1968.

Any good book store should be able to help you find at least two or three of these documents.

Spokesmen for the Church Family

During the last few months many men who fled to Canada to escape the draft have returned to the United States. A knowledgeable member of our group said that the American Catholic bishops have approved this; in fact, he said that a few years ago the bishops published a policy favoring amnesty.

I disagree; even more seriously, by what authority do the bishops of the country formulate a policy on amnesty? This isn't a religious concern. It's a national political concern and therefore should be restricted to our government.

Obviously the bishops disagree with you. While they have never proposed or defended a blanket approval of anyone who avoided the draft or other military activity, they do claim that religious issues loom large in the amnesty question.

This is so obvious, I find it difficult to believe that anyone could not agree. Numerous personal rights and moral responsibilities are involved: the obligation of individual human beings to follow their own religious consciences in matters of public morality, the circumstances under which a nation may wage a just war, the measures of punishment or revenge a government may morally pursue against individuals who oppose — on religious grounds — participation in a particular war, or in any war. All these are unquestionably religious concerns.

The bishops have authority to speak on these issues for the simple reason that they are the official "family" spokesmen for the church in matters of faith and morality. Jesus couldn't have made it clearer that not only his individual followers, but the whole group — his church — was to stand and be counted for what is right.

His love, his generosity, his pity and his passion for justice must be reflected in the life and commitments of his community of believers, as well as in the private life of each individual.

Bishops and others in the church may differ on what a specific position should be, just as they do in other Christian churches. But that does not absolve them of the responsibility to speak and to speak strongly, as they have on the amnesty issue, when they find it necessary.

Cloning

Several times in recent years I have read about "cloning," and that it is causing a big moral problem. What is it, and what's the problem?

The word comes from the Greek word, "klon," which means a twig or a cutting, and is used to designate a remarkable process which biological science has recently discovered.

It is common knowledge now that every cell in a plant or animal carries that special, unique "genetic code" of that individual. For example, the sets of chromosomes that are in the first cell when the sperm and ovum unite in human reproduction, divide and are duplicated eventually in the billions of cells in an adult body. Certain processes guide some cells to become arms, others to become legs, and others to become blood; but all the original genetic "information" is in each cell.

Not long ago, scientists began discovering that it is possible to take a cell from some living organisms and through an extremely delicate procedure, produce a new "beginning" cell that possesses exactly the same genetic make-up as the "parent." This cell would, in effect, grow into an identical twin of the parent body.

Until now, cloning has been successful only with some plants and lower animals. Some scientists expect the day is not too far distant when it will be possible with humans. Then science could, for example, pick out the ideal astronaut, let's say Neil Armstrong, and produce 100 Neil Armstrongs from his own body to form "ideal" teams for space flight. Other uses of the procedure would obviously be numerous.

The moral question, as with so many other newly-discovered scientific possibilities, is: Should mankind go ahead and do something just because it is possible? If so, under what conditions, and with what safeguards? Who will make the decisions? What human, spiritual, psychological, religious values are involved?

Unfortunately, as with so many other modern technical developments, from sperm banks to nuclear weapons, too many responsible persons consider such concerns irrelevant, or at least superfluous. Their thought seems to be: Let's try it and think of the consequences later. By that time, enormous and irreparable damage could be done to the bodies, psyches, and social structure of the human race.

For these reasons, moral theologians of all faiths are wrestling publicly and urgently with such questions.

Sterilization

If a young Catholic woman with three children, who has unsuccessfully used the rhythm method, had her tubes tied, has she committed a mortal sin? Has her husband sinned, especially if he agreed with her in wanting no more children?

Can she go to Mass and the sacraments? Do you think the Lord tries to understand the reasons why we do what we do? I pray to the Lord for answers, but they don't come very easily. I know many Catholic people hard-pressed for answers and we desperately need help on where to turn. The answers aren't in a Sunday sermon like they might have been years ago. I'm sorry my questions got so long, but many young couples need these answers and I'm number one on the list. I'm 28 years old.

Let's take your questions one at a time. First, and maybe the hardest to respond to: Did you commit a sin?

The Catholic Church teaches that any kind of direct sterilization (such as tubal ligation or vasectomy) is objectively seriously sinful. This means that such an action in itself, considered in isolation (if that were possible) from the circumstances of the individuals involved, is a serious offense against God, our Creator, since it deliberately destroys one of the major functions of our body.

Whether an act of sterilization is subjectively sinful — that is, did the person involved actually commit a grave sin? — is a far more difficult question. Involved here are such considerations as these: Did this person realize fully that the action was seriously sinful for him or her when the action was done? Were there alternatives that the individual was emotionally, intellectually and spiritually capable of choosing and carrying out? Worded more theologically, was the person morally free-willed when he acted as he did? Were there other circumstances present that might diminish full responsibility for any possible sinfulness in what was done?

While these are routine questions in determining moral responsibility for our actions, it is usually hopeless, fruitless and sometimes even harmful to attempt to untangle them after the fact, even for the person directly concerned. Usually the individual has a pretty good idea of how his action fit in with what his conscience told him was right and wrong. Once the thing is done, the right thing is to put the matter in the hands of Our Lord, ask his forgiveness for any sinfulness of which one may be guilty, and then move on.

How about your husband? Certainly, encouraging and assisting another in doing something that is seriously wrong can itself also be seriously sinful. However, the same questions discussed above would apply to him as well as to you.

Can you go to Mass and receive the sacraments? By all means! Not only can you, you should do so. With your enormous responsibilities as a mother and wife, and with your concern over your actions, you need the healing and forgiving love of Jesus which we experience so powerfully in the sacraments of penance and the Eucharist. Don't put it off any longer. Go to a priest you feel will be compassionate and honest with you, and talk with him.

After Vasectomy

I'm a Catholic who stopped attending the sacraments about five years ago. Two years ago, shortly after the birth of my daughter, I had a vasectomy — not as a protest against the church, but due more to my lack of faith in God's giving me the patience and understanding to raise more than the two children I have.

I've had many sleepless nights since then. I've been attending Mass for the past two years but have not received the sacraments. My children have both been baptized. What can I do now? My wife and I both want to be on good terms with the church and raise our children as Catholics.

Please go and talk to a priest as quickly as possible. Whatever wrong you may have done, there seems to be no reason that you cannot now receive the sacraments of penance and the Eucharist. The priest will help you work things out and get back where you want to be.

Sterility

What would be a wife's position if her husband had a vasectomy operation without her knowledge or approval? Would she be practicing some sort of sinful birth control by having sexual intercourse once she has been informed of the surgery?

Your question might more basically be phrased: May a married couple have intercourse even though they know their union cannot result in children because of a condition of sterility? Such a condition may be present naturally (as when one partner is unexplainably sterile), after a hysterectomy, at a later age when child-bearing years are past, and so on.

No moral obstacle to sexual relations exists in these circumstances. The possibility of the wife becoming pregnant and bearing a child is not a moral requirement for intercourse.

Regardless of how it started, you have a condition of sterility in your marriage which, at least on your part, did not and does not now imply any sinful intention or deliberate wrong action. There is no reason why you would be required to abstain from sexual relations.

However, you cannot ignore another element in the situation. Your married life, including your sexual life, is not carried on as two individuals isolated from each other. Therefore, since the cause of the sterility in your marriage was deliberate, it is important that you help your husband overcome and correct any sinful conscience and any continuing intention of violating his responsibilities in relationship to God in the matter.

Sacraments After Vasectomy

Under what conditions could a man receive the sacraments of penance and Holy Communion if, after sincere consideration of his conscience, he determined that a vasectomy was not wrong for his circumstances and, in fact, had such surgery performed?

Putting the question precisely as you did, the answer would have to be that nothing prevents such a person from receiving the sacraments. One does not commit a mortal sin unless in doing the action he believes and reflects sufficiently on the fact that here and now he is doing something that is seriously against God's law. Your statement implies that the individual in question is doing just the opposite; as he sees it, he is saying sincerely to God: This is what I believe you want me to do. Such a person is obviously not guilty of sin, and therefore has no reason to mention the fact in confession, or to keep from Holy Communion.

The joker in the whole question, of course, is in the words "sincere consideration of his conscience." If you recall another question about conscience, you know that an honest conscience necessarily includes many factors, not the least of which is the moral guidance given by our Christian faith, and by the church.

It also includes at least one most essential "consultation," the one with one's spouse. Even apart from any Christian morality, consideration of such decisions in isolation from, or against the wishes of, one's wife would be in itself a grave offense against justice and charity, whatever else it may be.

"Sincere consideration of one's conscience" with prayer, faith, and trust, is, of course, within the ability of each of us. It seems to me, however, that sometimes some of us are tempted to make it more spontaneous and simple than it in fact is, especially in matters of large, long-range importance. I would suggest that you have not fulfilled that responsibility until you have discussed the subject with a competent priest in whom you have confidence.

Abortion After Rape?

Does the Catholic Church advocate an abortion for a baby who was conceived as a result of rape? Did the Catholic Church ever approve of abortion for that particular reason, if it doesn't today? I heard that not long ago the church said it was all right if the abortion took place a short time after the rape.

The Catholic Church teaches that the deliberate killing of an unborn child is wrong under any circumstances, including a child who may have been conceived after a forced sexual intercourse. And it has never taught otherwise.

The basis of the church's position — and, incidentally, the position of almost all other churches and nations until this century — is that abortion is deliberately taking the life of another human being. Modern sciences, genetics and biology, and even the increasingly sophisticated field of pre-natal psychology which studies the physical and emotional reactions of children before they are born, increasingly support the conclusion that we are dealing with a human life during those nine months in the womb. This would be just as true of a child whose mother was a victim of rape as of any other child.

The second part of your question — concerning a "short time after rape" — deals with a procedure that could be permissible, but may not be very physiologically realistic. It is possible that some time may elapse before the sperm and ovum unite after sexual relations. This union never occurs in the vagina. It may occur in the uterus itself. More commonly it occurs in the Fallopian tubes, after which the new combined cell enters the womb (uterus), implants, and develops into the full-grown baby.

Some physicians, and others who are supposed to be experts in the field of physiology, assert that by using a vaginal or uterine douche (that is, by washing out the vagina and uterus), it is possible to remove the sperm before it has a chance to unite with the ovum of the mother — an ovum which is, of course, normally there only once a month.

Insofar as this is possible before the fertilization of the ovum, it would be a legitimate, moral procedure after rape. But sperm swim awfully fast. For this and other reasons, it is doubtful whether the procedure is at all practical as a method of preventing conception.

Church Approved Abortion?

Someone told me recently that the Catholic Church once taught that abortion was permissible, and in fact only took a strong stand against it recently. I've also heard this from some of the groups favoring abortion. Is this true?

Pro-abortionists like to resurrect this accusation in an effort to find inconsistencies in the church's position on this important moral issue. But the accusation is totally false.

A strong, explicit prohibition against abortion goes all the way back to the Didache (called "The Teachings of the Twelve Apostles," written probably around the year 100). This document declares, "You shall not slay the child by abortion."

Such a prohibition persists through the early fathers and teachers in the church, and has never been contradicted or mitigated by any church official.

It is true that many writers and theologians through the centuries followed the then current, and now obsolete, biology of their times which believed that the fetus did not become human until a certain point in its development.

St. Thomas Aquinas, for example, was simply following the scientific information of his day when he suggested, 700 years ago, that a male fetus isn't fully human, because it didn't look fully human, until the 40th day, and the female fetus until the 80th day.

All this has changed, of course, with the science of genetics and other disciplines which tell us much about prenatal human life.

Even in these earlier centuries, however, there was no approval of abortion. There is no foundation for stating that the church only recently came around to its position on the subject.

Anyone interested in more details on the history of how abortion has been viewed in the world and in the church will find much interesting and useful information in the excellent book, "Abortion — The Development of the Roman Catholic Perspective," by John Connery (Loyola University Press).

A Mother Regrets

The Question Box receives numerous questions concerning abortion. Many require answers far too long for this space. Included are questions relating to the personal aftereffects on a mother who has had an abortion.

Better than any reply I could give is the following letter. The mother who wrote it is not unique.

I have written her assuring her of God's forgiving love, but I hope our readers will remember her and others like her in their prayers.

Dear Father Dietzen:
Please, Father, don't throw this letter away. Let me talk to you. I need it, and perhaps if someone else in my situation reads it, she won't do the same thing.

After finding out I was pregnant I panicked because I picture a very insecure future for my children. I panicked because I thought we wouldn't have enough for everyone since now there are times we have just one complete meal.

So after coming back from the supermarket depressed because of the prices and the foods I couldn't get for my children, I decided I couldn't bring one more child into this world and then not be able to offer him a stable future. I know I was a big coward, but I did it thinking that this was the best thing to do for that baby and for the children I already have.

This was the hardest, the most painful decision I have ever taken in my life.

I cried during the "procedure," as it is called by the so-called counselors and doctors. With that child went part of my heart. I thought I would overcome that, but now I know I just tried to fool myself. I can't stop thinking about that 8-week-old baby I aborted.

I can't forget what I have done. It's just too much for one's conscience. Day and night I keep imagining that baby crying, telling me to let him live. I imagine the baby felt as if he was being caught by a "black hole" when the surgical vacuum was taking him out of me. I'm scared to be alone or in the dark.

Believe me, Father, I feel awful. I truly regret what I have done from the bottom of my heart. I ask God to please forgive me, to help me.

Instead of asking for that valium at the clinic when I felt I just couldn't go through it, I wish that I would have had enough faith in God, in the world, and that I would have left that place.

Is it possible that I can be forgiven — here on earth — at least a little bit? I don't dare go to church when there are people there. I pray alone and ask God for forgiveness.

I wish to advise any woman who, in my situation, thinks that abortion is the practical, easiest and most reasonable way to solve any problems. I know by my own experience that once in the clinic everything sounds "secure, simple, fast, confidential, practical, almost painless, etc."

You see so many women in there, all ages, colors and races, that you really believe temporarily that it is something normal to do, that it is the right thing to do. But, once everything is done, once one is out of there, then we can't fool our conscience, our principles.

It is impossible to ignore the conscience, to run away from it. It is an eternal nightmare. It is like having always the need to reach that baby, not to let him go. But, no matter how hard we try, we just can't reach him.

Yes, the procedure is fast but the pain and guilt are endless.

Don't think you have to accept abortion to do it. I always thought I wouldn't do such a thing, but I panicked. I didn't have faith. I was desperate and now I am paying the consequences. No matter how much I cry day and night, I will always feel sorrow for what I have done.

Father, I hope you can tell me I can be forgiven or where to go.

Help in Pregnancy

Your column recently quoted the deeply moving letter of a distressed woman who had had an abortion.

Nearly every major city has at least one emergency counseling center to urge pregnant women to consider alternatives before having an abortion. These may be found in the phone book under such names as Birthright, Alternatives to Abortion, Life-Line, The Society for the Preservation of Human Dignity, Help-Line, Pregnancy Guidance, Problem Pregnancy Help, Pregnancy Counseling, Help Inc., Guidelines, Personal Crisis Service, Alternatives Inc., Choose Life, Birth Choice Inc., Heartbeat, Pregnancy Aid, and Right to Life.

Perhaps it would be helpful if you could, from time to time when you write about this subject, publish some of this information.

Thank you for the suggestion and the information. I would add that the nearest Catholic newspaper, Catholic Social Service agency, and Catholic parish, as well as an increasing number of Protestant congregations and pastors, are also valuable sources for assistance in finding such centers. Look them up in the telephone book, or, if you wish, ask your parish priest how to contact them.

All these groups perform a continuing valuable service to numerous women with problem pregnancies, as you have also by sending your letter.

Priests and Abortion

I'm almost ashamed to ask this question. However, are there any priests who would approve of abortion?

I would like to know more exactly what you mean by an abortion. There are, and always have been, certain medical procedures which are sometimes called abortive (since they result in the death of the baby), but which are perfectly moral.

If you mean direct abortion of a human fetus, which the Catholic Church teaches is clearly and seriously immoral, there are priests who would question that, one way or another. I suppose it is their right to do so personally, as long as they are careful not to present themselves as Catholic priests teaching as official representatives of the church when they give their private opinion.

Unfortunately, this distinction is not always remembered or observed.

After Two Abortions

I must have an answer to this. It has been on my mind for so long, and rightly so. I was raised a Catholic and married a Catholic, though he wasn't practicing his faith. My problem is that I had two abortions, which I didn't want but finally had. I know it was very wrong, so I haven't been able to go to confession or Communion for 25 or 30 years. It's driving me crazy now. What should I do?

Abortion is a very serious offense against God and man, since it is the taking of a human life. I realize you know this, but I want to emphasize that what I say next is not meant to minimize that fact. The first step to forgiveness is an honest acknowledgment of our sin.

I hope you talk with a priest and receive the sacrament of penance soon. One of the strange things about sin is that it frequently seems to diminish in size when we're tempted, and then afterward it looms so huge that we fear even God can't forgive or heal the hurt that is done. In a way, that is an even bigger mistake than the sin itself.

God doesn't like the sin, and certainly doesn't encourage us to ignore his commands. But he does tell us often in Scripture that he considers the forgiveness of sins the greatest of all his works. In other words, he is quite proud of the fact that no sin, no evil, is beyond the reach of his goodness and his mercy. That is a joyous and basic fact of our Christian faith.

So, he is there, waiting for you simply to run to him and tell him you're back. Read prayerfully the story of the forgiving father (Luke, chapter 15), and then go to confession and receive the Eucharist. You've been away long enough.

Is Baby Unjust Aggressor?

In a recent group discussion on abortion, one member told us that some theologians have attempted to justify abortions on the basis that the child in the womb can be an "unjust aggressor." What does that mean?

It is a common and generally accepted moral principle that when someone is threatening my life (or someone else's) I have every right to take appropriate measures to defend myself. In this case the person who threatens my health or my life is referred to as an "unjust aggressor."

No theologian, at least no one of any standing, has, to my knowledge, seriously defended abortions on the basis of such a moral principle.

Even if the principle were accepted in this area of morality, it would apply only in those instances where the child in the womb constituted a direct threat to the life of the mother. In no way could it be used as a general justification for abortion.

Acceptable Abortion Laws?

I am much opposed to the Supreme Court decision legalizing abortion and am now planning to work with an organization called Right to Life.

However, recently a question came up about approving legislation that would allow an abortion to save the life of the mother. What is the church's position on this?

The position of the church is, as it has been, that deliberate killing of an unborn child is always wrong, even if it is intended to save the life of the mother.

However, a Catholic could quite properly approve and work for legislation along the lines you mention, because in practice (and perhaps even in theory) sinful abortions "to save the mother's life" are not generally likely to occur.

Let me explain what I mean. It is quite possible, for example, that a pregnant mother may be ill with a serious disease that the doctor must treat immediately. It is also possible that the doctor knows that if he does what is needed to heal the mother, she will lose the baby.

An obvious illustration is cancer of the uterus. If in the physician's prudent and good medical judgment that uterus must be taken out before the baby is viable, or the mother will die (or the cancer will likely spread critically), the uterus may be removed. Naturally, with such surgery the baby will die.

Some would incorrectly call this "an abortion to save the mother." It is, however, a perfectly moral procedure. Clearly, the baby is not killed, or aborted, in order to save the mother. It dies when the mother is treated as is medically necessary.

Other medical procedures may be less clear cut, but could fall into the same category.

As indicated before, in practice the problem hardly exists today. In the largest hospitals and clinics in the country which handle especially difficult cases, it has been years since doctors have faced a decision whether to save the mother or the child — if indeed they have ever done so in modern times. Medical management of pregnancy problems, to serve both the child and mother, has made enormous progress.

I would be quite happy, therefore, if abortion laws existed along the lines you indicate. The fact is they were in most states, until the liberalizing trend began.

Mother or Baby?

In my college ethics classes a thousand years ago, I understood that if there were a question of the mother or baby, the mother's life must be sacrificed. Others said that, since the baby is an unjust aggressor, the baby should be sacrificed. Who is right?

While my college and seminary days were somewhat less than a thousand years ago, I doubt that I'm much younger than you. The only thing I remember about that "mother or baby" position is that it is not, was not, and will not be taught by the Catholic Church as even remotely applicable to a medical dilemma during pregnancy — but there have been, and probably always will be, people who think that's what the church believes.

The history of medical science, biology, and moral theology on the subject is long and complicated, but to claim that a baby in the womb is an "unjust aggressor" in any moral sense of the word is out of the question.

Unfortunately, that term has been used sloppily on occasion in reference to other medical procedures possible during a pregnancy, and which might (or certainly will) result in the death of the unborn child. A classic, though somewhat unreal, example is a pregnant mother with a cancerous uterus which her doctor feels should be removed immediately. Such surgery would be morally permissible even though a non-viable fetus would surely die in the process.

I say it is a rather unreal example because this situation, as well as all those other "mother or child" problems, rarely if ever exist in modern medicine. Medical skills and routines provide a wide set of options today. After conversing with, or listening to, hundreds of physicians, including those in the largest obstetrics hospitals in the country, I have yet to find one who feels he has ever had to make a personal final choice to kill either the mother or the child.

There's an old axiom that remains true here: Good moral theology and good medicine go together, with emphasis on the word "good" in both cases. It is wrong, and unnecessary, to directly take the life of any innocent person, born or unborn.

Contemplating an Abortion

I have a friend who is seriously thinking of having an abortion. To me it's murder, but what can I say to prevent it? She says my church shouldn't dictate to her what she can or cannot do.

The whole abortion controversy has become ridden with almost belligerent emotionalism. In my experience, when a situation of real crisis arises in an individual's life, all rational argument is pretty futile. Deep convictions, faith, and the "feel" the individual has for other children and for life are what will determine her decision.

One observation may help. Participation in dozens of discussions, panels and ordinary bull sessions with people of all shades of opinion on the question has convinced me of one thing: Very few pregnant women, even those strongly pro-abortion, really believe they are not carrying a human baby. They know, regardless of the line they may give themselves, that what is in their womb isn't just a blob, a chunk of material that is as disposable as an appendix or gall bladder. Each knows it is a baby, already a boy or girl — her child.

Seen in this light, the words of one mother are, to put it mildly, impressive. "Apart from everything else, maybe I'm just too much of a coward to have an abortion," she said. "I know I'd have to live with it till I die.

"I don't mean just the abortion itself; maybe I could get over that. But what will happen later? Five years from now, when I see a little girl all dressed up downtown, or going to school, I will know she could be my daughter.

"Fifteen years from now, when I see a neighbor's boy growing into manhood, I would know mine could be just like that. And 30 years from now, when I see a young mother taking care of her home and children, I'd know she could be mine — if I hadn't ended it all before it got started.

"I know these thoughts would nag me for the rest of my life. And I'm afraid it would drive me crazy."

Maybe the mother who said this is unusually sensitive and perceptive. But we don't really know much about the satisfactions or regrets of women who have had an abortion, five or 25 years later, do we?

Encourage your friend, and pray for her. If she believes in God, urge her to pray before she makes her final decision.

Catholics For Abortion?

A panel discussing abortion several days ago included a member of one of the women's organizations who defended abortions. She said that the Catholic Church isn't united in its opposition to abor-

tion, and seemed to say that Catholics were free to make up their own minds about it. Is she right? Is there any support for liberal abortion laws in the Catholic Church?

It is obviously impossible to speak for every Catholic. I myself know some personally who vacillate greatly on the subject, especially when it hits their pocketbook.

There is, however, no basis whatsoever for saying that the Catholic Church is ambiguous or disunited on this subject. Or that it ever taught anything different on abortion than it does at present. Catholic people as a whole, including the experts in theology who do the exploration and teaching in subjects relating to moral life, as well as the teaching authorities in the church (bishops and popes) give no evidence of any division on the subject of right to life of an unborn child.

The United States bishops repeatedly insist on this tradition. In their statement of February, 1976, entitled "Political Responsibility: Reflections on an Election Year," they stress that "the right to life is a basic human right which should have the protection of law. Abortion is the deliberate destruction of an unborn human being and therefore violates this right."

They also, at the same time, repeated their support of a constitutional amendment to restore basic constitutional protection of the unborn child, a protection greatly undermined by the Supreme Court decision on abortion in 1973.

Natural Family Planning

I want to be a happy wife and mother, but my problem is I feel I have enough children to keep me worrying about their upbringing and making them good Catholics and providing for them. At my age, I'm afraid I couldn't cope with a new baby, and I worry about having babies later in life on account of retardation. I practice birth control, and feel guilt-ridden; but I wonder if the church recognizes this sort of problem. I can't see how an all-loving God could make a good mother and father burn in hell under mortal sin for doing what they feel is in the best interest of their family life. I'm confused, and have to know.

From your letter, it seems to me that you are asking help not so much directly about birth control as about how to come to a decision that will give you peace of conscience and peace with God. This sort of personal advice is impossible in a column such as this.

I urge you to talk the matter over with a competent priest (or someone else) whom you trust and with whom you feel comfortable. I hope you will do it soon.

If you haven't already, I urge you to look up the nearest Natural

Family Planning (NFP) information program in your area. Sometimes not very accurately referred to as the "new rhythm method," NFP is a far more advanced method of family planning increasingly used by people of many faiths and in several nations. It differs radically from the old calendar method of determining fertile and infertile times for sexual intercourse, utilizing several symptoms which occur in the ovulatory cycle as signals helpful to the husband and wife.

The method can be quite successful for the vast majority of normally intelligent and motivated couples.

Two excellent books on the subject are "Natural Family Planning," (general editor Anthony Zimmerman, published by DeRance Publishers, Milwaukee), and "The Art of Natural Family Planning," by John and Sheila Kippley, (published by Couple to Couple League, Inc., Box 11084, Cincinnati, Ohio, 45211).

Most larger communities have centers where instruction on NFP is available. Further information on NFP centers is available from the Couple to Couple League and from the Natural Family Planning Foundation, 205 S. Patrick St., Alexandria, Va., 22314.

No More Fast and Abstinence

Can you tell me why Catholics don't have laws about fast and abstinence and penance any more? Those laws (of fast and abstinence) always gave us something that other churches didn't have. I think we should still have obligations to do things like that, especially during Lent, so why did the church take them away?

Who says we Catholics don't have obligations to fast and abstinence and other penances anymore? If there is one thing every statement of the church insists on relating to this subject, it is that self-denial — including such things as occasionally limiting the amount or type of food we eat — is a serious obligation for all Christians, and that none of us can ignore that obligation without grave harm to our spiritual health.

What you mean is that the church is usually much less specific about the manner in which we carry out that obligation in our lives, which is a far different thing. In relaxing some detailed regulations about such matters, the Catholic Church, as well as other Christian churches, is simply responding to a very uncomfortable discovery during the past few decades: Far too many Christians so identified their Christianity with the meticulous fulfillment of minute church regulations that they lost contact with how these regulations are related to the basics of their faith in Christ — and thus, too frequently lost contact with Christ himself and what he stands for in our lives.

The church's concern is not simply that this *might* happen. Evidence that it has happened in many parts of the world, including our own, is overwhelming — and inspired much of what the bishops of the world did in Vatican Council II.

How can we claim to have no law of fast or abstinence or penance when Jesus himself tells us, "Whoever wishes to be my follower must deny his very self, take up his cross each day, and follow me." Or, "He who will not take up his cross and come after me is not worthy of me." One would be hard put to find a more clear, absolute statement of obligation in any church law, old or new. The New Testament abounds in such passages, either by, or in the name of, Christ himself.

The church may leave the details to us. But it points out these commands of Jesus and says to us: "Here is what the Lord says. Now you have to decide if he and his words mean anything to you. It's your commitment to him which is at stake. If he is your Lord as you say, his command is law. We will offer suggestions, even name a few special days for fasting. But you are adults, and you have all the information you need to be aware of how a Christian acts. The decision is yours."

Friday Abstinence

Is it a sin not to do other penance on Friday now that we have the privilege of eating meat on that day?

No. Eating meat on Friday is not a "privilege" any more than eating it on Tuesday is a privilege. The church had a law under which Catholics were to abstain from meat on that day. Now it does not.

From the earliest days of Christianity, Fridays have held a special character in the life of the followers of Christ as days of special effort at prayer and some sort of self-denial. Friday commemorated the day of Jesus' death. Christians considered it most appropriate, then, that a special effort be made on that day of the week to attend to his words: If anyone will be my Disciple, let him deny himself, take up his cross daily, and come follow me.

The obligation to heed that command falls upon all Christians — by accepting and carrying the crosses that are ours without looking for them in daily life as well as in some sort of occasional voluntary penance or self-denial.

There is no particular Catholic obligation, however, to observe this responsibility on any specific day of the week.

Mother Takes Pills

I would like to know if birth control pills are against the teaching of the church. My mother has been taking these for quite some time. I found this out when I stumbled onto them. If this is wrong, how

should I get her to stop? She is at Mass every Sunday.

Take it easy, now. You're jumping to a lot of conclusions. There are ways, of course, that "birth control pills" could be used wrongly. Perhaps you do not know, however, that there are certain women whose doctors prescribe such pills for perfectly legitimate reasons, many of which have absolutely nothing to do with birth control.

What are usually known as birth control pills are now more properly called by the broad generic name of progestational steroids. They are basically nothing but artificial hormones, hormones which some women need more of at certain times than their bodies produce naturally.

It's even quite common that these medications are needed on the same monthly regimen as they would be if they were being used directly for contraceptive purposes.

If it still bothers you, and you think it could help, why not ask your mother about it?

Passive Euthanasia

A newspaper referred to what was called "passive euthanasia." The article seemed to say that this kind of euthanasia is morally permissible. If it's mercy killing, it's still wrong, isn't it?

Passive euthanasia is a phrase used occasionally today in medical and moral literature to describe a situation in which a person is allowed to die rather than be provided with treatment or medication that would keep him alive. Thus, it is opposed to active euthanasia (euthanasia, or mercy killing, in the traditional sense) in which death is brought about by some positive, deliberate action of a physician or other person.

Using the word euthanasia in this double sense can be confusing. There is a huge difference morally between the two. For example, to administer a fatal drug to a suffering person (active euthanasia) may be called "merciful release" or any number of other pleasant sounding names. But it is plain intentional killing of another human being. It has almost always been recognized as seriously wrong by the human race in general, by moral theologians, and — until recently at least — by the medical profession almost without exception.

On the other hand, it is not always morally necessary to use every conceivable means to keep a sick person going a while longer. Treatment which would be extraordinary under the circumstances, because of immense cost, extreme pain, little hope for success, or other reasons, need not always be used.

A very old person might know, for example, that his life could be prolonged by several months only by a very expensive and exhausting operation. He would not be obliged to submit to that operation, nor would his doctor be obliged to perform it against the patient's desire.

Dozens of additional examples concerning other types of cases could be suggested.

Obviously, such a decision can be very complicated and difficult to make. What might be extraordinary, and therefore not required, for an aged grandmother, could be quite different for a younger father who still has a wife and family depending on him for support. All aspects of charity — to oneself, to others, and to God — must be carefully weighed in each instance to make the decision prudently.

Passive euthanasia, then, is not necessarily mercy killing in the immoral sense. Whether it is right or wrong depends on the circumstances.

What is Obscene?

My question has to do with morality I suppose — the meaning of "obscene." Obscene means something lewd or impure. But now I see it used to describe other things. A remark in our paper said that a recent speech by a high government official was obscene. How do you explain that?

The definition you give is the common one, but it is not the real, basic meaning of the word. The adjective comes down to us from ancient Greek (and perhaps Roman) drama. In many Greek plays, as you know, there were hideous crimes committed: eyes were put out, parents killed their children and vice versa, and the bloodiest monstrosities were perpetrated. However, these were always done *ab* or *ob scaenam* — literally, off the scene, or off the stage, because they were considered too loathsome, too cruel, too de-humanizing to be openly laid out before decent and civilized men.

Thus, whatever is repulsive, cruel, or otherwise excessively shameful in man's dealing with his fellow man, came to be labelled as obscene. Sexual immodesty is, therefore, just one — and perhaps one of the lesser — types of obscenity abounding in the world.

A good example from Scripture, incidentally, is Isaias' prophetic description of Jesus in his Passion. This future Servant of God, said Isaias, would suffer so violently that he would become as "one of those from whom men hide their faces." In that sense, what was done to Jesus, and the whole episode of his subjection to it, was truly "obscene."

Right to Die

Is there any recent church statement about the right to die with dignity — that there is no need to use extraordinary means to keep a

dying person alive, etc? I have a teacher who insists the Catholic Church demands that nothing be done in this way, in order to allow a person to die peacefully.

References of the kind you seek are numerous. One of the more recent appears in a letter written Oct. 12, 1970, in the name of Pope Paul VI by the Vatican Secretary of State to the International Federation of Catholic Medical Associations.

Pointing out that a doctor can never kill, the letter noted, however, that he does not have to use all the techniques of survival that modern science offers. "In many cases," it continues, "would it not be useless torture to impose vegetative resuscitation in the final stages of an incurable sickness? The doctor's duty here is rather to ease the suffering, instead of prolonging as long as possible, by any means and in any condition whatsoever, a life no longer fully human, and which is closing to its natural end...In this way, too, a doctor must respect life."

The position indicated here is not new; it dates a long way back in Catholic and other Christian moral teaching.

Born 30 Years Too Soon?

If now it is no longer a mortal sin to eat meat on Friday, what will happen to all those Catholics in hell who were sent there just because of committing this sin when it was still a sin?

Maybe we should all pray hard that God will grant them a general amnesty?

Seriously, and most importantly, we don't have any sure word from God that any particular person (or anyone at all for that matter) is in hell. Or if they are, we cannot know what specifically was the turning point in their lives at which they completely and knowingly separated themselves from friendship with God.

We do know that no one is eternally separated from God "just" for eating meat on Friday, even though it then involved a serious obligation. If mortal sin is what we say it is — a deliberate, final (unless repentance and reconciliation follow) rejection of the love and grace of God — it is obviously something that involves a whole change in the direction of one's life, of his deepest personal intentions and priorities.

Just as obviously then, it is not something accomplished in five minutes, even as a strong human friendship is not destroyed in five minutes, unless a lot of weakening, carelessness and selfishness has prepared the way.

The letter of St. James in the New Testament is pertinent. He says: "When passion has conceived, it brings forth sin; but when sin has matured, it begets death." Mortal sin, which is the death of God's life and love in the soul, is therefore the end of a long development — a maturing — of a sinful attitude.

Was a conscious, malicious rejection of the church's former regulation of Friday abstinence ever involved in such a "climax" of sinfulness? Your guess is as good as mine.

Bishops Oppose Capital Punishment

Our local newspaper says that in 1980 the U.S. bishops declared themselves against capital punishment.

I can understand that. What I can't understand is that the bishops compared capital punishment with abortion, and said that we should respect the life of criminals just as much as we should respect the life of unborn babies.

How could they do that? There's a lot of difference, it seems to me, between a man who is in prison for murder and a baby who isn't even born yet.

If your report of what was in your local paper is accurate, the truth got garbled somewhere.

It's true, the bishops did declare their opposition to capital punishment, not in theory, but because of the circumstances with which it is used in the United States. Their basis for this position is that capital punishment is disproportionately used in our country against the poor, racial minorities, and others on the lower levels of the social scale. They also question the claim that capital punishment is a deterrent to crime.

The bishops did not compare condemned criminals to innocent unborn human beings in taking their position, but rather to the principle that human life must be respected, and that this respect must apply also to the issue of capital punishment.

In taking this position, they referred to the taking of unborn human life. Opposition to capital punishment, they stated, "removes a certain ambiguity which might otherwise affect the witness that we wish to give to the sanctity of human life in all its stages. We do not wish to equate the situation of criminals convicted of capital offense with the condition of the innocent unborn, or of the defenseless aged or infirm, but we do believe that the defense of life is strengthened by eliminating exercise of a judicial authorization to take human life."

In other words, if courts are allowed to take human life in some instances, it too easily opens the door for an attitude that allows them to permit the taking of human lives in other circumstances as well.

Against Capital Punishment

Your column discussed the position of the U.S. Catholic bishops against capital punishment. I cannot understand the reasoning for this stand.

The bishops seem to think that if a person is poor, a member of a racial minority, or otherwise on the lower levels of the social scale, he has the right to commit any crime he wishes. I come from a poor family of six, and we were taught properly not to commit crime. Please tell me how you can give anyone the privilege of taking someone's life or raping someone, and then say they should not be punished.

The position of the bishops which I presented in that column in no way justifies criminal acts by anyone. Their point is that the laws applying the death penalty to certain crimes are not enforced in the same way for some groups of Americans as for others — as an examination of death sentences in nearly every state makes quite clear.

Every large community in the nation has its tale of heavy penalties given to the poor or otherwise underprivileged offenders, when richer offenders go free or receive token punishment for far more serious crimes. Bad enough when it results in prison terms or other sanctions, the situation becomes intolerable when it involves the penalty of death.

Apart from other serious concerns — for example, the real effectiveness of the death penalty as a deterrent from crime, or how much right the state has to inflict death on an offender — the bishops' argument was that since laws calling for capital punishment are applied with gross inequity, those laws should be taken off the books.

In taking this position, the bishops are simply asking for equal justice under the law for all citizens, a right guaranteed by the Bill of Rights. They do not condone any crime, regardless of who the offender may be.

What Is Sin?

Two priests have told me recently in confession that I am scrupulous. Both said I should ignore the times I thought I committed a sin, and go to Communion anyway. I don't understand how I can do that. I was always taught we have to go to confession before we receive Communion if we have a mortal sin. Can you tell me what to do?

Yes, I can. And I hope you will do it. Follow the directions the priests have given you!

Scrupulosity simply means that, for any of several reasons, an individual has lost his or her sense of good judgment about what is a sin. A scrupulous person tends to see sin where there is no sin, sometimes interpreting the most innocent action as seriously sinful because of "bad intentions" or wrong evaluation of the seriousness of the action.

A priest is — or should be — prepared to recognize signs of scrupulosity in confession, and to help the individual work through them. In some cases, where the problem has developed into a deeper neurosis, he may even suggest professional psychological assistance.

Your best course, in fact your only course, is to go to a priest in whom you have confidence and follow his directions completely, even about Communion. And don't float around looking for a priest who will "really understand" your situation. Chances are that one or both of the priests you mention do understand, and are doing the right thing to help you.

One final word: Don't be discouraged. This kind of difficulty always causes some anxiety and suffering. But there are encouraging signs in your letter that the problem is not yet too deep. If you pray and follow exactly the course I've outlined, you will either solve the difficulty or learn how to live with it peacefully. I hope you do.

Sin In Anger?

Is it a mortal sin to use God's name in vain in a fit of anger?

The traditional three requirements for a mortal sin are still good ones:

1. Serious matter — that is, the action must be one which is completely incompatible with a respect and love for God.

2. Sufficient reflection. One must realize when he is doing the action (or refuses to do it in a sin of omission) that if he does what he is contemplating, he is deliberately rejecting God's love and friendship. In other words, he must be fully aware that what he is contemplating is a mortal sin.

3. Full consent of the will. Realizing all this, he still deliberately wants to go ahead and do it anyway. Considering these requirements, it is difficult to see how the action, as you describe it, could ever be a mortal sin.

Answer to Scrupulous Lady

My husband has a heated reaction to your answer to the scrupulous lady who worried about what is a sin. Other priests had told her that she should go to Communion, no matter what sins she thought she committed. You said she should follow their advice.

We think you should have insisted that one does not go to Com-

munion with a mortal sin, and then approached the possibility that she may be scrupulous.

In the opinion of at least a few priests, the lady in question is a victim of some real scrupulosity. It also came through in her letter to me.

Such persons may be totally incapable of judging the seriousness of any sin, or even of judging whether there was a sin at all. It can be highly questionable whether an individual so distraught and emotionally entangled is psychically capable of serious sin. If you recall, two of the requirements for mortal sin are sufficient reflection and full consent of the will.

My response, therefore, described how a scrupulous person may react. The answer obviously does not apply to anyone not afflicted with this emotional problem.

Gossip

When does an injury to another person by true gossip become sinful? If the information is strictly true and has taken place, where is the injury or the sin?

In my experience as a priest, no crimes of speech (perhaps no crimes of any kind) are more destructive to our social relationships than the one you mention — and the feeling that simply because a thing is true about someone else, we are free to say whatever we like about it, whenever we like, and to whomever we like.

One who thinks and acts this way is grossly in error. When the topic of our loose gossip is true, we're dealing with the sin of detraction and contumely (insult), as distinct from the sins of calumny and slander, which involve lying about the faults of another.

One commits the sin of detraction when he makes known the faults of another without a very good reason for doing so. It can be a serious moral offense if it does great harm to that other person's reputation by having his or her faults spread about when they otherwise would not be.

The same sin of insult is committed when the other person is refused ordinary decency and respect whether face to face in private, or in public, such as in newspapers or on television.

Even when the other person's faults are public knowledge, it still can be sinful against charity to speak unnecessarily about those faults.

Occasionally there may be good reasons to tell another's faults, to a child's parents, for example. It is grossly wrong, though, to imagine that just because a story about another is true, one is at liberty to spread it around. A person's good name is among his most precious possessions, and the fact that one gets a kick out of being always there with the latest tidbit is no justification for tarnishing that good name. A person's faults are a matter between himself and God. The rest of us should keep our noses out.

Scripture has many strong, condemning words for gossips. In one of the psalms, God doesn't mince words: "The slanderer of his neighbor in secret — him will I destroy."

Already in his own time, St. Paul recognized the poisonous effect of this kind of conversation. He found himself forced to warn against it frequently. His advice to Titus is still valid: "Tell them not to speak evil of anyone." Which means in blunt language: "If you can't say something good about someone, keep quiet."

Sunday Rest

If one has fulfilled his Sunday obligation of hearing Mass, is it sinful to perform some work that day? I am a widow and working, and find it necessary to do some of my work on Sunday as I cannot accomplish it all otherwise.

Necessary work such as you speak of is certainly permissible on Sundays. Anyway, we should not consider "keeping holy the Lord's day" as only, or primarily, a matter of fulfilling laws.

Whatever obligations the church has asked us to observe on Sunday are meant as an aid to keeping the spirit of reverent reflection, worship and rest. Vatican Council II calls Sunday "the original feast day," and urges that its observance should always be proposed and taught "so that it may become in fact a day of joy and of freedom from work." (Constitution on the Liturgy, 106.)

Sacraments for Criminals

Can a murderer, rapist, or a robber, who is not Roman Catholic, be converted to Catholicism and receive all the sacraments after living a sinful life for 10 or 20 years?

No question about it: Of course he can. It is hard to believe that some Catholics or other Christians may be surprised at this, considering the times Jesus insisted that he came "not to call the just, but to call the sinner to repentance."

If one has to be perfect, or sinless, to become or remain a Catholic, we are all in deep trouble. In fact, if we are to have the spirit of Christ, our best efforts at charity, patience, and acceptance should be directed to those who have (at least as far as our human eyes can see) the most to overcome, and who have the most difficult struggle to become what God is calling us to in this pilgrimage on earth.

No one of us has any right to act otherwise than Christ himself, who was overjoyed and went out of his way to lend a healing word when a sinner showed he was ready to try to find his way back. I suggest you reread chapter 15 of St. Luke's Gospel.

Death Penalty A Favor?

I hold that the death penalty is good for murderers because it would save them from hell and eternal damnation. The only time a condemned man would examine his conscience is just before he passes on to his reward, and in nearly every case not before.

Once he admits that wrong was done by taking the life of another human being, and asks for forgiveness, his soul is not lost but is admitted into paradise. So the death penalty for criminals need not be viewed as cruel or unusual punishment, but as a favor. They will inherit eternal life.

Remarkable! You have just given a perfect reason for hanging at least half the human race. Many non-murderers commit crimes just as serious and just as destructive as murder. Why should they or even lesser sinners be deprived of this potent encouragement to repentance?

What makes you think people become so remorseful before execution? The disciples frequently urged Jesus to force reluctant Jews to accept him through physical coercion. But Our Lord adhered firmly to his conviction and policy that no worthwhile conversion is brought about by violence of any sort. There's no evidence that people are any different today.

Catholic Social Doctrine

I have seen many references to "Catholic Social Doctrine." I don't remember anything like this from when I learned the catechism, or in religion classes. What does it mean?

The phrase "Catholic Social Doctrine" signifies the large body of official Catholic teaching dealing with such "social" matters as economic life, rights and responsibilities of private property, political systems and their relationships to the individual citizen, labor unions, war and peace, and many others. These teachings have developed over many centuries, but have been made more specific during the past century, especially in formal teachings of the modern popes.

Pope John XXIII summarized the basics of this complex body of doctrine in one of his great social encyclicals, "Mater et Magistra." First, he says, all aspects of economic life in a nation must be regulated not for "the special interests of individuals or groups, nor (by) unregulated competition, economic despotism, national prestige or imperialism, nor any other aim of this sort. Rather, all forms of economic enterprise must be governed by the principles of social justice and charity."

Second, all social institutions (governments, welfare programs, international bodies such as the United Nations, etc.) must aim "to achieve in social justice a national and international juridical order, with its network of public and private institutions, in which all economic activity can be conducted not merely for private gain but also in the interest of the common good" of all people.

Can Catholics Join the Masons?

Your Question Box told us several times in recent years that under certain conditions it is possible for Catholics to belong to the Masons. However, in February, 1981, our local paper reported that the Vatican had reaffirmed its "200-year-old ban against Roman Catholics joining the Masons," and said that those who do so still suffer the penalty of excommunication.

Don't you think you should print a correction retracting what you said? Obviously, it is still wrong for Catholics to join this organization and you should say so clearly.

On the contrary. What I have said during the past few years about the possibility of Catholics belonging to the Masons is still valid.

Since I received questions similar to yours from many states, perhaps some explanation of exactly where the church is on this matter would be helpful. News articles reporting the Vatican action have been, at best, grossly misleading.

Part of the church's code of law states that anyone who joins a Masonic sect, or other society which plots against the church or against legitimate civil authority, incurs automatic excommunication from the Catholic Church. (Canon 2335)

However, this proscription is not nearly as absolute and universal as it may appear. The interpretation and application of penal laws (laws which in some way limit human freedom and apply sanctions) are nuanced and limited by many principles which form part of the church's tradition of jurisprudence.

One such principle is that any regulation or censure which would forbid actions otherwise open to Catholics must be interpreted in its narrowest sense. Such a regulation usually applies, for example, only where the reason for the law clearly exists in a particular situation. Thus, membership in a particular Masonic group is forbidden only when that organization does, in fact, oppose the church or government by open prejudice or persecution, undermining legitimate civil authority, and so on.

Anyone familiar with the history of Europe and America during the

past 200 years is aware that the character of Masonry changes drastically from one place or time to another. Political and anti-religious
activities so common to Masonry in Europe and Latin America, have,
with some notable exceptions, hardly been evident in most parts of the
United States. Strictly speaking, therefore, the prohibition against
membership in the Masons has never been as absolute as most people,
including most clergy, presume.

In 1974, the Congregation for the Doctrine of the Faith re-
emphasized this fact. Speaking explicity of membership in Masonic
societies and other societies of this kind, a letter from the congregation
to presidents of bishops' conferences said: "In considering particular
cases, it must be kept in mind that the penal law is subject to strict
interpretation. Accordingly, it is sound to teach and to apply the opinions of authors who hold that Canon 2335 refers only to Catholics who
enroll in associations which truly plot against the church."

The declaration reported in the news articles you mention points out
that the 1974 statement made no changes in church legislation. This
more recent statement of the same congregation, dated February 17,
1981, referred to the 1974 statement as follows:

"Insofar as the aforesaid letter refers to the interpretation given to
the canon in question, it must be understood as an appeal to the
general principles of the interpretation of penal laws for the solution of
cases for individual persons."

The letter observes that the congregation did not intend bishops of
different countries to make sweeping statements about membership in
the Masons, either for or against. Traditional norms interpreting the
law must be applied in each case.

What does all that mean in plain talk? Unless there is an explicit
statement to the contrary by his own bishop, a Catholic man who is
certain in his own mind that a particular Masonic organization is not
anti-Catholic, and that his membership would not support irreligious
or harmful political activities, has a right to join the Masons. The
wisdom of his joining is another question, but it would not be sinful,
nor would he be excommunicated.

Apart from the 32nd degree Southern Jurisdiction of the Scottish
Rite which often has been accused of actions and attitudes prejudicial
to Catholics and the Catholic Church, Masonic organizations in the
United States generally avoid the more sinister characteristics of international Masonry. In fact, individual American Catholic bishops have
publicly praised the attitudes and good works of Masonic groups in
several parts of the country. In 1976, for example, Cardinal Terence
Cooke of New York told the New York State Masons, "Here in
America our principal bulwark of freedom has been voluntary groups
like the Masons, dedicated...to order in the soul and order in society.
These free organizations are well-organized groups of people who

believe in a community of spirit, and who labor to reconcile the claim of duty and the claim of liberty under God."

Bishops who commented on the February, 1981, letter saw nothing in it that would require a more restrictive policy on Catholic membership in the Masons.

Because of past and present conflicts between the Masons and the Catholic people in many parts of the world, a more general ban ("in every case") against membership remains in effect for clergy and members of Religious communities.

Believing in Dreams

An article in a Catholic magazine recently talked about dreams and said that we should think about our dreams, "befriend" them, and that we would learn things this way. I thought that it was superstition to pay attention to dreams. Is it all right to do what this article suggested?

To think about our dreams, and even to learn something from them, is surely not sinful. We have ample proof even in the Bible that God has used dreams to help people understand his will for them.

Psychological sciences still cannot tell us very much for sure about where dreams come from, or precisely what makes them happen. It is now widely agreed that reflection on one's dreams, trying to enter into their imagery and moods and understand them, can often contribute much to a person's self-knowledge, his perception of his own emotions, and so on. One author who has written much on the subject of psychology and religion coined the term "befriend a dream" — which is probably where your article picked it up.

Some persons who are responsible for formation in Religious orders and communities have found that such "listening" to one's dreams, and even sharing them very simply and non-judgmentally with another, may be quite helpful to both persons.

Of course, dreams could be used wrongly, for example, if one pretended to tell fortunes from them, or if one allowed himself to become obsessed with a fantasy world. But it would be just as wrong not to accept dreams as a very natural, if puzzling, part of life, or to assume that there is automatically something magical, even diabolical, about them.

Destined to Sin

We visited in a parish around Christmas time where the bulletin had an article on St. Nicholas and the help he had given to some poor girls. The bulletin said these girls "seemed destined for prosti-

tution." Is there any person who is "destined" for something like that? Isn't it always a grave sin for any reason?

Being destined can mean several things. We might be destined to something because it is predetermined by God's providence, and will happen regardless of what else happens. Thus, for example, we are destined to die.

Being destined can also simply mean that we are headed in a particular direction, like a plane is destined for Los Angeles. It will arrive there unless something happens to change its course.

Many lives are somewhat the same. To all appearances, they seem destined for greatness or tragedy unless something happens to change their course.

Dressing for Church

If a church — St. Peter's in Rome, for instance — has become a public museum, do church authorities have a right to set standards of dress for those who come in?

St. Peter's, and other churches like it around the world, are *not* museums. They are houses of worship, especially sacred and dedicated to the service and praise of God. If we make the comparison, they are no more museums than the golden-domed Mosque of Omar in Jerusalem is a sightseer's playground; it is a mosque, a house of prayer. Ask any Moslem. Rules of propriety and decency are not only tolerated, they are expected and honored by thoughtful and civilized visitors.

Nevertheless, it might not be out of place to remind the proper authorities that some major church-shrines like St. Peter's in the Vatican are as much the domain of Americans and Japanese as of Italians. Wider representation on the rule-making committee might help toward understanding that many exemplary Catholics do not consider a lady's bare elbow a sign of moral degeneracy, even in church.

Rosicrucians

I see many advertisements for a religion called the Rosicrucians. They use the initials AMORC. But I can't find any information about them. Who are they, and are they really a religion?

The Ancient Mystical Order Rosae Crucis (AMORC) is a modern form of gnosticism. Coming from the Greek word "gnosis" (knowledge), this kind of philosophy has cropped up in many forms and in many places for about as long as man has been wondering about the world outside of himself. We even read in the New Testament of the problems the early church had with the Gnostics.

The style of gnosticism varies, but always the promise is that secrets of the universe will open up through some profound mystical experience. The initiates — those "in the know" — are believed to have a grasp on the meaning of man and his world that remains unknown to the rest of mankind.

The order of the Brotherhood of the Rosy Cross (Rosae Crucis) appeared perhaps 500 years ago, though many of the earliest documents are now known to be hoaxes written much later. As it now exists, the AMORC was organized about 100 years ago. Units (they call them "colleges") are organized in the United States and Europe. Rosicrucian General Statutes identify it as part of Freemasonry.

AMORC doctrine appears to be a strange mixture of Christian and non-Christian ideas. Many elements are incompatible with Christian faith. There is, for example, a strong pantheistic strain in such movements holding that all creation, man included, is somehow an extension of God. Such doctrines do not appear in so many words, but they are implied throughout the philosophy.

The church has not taken an official position on the Rosicrucians, just as it has not against numerous other quasi-religious groups. It seems impossible, however, to accept and believe the truths of the Catholic faith and at the same time the teachings of this Mystical Order.

Shower for Divorced Person?

Recently I was asked to help at a shower for a Catholic bride who was marrying a divorced man. The wedding was to take place in a Protestant church because it couldn't be performed in a Catholic church. I refused. Did I do wrong? Could a Catholic who knew all this attend the wedding in good faith?

A person's decision in a situation like this is never an easy one because it involves so many seemingly conflicting obligations of charity.

Of course you are not acting in true friendship if a friend is doing something you consider seriously wrong and harmful, and yet you pretend that you consider it blameless or a minor matter of personal difference. In the all too common circumstance you face, it is generally easier for a close friend or relative to be involved in such a wedding, and at the same time have the bride and groom perfectly aware that their involvement in no way implies agreement with the couple's attitude toward marriage and divorce, but is simply a gesture of friendship and affection. For a more distant acquaintance it may be more difficult to do this.

In my own experience, I have found that individuals are often confirmed in their easy attitude toward divorce and remarriage by the ready and unquestioning "approval" of their friends and relatives.

Some sad, complicated family tragedies have resulted.

Of course, there may be obligations in charity to others, too, such as your family, your children — and not least of all to yourself. You have your own convictions and you don't have to be ashamed of them. It's not hard to feel pressured in such situations today by the claim that everyone has the right to "do his own thing." Fine. But that goes both ways. You have just as much right to do your own thing, even if it means saying, "I don't agree with what you are doing." With a little thought, I'm sure you can make your point with tact and kindness.

I'm sure you are aware that there are circumstances in which a Catholic may quite legitimately be married in a Protestant church. That would seem ruled out by your question, however, if you are sure, as you say, that her marriage "couldn't be performed in a Catholic church."

Ku Klux Klan

A friend of mine from one of the southern states claims that some Catholics are members of the Ku Klux Klan. I thought this was an anti-Catholic group, and that Catholics were forbidden to belong to it.

The KKK did form a large part of the wave of anti-Catholic bigotry which lasted through several decades of the last century in our country. It was one of four or five major "native American" organizations which sprang up after the economic panic of 1819, and along with the large immigration of mainly Catholic Europeans.

In spite of its heavily anti-Catholic beginnings, however, the KKK's focus today is largely racial. Catholics have never been forbidden to join the organization, and undoubtedly some now do. To my knowledge, however, none have ever attempted to explain how Christian beliefs and principles can co-exist with the policies and activities of the KKK.

Healing on TV

What is the Catholic Church's view on the miracle services performed on television by many ministers? I know that whenever there is an alleged miracle, the Catholic Church expects much proof before the said miracle is claimed authentic.

But is this really necessary if there is simple faith that God can heal and will heal? Why cannot we just accept these healings as the real thing without all the proof?

The Catholic Church surely does believe that miracles of healing are not only possible, but are perhaps much more frequent than many of us suspect. The rite for the sacrament of the anointing of the sick, for example, clearly states the church's prayer and expectations for healings of various kinds as a result of the petitions made by the people of God.

The church is concerned in the matter, however, because true miracles (healing or otherwise) are not simply haphazard, frivolous intrusions by God into nature. As Jesus made clear, miracles are, above all, signs — signs of our Heavenly Father's presence and his approval and "authentication" of the person or truth in whose favor the miracle was performed, and signs of his lordship and supreme power over evil.

This is why he once told the people, "If you do not believe me, believe the works that I do." In other words, his miracles showed that Jesus was the messenger and Son of God he claimed to be.

As you must be aware, experience has taught us that many things can appear to be miracles when they are not. "Mysterious" cures can often have quite non-miraculous physical or psychological explanations. Certain religious con-men have sometimes staged outright fake "miracles" to establish their religious credentials.

Thus, the church intends no disrespect to God or man when it exercises — and suggests — caution in accepting at face value every apparent miracle that comes along. It has too much belief in God's power to allow supposed exercises of that power to be used as entertaining curiosities or religious gimmicks.

Defense Attorney's Duties

Several trials which have been widely publicized — some nationally and some in our area — have made me wonder about what a Catholic lawyer is allowed to do. Many times, from things that come out during a trial, it sure seems to me the lawyer must have known the person who hired him was guilty. Suppose a lawyer does know, is really sure, that a person committed the crime he is being tried for. Could the lawyer take the case and try to get his client off? Isn't it wrong for a lawyer to lie and say things he knows are not true, just because he is the defense attorney?

It is, of course, wrong for an attorney to lie, especially in circumstances such as this. But that doesn't really answer your question.

In our system of justice, a person is legally (even if not morally) innocent until proven guilty. An attorney may take up the legal defense of an individual he knows is morally guilty, and attempt to block a conviction.

To accomplish this, the defense attorney may use any legal means that are just. For instance, he may attempt to hide information that would be detrimental to the client, and he may attack or take advantage of weak points in the prosecution's case.

At least two actions, however, would obviously be wrong and professionally unethical. One would be an attempt by the lawyer himself to falsify information or documents, or lie about the case or anyone connected with it.

The second is where perhaps the greatest danger lies for an attorney who is trying to prove to a jury something he knows is not true. He has no moral or legal right to deliberately attempt to confuse or intimidate a witness into giving testimony that the witness really knows is not true. It goes without saying that the attorney acts immorally in bringing a witness who has the deliberate intention of perjuring himself.

Another consideration is the character of the defendant himself. An attorney would act immorally, for example, if he designedly brought about the freedom of a psychopathic individual who would clearly constitute a menace to people around him, without, in some significant way, attempting to alleviate that danger.

Origin of Species

Our study club is thinking of discussing the book "Origin of Species" by Charles Darwin. What do you think of this book? Someone said that we, as Catholics, should not read it.

Darwin's book is naturally of importance in the history of modern science. He was a brilliant observer and had a phenomenal capacity for putting his findings together in a creative way.

The sciences which deal with the development of life on earth have made enormous strides since "Origin of Species," however, and have corrected many of Darwin's theories. I believe certain other books in the field would be more enjoyable and helpful, unless you're interested in the historical approach.

Some people tried to use Darwin's findings in an anti-religious manner, but the book's approach is quite scientific. It's not the usual bedtime reading, though, so be prepared to work if you choose to read it.

Habit of Masturbation

Several years ago, because of the incapacitation of my wife, our sex life was over. We still have a warm and loving marriage of over 30 years, but during the last few years I have fallen into the habit of masturbation.

Because I was unable to control this, I no longer received the sacraments and then gradually stopped attending Mass. I despair of

ever breaking this habit. A few weeks of control are invariably followed by yet another act or two. Is there an answer for me?

I'm sure there is. The details will have to be worked out gradually, but a most important part of the answer is to return to the sacraments of penance and the Eucharist. Where there is good will, as there obviously is in your letter, the life and grace available to us in these ways is valuable and powerful.

I suggest you try to find a priest, a confessor, who is willing to take the time and give the attention to assist you. Several explanations are possible for your development of this habit.

Considering your faith and your desire to live a good life, there is serious question about how deliberate, and therefore how sinful, such actions may be on your part. A kind and willing priest will help you sort this out. Be calm and peaceful about it and trust that God knows where your heart is. I'm sure that with prayer, the Mass and the sacraments, you will find a way to deal with this that will give you peace of mind.

Sinful to Attend Anniversary Party?

A friend of mine, a divorced Catholic, will be celebrating the 25th anniversary of her second marriage soon. Would it be a sin if I attended the celebration?

Such decisions can cause us concern, but it isn't a question of sin or not. You obviously are giving it serious thought and want to do the right thing.

The question is rather, "What is the better thing to do?" After 25 years, the likelihood that she will interpret your presence as your personal approval of her whole past life is small indeed. It would be considered a gesture of friendliness and love for the couple.

Unless you feel other circumstances involved should strongly influence you, make your decision on the basis of your friendship and support for her.

Trans-Sexual Surgery

We hear so much these days about trans-sexual operations. Is this a moral procedure — to change a man into a woman, or a woman into a man?

Your question allows of no easy or simple answer. But a couple of things will be significant factors in any such operation.

First, let's suppose we are dealing with a reasonably normal person whose male or female identity is well established — emotionally, psychically and physically, both internally and in relationship to others.

For such an individual to attempt a sex change, even to whatever slight degree that might be possible, would be a gross abuse of his or her person, and morally wrong.

Few if any such cases are that clear cut, however. It is possible for an individual to possess a clear genetic sexual identity (male or female chromosomes) as well as major physical male or female sex characteristics, and still suffer from a quite confused sexual identity. The complicated system of internal secretions (hormones) which interact from one organ or gland to another, is subject to all sorts of imbalance; if this imbalance is extensive enough, it may cause serious difficulties in an individual's ability to function in his or her "proper" sexual relationships.

In light of this, many other factors enter. Certain remarkable surgical procedures are, or soon may be, available to deal with these kinds of pathologies in men or women. For one thing, however, there's room for question in some cases how much "sex change" is really involved. More importantly, procedures are increasingly available to deal with such physical ills by therapy far less drastic and questionable than surgery.

One gets the impression that most of these radical "treatments" have been carried out, up to now, with almost no serious consideration of the moral implications for either the individual or society. And that in itself must be deplored. But it is too soon, and too many variables are involved, to conclude at this point that every operation labelled a "sex change" is always automatically wrong.

Widow Worries About the Past

I have been a widow for many years and something from my past haunts me. I married a man who told me he had a vasectomy. I married him knowing this and received the sacraments every Sunday without confessing that I was guilty of practicing birth control.

I have confessed this sin since I became a widow. The priest made no comment, gave me absolution and that was all.

What else am I to do? Every time I go to Communion I feel I am committing a sacrilege.

It might have been helpful to you if the priest had explained a little bit. But probably the main reason he did not comment was that there really was nothing to comment about.

Often in the sacrament of penance, particularly when dealing with something that is past, it is futile (and probably impossible) to sort out how much guilt there may have been over something done that was wrong. This certainly is true in your case, as the priest probably realized. He knew that to go into the past and try to unravel degrees and qualities of guilt would really serve no purpose.

The only important thing was that you were confessing that, insofar as you were guilty of any sin before God, you were sorry for it. God certainly accepts that, and the priest did too. Whatever sin there may have been is now forgiven because of your sorrow, and through the sacrament of penance. It is all past and you are certainly forgiven.

I realize it is easier to say this than to accept it in our hearts. When we feel we have done wrong over a period of time, it is difficult to believe that we can lay it all out before God and know that his love and mercy are larger and stronger than any of our weaknesses.

But that is precisely the message that Jesus gives us and which he carries out through his church in the sacrament of penance.

You are perfectly correct in receiving Holy Communion as often as you can. You might make an additional intention in this sacrament and in your prayers asking God for the grace of full acceptance of his forgiving love for whatever wrong intentions or actions there may have been in your past life.

Alcoholic Beverages

By what authority does the Catholic Church approve drinking when the Holy Scriptures are so clear regarding the Lord's attitude toward it? Has no one ever questioned this before? With all the heartache, sin, and irresponsibility that drinking causes, how can one honestly believe that it is approved by the Lord?

Certainly it has been thought of before. A number of Protestant sects, as you must know, consider any drinking of alcoholic beverages a sin.

It is impossible, however, to use the Bible in any way as a basis for this belief. There is no denying that the misuse of alcohol causes enormous suffering and is wrong. Indeed, the Scriptures say as much several times. But Scripture also has numerous good things to say about wine, and encourages its proper use for everything from celebrations to bodily health.

There is no scholarly basis whatsoever for saying that the word most often used in the Bible for wine (in both Greek and Hebrew) means anything else than fermented, alcoholic "fruit of the vine." That includes the wine miraculously presented by Jesus to the bride and groom at Cana, as well as the wine St. Paul tells Timothy to take occasionally for the good of his stomach. (I Tim. 5,23).

"I'll Go When Time Is Up"

I irk my relatives and friends because I won't seek medical help. They claim it's due to stubbornness. My argument is that I'll go

next week if my time is up, whether I seek help or not. Am I right or wrong?

Sorry, but you don't give anywhere near enough information for any answer to be very helpful. How serious is your illness? How much help will the medical service be? How old are you, and what responsibilities to others have you in your present life situation? A father at age 45, for example, with six growing children, obviously has a far more serious obligation to seek medical help than an old man of 80 whose children are all adults.

However right or wrong your conclusion may be, though, I can't say much for your argument. By the same logic, you could drive your car recklessly, or stop eating, arguing that when your "time is up" you'll die anyway. Our responsibility is to take reasonable care of our health, and protect it as well as we can, whether the dangers to it come from inside or outside.

Marriage and Family

Origin of Marriage Vows

Would you know where the words of the marriage vows originated: "I take thee...till death do us part." Did they come from Christ or officials of the church?

The language of the marriage vows did not come from Christ. In fact, the words or actions by which marriage consent is expressed by the bride and groom have varied greatly from one time to another, and even today from country to country and from one Catholic rite to another.

The only essential in our Christian context is that the couple declare to each other in some external way their intent to join now in a permanent marriage union with faithfulness to their spouse. This declaration may be in words, or, as in some rites, almost entirely in symbolic actions — such as drinking from the same cup, conferring of the wedding rings, etc. The significance of these actions is as clearly understood by all the participants as words would be.

Are Marriage Laws Same For All?

What is the church's present stand on mixed marriages? There are two cases, seemingly similar, but handled by our church in a contradictory way. One was a single Catholic woman who wanted to marry a divorced man. His divorce was 15 years ago after a brief marriage with no children. She could not have a church wedding, but the marriage took place anyway. She lost her job with the local Catholic school.

The other case is the same. The woman is Catholic, and the man was married before. But this marriage was of long standing and he had grown children. This marriage was approved and the "big event" took place in church. They were much more prominent parishioners, incidentally.

How do you explain this paradox? Could you enlighten us as to where we could look to find current church law about such things?

You say the two cases are the same, but you don't mention many facts which would affect any judgment. Were either of the partners in the first marriages baptized Catholic? Were the spouses in either of the first marriages married before? Was there an impediment in either of the first marriages that would make that marriage invalid and therefore able to be annulled? If neither, or only one of the partners in the first marriages were baptized Christians, was the Pauline Privilege or Petrine Privilege possible in the second case but not in the first? Different answers to any of these questions could explain the difference in the result.

One thing is certain from your letter. The two cases are by no means the same, in spite of the similarity of the few superficial facts which are probably common knowledge.

Laws and policies by which the church attempts to respect marriage, and those who have committed themselves to that state of life, are many and complicated. Their application and interrelationships cannot be simply explained, anymore than an important area of civil law can be capsulized in a small pamphlet.

Two sources which might fill in some of the major gaps in understanding, however, are the following: "Are Catholic Marriage Laws Changing?" — a publication of Catholic Update by St. Anthony Messenger Press, 1615 Reynolds St., Cincinnati, Ohio, 45210, and the booklet, "Mixed Marriage: New Direction" published by the United States Catholic Conference, USCC Publications, 1312 Massachusetts Ave., N.W, Washington, D. C., 20005. Try one or both of these and see if they help.

Summary of Marriage Rules

I know you receive and answer a lot of questions concerning marriage. Some people divorce and remarry in the church, some cannot, and some have marriages annulled. Frankly, it's darned confusing to me, maybe because I've really never seen a list of all the rules in one place. Is it possible for you to tell us what these rules or laws are? I think it would help me and probably many others to understand some of the situations in our families.

Yours is probably one of the most sensible questions I've ever received, and one of the most difficult to answer. The marriage legislation of the church is long and involved, reflecting at once its concern for the sacredness of marriage and its concern for the people in painful or impossible marriage situations.

From my experience, however, the following summary of the

church's present marriage laws should go far in answering questions about specific cases, as they would apply normally to our country:

1. Any person who is baptized a Catholic must be married before a priest in order to be truly (i.e. validly) married. The only exception is when the bishop himself gives a dispensation for a Catholic to marry elsewhere, such as a Protestant church, before a civil judge, etc. Without such a dispensation, any marriage involving a baptized Catholic that does not take place before a priest is not valid in the eyes of the church.

2. If neither marriage partner is Catholic and both are free to marry (for example, if neither one has a previous marriage), the Catholic Church recognizes the union as a true, valid marriage. Thus, contrary to what some people still believe, the church definitely considers the marriage between two Hindus, for example, or two Baptists or Lutherans, as real marriages.

3. Furthermore, if both non-Catholic partners in a marriage are validly baptized Christians, the Catholic Church views that marriage as a Christian sacrament. They receive the sacrament of marriage, and have what we call a sacramental marriage.

Because they are Christians, their marriage carries with it that special reflection of the covenant of love that Jesus has for his people, his church. As the Second Vatican Council put it so beautifully, "Christian partners are strengthened, and as it were, consecrated, by a special sacrament for the duties and dignity of their state...The spirit of Christ pervades their whole lives with faith, hope and love."

This unique character of all Christian marriages has special significance in our marriage laws, as the next point makes clear.

4. While the church does claim authority to dissolve certain marriages "in favor of the faith," it considers any sacramental marriage, in the sense explained above, entirely beyond its reach or power to dissolve.

Thus, if it is certain that two people in a valid marriage were truly baptized in any Christian church, there is no possibility of the church's dissolving that marriage to allow either of the individuals to marry again. (Remember that "dissolving" a marriage is different from an annulment, which is a declaration that there was never a valid marriage at all.) This rules out such procedures as the Pauline Privilege or Privilege of the Faith which might be used in other circumstances, and which we'll talk about next.

Remember that in any case involving someone who has been married before and who now wishes to marry someone else in the Catholic Church, all pertinent facts (such as baptism, previous marriages and divorces, etc.) must be substantiated by appropriate documents and, if necessary, by testimony of people in a position to know. This is one way the church attempts to assure that the persons involved do not get into a new situation that will hurt them again, perhaps even worse than before.

The church does, as I said, claim authority to dissolve certain marriages so that the partners may be married again. This is what happens in most situations where a person who is Catholic marries for a second time.

If one of the partners in a valid marriage is not baptized (wherever that marriage took place), such a marriage may be dissolved by the church so that a later marriage may be true and valid. This procedure is based on a passage in St. Paul (1 Corinthians 7, 12-15) in which Paul discusses marriages and remarriages of new converts to Christianity.

For at least 1,500 years, the church has interpreted this teaching as giving it the right to dissolve marriages of unbaptized people "in favor of the faith" — that is, for the good of their faith.

Such procedures may be of two kinds:

1. Pauline Privilege, named after St. Paul. This method is used to dissolve the valid marriage of two non-baptized persons if one of the partners wishes to become a Catholic and marry a Catholic. These cases are usually decided by the marriage tribunals of the local diocese.

2. Privilege of the Faith. Through this approach, the church dissolves a valid marriage of a baptized person (whether that individual is Catholic or Protestant) with a partner who is not baptized. Here, one spouse is baptized at the time of the marriage; in the Pauline Privilege procedure, both are unbaptized.

Normally, Privilege of the Faith cases are decided by officials in Rome.

Finally, one more word about annulment, which is a formal declaration that what seemed to be a valid marriage was never really a marriage at all. Note carefully that this is different from dissolving a marriage that is truly already in existence.

In most annulment procedures it makes no difference whether the people involved are Catholic or Protestant, baptized or not. What must be proven is that some condition was present in the marriage that made real marriage promises impossible.

One example of such a condition would be if one or both spouses intended never to have any children in their married life. Another example would be an emotional or psychological instability so serious in one of the partners that he or she simply was incapable of genuine, full commitment to the kind of life together that marriage involves.

Annulments are discussed more fully under other questions.

A Sacrament Without Believing?

I am greatly disturbed by an answer you gave about marriage. You said that non-Catholics are considered to have a sacramental mar-

riage if they are validly baptized Christians. Is this true if they do not believe the marriage is a sacrament? And suppose the ceremony is witnessed by a clergyman who also does not believe it is a sacrament? You seem to answer in the affirmative.

If this is your belief, it would seem to make the sacraments simply magic. I suggest you reconsider your answer to a very serious question.

The answer I gave is correct according to present Catholic belief and practice. The questions you raise are, however, truly serious and are, in fact, being studied intently by theologians and canon lawyers.

The position of the church concerning sacramental marriages is loaded with some critical problems. According to our theology, marriage is the only sacrament that individuals can receive not only without knowing it, but even without believing in it — in fact even deliberately rejecting a belief in the sacramentality of their marriage. Your question pinpoints the precise situation in which such an anomaly might occur.

At least part of the solution seems to lie in a clarification of the meaning of the word sacrament. That there is a significant and profound difference between a marriage of non-Christians and the marriage convenant and life of two Christians who meet and live with each other as committed members of the family of Christ, would not be denied, I believe, by anyone. As St. Paul said in the Letter to the Ephesians, the marriage of a man and woman who are already brother and sister in the family of Christ is itself a sign — a sacrament — of the love that flows between Christ and his church.

So the church is attempting to polish its understanding of Christian marriage.

The problem, incidentally, arises not only in the type of situation you describe. A similar question must be asked of a marriage which involves an individual who calls himself a Catholic, but whose beliefs and practice of the faith are nearly non-existent. How realistic or honest is it to call such a marriage a sacrament — that is, a proclamation and commitment to live out their faith as members of the body of Christ?

Your question is an excellent one. Frankly, I'm surprised more people don't ask it.

Divorced Not Excommunicated

A columnist in our local daily paper recently discussed the remarriage of divorced Catholics and whether they could go to Communion. Several times she quoted a priest, whom she named and identified as a "widely known Catholic authority on separation and divorce."

After explaining that such people were no longer excommunicated from the church, the priest said that Communion is "not a gold star, not a badge for having it all together...We say that the meal (Communion) is not supper for those who have it all together, but for those to whom the Lord is reaching out in their struggles. This is not a relaxation of formal rules, but a greater degree of understanding of the Eucharist, that it is a meal of healing, of reconciliation for people trying to do their best under the circumstances."

What is your opinion of his attitude?

Again, divorced and remarried Catholics are no longer excommunicated. That change says nothing about the validity of their new marriage. It simply says that they are still members of the Catholic Church, except that they have done something seriously wrong in violation of its laws and, perhaps in most cases, divine law.

Generally, I must agree with the priest you quote. If one is a Catholic (which a remarried Catholic still is), the only other requirement for receiving the Eucharist is that he or she is not deliberately in the state of mortal sin.

Note that this does not say they have not committed a serious sin. Perhaps they have, if all necessary conditions were present. But being in the state of sin means that one deliberately continues in a sinful situation from which he is morally able to remove himself. This means that the individual is physically and emotionally and spiritually able to remove himself from that situation, and able to do it without causing even more serious harm.

To use an obvious example, a remarried man, for instance, may have extremely serious responsibilities of every kind to his present family. Even though all this may have come about because of a sinful action, those responsibilities are there now. If he simply cannot leave his home without serious physical, mental and even spiritual harm to his present wife and children, I know of almost no one who would claim he must break up that family in order to get himself straight with God.

The illustration points out that such situations are possible, and that no one is in the position to judge another.

Your priest's final phrase, "trying to do the best under the circumstances," must be understood seriously and correctly. Like the expression, "follow your conscience," it can mean many things. But understood rightly in the light of the teachings of the church, it summarizes one's responsibilities before God quite well.

Required Marriage Instructions

In connection with the approaching marriage of a relative, I was told that there would be no instructions for the couple by the priest.

With so many marriages ending unhappily or in a divorce, I find this hard to believe. Aren't priests required to give some sort of instructions or help to people before they are married?

Two Catholic Church laws apply here. One, Canon 1018, prescribes that the parish priest must instruct his people concerning the meaning of Christian marriage and marriage impediments. This refers to the continuing education of people in the parish through Sunday homilies, courses concerning marriage for grade and high school students, adult education programs, and so on.

The other law, Canon 1033, deals with instruction of the individual couple before their own marriage. This places responsibility on the parish priest to instruct them more in detail about the meaning of marriage, the mutual obligations of husband and wife and the duties of parents towards their children, and to encourage them to make appropriate spiritual preparations for their marriage.

The parish priest is not required, of course, to provide all this instruction personally. The range of subjects on which the couple should have some assistance is vast, including topics like finances, interpersonal communications, in-laws, sexual and other physical expressions of their love, attitudes toward children and their care and proper upbringing, recreational activities, and numerous other elements of life together that will be significant during the first months and years of their married life.

Few, if any, priests have the time, experience or insight to handle all these subjects adequately without assistance. Thus, most parish priests today rely heavily, for example, on Pre-Cana conferences (presented by doctors, clergy and married couples), Engaged Encounters, or similar extensive programs which assist them in fulfilling this responsibility. Engaged couples are frequently required by their parish, or by their diocese, to participate in such programs before marriage.

No particular number of "instructions" are demanded by the general law of the church.

Pre-Marriage Requirements

Different rules for different churches in the same city have always troubled me. But recently this affected me personally.

Our daughter was to be married late last year. We tried to have a Catholic wedding, but there was no way because no one would allow it without the required pre-marriage conferences.

My daughter and I were in a local florist shop before the wedding, and a lady friend of mine told me that her son's wedding was arranged with only three week's notice. She said they were allowing

her son and daughter-in-law to take the pre-marriage course at a later date after the wedding. None of the priests in our parish suggested this. Please explain how this was allowed to happen.

The purpose of the pre-marriage conferences which are required in most dioceses of the United States today is to help a couple evaluate their strengths and weaknesses, and to assist them in the final decision concerning their marriage. It makes little sense to do this sort of reflection after marriage, even though the ideas may be helpful to a couple any time.

The priest in your parish followed the regulations for your diocese, and from what you reveal in your letter concerning your daughter's faith and maturity, my first reaction is that he acted quite correctly.

It is possible that under certain circumstances, in the judgment of the priest involved, some preliminaries required in an area or diocese may be dispensed with. Perhaps the priest in the other parish followed proper procedures in doing what he did also.

Your letter emphasizes the urgency of following diocesan guidelines in these matters to prevent confusion to everyone involved. If you want a fuller explanation of why the priest in your parish made the decision he did, and another priest made a different decision, ask them. They will explain the reasons to you.

Annulment No Privilege

I am not the only Catholic who has been almost destroyed by the decision of the Roman Catholic Church to annul the marriage between a famous public figure and his wife, who bore him three children. How can the church do this when it hurts so many people?

A declaration of annulment is not a "privilege" the Catholic Church chooses to give to one person rather than another. It is a declaration, after long and serious study by psychologists and others who are competent to make such judgments, that no marriage ever existed between the two people involved.

Most of the time today this judgment is based on evidence that one or both of the partners in the marriage were, because of serious psychological or emotional deficiencies, completely incapable of real honest marriage consent. This may be true even if several children were born of the marriage during the intervening years.

If the evidence brought forward through painstaking investigation reveals that the husband or wife (or both) were suffering from some emotional or psychological instability so severe that the genuine consent to the common life together that we call marriage was impossible, then the church has no alternative but to declare that marriage invalid.

I sympathize completely with the frustration and pain you feel over these kinds of decisions. That pain and anxiety are understandable in light of the sacredness in which we hold the sacrament of marriage.

However, I hope you can understand that it is respect for that very sacredness which prompts the church to require that people honestly know what they are doing before such a union can be a genuine Christian marriage.

In the case you mention, and in all other declarations of annulment, the church, after long investigation of all the people involved, comes to the conclusion that there simply was never a marriage.

The hurt in such decisions can be very great. But the answer is to work toward making sure in the future that couples entering into marriage have enough preparation and knowledge to know thoroughly what they are doing so that annulment, or what is called "lack of due discretion," will be less possible in the future.

Futhermore a declaration of nullity makes no moral judgment one way or the other about either of the partners. It simply declares, not that the couple will not, but rather that they could not, commit themselves to, and live in, a true marriage relationship with each other.

Defect of Form

A problem has recently surfaced within our family which has us all puzzled. Our daughter was married by a justice of the peace early last year. The marriage was a tragedy for many reasons, and they are now separated. She is filing for divorce.

Our parish priest tells us we must provide copies of baptism, confirmation, and other certificates, and after a hearing she will be granted an annulment.

How can this be? If the Catholic Church does not recognize her marriage and she cannot receive the sacraments in this unrecognized marriage, how can it issue an annulment? We'll appreciate any light you can shed on this.

Your questions reveal a good bit of confusion about annulments. An annulment is simply a declaration (by the church or civil authorities) that no marriage ever existed. Numerous reasons might exist for such a declaration, ranging from purely legal impediments through such conditions as a serious lack of proper intention for marriage, or psychological inability to commit oneself to marriage.

In your daughter's case the annulment would be granted because of what is technically called "defect of form." This means that a Catholic was not married before a priest and therefore, according to church law, the marriage is invalid. It is the simplest kind of annulment case since one needs to prove only that he or she was baptized a Catholic and that the marriage ceremony never took place before a priest. The documents you are to obtain are mainly to substantiate those facts.

It is possible for a Catholic to be validly married before a minister, or justice of the peace, if a dispensation for such a marriage has been received from the bishop of the diocese. You give no indication, however, that your daughter obtained such a dispensation.

Judging from your letter, there is no reason whatsoever that your daughter is not now perfectly free to receive the sacraments of penance and the Eucharist.

Annulment Delayed

In December, 1978, my boyfriend spoke with the pastor of our Catholic church regarding an annulment of his first marriage. In April, 1979, he filled out a questionnaire explaining the reasons why the marriage should be annulled, and also listed witnesses. This petition was filled out and returned.

None of the witnesses have been contacted after seven months of waiting. I hoped perhaps you could tell us what is causing the delay.

I don't know what might have caused the delay between December and April, but the procedures in such a case do not even begin until the petition is formally presented and a list of witnesses has been provided for supporting testimony.

If you returned the petition form immediately and the parish priest sent it out shortly afterwards, it would not be unusual that some witnesses would not have been contacted at the time of your writing (July). How quickly all this can be done depends on several factors: the volume of cases active in your diocesan tribunal, the location of the witnesses, and the ease with which a parish priest near the witnesses is able to make an appointment with them to complete the necessary forms.

I, personally, am never disturbed when someone with a pending marriage case asks me how it is progressing, and whether there is anything else they might do to assist the procedure.

Perhaps an inquiry to your own parish priest would help you to understand how your case is moving. Remember, however, that the final decision on such a case takes a long time, normally considerably more than four or five months.

Getting Back into The Church

My husband and I were both divorced before our marriage 23 years ago. Now, in our late 60s, we would like to receive the sacraments without a lot of red tape of bringing in previous wedding and divorce papers.

We are practicing Catholics and attend church regularly, with the exception of receiving the sacraments of Communion and penance. Can you help us get completely back into the church?

As much as it would please me to do so, it is normally impossible for me or any other priest to personally pursue marriage cases at a distance. I am happy to be able to supply any information that could be helpful, but church law requires that such marriage procedures be pursued through the parish or diocese of the individual involved.

Please contact your parish priest or another priest in your area with whom you might be better acquainted. He will help you learn if something can be done in your case and assist you in doing it with as little hassle as possible.

Remarriage After Divorce

Is it true that a divorced Catholic couple can remarry (to different partners) in a Catholic church if they are married in a Catholic church the first time? A co-worker has told me that someone in her family remarried that way. I have members in my family who are divorced and would like to remarry in the church. How can some people be allowed and others denied?

If a Catholic couple are married in a Catholic church, there is only one way either of them could marry another partner later on in the church. It would require a declaration of nullity (annulment) for the first marriage, a declaration which must be determined by the marriage tribunal of the diocese where the people live.

To determine whether such a procedure is at all feasible in a particular case, the individual must talk to a priest, explain the situation thoroughly, and he will assist in taking whatever steps are possible.

Children Legitimate?

If a man and woman have been legally married for a number of years and an annulment is obtained, for whatever reason, are the children born to this couple considered illegitimate?

If the man and woman in question were free to marry in the first place, any children born during their legal union would be considered legitimate by the church, even if the marriage was annulled sometime later.

Such a union is called a "putative" marriage; that is, everyone thought it was a marriage and there was no overt reason to think otherwise. The fact that some condition was present throughout the marriage that enabled it to be annulled some years afterward does not change the fact that this couple was thought to be married by everyone, probably including even themselves.

Their children would be considered legitimate for all purposes of church law and, to my knowledge, also of civil law.

It is quite possible, of course, that children could be injured emotionally more or less seriously by the awareness that their parents, at this late date, feel they were never married at all and that such a declaration has now been made by the church or civil law. Legally, however, no stigma whatsoever devolves on the children because of annulment.

Do Children Prevent Annulment?

Where and how do I get information on starting an annulment? A priest told me I have no chance because I have two children. Is this true?

Annulment proceedings should begin with a priest in your area, preferably in your parish, although another priest friend or acquaintance could begin the process.

The priest will then submit your story to the diocesan tribunal, which will decide whether there is enough basis for a possible annulment to begin the many steps involved in this procedure. Only after these investigations are completed and evaluated can a final decision be given.

Two children, or 10, are not necessarily an obstacle to obtaining a declaration of nullity. Many circumstances which might be bases for annulment have nothing to do with whether the couple have children or not. If, for example, one of the spouses proves to have an emotional deficiency so serious that a true married life was, and is, psychologically impossible for him or her, the marriage tribunal would be required to declare that no marriage ever existed (in other words, issue a decree of annulment), even though the couple went through the marriage ceremony, lived together for several years, and had several children in the meantime.

Annulments Explained

In reponse to a question about annulments, you said:
"If one spouse proves to have an emotional deficiency so serious that a true married life was and is psychologically impossible for him or her, the marriage tribunal would be required to declare that no marriage ever existed, even though the couple went through the marriage ceremony, lived together for several years, and had several children in the meantime."

Why don't all the so-called Catholic periodicals get together and submit a proposal to Rome that the phrase, "I take you for richer or poorer, for better or worse, in sickness and in health," be eliminated from the marriage vows?

You are only one of probably many thousands of Catholics who are terribly confused about the meaning of an annulment of a marriage.

It is precisely because the church considers those marriage vows so serious and so essential that it requires couples who enter marriage not only to be sincere, but to have at least a minimum ability to know what the words mean and be able to live by them.

A 12, or 14-year-old girl or boy may love someone very much and be quite sincere in wanting to get married. The church says, however, as do most states and countries, that no matter how sincere such a child may be, he or she lacks the experience of life and the emotional and psychological maturity to realize the implications of those words. He therefore lacks ability to commit himself to a genuine community of life that we call marriage, even though he may say the words clearly and beautifully.

Surely you are aware that this kind of immaturity and lack of capacity for commitment are quite possible in someone considerably older than 12 or 14. These defects, however, are not always easily discernible; they may, in fact, only be evident some time after the couple begins to live together as husband and wife.

It will help, perhaps, if we recall that Religious orders of men and women are allowed to call a candidate to final perpetual vows not only when that candidate has reached a sufficient age, but also only after some years of thought, study and prayer — and after a good while of living the reponsibilities that kind of life will require.

Yet we regularly accept young couples for marriage when they have known each other but a few months, and almost nothing is known about whether or not either of them really understands or knows what marriage is all about, or can live up to the responsibilities that marriage entails.

I'm certainly not suggesting trial marriages; in my opinion there is no such thing. Nearly every diocese in the country, in fact, provides an increasing variety of helps to assure a young couple that they are prepared as much as possible for a valid, honest Christian marriage.

I only suggest that, given the fact of our upset and confused culture today, we should not be surprised, or for that matter even scandalized, that some number of couples were simply incapable of marriage with each other, and that this fact becomes inescapably clear through proper investigation.

While annulments in the Catholic Church today derive from this sort of psychological incapacity, other reasons are also possible.

Among these would be a clear intention by one of the partners contradicting an essential value of marriage, such as permanence, fidelity or openness to children.

One last remark. I strongly urge you and everyone else to resist the temptation to harsh and rash judgments about annulments and those who receive them. Believe me, annulments are no "easy way out." Behind every one lies a sad story of tragedy, broken hopes, defeat and heartbreak.

But there is another story of faith, love and deep concern for what is right that is able to sustain the individuals involved through the long and often painful annulment process. God is the only one who knows our hearts and he is, after all, the final judge.

Married and Divorced Twice

If an unbaptized person has had two marriages and divorces, must both be investigated, or only the first, to see if he can be married to a Catholic in the church.

In any situation involving someone previously married who now wishes to marry in the church, all former marriages must be examined and decided upon before a new wedding can occur.

Sometimes the procedure for one or the other (or all) of the previous marriages may be quite simple. Other times extensive investigation and examination of each one is required. The only way to know for sure is to talk with a priest, give him all the facts, and listen to his advice.

Can My Son Marry in the Church?

Several years ago my son, a Catholic, married a girl who had been baptized a Methodist and had been previously married.

Her first husband abused her and their child, which caused her to divorce him. When she and my son were thinking about marriage, they went to a priest who told them they could not get married in the Catholic Church because she had been baptized a Methodist, so they ended up being married by a justice of the peace.

This is a real heartbreak for me, and I think to him, too. Is there anything they can do to get married in the church?

The mere fact of her being baptized a Methodist would not create an unsolvable problem unless her first husband were also a baptized Christian. If he were not, a procedure might be possible that would allow the marriage.

Other significant factors would be whether her first husband had been married before, what circumstances existed in the first marriage that might suggest the possibility of an annulment, and so on.

Presumably a priest consulted by someone like your son would ask all the necessary questions to explore any avenues for marriage in the church. If your son hasn't talked with at least one other priest during the past few years to obtain his opinion, I'd suggest he do that. Sometimes one priest will see a chance where another does not.

During Annulment Process

I would like your opinion on whether our son may receive Holy Communion. He and his wife were divorced, at her insistence, several months ago. He goes to church regularly, dates occasionally, and has begun a process for annulment of their marriage.

A priest apparently told him that he cannot receive Communion now. This is certainly not what I was taught, and is contrary to what I read in your column. Isn't it possible for him to receive the sacraments unless he remarries?

I suspect either your son or the priest seriously misunderstood the situation. According to the information given in your letter, there is nothing in your son's present life situation that would prevent his receiving the sacraments as a Catholic in perfectly good standing.

Remarried Same Man

If I was married by a justice of the peace to a Catholic, later divorced, and then was remarried to the same man by the same judge, can we be married by a priest now? I am a Catholic, too.

If neither of you were ever married except to each other, there is nothing preventing your being married in the church at this time. This assumes, of course, that all the other usual requirements and intentions for a marriage are present.

If either of you have been married to someone else somewhere along the line, that problem would have to be discussed with your parish priest.

A Misunderstanding

My son married a divorced girl five years ago. At the time they wanted to be married in the Catholic Church but the priest told her she must first sign a paper saying she was not married before. Even my husband would not go along with that.

Now she refuses to allow the three children to be baptized because

the church will not accept her and allow her to become a Catholic. What can be done? My son has spoken to a priest who did not seem able to do anything in their favor.

Somewhere along the line your son and his wife grossly misunderstood either the process the priest was following, or the questions they were being asked. Nowhere in any of its procedures does the Catholic Church ask or encourage any statement that is contrary to the facts as that individual knows them.

At some stages of certain marriage procedures, an individual might be asked if a previous marriage had ever taken place in the Catholic Church. In itself, however, this implies no statement concerning the validity of that previous marriage, since marriages of non-Catholics are recognized by the Catholic Church as perfectly valid, presuming, of course, they are both free to marry.

Your letter gives nowhere near enough facts for me to make even a wild guess at whether a Catholic marriage for your son and his wife is possible. I suggest he lay the whole matter before some priest in his locality and determine if a validation of their present marriage is possible. I hate to see them missing so much spiritually simply because of a misunderstanding.

Need to See Parish Priest

I am 33 years old and have been married 16 years. We have four children who are practicing Catholics, but I cannot be.

I was 16 when we were married and was raised a Catholic up to that time. My husband was a Baptist who had been divorced, so we were married by a justice of the peace. For years now I have been taking our children to church, but have been unable to receive the sacraments of penance or Communion, which I would like very much to do.

Is there any way that I can become a practicing Catholic again? If my husband were willing to become a Catholic, could we be married in the church? Please answer this letter as soon as possible because my present situation bothers me very much.

There is some possibility that you could return to the sacraments and that your marriage could be validated by the Catholic Church. However, to explore the possibility of any marriage case, or other solution to the problem, you would have to talk to a priest either in your own parish or one nearby. I seriously urge you to do that right away.

Dispensation From Form

A devout Catholic friend of mine is marrying a Jewish girl in a civil ceremony presided over by a justice of the peace.

I've spoken to two priests on his status with the church after his marriage, and received two different answers. Will he or will he not be a Catholic in good standing after this ceremony?

The answer is not that complicated. Perhaps each of the priests you consulted was right, depending on the circumstances.

If the Catholic has received a dispensation from the bishop not to be married before a priest, then his marriage will be valid in the eyes of the Catholic Church. Normally Catholics are obliged to be married before a priest, but under certain conditions the bishop of the diocese may dispense them from that obligation. Technically this is referred to as a dispensation from the form of marriage.

If the Catholic partner in this marriage has not received such a dispensation, the marriage would not be valid according to Catholic Church law. He then would be acting in violation of a very serious obligation as a member of the Catholic Church. In making such decisions he would, among other things, withdraw himself from any right to receive the sacraments until his marital situation were somehow corrected.

Why Not Remarried?

A Catholic friend of mine married a non-Catholic, unbaptized divorced woman. They now have three children. After their marriage the lady converted to the Catholic faith and was baptized. Her first marriage was annulled by the Catholic Church.

Up to now the couple have not remarried in the Catholic Church, yet they both regularly receive the sacraments. My understanding of the church's teaching is that, in the eyes of the church, he is not really married to this woman. Even though he has the annulment, they are not yet married according to the church since there has been no Catholic ceremony. This is all confusing to me as a Catholic. Can you explain?

After the first marriage was annulled, this couple certainly should have had their marriage validated in the Catholic Church. I suspect there may be some facts here you are not aware of. Perhaps they have indeed declared their marriage vows before a Catholic priest.

This validation ceremony can be very private and simple. Sometimes couples do not wish to make a big ceremony of this validation, though they should have some way of making known to their close friends that their marriage has been validated in the Catholic Church.

Are you certain the annulment process is complete? I find it difficult to believe that a couple who would persevere in the tedious, lengthy annulment process would not take the final simple step of declaring their vows before a priest. If they have not yet been married before a priest, they should not, of course, be receiving the sacraments.

If your friendship is intimate enough, ask them. If not, I suggest you give them the benefit of the doubt and assume they have fulfilled all of the requirements making a full Catholic life right for them.

Annulment and Physical Abuse

About five years ago we brought our daughter and her 18-month-old child from Florida to live with us. A neighbor of our daughter had called telling us she had taken our daughter to get stitches in her chin. We didn't realize the situation, but our daughter's husband had been abusing her for over a year. She had tried to stay with him since she felt she should live with her husband.

Now it seems there is no hope for that. We understand that the diocesan marriage court decides if there are grounds for a marriage annulment. Could you suggest what action we might take?

You do not give many details, but I have found that whenever there is serious physical abuse, particularly early in marriage, there are often also other psychological problems that make an annulment at least worth investigating.

Your first move should be to contact your parish priest, explain the situation, and ask his advice. He will guide and help you through the procedures which, as you indicate, are under the responsibility of the marriage court of your diocese. If it is impossible to contact a parish priest near you, you may write directly to the diocesan marriage court and explain the circumstances. I am sure they will help arrange at least an initial interview with someone.

Divorced and Remarried Parents

I have a niece who was married to a non-Catholic boy in a big church wedding. They were divorced after a year, and she wanted to marry a Catholic. The priest told her nothing could be done. So they got married by a justice of the peace.

I know their marriage is not valid according to the laws of the Catholic Church. Now they are expecting a baby. Will their child get to be baptized as a Catholic?

As has been stressed in previous pages, being baptized as a Catholic means much more than simply that a priest performs the ceremony. The newly baptized commits himself, personally or through parents and godparents, to a life of faith, worship and mutual support within the Catholic community. His fellow Catholics oblige themselves to the same for him.

At least twice during the baptism ceremony, the parents formally and explicitly profess that they understand and accept this belief of what is being done, and they promise that they will assist their child in fulfilling that responsibility through the coming years. Also, immediately prior to the solemn profession of faith before the pouring of the baptismal water, parents receive the serious admonition: "This is the faith of the church. This is the faith in which these children are about to be baptized."

Are the parents you describe able to make such a promise? It is entirely possible that they can if they themselves are committed to living as full a Catholic life as circumstances permit. One point in their favor is that they both have at least some Catholic background and roots in the Catholic faith. That doesn't remove all the problems, but it does give them a bit of a head start in a difficult task.

The final decision, of course, rests with the parents and with their parish priest.

Are Parents Still Responsible?

Doctrines taught in religion classes of Catholic schools today seem so often to differ with what I and other parents think. Is our responsibility for the Catholic education of our children lessened, since we don't know what's happening?

Absolutely not. While parents, as well as teachers and school officials may often forget it, parents remain the ones with the primary right and responsibility for the growth of their children, and that includes their education. A mother and father no more surrender this responsibility by sending their children to school than they surrender primary obligations for their child's health by sending him to a doctor.

Certainly the faith is "taught" today much differently than when we were in school. (Considering the unspeakable tragedies of the past 30 years, both at home and abroad, by the failures of supposedly religious people, one would think, incidentally, we might welcome efforts at a few changes.)

But, to be frank, why don't you know what's happening? Special programs for parents of students, even series of classes, are common today in Catholic schools and other religious education programs. Annual or semi-annual Masses are scheduled for students and parents to help parents better understand the liturgical implications of the faith their children are building. Attendance at all such activities is typically poor — unattended mainly by parents who openly admit their confusion over what their children are being taught.

Such parents often stay away because they fear they will learn something that will shake them up and make them do some fresh thinking.

It may be an explanation, but it's hardly a responsible way to act.

If your school or religion class is doing something you don't understand, ask your child or his teacher to try to explain it more fully. You might even attend a class or two and show them both, at least, that you care.

Married a Transvestite

A friend married a transvestite — a person who dresses in clothes of the opposite sex — but didn't find out until after they had been married for some time. She tried living with him, but after a few years she was in such a state the doctor recommended divorce.

She is a good Catholic, but would like to remarry. Could this be grounds to have the marriage annulled? Priests I have questioned doubt it.

It is possible for such a marriage to be annulled. There's absolutely no way of knowing, however, until the facts are sufficiently investigated.

A major element in the case, of course, is the depth and extent of the psychological illness and incapacity which her husband suffers. In certain instances, this type of person is so emotionally crippled that true consent to marriage, with the relationships and responsibilities this implies, is not possible.

Only appropriate psychiatric and legal consultation can determine that. A decision concerning the nullity of the marriage would then be made based on the results of such investigations.

Suggest that your friend discuss the matter personally with a priest in her area in whom she has confidence, and follow the procedure he suggests.

"Unofficial" marriages

Is there any way a couple can be married in the Catholic Church without having the marriage registered with the state? My first husband died, and I have been raising our three children on an annuity from his former employer. However, that annuity stops when I remarry.

I have met a fine gentleman who wants to marry me, but he is on a low income, and we would need the annuity money for the children. Could we get married without having it "official?"

There's no way you could do that, to my knowledge. Any person empowered to officiate at marriages (clergyman, judge, etc.) is obliged by law to notify the proper state office of the fact of the marriage. This is normally done through completion of the marriage license which the couple must acquire before they can be legally married.

Failure of a priest, minister, or anyone else, to notify the state that he has performed a marriage, is a violation of the law for which he may be punished, at least with a fine.

Common law marriage, by which a couple would simply begin to live together without benefit of a properly performed and registered marriage ceremony, is not recognized in most states. Therefore, attempting an "unregistered marriage" could create serious legal problems for the clergyman and yourselves.

Should you still have questions, it would be best to discuss the matter with an attorney.

You didn't ask about the morality of what you are contemplating, but have you considered that this might be stealing from your former husband's employer in taking money that does not rightfully and contractually belong to you?

A Sin to Catch V.D.?

Do I have to tell the priest in confession that I have contracted V.D.? Is it a sin to catch V.D. from your husband?

It is obviously no sin to catch V.D. The sin, if there is one, is in the morality of the sexual relationship itself, which transmitted the disease. It is very wrong to expose someone else to the disease, or to refuse to obtain proper care for oneself when it is known the disease has been contracted.

Disappointed Parents

If a son has knowingly entered an invalid marriage, are his parents obliged to accept this? Can they refuse to forgive him? Can they receive the sacraments worthily without forgiveness in their hearts?

You are suffering a deep personal tragedy. All good parents want the best for their children, and for mothers and fathers who have a deep religious faith, that means hoping their children will share in the benefits that come from a committed belief in God and his teachings.

You feel that your son has lost all this, at least for the present. I believe you are more hurt and disappointed than embittered or unforgiving. Remember, there's a big and important difference between accepting and approving what has been done, and accepting your son himself — and even his new wife insofar as you are able to do that.

You have every right to your own convictions, of course. You also have a right to make sure those convictions are clearly understood by your son. But that does not preclude your accepting him where he is, loving him, and supporting him as you can in the heavy responsibilities he has undertaken. This is a matter of simple Christian charity. Without betraying our beliefs, we must leave judgments to God.

Don't hesitate to go to the sacraments, and keep praying for true peace of mind and peace with God for him and for yourselves.

Priest Doesn't Marry You?

An 80-year-old friend told me recently that a relative was married and praised the priest who "married them." I replied that even the pope cannot marry someone; the couple marry each other and the priest simply receives their vows.

Would you please tell me if I'm correct in believing that an ordained priest can administer only six of the seven sacraments?

Technically, you are right. The bride and groom, by their exchange of marriage vows, administer the sacrament of matrimony to each other; the priest is there as the official witness and representative of the church.

Therefore, in the Latin Rite, ordained priests can administer only six of the sacraments. (In some other Catholic rites priests may marry, in which instance, of course, they would also administer the sacrament of marriage.) Thus the expression to be married "before" a priest is theologically preferable to "by" a priest.

Don't get your hopes up though. Your chances of reversing several centuries of English tradition on the subject are somewhat less than promising.

Formerly Married Catholics

A parish in our area has announced a series of meetings for "formerly married Catholics." Isn't this dangerous for the church to give recognition to the divorced and separated? Can a divorced Catholic receive the sacraments?

The church — which means all of us Catholics — has a serious responsibility to provide what assistance we can to those who are trying to adjust to a "single" style of life, and often trying to raise a family without the help of a spouse.

This responsibility has been delayed far too long, perhaps because of this attitude that such Catholics are somehow "untouchables." Whether such an attitude was ever justified or not, and I doubt it, you must know that with the pressures and conditions of married and family life today, many are divorced or separated through no fault of their own. Some factors in marriage relationships are as much out of one individual's control as the death of the spouse was out of control of a widow or widower.

Furthermore, the end of their marriage does not mean the end of their need to love and be loved — especially, incidentally, by their still-married friends.

When widows and widowers and separated Catholics were relatively few in number, perhaps there was some excuse for not recognizing their special needs and trying to meet them. That is no longer true. Rather than "dangerous," the series of meetings of divorced, separated and widowed Catholic men and women is, if anything, long overdue.

There is nothing in itself that prevents a divorced man or woman from receiving penance and the Eucharist. In certain ways they may need the sacraments more in learning how to move away from their accustomed married life style. The same rules apply to them in this matter as to any other Catholic.

Here, as elsewhere, we have no right to judge or condemn, but rather to do all we can to strengthen and heal and support.

Should Priest Have Attended?

How would the church view the attendance of a priest at a large reception following a wedding, performed by a judge, of a Catholic couple, one divorced and the other a widow?

The action taken by this Catholic couple in planning their wedding and reception in advance, being aware of the fact that their wedding would not be sanctioned by the church, their attendance at Mass and receiving Holy Communion on the morning of their wedding is, in my opinion, a source of scandal to the community.

Under the circumstances of the wedding, doesn't the presence of the priest at the reception constitute his approval of the wedding?

It is possible that, for some reason, both individuals were free to marry and that they received a dispensation to be married before a judge. In the circumstances you describe, however, the likelihood of that is quite remote.

If the marriage was invalid according to the laws of the church, as most Catholic people would understandably assume, it would seem that the attendance of a priest at the reception would be at least extremely confusing. Attendance by certain friends, or even a family, might be interpreted a little more easily as simply an expression of friendship — though even that would have to be thought through very carefully beforehand by each individual.

The priest's attendance would normally be interpreted as an apparent celebration and congratulation concerning a marriage that, according to Catholic Church regulations, simply does not exist.

Your comment about their attending Mass and Communion on the morning of their wedding is what makes me wonder if perhaps there was not some permission given for this ceremony. Whatever the policy of your diocese, I cannot imagine a priest sanctioning that kind of contradiction between the individuals' life of prayer and worship and what they professed by their open rejection of church law later in the day.

Approving such a course of action would be no favor even to the couple being married, who appear already to have an awfully mixed-up conscience. Ignoring for the moment the scandal to everyone else, someday they will have to sort out their beliefs and actions, and straighten themselves out on who they are and what they believe. Confusing the couple further by apparent approval of their present action can only hurt them in the long run, it seems to me, and is surely no favor to them.

Excommunication and Remarriage

I still don't understand a few things about the possibility of divorced and remarried Catholics returning to the sacrament of Communion.

Does the church now consider second or third marriages all right, since these people are no longer excommunicated? If not, how can the church say it is possible for them to receive Communion if they are living in sin?

I realize this matter sounds extremely complicated and confusing to most Catholics.

First of all, be clear on one point. In eliminating the excommunication of divorced and remarried Catholics, the American bishops explicitly stated that their action could in no way indicate acceptance of these second marriages as valid and sacramental. The fact that persons in this situation are no longer excommunicated simply means that they remain members of the church and may share in many ways in its life and worship. (Actually, many remarried Catholics were doing this already, which only increased confusion over the significance of the bishops' action, which they intended as an expression of concern and care for these members of our faith.)

To your second question, it is true that divorced and remarried Catholics are living in an objectively sinful situation according to the church's laws, which reflect its beliefs in the permanence of marriage. For this reason, of course, the general rule of the church is that they cannot receive Communion.

However, whether the individuals involved are, as you put it, "living in sin" as far as their own souls are concerned, is something only God can know and judge. It is possible they are not, if, for example, they sincerely wish to do everything necessary to get straight with God but find it morally impossible to leave the present spouse without proportionately serious emotional, spiritual, or physical harm to others. This is simply good traditional moral theology.

Applying, then, our traditional theology of the Eucharist, it becomes clear that receiving Communion may be considered in some instances. As the bishops said, the lifting of the excommunication does not "of itself" permit divorced and remarried Catholics to receive the sacraments of penance and the Eucharist, but the possibility is not ruled out.

Why Won't Church Go Along?

I brought my family up under strict Catholic teachings, and my daughter is a very strict, dedicated Catholic. She now loves and plans to marry a man who has been divorced for seven years.

They explained their situation to a priest who told them they cannot be married in the Catholic Church. This is a great shock to me and my daughter, who thought she would bring her husband into the church and now she is being rejected.

It's no wonder the church is losing attendance. I see Catholics who are divorced and some remarried, and still receiving Holy Communion. Why? Why cannot my daughter at least be married at the side altar?

I'm not sure precisely what you mean by strict, dedicated Catholic. But either there are some awfully big holes in your daughter's (and apparently your) knowledge of the Catholic faith, or your daughter deliberately ignored some basic beliefs about marriage and now is bitter because the church cannot agree with her.

Any Catholic even minimally educated in the teachings of our faith must be aware of the basic teachings of the church concerning marriage, and therefore aware that he or she is looking at possible big problems when a serious relationship is allowed to develop with a divorced person.

Sometimes an annulment or other procedure may be implemented by which two such individuals might marry according to the laws of the Catholic faith. But the church has absolutely no power or authority before God to do what you are asking, that is, to approve the marriage of a man and a woman, regardless of previous husbands or wives, simply because those two people are in love and want a Catholic wedding.

The priest you mentioned apparently gave good advice. The place where the marriage takes place — side altar, high altar, or park bench — is irrelevant to the validity of the marriage. As long as a former spouse is living, no marriage according to church law is possible without an annulment or other formal procedure which would assure that both partners are now free to marry.

If your daughter does have the strong Catholic roots you seem to indicate, I would strongly urge her to go back to the priest, or to another priest, and ask him to investigate the possibilities of one of these procedures.

Baptism and Mixed Marriage

Can a marriage between a Catholic and a non-Catholic be dissolved because the non-Catholic was never baptized?

In his long discussion of marriage and celibacy in the first letter to the Corinthians (chapter 7), St. Paul says that if the non-Christian spouse of a recently baptized Christian is willing to continue living together in harmony, there must be no divorce. If the non-Christian spouse is unwilling, however, the couple may separate for the good of the faith and presumably for the benefit of both.

Since the fourth century — in other words, for about 1,600 years — Christian tradition has (sometimes with considerable hesitation) seen this as a biblical basis for allowing a divorce and remarriage in the situation you suggest. In church law it is called the Pauline Privilege.

The procedure is not an overnight one, however, and sometimes can become quite complicated, involving problems of previous marriages, the question of whether or not the husband and wife were baptized Christians, and so forth. Each case is different and is handled separately through agencies set up in the church for that purpose.

If I Marry Out of the Church?

My situation is somewhat different than the one you discussed recently on divorce and remarriage. I am a Catholic and have never been married, but the man I'm interested in is a divorced non-Catholic. I would like to know, if I enter a marriage of this kind, will the sacrament of Communion be denied me? He has even mentioned that he would consider becoming a convert if it would help.

The answer to your main question — whether or not you could marry this man according to the rules of the Catholic Church — can only be given after discussing all pertinent details with your priest. So many factors (previous marriages, baptismal status, etc.) are involved that not even a wild guess is possible in this column.

In fairness to yourself, I strongly suggest you keep a couple of things clearly in mind. First, remember that the answer may quite possibly be no. Often an individual pursues a course like this with a vague feeling that somehow "something will work out." Such may not happen, resulting in considerable suffering for yourself and others.

Second, if you do something you believe is wrong, Communion "would be denied" you only by yourself, not someone else as you seem to imply. There is no police force guarding the Communion table. Normally the only obstacle to Holy Communion for a Catholic is a serious offense against God's law that is unrepented and unconfessed. The individual himself is the only judge of that.

Witness at Civil Marriage?

Is it permissible for a practicing Catholic to be the main witness at a wedding between a divorced Catholic and a Protestant in a civil ceremony?

I have heard that this is not allowed by the church, but have been told that I am misinformed.

It is wrong for a Catholic to be a witness at a marriage ceremony which is invalid and wrong according to church law, as this marriage seems to be.

It is possible, though unlikely according to your letter, that the marriage will be in accord with church legislation. This would have required action by a Catholic marriage court relating to the first marriage, and a dispensation for the new marriage to take place in another church or court.

If you're not certain, your parish priest can help you find out.

Is It Your Business?

My question concerns two people who were married in the church. After 12 years, and one child, can the father ask for a divorce and then marry a non-Catholic and still take Communion? Also, the non-Catholic wife was told she could receive Communion in the Catholic Church. She was also divorced. They now have two children and these children are baptized in the church. Please explain.

If you're asking whether such a series of marriages is possible within the regulations of the Catholic Church, the answer is yes. It is very possible, for example, that an annulment of the first marriage was obtained for several possible reasons, which would mean that both partners would be free to remarry.

If you ask how you can find out for sure, I'd have to give you two answers. First, if you feel you have a right to know the background of the matter because it involves a close friend or family member, you might ask them about it. If it does not involve such an individual, then the personal aspects of the case are really none of your business. Parish priests and Catholic marriage tribunal officials are trained to deal with such cases with extreme care and concern so that the sanctity of marriage and the rights of everyone involved are fully respected. As for the rest of us, when we see a tragic personal problem worked out in a manner that seems to be for the spiritual good of people, we should be happy for them and let it go at that.

One item I do have a question about is your statement that the non-Catholic is receiving Communion. If your information is correct, she may be acting entirely on her own. If she says she is receiving Communion with some sort of approval, I have no explanation for that in the light of current Catholic regulations concerning the Eucharist.

Permanence of Marriage

If two people were divorced, one Catholic and one non-Catholic, and they want to marry each other, why can't they be married in the Catholic Church? Why must the sacrament of Communion be denied the Catholic for life?

A thousand factors may determine whether or not a particular second marriage can be performed in a Catholic church. This answer, therefore, must speak only of general and basic truths; it cannot attempt to explain specifically about your son's marriage.

When two people marry, the presumption of the church is that they are promising and uniting themselves to each other, as they themselves say, for life. This commitment is religious and most serious and binding in conscience. Certainly no one is married in the Catholic Church without being reminded that this is what marriage involves.

When this commitment is broken, the church takes the position that, whatever private and personal justification the individual may give to himself, facts must be accepted and acted upon as they appear in public.

In other words, without judging the person's interior relationship to his own conscience and to God, as far as the church's society is concerned a second marriage cannot take place when one or both partners already have spouses to whom they have united themselves in marriage. (The fact that a civil divorce has been granted would not change the matter.)

The same facts explain why such persons should not go to Communion. The church accepts at face value the individual's personal and religious commitment in the previous marriage. In such a presumption, a second marriage would be seriously wrong. And, as you know, continuing to do something one knows is seriously wrong rules out the worthy reception of Holy Communion.

It should be noted, of course, that some couples in such marriage situations sincerely do not believe they are wrong, or find it impossible to get out of the situation without gross injustice to others. Later questions will deal more explicitly with some of these situations.

"Promises" in a Mixed Marriage

Your answer concerning the marriage of a Catholic with a non-Catholic sounded so simple.

Why didn't you mention that the Catholic party must sign a statement that the children of that marriage must be raised Catholic? Some young people are surprised to learn that such papers must be signed before the marriage can take place before a Catholic priest. If one of the parties does not agree to this, the marriage cannot take place.

What you say is true, and I adverted to it briefly in my answer. But obviously the matter needs a little more explanation.

Formerly, both the Catholic and non-Catholic partners signed promises to raise the children Catholic. This practice was changed by Pope Paul VI in a document on interfaith marriages ("Matrimonia Mixta") in 1970.

While the procedure is different, the intent of the church is the same: to prevent, at least as much as possible, any serious harm to the marriage because of religious differences between the husband and wife. Let me explain.

The procedure today is this: The non-Catholic partner signs or promises nothing. The Catholic partner signs two statements. The statements are basically as follows:

1. I reaffirm my faith in Jesus Christ, and intend to continue living that faith in the Catholic Church, and

2. I promise to do all in my power to share my faith with our children by having them baptized and raised as Catholics.

The non-Catholic partner is not asked to sign or promise anything. The priest who is helping the couple arrange for the wedding is required to sign a declaration that the non-Catholic partner has been informed of this affirmation and belief of the Catholic.

Normally, the priest will also explain what these beliefs mean to the Catholic, and how such beliefs affect the Catholic's life, and then urge the couple to be sure before their marriage that their respective faiths and convictions can be preserved and honored in their marriage.

Several points need to be noted about the "promises" made by the Catholic. First of all, they add absolutely nothing to what a Catholic already believes if he or she is truly Catholic. When an individual presents himself to a Catholic priest for marriage as a Catholic in the Catholic Church, the priest and the church have the right and obligation to assume that that individual is a Catholic — which means there are some things that person is honestly convinced of and adheres to as his personal faith.

Among these are the two statements given above. Any Catholic who does not hold these as basic beliefs is either grossly ill-informed about his religion, or is very shakey in his faith.

Why then are the declarations asked at all? One reason is as a reminder. But more importantly, they are meant to help the couple identify any differences in their religious beliefs or expectations from the marriage, so that these differences can be dealt with and resolved before the marriage takes place.

In other words, while the church knows what a good and knowledgeable Catholic believes, it does not pretend to know the religious beliefs of the non-Catholic. It presumes, however, that the non-Catholic has some beliefs about God, family, marriage, and other religious matters. And it is concerned that these beliefs of the two people be confronted by them before the marriage so that any critical differences may be ironed out.

Ultimately, of course, this must be done by the two people themselves, acting from the base of their own convictions. They must be sure that any conflicts of belief (for example, about their own personal religious obligations, the baptism and education of their future children, and so on) can be resolved without either of them being asked to compromise what their conscience tells them are serious moral obligations before God.

If such resolution proves impossible, the couple could not, of course, enter the marriage with a good conscience.

The entire procedure is simply another expression of the church's loving concern for the faith and conscience of the Catholic, first of all, but also of the non-Catholic, whose convictions are, one would hope, just as serious to him as ours are to us.

"Church's Laws Will Change?"

My father is deceased and my mother has married a divorced man who is not Catholic and was never baptized.

I'm not sure whether this man would become Catholic or not. But when they were married the priest told my mother (according to her) that they should go ahead and marry since the church's rules would change in five years.

It's now five years later. What chance is there for her to get married in the church and return to the sacraments?

I am fairly confident that the priest could not have advised your mother to act on the basis of such speculation as a rule change in church marriage laws. Many times we hear, with no deliberate dishonesty at all, what we would like to hear in matters that deeply affect us. My suspicion is that this is what happened to your mother.

Whatever happened five years ago, if the facts you give are accurate, I suggest you ask your mother to talk the matter over thoroughly with a priest first, or, if you would feel more comfortable, you discuss it with the priest yourself first. If your mother's present husband had only one previous marriage, and if there is no other impediment, a procedure exists which might allow the marriage of your mother to be validated in the church.

The procedure is not new, by the way, though it is used more now than formerly.

First-Cousin Marriages

I hope you can help our family with a problem. Our son has been dating a lovely girl who is also a student at the college he attends. They are both intelligent, family-oriented people, but the difficulty is they are first cousins.

We parents on both sides have discussed the matter with them, but they see no moral problem at all. Isn't it still Catholic doctrine that we are not to marry "within the third degree of kindred?"

Your problem may be solved simply by civil law. In most states of the country, the kind of marriage you describe is illegal. Relatively few states allow marriage between first cousins.

The prohibition against such close intrafamily marriages is based on the negative genetic and social consequences which can easily occur should such marriages become prevalent in any society. The Code of Canon Law which governs the Latin Rite of the Catholic Church still prohibits marriage within the third degree of relationships, which would include all grandchildren of a common grandparent — in other words, first cousins.

However, dispensations for a marriage between first cousins can be granted. In fact, marriages of first cousins are still quite common today, even among Catholics, in certain parts of the world.

Can I Remarry?

I have been a Catholic all my life, and am keeping company with a lady, also Catholic. In 1927, I was married by a justice of the peace and later had the marriage validated in the church. We were divorced in 1932.

Since then my first wife has been married eight times. In fact, the

reason we separated was that she was running around with other men. I've been told that we could not get an annulment, but I've also been told that anyone marrying that many times is unbalanced.

The lady I'm keeping company with and I would like to be married in the church. We're both in our 70s, and nothing would make us happier than to be married in our religion. What can we do to make that happen?

Getting married eight times, even over a period of 50 years, may well be a symptom of mental or emotional unbalance. At the very least it is a symptom of a pretty shakey idea of the meaning of the marriage promise, and for that reason of a questionable capability for entering into a true marriage with anyone.

In other words, judging, of course, only from the information you offer, this is the kind of case that seems well worth submitting to your diocesan authorities for further investigation. You don't mention who told you an annulment was possible. If it was not your parish priest, or another priest in whom you have confidence, I certainly urge you to discuss the situation with him now.

The fact that all this happened nearly five decades ago complicates matters somewhat, since some of those whose testimony would be desirable have surely died by this time. It's still worth bringing to the priest's attention, however, and let him see what might be done. Good luck!

Are the Rich Privileged?

Isn't the Catholic religion the same for all, or do the rich people have more privileges? A book on the Kennedy family tells how Jackie Kennedy was allowed by Cardinal Cushing of Boston to marry Aristotle Onassis after she gave the cardinal some expensive gift. This was after President Kennedy died, and Mr. Onassis had been divorced. I have a dear friend who could not get permission to marry a divorced person. Why the difference?

First of all, church officials who make the final decisions on marriage cases are extremely careful to try to keep their deliberations free of any influence that might arise from the financial condition of the individuals involved.

The Roman Rota, for example, the highest Catholic "court" dealing with marriage matters, publishes a yearly report on the decisions it has made, and on the number of those for which no financial compensation was received. Each year it is clear that ability to "pay" has no relationship to the outcome of the case. From my own experience, the same is true of tribunals at other levels.

As we have pointed out, few marriage cases are exactly the same, no matter how similar they appear to the outside observer. You and the author you are reading apparently assume the Jackie-Aristotle marriage was approved and blessed by the Catholic Church. This was not the case, since his divorce from his former wife was not recognized by the church. (In fairness, however, it should be said that the marriage laws of the Roman Catholic Church differ in this matter from those of the Eastern Orthodox Church to which Mr. Onassis belonged. It seems that according to his church he was free to marry Mrs. Kennedy.)

As for Cardinal Cushing, there is no record, to my knowledge, that he "allowed" her to enter the marriage. He merely noted that only God knows who is a sinner and who is not, and that the occasion called for an exercise of "charity, love, and mutual respect and esteem." That's still good advice.

Can Aunt Receive Communion?

I am a Protestant writing on behalf of my Catholic aunt who married my uncle, a Protestant, in 1935. Her first marriage was annulled in 1934.

My aunt is now 75 years old, and has never taken Communion since she married the second time, which grieves her very much. I have told her about the articles I've read concerning the changes in your church's ruling, but she feels she should have official sanction. Can you advise me how to help her?

I wonder if your aunt has ever talked with someone about her concern. Judging only from the information in your letter, I see no reason for her not going to Communion. I'm presuming that she married your uncle in the Catholic Church, and there appears to be no reason she would have done otherwise.

Please ask her to discuss the matter with the nearest priest, who, I'm sure, could settle her conscience in a few minutes. Many previously married people, who are in perfectly good standing in the church, mistakenly feel they cannot receive the sacraments of penance and the Eucharist. Your aunt may well be one of them.

Husband Has Been Unfaithful

I am reluctant to talk to my parish priest about this problem, but I need help from someone. Two months ago I found out that my husband was involved with a white woman. (We are black.) Later I found out that she is pregnant by him. What do you advise me to do? At this point I'm confused. I can't forgive him and am very unhappy living with him now. He's a truck driver and is away five days out of a week. Of course, he blames me for what happened; he says that I

neglected him and that is why he turned to this woman for love and companionship. We have six children, aged five to 16.

Please help me make a decision. I can't do it alone.

I understand how terribly hurt you must be by this tragic action on the part of your husband. Certainly you cannot make a wise decision without sharing the problem and exploring your alternatives with someone you can trust.

On the other hand, it is impossible for me to advise you helpfully at this distance. So many feelings of all involved must be explored, and so much of the past and present history of your relationship with your husband needs to be considered that you need someone with whom you can sit and talk out the problem.

Don't be too quick to count out your parish priest as a consultant. I realize the situation is embarrassing to you, but you will not scandalize him and he has probably helped many others in similar dilemmas. Beyond that, try a wise relative or friend, or a professional counselor you can have confidence in. But don't try to go it alone. You need all the support and encouragement you can get from someone who is interested in you and your children.

Son in New Church

Our son has become a "born again" Christian, who plans to marry in his new church in a few months. Do we as parents go to the ceremony, or stay away.

It used to be wrong to attend such affairs, but now we don't know. Our nephew was in a similar situation recently, and his parents received all kinds of different answers including "Absolutely not" and "Do as you like." I'm truly confused. Where do we go from here? We love our son and we love our religion, and we want to do what is right.

This kind of situation is always anguishing for a family. I'm afraid my words may not ease your decision as much as you would wish.

First, however, be assured that there is no black-and-white, right-and-wrong answer to your question. It requires weighing several factors and then making as prudent a judgment as you can, all things considered.

One element I am sure you wonder about is the possibility of scandal. What will your action say to your son, and to the rest of your family and your friends, about your own approval of the marriage, and about your attitude toward his leaving his old faith and changing to the new religion? On the other hand, basic charity and your parental love urge that you let him realize you are not ostracizing him from your family, and that you keep lines of communication open to him.

Remember that you have your own convictions, too, and you do not have to apologize for them. You have as much right to your beliefs as your son has to his. If you feel that merely going to the wedding would indicate your approval of the marriage or of the religion in some way that would compromise your own faith convictions seriously, then you should not go.

However, you may be able to make your position absolutely clear, and still attend the wedding without being misunderstood.

Obviously, the solution you reach will depend on these and other factors — such as the nature of your relationships within your family, who else will know about it or be at the wedding, and on your judgment as to how your friends would understand your presence there.

Other children in your family, especially younger ones, are also a consideration. You naturally do not wish to do anything to confuse or mislead them about your faith and what it demands of them and you.

Perhaps today there is less danger than before in the attendance of parents at such affairs because of the widespread confusion and radical religious searching in many of our young people. One wonders on occasion, to put it bluntly, if they ever had any faith to lose — and this through no moral fault on the part of the parents. Emotional and spiritual maturity of the kind required for a genuine, internal faith commitment seems to arrive awfully late for many young people today.

Think and pray about it, decide, and then don't fret over your decision.

Rash Judgments About Remarried

You stated that, by present church law, divorced and remarried Catholics are unable to receive the Eucharist. You give the impression that this is just church law.

I thought it was divine law that we had to be in the state of grace to go to Communion. People who were validly married, got divorced and are now remarried, are objectively in the state of mortal sin. That condition lasts until they are willing to give up their sinful relationship. How can you say such people may at some time be able to receive Communion?

You are right in everything you say. You omit, however, some critical additional truths which you have apparently forgotten.

One essential requirement for a serious (mortal) sin is that the individual deliberately remains attached to that sin, or deliberately remains in a sinful situation from which he is morally capable of removing himself. Those last nine words are important. They mean that the person must have not only a theoretical possibility, but a real honest-to-God choice available for getting out of the situation that is objectively sinful. If he does not have such a choice, it cannot automatically be declared that he is in what you call the "state of mortal sin."

The very case you protest, in fact, that of a divorced and remarried Catholic, might present one of the more apt examples of such a condition. Let's suppose a Catholic woman is divorced and remarried contrary to the laws of the church. Fifteen years later, she knows she has done something wrong and wants to do everything possible to get straight with God. By now, however, there are four growing children living in what appears to be a good home with a reasonably happy and stable mother and father. By every human appearance and judgment, at least, the children are dependent upon both parents for the right fulfillment of their basic social, physical, psychological and perhaps even religious needs.

I know of almost no moral theologians and very few, if any, parish priests who would claim that this woman has a serious moral obligation to break up her home, take her children (if she can) and divorce her husband so she can get back to Communion. In fact, most agree today more than ever that the very suggestion of such a solution is grotesque.

(I will not discuss here such solutions as a brother-sister relationship between the husband and wife, which are increasingly recognized as having limited validity in such situations. At any rate, they are private matters between the couple and are therefore irrelevant as to how that marriage looks to outsiders.)

From this it should be obvious that to view all couples in a divorced and remarried relationship as living in mortal sin is plain and simple rash judgment. Admittedly not all such relationships are the same or equivalent to the one example I give, but this type of situation is by no means uncommon.

We should be careful not to pass judgment. It is well to remember Christ's words: "Be compassionate, as your Father is compassionate. Do not judge, and you will not be judged. Do not condemn, and you will not be condemned. Pardon, and you shall be pardoned." (Luke 6:37)

The absolute prohibition against divorced and remarried Catholics receiving the sacraments is a church law, or, if you wish, the church's interpretation and application of a divine law. In taking this stand, the church must consider many factors, such as preserving clearly its teachings on the permanence of marriage, and the meaning of the Eucharist as an expression of faith and unity with the church.

The fact remains, however, that this prohibition is perfectly open to change or mitigation by the church, with no violence done to divine law concerning the Eucharist.

As for those of us who are not directly involved in a situation like this, we should remember that every case is different, and there may be many aspects of a case that for reasons of justice or privacy cannot be explained to anyone else. In other words, we ought to just plain mind our own business and remember that God is perfectly capable of watching out for his own interests.

It should be enough for us to hope, and be thankful that a fellow Christian may be able to work out something that can give peace of soul to himself and his loved ones.

Still Have Nuptial Masses?

I seldom see a reference to a nuptial Mass any more. Does it still mean a regular Mass centered around a wedding? Does it have to be performed in the morning? And do both parties have to be Catholic?

Nuptial Masses are generally referred to today as simply the Mass on the day of marriage. The wedding ceremony takes place after the Scripture readings and homily, but most of the variable parts of the Mass such as the prayers, Bible passages, prayers of the faithful, and so on, center on the theme of marriage.

According to general church regulations, wedding Masses may take place any time of the day or evening, but individual dioceses may have local rules limiting this in some way. In many parts of the country, for example, wedding Masses are not allowed on Sundays without special permission from the bishop.

Catholic Marriage in Protestant Church?

Recently a Catholic friend of ours was married to a divorced man in his Presbyterian Church by a Presbyterian minister. We understand that a Catholic priest attended and blessed the couple after they were married.

Does the Catholic Church recognize this marriage as valid, and can she receive the sacraments of penance and Communion? If so, we would like an explanation.

The situation you describe is entirely possible within the legal framework of the Catholic Church, and (except for being married in the Protestant church) the possibility is by no means new in the Catholic Church.

There are two ways the second marriage might take place in light of his previous union. First, there could have been an annulment of that first marriage. This means, as is discussed more at length elsewhere, that some impediment existed from the beginning of that first marriage so that in the eyes of the church, and possibly of the state as well, there was never a marriage at all.

The other way is through a process called Privilege of the Faith. This process is similar to the Pauline Privilege (see 1 Corinthians, chapter 7) which would allow a second marriage in certain circumstances when it would be helpful to the faith of one of the parties. Privilege of the Faith cases are used to dissolve the marriage of a baptized Protestant (or sometimes Catholic) and a non-baptized person so that the partners in that marriage may marry again.

Neither annulment nor Privilege of the Faith cases are new in the church, though the average Catholic doesn't even hear about them until it involves a friend or member of the family. The marriage you speak of quite probably involved one of these processes, and therefore was perfectly legitimate according to Catholic marriage laws. There is no reason the Catholic wife could not receive the sacraments.

Most Catholics surely know by now that a marriage of a Catholic and a Protestant can take place before a Protestant minister, provided the proper permission (technically called a Dispensation from the Form of Marriage) is obtained from the local bishop. When this happens it is quite common for the Catholic priest to share in the ceremony. I myself have done it several times when members of our parish were married in the church of the Protestant spouse.

Is My Marriage Valid?

I met my husband in 1964, and after many ups and downs through several years, we decided to marry. It was then I found out he was never baptized and really seemed to be what he always called himself — an atheist. A nun in my school had said that Catholics cannot marry someone unbaptized, so I encouraged my fiance to join a church, which he did; he was baptized in the United Church of Christ. We took his baptismal certificate to the priest, and were married.

Now I've begun to worry about our marriage, whether it is truly a marriage since I am not sure how much he wanted to be baptized in the first place. Our two children are being raised Catholic. My husband encourages their prayers and participates in the celebration of our Catholic feasts.

What can or should be done to, or with, our marriage? Is it valid? I don't know any priests here well enough to ask.

I understand your feelings, but can put your mind at ease. From what you told me, there's no question that your marriage is valid.

First, it is possible for a Catholic to marry a non-baptized person. It's done all the time. You are probably aware that a dispensation is required for a Catholic to marry one of another faith, or of no faith. Different kinds of dispensations are needed when the non-Catholic party is baptized, and when he is not baptized. However, to avoid the very problem that bothers you, normally both of these dispensations (technically called, respectively, dispensations for Mixed Religion and for Disparity of Cult) are granted in a mixed marriage. This way, whether the non-Catholic is baptized or not, the marriage is perfectly valid.

You have nothing to worry about on this score. Continue receiving the sacraments, and be happy your husband takes the supportive attitude he does concerning the faith of you and your children.

Marry "in the Church?"

My daughter plans to marry a divorced Protestant. He was baptized in the Baptist Church. Since they were told that they cannot marry in the Catholic Church, should my daughter obtain special permission from the bishop in order to marry in a Protestant church?

Is it possible that a priest can be present at the ceremony and give them some special blessing?

When the priest said your daughter and her fiance cannot marry in the church, he meant that they cannot be married according to the laws of the church, not simply that they cannot have the ceremony in the church building. A dispensation from the bishop to marry without a priest, in a Protestant church or elsewhere, is possible only when a couple are free to marry each other validly within the framework of Catholic marriage laws.

Therefore, without a declaration of nullity or other procedure (which apparently your parish priest considers unlikely) no such permission could be given, nor would a priest be present.

As a possible help to others, I should point out that your question, and your daughter's situation, is just one more illustration of the need to consider these facts of life before, not after, a person gets seriously involved with another with the possibility of marriage. The church's basic teachings and regulations concerning marriage are clear, long-standing, and readily available for the asking.

Therefore, if an individual's Catholic faith is considered personally valuable and essential, some principles and rules for personal guidance on dating and courtship must be set for oneself long before things have come to the point of planning the marriage.

Origin of Teachings on Birth Control

I know there is much controversy about birth control today, and the church is officially against it. I'm puzzled, though, on how it

came to teach what it does. Was it originated by a pope, or a council, or what? And what is the scriptural basis for it?

Thousands of pages have been written on the questions you ask.

As far as we know, Jesus never taught anything explicitly on the subject of birth control. The church's position on birth control, as well as its other moral teachings, developed gradually. Questions confronted people at various times, and the church responded.

From the time of Saint Paul, Christian teachers placed enormous emphasis on virginity, often even inside marriage. Largely as a result of this emphasis, a number of strange sects arose who attacked marriage from any of several directions. Some were materialistic and sensual; others were quite "spiritual," claiming that marriage, and especially sex, were evil and beneath the dignity of enlightened Christians.

To counteract these groups, the church had to answer the question: If virginity is so ideal, how does the church avoid being in the position of condemning marriage and sexual procreation?

The manner in which Christian teachers and theologians answered this question proved critical and significant in the church for nearly 14 centuries. One option open to them was the one suggested in St. Paul's Letter to the Ephesians: Sexual intercourse is closely associated with married love and is, among other things, important for the growth and development of that love.

However, under pressures from the social structures of the time and from the great emphasis on virginity in the church, and in order to compromise with the contempt for sexuality among these heretical groups, theology and preaching took on an entirely different direction. Sexual intercourse can be good and holy, said Christian teachers. But what makes it good and holy is procreation, the desire for a child. Thus enjoyment of sexual relations, or having intercourse as an expression of love for one's spouse, is sinful unless the couple desires to conceive a child.

Additional support was claimed for this attitude by an appeal to "nature." The obvious physical function of any organ (including sex organs) was considered "natural," entirely divorced from any relation to the whole person. As some of the great early preachers and doctors of the church put it, the natural way is the way animals do it — and animals have sexual union to procreate other animals. Human beings, therefore, should do the same.

St. Augustine, who died in the year 430, crystallized this basic attitude toward sex in his writings. His approach generally predominated in the church until perhaps 150 years ago; contraception was included in the lists of sins (penitentials) drawn up by various theologians since about the eighth century.

Until modern times, official teaching on the subject has been generally informal and local, but it has followed the attitude I just explained. In his famous Pastoral Rules, for example, Pope St. Gregory the Great (590-604) taught that married couples may have intercourse to have children, but if any enjoyment is mixed with it, they sin against the "law of marriage."

As anyone knows who has read St. Thomas Aquinas, Chaucer or Dante, this rather severe approach came under considerable suspicion, not to say disregard, through the centuries. Only since the first part of the last century, however, thanks largely to one of the great theologians of modern times (St. Alphonsus Liguori), has respectable Catholic theology accepted the fact that married love and affection possess an essential, even primary, significance in sexual intercourse.

Traditional teaching on contraception has, of course, been adhered to in all papal documents. But the essential role of the love and affection between husband and wife in sexual relations is increasingly emphasized, especially by Popes Pius XI, Paul VI and John Paul II.

Both the Old and New Testaments tell us much about the meaning of sexuality and sexual relationships between men and women. No one seriously claims today, however, that scriptural texts can solve the birth control controversy one way or the other.

Catholic teaching on the subject was summarized and repeated in the historic encyclical letter of Pope Paul VI, "Humanae Vitae" (1968). The Holy Father surveyed the traditions of the church in its respect for the conjugal and parental designs for marriage, noted the many ways nature itself causes "a separation in the succession of births," and concluded by reiterating the position of the Catholic Church: "Nonetheless, the Church, calling men back to the observance of the norms of the natural law, as interpreted by her constant doctrine, teaches that every act of marriage intercourse must remain open to the transmission of human life."

Purposes of Marriage

Your background on the church's position on birth control was very informative.

The natural sex drive and the parent instinct has a beautiful result, a new life. Isn't a secondary but nonetheless beautiful result of sex between husband and wife the relief of the stimulation of the sex urge, resulting in bodily peace, feelings of love and mental balance between the couple? That is, of course, for those who choose the married path of life.

What are the church's views on this?

You stated the church's view beautifully, with one exception. The church would not be so anxious about that word "secondary." The development of married love and peace between husband and wife is more than a secondary purpose of their life together, including the sexual side of it.

In his impressive and historic encyclical on Christian marriage ("Casti Connubii," 1930), Pope Pius XI taught that the mutual fulfillment and holiness of husband and wife is itself a "primary purpose" of the married state.

Vatican Council II, in all its statements on marriage, avoided the "primary-secondary" approach completely. All essential aspects of marriage — openness to children, mutual affection, sexual relations, and the rest — depend on and support one another.

Birth Control Interpretations

I realize that there are many opinions and interpretations about the morality of birth control since the pope spoke in his encyclical a few years ago. With so many different ideas around, has the church (and by that I guess I mean the pope) approved or rejected any of them? It would help to know where we stand.

There surely have been numerous interpretations of the church's stand since Pope Paul's "Humanae Vitae" (1968) on contraception. Many have been "official," that is, they have come from bishops, and especially from the national conferences of bishops.

Shortly after "Humanae Vitae," the bishops of Canada prepared a document on the subject for their people. They emphasized the responsibility of the Holy Father and the bishops to give direction in such an important matter. They also stressed that man's dignity lies "precisely in his ability to achieve his fulfillment in God through the exercise of a knowing and free choice."

In making these choices, they said, man has the responsibility "of forming his conscience according to truly Christian values and principles. This implies a spirit of openness to the teaching of the Church."

Then, speaking of married couples themselves, they said that couples may accept the teaching of the pope, and yet find themselves in a dilemma. Such couples "find that because of particular circumstances, *they are involved in what seems to them a clear conflict of duties,* e.g. the reconciling of conjugal love and responsible parenthood with the education of children already born, or with the health of the mother.

"In accord with the accepted principles of moral theology, if these persons have tried sincerely but without success to pursue a line of conduct in keeping with the given directives, they may be safely assured that *whoever honestly chooses the course which seems right to him does so in good conscience.*"

The Canadian bishops also noted that, because the encyclical only briefly indicates the argumentation and rational foundation for its stand, men of science, culture, and education "in some cases" find it difficult, even impossible, to accept as their own all the elements of this teaching.

"We must appreciate the difficulty experienced by contemporary men in understanding and appropriating some of the points of this encyclical," they wrote, "and we must make every effort to learn from the insights of Catholic scientists and intellectuals, who are of *undoubted loyalty to Christian truth, to the Church, and to the authority of the Holy See.*

"Since *they are not denying any point of divine and Catholic faith, nor rejecting the teaching authority of the Church,* these Catholics should not be considered, or consider themselves, shut off from the body of the faithful." (The Canadian document is considerably longer. Only the key passages are quoted and emphasized here.)

Pope Paul, of course, received a copy of the Canadian statement. Shortly afterward, Archbishop Clarizio, Apostolic Delegate to Canada, informed Canada that the pope was quite satisfied with their interpretation, and expressed his own (Clarizio's) appreciation to the bishops for explaining "such an important document with due fidelity and respect to the pope."

The bishops were also assured by Cardinal Cicognani, then papal secretary of state, that Pope Paul had seen the document and viewed it "with satisfaction."

The same situation was recognized, in fact, some years earlier by the bishops at Vatican Council II:

"This council realizes that certain conditions often keep couples from arranging their married lives harmoniously, and that they find themselves in circumstances where at least temporarily the size of their families should not be increased. As a result, the faithful exercise of love, and the full intimacy of their marriage, is hard to maintain.

"But where the intimacy of married life is broken off, its faithfulness can sometimes be imperiled and its quality of fruitfulness ruined, for then the upbringing of children and the courage to accept new ones are both endangered." (Gaudium et spes — the Church in the Modern World, no. 51)

Bishops conferences of several other countries recognized the same difficulties for married couples. The Austrian hierarchy wrote that if a married person, after full and honest reflection before God, should act against the church's teaching on contraception, "he must not feel cut off from God's love in every case, and may then receive Holy Communion without first receiving the sacrament of penance."

The American bishops "urge those who have resorted to this never to lose heart, but to continue to take full advantage of the strength which comes from the sacrament of penance, and the grace, healing and peace in the Eucharist."

The German bishops acknowledged that many cannot accept the teaching of "Humanae Vitae," and that "many priests and lay people who want to remain loyal to the Church are greatly perplexed." The bishops continue, "Pastors will respect in their work, especially in the administration of the sacraments, the decisions of conscience of the believers made in the awareness of their responsibility."

Shop Around for Birth Control?

A person asked a priest, "What do I do if a priest tells me in confession it is wrong to practice birth control?" The priest answered that all priests in the diocese are not well versed in this, and to shop around till he found the answer he wanted. Do you agree with this?

I agree with the first part, but certainly not the second. A Catholic manifests utterly no honesty with God by shopping around to get the answer he has already decided he will accept.

It is quite another thing to look for a priest you consider compassionate and informed, a priest who knows what's going on in the field which concerns your conscience, and whom you feel you can count on to respect and reflect the teaching of the church as it applies to you, with every possible consideration of your own needs.

To "shop," if necessary, for such a priest is wise. He'll be the biggest help to you in reaching a good decision.

You are, I hope, aware that several different legitimate approaches are possible in reaching a moral decision about birth control, a fact clearly evident if only from the various directions offered by national conferences of bishops as guides to priests and laity. It is, therefore, no surprise that varying approaches will be manifested by priests in their counseling. Every priest dealing with lay people has a serious obligation to be aware of the possibilities, and how his own advice is consistent with the basic principles of moral theology, especially as they permit any imposition of serious obligations.

Lay people, of course, cannot and should not rely solely on a priest for this guidance. They have a duty to make themselves at least minimally knowledgeable about essential factors in any serious decision which, after due prayer and reflection, they will be responsible for to God.

Onanism

In your history of the church's teaching about contraception, you failed to bring in the Bible. Look in the book of Genesis about con-

traception: "A detestable thing, a conjugal blasphemy that offends the highest attribute of the Father, Creation."

First, I'm not sure where you found the quote, but it is not from Scripture. Among a few things wrong with it, Creation is certainly not the highest attribute of the Heavenly Father. (His greatest attribute, by his own declaration, is his merciful, forgiving love!)

Scripture was not included in the brief history to which you refer because it has little, if anything, to say directly that is helpful regarding the morality of contraception. Indirectly, of course, it says much about the meaning and value of life, the relation of children to the love and hopes of parents, the lordship and authority of God, the importance of generosity and faith, and so on, all of which play a role in any moral decision including this one.

Presumably your reference to the Bible is to Genesis, chapter 38. Onan's brother had died. According to God's law in the Old Testament, Onan was bound to marry his brother's widow, Tamar, and have children by her if possible. The 'Levirite" law prescribed that these children would legally be not his, but his brother's. For this reason, says Genesis, whenever Onan had relations with his brother's widow, "he wasted his seed on the ground, to avoid contributing offspring for his brother. What he did greatly offended the Lord, and the Lord took his life."

The passage has often been wrongly interpreted as an explicit condemnation of contraception, and even more of masturbation. It is commonly acknowledged, however, that not the "wasting of the seed," but the refusal to observe a most serious family and tribal law was primarily responsible for Onan's condemnation and punishment.

"Worthy to Take Up Gifts?"

What do you think of divorced Catholics, who have remarried divorced persons, taking up the gifts to the altar at Mass? These people were married in the Catholic Church the first time with a Mass.

I think the proper and Christian attitude in such circumstances is:

1. happiness that the people involved are still trying to keep active in their religion and their spiritual lives, and gaining some consolation and help from their parish in what must be an extremely painful situation;

2. satisfaction that, while these persons may not be free to receive the sacraments of penance and the Eucharist, some ways have been found for them to share in the worship of God as much as possible;

3. and, the details of the divorce and remarriage, and how things

were worked out for their activities in the parish, should not be of excessive concern to you.

No one knows the full background in these cases except the individuals themselves, God, and perhaps to some degree the parish priest. And it is really nobody else's business. Only God knows how guilty of sin a person is in his or her heart for what happened in the past, or how much they may regret whatever wrong has been done.

We should regard these people, then, with the same respect and kindness we owe others — and encourage them to participate in every parish activity that is open to them.

Can Daughter Be Married in Church?

Our 21-year-old daughter has drifted away from the church in the past three years. She's now seriously interested in a young man of another faith whom we believe would be a very good husband.

Could they be married in the Catholic Church? I recall that a Catholic is not really married unless he or she is married before a priest.

Ordinarily a Catholic must be married before a priest for the marriage to be valid in the eyes of the Catholic Church.

The bishop of each diocese has authority to dispense from that requirement under certain circumstances. Sometimes, for example, the non-Catholic partner may have a particular personal or family connection with a congregation of another faith. There might even be serious prejudice against Catholics on the part of the non-Catholic or his family.

Ignoring, for the sake of your question, whatever consequences such attitudes might have on the marriage itself, the bride and groom could petition the bishop for a dispensation to be married other than before a Catholic priest. The petition is made through the Catholic partner's pastor during the time necessary papers are filed and other preparations are made for the marriage.

When such a dispensation is given, the marriage might take place before a minister, justice of the peace, or any other legally-qualified religious or civil official. The priest may, of course, be invited to the wedding, but his presence is not required for the validity of the marriage.

Nephew Married Out of Church

My niece's boy is married outside the church to a divorced girl. They tried to arrange to be married by a priest, but it took too long, so they were married at her Protestant church.

As a Catholic, am I permitted to give this boy and his wife presents or money for Christmas and their birthdays? I think a lot of him, and want to be sure I am doing the right thing.

These kinds of situations always call for difficult and often painful decisions. While one cannot presume to judge another individual before God, you obviously believe, based on your Christian convictions about marriage, that the boy has done something seriously wrong.

Surely, if he claims the right to do his thing, you have at least as much right to do yours. In no way should you be expected to deny your beliefs, or act contrary to them, or pretend you approve his actions. At the same time, you wish to preserve a good relationship in the family, and to let him know he still has your love.

My own conviction is that in such circumstances much more is gained by honey than vinegar. Give the gifts that you feel appropriate, and make sure he realizes your affection for him.

I think you owe it to him, though, to let him know clearly (and this need be done only once) how you feel about what he has done, especially since there seems to be a respectful attitude toward you as his great-aunt. You should not be in the permanent position of wondering whether he is misinterpreting your actions as an agreement with what he has done.

Should he become angry with you for saying what you think, chances are good this will be because he feels a genuine guilt over his actions, and resents being reminded of it by someone close to him. If this happens, hard as it may be for you, you will have done a considerable favor for him, both psychologically and spiritually.

Honor of One's Parents

What is meant by the commandment: Honor your father and mother?
Does this mean that if you are disobedient at home you are breaking the commandment and therefore committing a mortal sin?

Obedience to parents is surely a significant element, but we should not start with that word when we discuss the fourth commandment.

It is worth noting that in both listings of the commandments in the Old Testament (Exodus 20 and Deuteronomy 5) the word honor is used. Thus, obligation to respect and love one's parents, to care for them as necessary, lasts throughout life.

The duty of honor is a serious one. The integrity and strength of family life depends upon this relationship and, by extension, much of the respect for authority in human society grows out of that kind of family relationship.

Obviously obedience is part of this honor and respect when one is growing up under the care of one's parents, who have the primary responsibility of guiding us toward adulthood. When we are young, and when we are living within their home, their regulations and commands should be obeyed, unless, of course, those commands involve something sinful.

The seriousness of violating this or any other commandment depends on many factors. To neglect one's parents grossly, to refuse continually to show them the respect and love which they deserve simply because they are our parents, to disobey a serious and important rule — all these may be serious sins if, of course, they are fully intentional and deliberate. Most "disobediences" against parents in the normal process of daily living are a long way from this kind of serious sin.

Banns of Marriage

Are the banns of marriage announced any more? I know of several marriages of friends where they were not given in church at all. Will they be announced only if the family asks for them, or what?

The "banns of marriage" are announcements of the intended marriage of two people, with the intention that anyone aware of any impediments to the marriage will make that fact known. According to present church law, the banns are proclaimed for three successive Sundays before the marriage date in any parish where either of the two partners has a home.

There seems to be less stress on banns today than in the past, perhaps because our population is much more mobile than formerly; people who know the bride and groom are likely to be spread out much more. Also, the testimonies of family and friends required before the marriage can take place are more extensive than they used to be. However, the law concerning the banns is still in effect.

Two major reasons you will not hear the banns as often as you might expect are that they are announced only when both partners are Catholic. Even then, dispensation from publication of the banns is easily obtained from the bishop of the diocese for a good reason.

Illegitimate Child's Father

Our unmarried teen-age daughter had a child more than a year ago. Our pastor, a Catholic social worker, and a lawyer said the father's name need not appear on the birth certificate or the baptism certificate.

We moved shortly before the baby was born. The parish priest at

the new church insisted that our daughter name the biological father
or he would not baptize the child. She was upset, but wanted the
child baptized so she named the father.

This still upsets her and she would like to have this man's name
removed from the official church record. The biological father was
not Catholic and has, in fact, never even seen the child.

You had the correct advice in the beginning. The father's name
definitely does not need to appear on the birth certificate or the baptism certificate. To my knowledge, all states require the name of only
one parent on the birth certificate.

Neither is the name of the child's father required on the baptism
record. In fact any name could be given, which could easily result in
serious injustice to innocent people, so in such circumstances the
father's name should never be on a baptism record.

There really appears to be only one thing that can be done and that is
to write to the bishop and explain the situation. It is possible, however,
that at this time even the bishop could not have the name removed.

For others who might sometime be in this unfortunate situation, the
name of the father need never be on the birth certificate or the baptism
certificate. Indeed, such information can very legitimately be refused.

Guise of Annulment?

**Would any priest approve of divorce under the guise of annul-
ment?**

No individual priest, even in a marriage tribunal, makes decisions
about annulments. It would therefore be impossible for any parish
priest, for instance, to "approve of divorce under the guise of annulment." The investigations and consequent judgments in such cases go
far beyond the personal inclinations and feelings of any individual
involved in that process.

Children No Longer Go To Mass

**During our 40 years of marriage, my husband and I have had
some rough times, but we felt we had a good family.**

Three of our children survived. They all had a good Christian education and training. Our sons went to Mass often and served sometimes nearly daily. Our daughter was in the convent nearly 10 years
and left. She married, divorced, and is now living with a man. Our
children are basically good, but none of them goes to church anymore.

After years of daily Mass and Communion myself, this troubles

me greatly. My conscience is really bothered by it and I feel I must
have done something wrong. Can you give me any ideas on how to
deal with all this?

Your disappointment over your children's religious attitudes and
lifestyles is shared by many parents — which is, I realize, no great consolation to a mother and father. I have two suggestions.

We must admit genuinely that there comes a point when children
become responsible for their own lives. There comes a time at which
parents, after having done their reasonable best for their sons and
daughters, allow that responsibility to shift to their children's
shoulders.

They need not agree, or pretend to agree, with all those children do.
But a great load is lifted once we accept the fact that they are now adult
persons in their own right and must answer for their own lives.

Furthermore, parents (and for that matter, anyone who has responsibility for others) should find great consolation in knowing that
nothing done out of love for another person is ever lost. From our
human experience, and particularly as Christians with the example of
Christ before us, we believe in the transforming power of love.

The effects of our loving actions may not always appear in the way,
or at the time, we would wish. They are there nevertheless, and will
show themselves in times and places we never expect, and perhaps will
never even know about.

Even sociologists agree that children possess an uncanny instinct for
absorbing and retaining the values they perceive in their parents. Once
again, however, these effects may not reveal themselves in manners
that will easily lessen the pain of disappointment and sense of failure
on the part of parents.

In other words, when our work of being parents and nurturing does
not produce the visible results we would wish, by no means does it
follow that this work was a failure.

As the first letter of John says in the New Testament, we believe in
the power of love — the love God has for us and the love we have, in
him, for each other. This means that we do the best we can with our
admittedly limited abilities, and then trust that love will accomplish, in
its own time, place and manner, everything we hoped for.

May Godparents Overrule Parents?

My goddaughter wants to go to a public high school. Her parents
think this would be perfectly fine but I am 1,000 percent against it.
As a godparent, how much responsibility do I have? May I overrule
the parents? Our future personal relationship is at stake.

First, you are to be commended for your concern about your

godchild. Often the baptismal sponsor considers it a mere formality and considers his responsibility fulfilled if the godchild is remembered on Christmas and birthdays.

The church prescribes that baptismal sponsors assist in the preparation for baptism and help the newly baptized person persevere in his life as a Christian. When the baptized individual is a child, the sponsor is "added spiritually to the immediate family of the one to be baptized and...as occasion offers he will be ready to help the parents bring up their child to profess the faith and to show this by living it." (Introduction to the Rite of Baptism).

This fairly clearly sets the extent and the limits of the sponsors' responsibilities. The parents remain responsible for their children's upbringing, and a godparent has no right to "overrule" them if he could. Even with the person for whom he is sponsor, the godparent's authority will depend primarily on the respect and honor he has gained from his godchild by his continued, thoughtful interest, his example and his prayers.

The sponsors' obligations are always, therefore, serious, but they differ considerably from the obligations of parents. Your respect for your godchild and her family, the ease with which she is able to confide and trust in you, your sincere and persevering interest in her welfare, your example of a good Christian life, and your prayers — all these are your contributions to her in this decision which she and her parents will have to make.

Parents Reject Daughter

I would like your interpretation of the words "judge" and "condemn" in the following example.

If a girl has been married in an enforced marriage, it is obvious she has committed a sin against purity. If an accusing person (a parent of the girl) states that because she has done wrong she will never be forgiven and may never come home again, and that they never want to see her — is the parent "judging" or "condemning?" Is condemning or judging ever justifiable?

Your statements cry out for comment on a number of aspects besides your actual question. For example, under any circumstance — including pregnancy — there is no such thing as an "enforced marriage." Until the marriage ceremony itself, both partners are entirely free to marry or not. In fact, in some instances the circumstance of the girl's pregnancy might increase the urgency that they *do not* marry, and deal with the situation in a different way. Anyone who encourages such a couple in the belief that they "have to get married" is guilty of a sinful and grave injustice toward them.

Young couples whose sexual activity leads them into an unmarried pregnancy generally never stop to think of the many people they hurt, and the lives they distress in addition to their own. Among those who suffer much are, in most instances, their own parents. Even so, I find it difficult to grasp how supposedly emotionally stable parents can react to their child in the manner you describe, though I know from unhappy experience that it does happen. The Gospels, beginning with the Sermon on the Mount, abound with clear statements from Christ that this kind of attitude toward *any* sinner is unjustifiable and sinful.

Any sin committed by the two people may have been repented and forgiven long before anyone knew of the pregnancy. If God has forgiven, by what contortions of conscience could anyone assume the right to withhold forgiveness, to play God in this brutal way? And this at a time when genuine unselfish support and love from the parents may be needed more than ever!

There is, after all, still such a thing as hating the sin — which we must — and loving the sinner, which we also must. Each time we pray the Our Father, we ask God to "forgive us as we forgive" those who offend us. Do the parents or others you describe really want God to treat them as sinners, the way they treat someone else?

An Alcoholic Husband

My husband and I have been married about 40 years. Before we were married I had an affair that was a very unpleasant situation.

Eighteen months after we were married, my husband, who was in the service, wrote to ask me if I had sexual relations before our marriage. I confessed. He came home permanently about two years later after our second child was born.

When my husband is sober and working, he's a fine person. But when he is drunk, he accuses me of having affairs and other things I would not think of doing. As a child I lived a good Christian life and I still go to Mass and Communion almost every day. Yet he still accuses me of these awful things. I have never cheated on him, and have kept my marriage vows.

When I told my doctor about this situation with my husband, she said he was using me for some guilt he had. This man has never told me in person that he loves me; he has written it, but never said it. Forty years is too long to do this. I need your help or advice on handling this. It's getting too much for me anymore.

Your letter is one more proof of something that cannot be said often enough. Confessions by husbands and wives of what went on before the marriage generally accomplish nothing except to threaten the atmosphere of that relationship for the rest of their lives.

This is particularly true when one partner prompts, or tries to force, such a confession from the other. So many negative factors are at work here that pushy questioning about such matters offers a quite sufficient reason to wonder about the love or emotional stability of one's partner. A normal person would possibly not want to know such information, and even more would not want to inflict the pain that such a confession would cause someone he loves.

These things are, and should be, kept between oneself and God. You cannot go back and relive your life, but maybe what I've said can help put your situation in a little better perspective.

I agree with your doctor. Your husband's attitude through all these years says something more about him than it does about you. From your letter it seems to me you are handling the situation as well as possible. What you're saying is that his continued lack of consideration, to put it mildly, hurts you deeply. I understand that. But your own persevering patience, love, prayer, and understanding will enable you to go on coping with it.

You cannot do this alone. Friends or counselors whom you can trust are essential. From my mail and my personal experience, however, I can't be too insistent in recommending Al-Anon, a group related to Alcoholics Anonymous, but consisting of the spouses and children of people who are addicted to alcohol. Members can help you cope with the Jekyll-Hyde personality your husband displays, and help you understand how to depend on God and others for help.

Al-Anon or Alcoholics Anonymous should be listed in your phone book. If not, write to Al-Anon Family Group Headquarters, Box 182, Madison Square Station, New York, N. Y., 10010.

Help After Divorce

I need your advice desperately. I am a Catholic and my family has been Catholic for generations. About nine years ago I married a non-Catholic man. After seven years of heartbreak and disappointment, I finally got the courage to face defeat and get a divorce. I know I should have done it sooner, but I felt like I failed. Even now, after two years, I feel ashamed of it and hate the word divorce; it's like death.

My former husband did not want to give up his single lifestyle after marriage, like drinking with the boys regularly and coming home when he felt he wanted. A lot of other things were involved, but the hardest part was when I found out after we married that we could not have children. I thought we would adopt, but he absolutely refused. I prayed for a long time that he would change his mind, but he didn't.

I'm going on 34 years old, and if it's God's will, I hope to marry again and have a child before I get older. I do, however, want to marry in the church and with God's blessing. I'm writing to you to say I would like an annulment and I feel I really deserve one. I need your advice on this greatly.

You obviously have been hurt much during the past years and feel frustrated and betrayed. I hope you will be able to find the way toward new hope in your life, and a way to put things back together for yourself.

The first thing you should have, even more than an annulment, and which I am sure you want deeply, is a healing of all these past hurts and some serenity of mind so that you can make a new beginning in your life. I urge you as strongly as I can to search for some assistance to achieve this healing. Whether it is through confidences you can share with a wise friend, or with one of the many groups that are designed to help people such as yourself get a new start, or perhaps both. Many people have suffered the same kinds of collapse you experience and have learned much about how to help others through these same tragedies.

A new movement called "Beginning Experience" is gradually spreading around our country to give precisely this kind of support and guidance to divorced, widowed and separated Catholics. You may obtain information about this movement by contacting Beginning Experience, 3100 W. 41st St., Sioux Falls, S.D., 57105.

The details you give in your letter make me strongly suspect that the marriage tribunal of your diocese would accept your case to investigate for a possible annulment. This would require, however, that you discuss the matter with a priest in your area who would begin the process.

I understand your reluctance to discuss the matter with a priest who knows your family well. Ask a friend in another area of the city to suggest a priest who may not be an acquaintance of yours, but who would be open to talking with you. Follow his advice. You might also ask him to suggest ways of finding the type of personal assistance I spoke of above.

The Church

People of God

Why is there now so much talk in the Catholic Church about the "people of God?" I presume the phrase means to include us. Is it the same as "the church?" If so, why not just say so?

The term "people of God" — used quite prominently by Vatican Council II — is a much broader name than "church," particularly if we mean it in the very limited sense of Roman Catholic Church.

The phrase comes from the Old Testament, where the people of Israel frequently are called the people of God: that is, a group set apart by God as recipients of special blessings from him.

In the New Testament, the death and resurrection of Jesus and the proclamation of this great event by the preaching of the Gospel gave rise to a new "people of God," brought together not by their own initiative, but by God's own action. (The Greek word for church, "ecclesia," means literally a group called out, or called apart.)

The church, in the sense of the recipients of God's saving work in the world through Christ, obviously can be looked at in different ways. As any mystery, no one description or definiton can convey the entire meaning. The phrase "Mystical Body of Christ," for example, as generally understood, focuses on the more *specific* claims an individual may have for union with Jesus, such as baptism, membership in the "organized" church, explicit belief in certain doctrines, and so on.

"People of God," however, focuses rather on the more *general* claims that give to mankind a right to God's mercy and other blessings — the Incarnation, and the death and resurrection of Jesus. This seems to be the reason for increased use of that name today, especially by Vatican II, which clearly preferred "the people of God" to other titles, such as the Mystical Body of Christ.

"The One, True Church?"

Can we as Catholics still say that the Roman Catholic Church is the one, true, Catholic and apostolic church? And that we alone possess the truth?

Understanding these qualities in a very carefully defined way, as the church understands them, the answer would be yes. However, I'm afraid that in the sense you mean (and as many Catholics and most Protestants probably think the church means them) the answer would have to be no.

When we call the Catholic Church "true," for example, it certainly does not mean that we believe that we alone possess the truth. Catholic theology not only holds that other churches can profess and teach truth, but also that the Holy Spirit is working within them in a real way with his light and love. This is especially true in Christian churches, but can be true of other religions as well — most certainly and obviously, of course, of the Jewish faith, which shares many essential traditions with Christianity.

Any sincere Catholic does believe that in the Catholic Church there are certain channels of truth and grace and intimacy with Jesus that normally are not present in the traditions, liturgy, and life of other churches. If he did not believe this, one would assume he would belong to another church — or none at all. The same would presumably be true, of course, of any sincere Methodist, Baptist, or Lutheran — for the same reasons.

Our beliefs in this matter were stated well and often in Vatican Council II. We believe that "the one true religion subsists in the catholic and apostolic church"; that truth imposes its demands on the human conscience "by the power of its own truth" and not by coercion, and that the Spirit's gift of truth must be honored wherever it is found. (See the Declaration on Religious Freedom, Art. 1, which is quoted here, and the Decrees on Ecumenism, Art. 2, and on the Church, Lumen Gentium, Art. 15.)

Explaining the Catholic Religion

Can you recommend a book that explains the Catholic religion? I was born and raised in the faith and suddenly realize I do not understand much of it. Maybe it's because of the changes in the church over the past 10 or 15 years, but I'm confused a great deal and need something to explain Catholic belief to me as an adult. I think that there are a lot of others who will appreciate the same help.

I'm sure other priests have their favorites, too, but since you're asking me, my recommendation would have to be a book called "Christ

Among Us: A Modern Presentation of the Catholic Faith" by Anthony Wilhelm. It treats all the major areas of Catholic liturgy, belief, and practice concisely yet with enough explanation and background to satisfy any adult Catholic wanting to review the fundamentals of his faith.

It is published by Paulist Press in paperback. Be sure to get the latest revised edition.

An adult religious education series, "Know Your Faith," is carried weekly in the majority of diocesan papers in the United States and Canada. This series is another valuable source of information on many current aspects of Catholic life and beliefs.

What Is The Magisterium?

I am a fairly recent convert to the Catholic faith, but I keep coming across a word in our Catholic paper which I never heard during my instructions. What (or who) is the "magisterium?"

The word "magisterium" comes from another Latin word, "magister" (teacher); it means the power, or duty, of teaching and leading.

Before Our Lord died, he promised his followers that the Holy Spirit, whom he would send, would bring to their minds all that he had told them. Magisterium is the word we use to indicate the authority and responsibility the church has in fulfilling that promise of Christ, the responsibility and charismatic power to be the faithful interpreter of God's word to mankind. It is, in other words, the human instrument Jesus uses to keep his people from serious and dangerous mistakes in their understanding of God and of man's salvation.

This responsibility is personalized and focused in the Holy Father, and in the bishops of the world together with him — a tradition we Catholics believe continues the pattern set by Jesus in placing this responsible authority in Peter, and in the other apostles with him. Because they are in this way the official interpreters and guardians of revealed truths, the bishops and the pope are also often referred to as the church's Magisterium.

This duty is, of course, not carried out in a vacuum. As Pope Paul VI noted some years ago, the Magisterium reveals no new truths, but is to be a "faithful echo" of the Divine Word and of Holy Scripture. In this, pope and bishops need the input, support, and assistance of all others in the church. These would include laity and clergy — who, by the witness of their daily lives help toward a deeper understanding of the teachings of Jesus — theologians, other teachers, and so on.

The Magisterium is one always-living way Our Lord honors his promise to his followers, to "keep them in the truth."

Next Ecumenical Council?

When was the last Ecumenical Council before the one a few years ago? When will the next one be, and do you think it will cause as much confusion as the last one?

The last Ecumenical Council before Vatican II (1962-1965) was Vatican I (1869-1870). Since the councils are called only when the need arises, the next one may be 10 or 100 years from now.

As for confusion, the next one will likely be similar to most past ecumenical councils; as much will depend on the preparation and renewal that happens before it, as what happens during it. Ecumenical Councils are not known for their settling effect on the life of the church, at least at short range. They usually deal with major historic challenges facing the Catholic people, so one would not expect them to be characterized by tranquility and lack of controversy.

Accepting the Changes

I converted to the Catholic faith about 23 years ago. Since then, so many of the things I identified with the church at that time have changed. It's hard, not only for me, but even for some of my friends who were born Catholics. How do we keep our balance in all these changes, especially the differences in Catholic teaching, and learn to take things in stride?

This question is among the most common I receive, and one of the most difficult. For one thing, any answer must be a quite personal one. Much depends on one's own temperament and faith.

The first requirement is a positive and hopeful attitude about the revolutionary developments going on around us. It seems clear that mankind is on the threshold of a new age; its life on earth — socially, politically, economically and even religiously — will be drastically changed from what we have known. Such a time in history always brings confusion, false starts, tentative hopes and many frustrations, as well as widely conflicting views on how to move into this future creatively without losing what is good from the past.

It shouldn't surprise us that Christians, including our Catholic Church, share in this turmoil and suffering. In fact, it would be cause for alarm only if the church (and that means you and I) were placidly going its own way, not being involved and hurting with those pains and fears that today tear at men's hearts.

In spite of the suffering and upset that accompanies it, this process of change and new birth has been a positive and incredibly revealing experience for the church, and it can be a beautiful and rewarding experience for us, too, if we let it.

The differences you mention are surely real. The difference between the way previous councils (for example, Trent in the 16th century, or Vatican I in the 19th century) talked about such things as the church, God, man and his human sacredness, and the meaning of the Incarnation of the Word of God, and the way Vatican Council II discussed them, is unprecedented in the church. This development has pointed the way toward a vastly enriched approach to prayer, to faith and hope, and to love of God and the world.

These happenings in theology and other areas of Catholic life are not a denial of what was taught in the past; they reflect rather a growing awareness that there is room for many more varieties of approach to the great mysteries about God and man than we once thought. The life of the church, as any other life, is not simply a handing down of neatly tied truths and practices. It is a continuing, adventuresome opening up to truth as the events of history and the grace of the Holy Spirit reveal it to us.

There's risk in all this, of course, and that's where the scope of one's faith comes into the picture. It becomes, frankly, a question of whether one really still believes in God — and of how big a God (and church) one believes in. We Christians know that, by his coming as man, Jesus embraced this poor earth and all creation — including the persons, events and processes of today. We believe that by his resurrection and exaltation with the Father, he is vitally present — today as in the past — as healer and savior, and that he already stands at the end of history as the Lord and Victor-King for all his people. This is the absolute heart of the matter.

It seems to me that God is much more honored by our keeping our eyes and our work focused on that great fact of his lordship, than by our being picky and fearful that every change (or every new weird idea, for that matter) signals the imminent collapse of the church, or of God's influence in the world.

To paraphrase a recent bumper sticker, I don't know about yours, but my God isn't cringing in the corner — and neither is my church.

I hope this approaches a helpful response to your question. Work hard for those things we Christians stand for — justice, truth and down-to-earth love for God and our fellow man — and then learn to be a little serene and enjoy the excitement. I have a feeling that's somehow what Jesus is doing, so why shouldn't we?

What Is the Roman Rota?

Our daily paper carried a story not long ago about the Roman Rota. We have also seen it mentioned several times in reference to reform in the church. What is it — and why do some apparently think that it is a problem?

The Roman Rota is the name of the highest standing "court" in the Catholic Church. It goes back about 800 years, and at one time had enormous power. Appeal from its decisions even to the pope himself was impossible without the establishment of a special papal commission.

Today, the Rota hears all types of cases, most of them dealing with marriage, and almost always on appeal from a lower church court. It is made up of about 18 judges (called auditors), who are divided into groups of three to hear and decide cases.

In general, objections to the Rota simply reflect the belief of many that a decentralization of court procedures would be desirable; for instance, it might be arranged that most judicial cases which now must go to Rome for final action would be handled instead entirely within each country.

Among other things, it is argued, such decentralization would reduce considerably the time required (often several years) to obtain a decision from the over-worked offices in Rome.

Can A Priest Marry?

We recently received word that a close friend who is a priest is planning to marry. This disturbed me greatly because I believed that the priests who did this were not good priests anyway, and I always thought he was a good priest.

What is his status in the church now? What should be our attitude toward him? Can we in good conscience retain his friendship?

Many Catholics still do not realize that it is possible for a priest to be released from his promise not to marry. Unlike marriage, whose nature and permanence are established by God himself, the celibacy of the priesthood is something the church could change, and has changed, in various ways through the centuries.

Jesus established the priesthood to serve his people in various ways, but he never made it his absolute rule that priests could not be married. In fact, married priests have been common in some parts of the world since the beginning of Christianity.

If a priest simply ignores the solemn promise he has made to remain unmarried, it would be wrong. It is entirely possible for him, however, to ask for and receive a release from that promise; in that case, he could marry and remain in perfectly good standing in the church as a layman.

Without his telling you, there's hardly any way you can know what his status is now, since these matters are naturally handled very privately. If you are a close friend, ask him. I think it is only fair that you should know, as it inevitably affects your feelings toward him.

Whatever the answer is, it doesn't mean he was not a good priest. If he did abandon his promise of celibacy without a dispensation, he possibly cut corners and neglected prayer a lot more than he should have, but God is the judge of that.

As for continuing your relationship with him, it can never be anything but right to be a friend to anyone — a thoughtful and honest friend. Try to understand and have the courage to be, and say to him, what you believe is best for him and for the others you must think of.

No Franciscan Monsignors?

Recently a number of priests in our archdiocese were named monsignors. There were no "order" priests among them, though we have many Franciscans in our area. Why is it that members of religious orders are not named monsignors?

The word "monsignor" is from a French word meaning "my lord." It apparently was first used in anything like the current sense during the "exile" of the popes in Avignon during the 14th century, and has been an honorary title for a wide range of laymen, priests and bishops who served as part of the papal household. More recently it has become somewhat of a gift to certain priests from their bishop, who wished to reward them for work or reponsibilities by petitioning the Holy Father to designate them honorary members of the pope's household, with the title of monsignor.

It seems that, because of the honorary nature of the position and because it would appear to set some members of the order above others without any real authority, members of religious orders and congregations have traditionally declined such honors.

Was Vatican II A First?

I recently read a remark by a prominent writer that the second Vatican Council was actually the first really ecumenical council. I understood that there were many before this one. What did he mean?

It's true that there were many ecumenical councils before Vatican Council II. It's also true, if one wishes to be geographically and numerically literal, they were not truly ecumenical — that is, worldwide. Possibly the most significant council in modern times, for example, at least in its long range influence on Catholic life and belief, was the Council of Trent. It started in 1545, after eight years of agonizing preparatory work, with only 25 bishops and four cardinals at the opening Mass. Dragging out for 19 years, with 25 separate sessions, it never enjoyed — for various political and religious reasons — the presence of more than a small minority of those eligible to attend.

More recently, the first Vatican Council opened in 1869 with about 700 bishops, out of about 1,050 eligible, on hand, and 500 of these were from Europe. At some sessions, only around 100 bishops were present.

During Vatican II, however, about 2,900 bishops and prelates were invited. Over 2,500 attended the opening in 1961, and 2,400 the closing in 1965. Based on numbers and on areas of the world represented, it was by far the most "ecumenical" council in history.

It is not primarily numbers or geography that makes an ecumenical council. The other councils were ecumenical insofar as their actions were at least accepted and approved by the Bishop of Rome, and were applicable to the whole church.

Women Counselors in the Church?

Don't you think we need women counselors in the church? No matter how hard a priest may try to listen to a woman's problem, especially a marital one, he will ultimately dismiss it as trivial because he cannot understand the importance of it to her.

The first important requisite for effective counseling is at least some degree of competence — that is, the ability to identify a problem when someone presents it, and to have some clear ideas on how to treat the problem or help the client to handle it. It also includes an awareness of one's limitations in providing assistance or therapy, and how and when to guide a client to appropriate further assistance.

Most priests today are very much aware, perhaps far more than most lay people are, that ordination of itself does not carry with it this kind of competence, especially for more complicated personal or family pathologies, which is why a large number of priests continue their studies to increase their ability in this phase of their work.

Much depends on the individual you consult — his kindness and understanding, and your confidence in him. Perhaps your first mistake, therefore, was in failing to search around for a priest who you would have reason to believe had some kind of experience, competence, and wisdom you could trust.

While a qualified counselor of either sex (whether married or unmarried) ought to have sufficient basic insights to help an individual of the other sex, it can easily be that for some individuals the most help will come from a counselor of the same sex, if for no other reason than that client feels more comfortable with the arrangement. At any rate, most counseling services, including Catholic social agencies, generally try to staff both men and women, who are available if you ask.

Women's Role in Church

Women in the Catholic faith are encouraged to participate in church activities which include serving on school boards, parent-teacher organizations, parish councils, liturgy committees, and other planning groups.

Others play a vital role in religious education as nuns, CCD teachers, or just plain Mom. Women have been the backbone of many right-to-life groups. They are also asked to be readers at Mass and distribute Communion.

And yet, our daughters are not permitted to serve Mass. What is the reason? Does the church really teach that women are inferior? (One priest I asked said that was nonsense; but I wonder.) Perhaps this restriction was reasonable in the past, but it certainly does not make sense today.

Yours is a difficult question to deal with because the picture of the ministry of women in the church is thoroughly confusing.

The law, of course, is clear: Women are not eligible for ordination to the diaconate or the priesthood, or for installation into the ministries (formerly minor orders) of lector (reader) or acolyte. Other liturgical regulations, however, allow women, at least in some circumstances, to perform nearly all the functions of both reader and acolyte, except what we would call serving Mass.

In his Apostolic Letter on the reform of Minor Orders (Aug. 15, 1972), Pope Paul lists the duties of reader: reading the Scripture and responsorial psalm, presenting the intentions of the prayer of the faithful, directing singing and other participation by the faithful, preparing other Scripture readers, and "instructing the faithful for the worthy reception of the sacraments." All these can be and are done by women.

Acolytes serve as special ministers of the Eucharist, and as assistants to the deacon and priest during the Eucharistic Liturgy. They may also expose the Blessed Sacrament for adoration, and instruct others in their function in the liturgy. Again, of these four acolytes' duties, church law now allows two of them, the first and fourth, to be performed by women.

No one, to my knowledge, has given any reason this should be. If closeness to the Eucharist is the criterion, distributing Communion seems of higher dignity than bringing the wine and water and holding the paten.

Concerning the inferiority of women, there are some embarrassing theological traditions that must be faced, because they cannot help but influence attitude and regulations about women's role in the liturgy.

For example, one of the latest comprehensive series of Latin theology textbooks was published only within the past few decades by an American theologian. The volume on the Sacrament of Orders reflects a long theological trend when it says that women should not be allowed to have the office of teacher because of their "natural condition of inferiority and subjection." Being weaker, they "are inept for the heavy labors of the social and ecclesiastical life." (!!) Their moral feebleness "is manifest in the lightness of judgment, in credulity, and in the fragility of spirit by which she is less able to reign in the passions, particularly concupiscence."

This was written in 1962, but the idea is not new. St. Thomas Aquinas said women cannot really be said to be continent, "just as brute animals are not able to be continent, for there is nothing in them that is able to oppose the appetites."

No wonder so many Catholics feel there's an urgent need for some radical rethinking of the position and role of women in the church.

Altar Girls

Is it permissible now for a parish to have altar girls at Mass? A parish in our area has had altar girls for a long time, and I know the bishop is aware that this is going on.

It is definitely still against the regulations of the church for girls or women to function as servers at Mass. The ruling was reiterated by the Vatican in the past few years. As I remarked above, this regulation is understandably confusing since nearly every other ministry at Mass, except that of deacon and priest, can now be filled by women as well as men.

I suppose you are right in saying the bishop is aware of the situation. But don't draw any conclusions from that. One day Pope John XXIII was asked how he managed to deal with the overwhelming responsibilities of the papacy. He said, "I try to see everything, overlook much, and change a little." Most bishops with whom I am acquainted try to follow that wise philosophy.

Ordained After Sex Change?

If a woman has an operation to change her sex, can she be ordained a Catholic priest? One priest I asked about it said no, because his/her baptismal certificate would indicate the child was female. Another told me there were a lot of technicalities involved. Do you know the answer?

The present canon law of the church requires that one be a member of the male sex to be ordained to the priesthood (Canon 968.) Thus, the critical question is: How does one decide whether an individual is a man or a woman? — a question, one might imagine, that caused little loss of sleep for those who drew up the code of church law 60 years ago.

The baptismal record might be one way, but it could be objected by some that the sex identity evident in infancy did not reflect the real psychological make-up of the child.

One might ask how the psychology of the person matches up against a description of male or female characteristics. But many psychological experts, unable to integrate into their doctrines the general common sense of human experience, aren't able to agree that there even are such characteristics.

A more physical criterion would be genetic analysis. Every cell of the human body carries a sex-signature in the genes which identify that person as physically male or female. No "sex-change" operation changes that genetic identity.

Administration of sex hormones and cosmetic surgery may modify external sex characteristics to some extent, but not to a degree significant enough to influence a decision like this.

If the question ever arises, the answer to whether such a person could be ordained to the priesthood would, of course, come from the Sacred Congregation for the Discipline of the Sacraments. For the above reasons and others, I would give about 1,000 to one odds the answer would have to be no.

What Is the Hebrew Rite of the Church?

Can you explain what the Hebrew Rite of the Catholic Church is? I have heard that this is a way for Jews to remain Jews and still become Catholics. How can this be?

There is no such thing as a Hebrew Rite of the Catholic Church. An intriguing suggestion has been made in recent years from some private sources that the formation of such a rite be considered, but no serious study of the matter has been made, to my knowledge, by any Catholic authorities.

The proposed rite would function much as other non-Latin rites of the church (Byzantines, etc.) Ultimately subject to the Holy Father, they would have their own patriarch in Rome or Jerusalem. All Hebrew Roman Catholics would be eligible to join the rite. Jewish feasts would be observed in a manner compatible with Catholicism; the rite would have church buildings in harmony with its own traditions, and eventually a Hebrew liturgy would be prepared and used.

In other words, the purpose would be that Catholics of Hebrew descent might maintain their racial and cultural identity for themselves and their children, removing what is presumed to be some of the main objections Jewish people have to becoming Christians and Catholics.

The idea is innovative and interesting. No one knows yet how acceptable the proposal might be to Jewish men and women who may be inclined toward the Catholic faith, or to the church officials.

Priests and Politics

I've never heard a good answer to this, and it seems to be getting worse instead of better. Why do so many young, modern priests feel they have to demonstrate, march, and get involved in all these political causes? It seems to me they ought to leave that up to us lay people.

When was the last time you yourself demonstrated, spoke out courageously, or in some way, as the saying goes, "put your body on the line" for mankind's great needs like peace, racial and social justice, or feeding the hungry? In all candor, the answer to your question may lie in your answer to mine.

Our individual temperaments, abilities and personal inclinations will determine how we each should fulfill this obligation. One doesn't necessarily have to carry signs to be a good Catholic. But if our Christian and Catholic faith has anything significant to offer in forming policies about these great concerns, someone has to shout it from the housetops — or whatever else is needed to get these ideals out in the daylight and prompt men to consider them.

You'll notice that even the pope and bishops find it necessary today to take "political" positions on matters that were not considered the church's business only a generation ago. If in doing this they seem to be moving too much out of the sacristy, perhaps it's because they're trying to teach us that when it comes to justice, peace, and civic responsibility, our faith demands more, and more specific, things from us than we thought.

Why Don't Priests Keep Up?

I know our priests have more than enough to do, but I think there should be some kind of courses or classes to help them keep up with what is happening in the church.

A lot of parish problems seem to come because a priest does not accept, or even know about, things that a lot of the people know. Why aren't there required classes or programs to keep the priests up-to-date, like the ones doctors and lawyers must attend?

The assumption has been that priests, just as others whose work involves a good deal of professional competence, will have sufficient intelligence to know that their special field is always changing and developing, and that their competence will soon deteriorate unless they keep themselves sharp on these developments. By far most of them, I believe, do recognize this need and responsibility and seriously continue their education year by year.

Numerous seminars or other educational programs are available to American priests annually to help them remain aware and competent in the subjects needed in their work — theology, counseling, Scripture, the spiritual life and so on. Priests are urged, sometimes by diocesan regulations, to take advantage of these opportunities regularly.

Because many do not, however, there is increasing discussion of making some sort of continuing education plan obligatory for all priests, just as associations of physicians, attorneys, and other professionals are putting more teeth into similar requirements for their members.

Priests in Ties?

In newspapers and magazines, we see a lot of priests, especially theologians, in non-clerical dress. Father Hans Kung is one that we never see in a collar. What's happening? Are they still priests?

Yes, they are still priests. And, as far as priests' clothes are concerned, there isn't that much happening.

Clergy dress is a very mixed bag. Much depends on where and when the priest happens to live. For centuries priests and bishops wore no distinctive garb at all, even when celebrating the liturgy. Later, liturgical vestments developed, and even later, the clergy's daily wear was "clerical" only in that it reflected the fact that many of them were either monks or professors.

The Council of Trent (in the 1500s) simply said clergy should wear clothing "comformable to their order, that by the propriety of their outward apparel they may show forth the inward uprightness of their morals." No color or style was required. A rule made for the American Church in 1884, and theoretically still in force, required that priests wear a Roman collar with a dark coat that reached the knees!

In recent decades, while American priests were in Roman collar, priests in Germany quite properly wore white shirt and tie. (The Protestants wore the Roman collar.) And in Italy, priests wore a black cassock everywhere, except, I presume, in bed.

In my own diocese, our regulation is that "lifestyle, dress, leisure activity and public behavior should be left to the mature judgment of priests themselves."

By no means do I imply that some sort of distinctive dress is not valuable or appropriate. But don't be too quick to jump to conclusions because of what you see.

"Resigned" Priests and Mass

This question caused quite a disagreement at our study club: When a priest leaves the priesthood, can he still offer Mass and hear confessions? I am a convert to the Catholic faith, and I remember the priest saying, "Once a priest, always a priest." But some of my friends disagree.

When a person is baptized, he is, as you know, established in a permanent basic relationship and identity with Jesus Christ — an identity that will always be there. No matter what good or evil he may do in the future, he remains a baptized Christian with all that implies.

Something very similar happens when a man is ordained to the priesthood. When he receives this sacrament, he is established in a new and special relationship to Jesus and his church, which involves certain functions and responsibilities in the service of other Christians and of all people.

The "power" to fulfill these services — for example, offering the sacrifice of the Eucharist or administering the sacrament of penance — is, therefore, never lost. Some old catechisms used to say that the sacraments of baptism, confirmation and holy orders "placed an indelible mark on the soul." The phrase is a poor one because it can be so easily misunderstood in a variety of ways; but it does carry the message that something permanent happens in our relationship to God and our fellow Christians when these sacraments are received.

Hence, personal priestly powers to fulfill these services are never lost. However, a man who has "left the priesthood" may not normally offer Mass or hear confessions. For excellent and obvious reasons having to do with the spiritual good of all, the church forbids such a man to exercise these functions except in extreme emergencies — for instance, if a dying person wished to go to confession or receive the Eucharist, and no other priest were available.

Mary, the Mother of God?

I am a Protestant reader of your column. Most things about the Catholic faith, even your dogmas, I can pretty much agree with. But calling Mary the mother of God really turns me off. How can anyone be God's mother?

Your misgivings are understandable. On the face of it, such a title for Mary sounds at least ridiculous, if not blasphemous.

Perhaps it will help if you understand when and how that phrase was first officially applied to her. In the early centuries after Christ, a large and powerful Christian sect, called Nestorians, taught that when Jesus was born he was just a man. As he grew up, they said, God sort of "saddled" him somehow, and "used" him to perform the work of our salvation.

The main body of early Christians had come to realize and believe that Jesus was both God and man from the very beginning of his life. They recognized that this Nestorian doctrine was dangerous to the whole theology of salvation. If Jesus was not really God, or was not really and fully human, something essential would be lacking in the saving work of reuniting God and mankind, which we believe was accomplished by Jesus.

The matter came to a head in 431 at the Council of Ephesus, the third Ecumenical Council. After long and often heated discussion, the council decided that the shortest and most direct way to pinpoint the basic belief that Jesus is truly God is to say simply: Mary is the mother of God — not from eternity, of course, but as he comes into this world in his human nature, in the womb of Mary. No one can accept that brief statement without believing that Jesus is both divine and human. He had a *mother* as we did, and therefore he is one of us. And yet the child of that mother was *God*, not by some later fiction, but as he came from her womb.

The Greek title "Theotokos" (God-bearer) was already commonly applied to Mary in Christian worship and devotion long before the Council of Ephesus.

As you can see, the title "Mother of God" came into official Christian doctrine as a vital part of belief about Jesus himself, not primarily as a way to honor Mary. It does, of course, reflect much honor on her to have had such an intimate share in God's plan of salvation.

Can We Change Parishes?

If the priest of one's parish does not allow certain liturgical practices approved by the church, is it permissible to go to another parish for Mass? Could I join that parish?

These are big questions, but they are closely related. Without getting too involved in theology, we must remember that the church, while made up of millions of members, only really "lives" in the comparatively small community of Christians who pray and especially offer the Eucharist together. This is where the church finds its identity, where it meets Christ, where it becomes identified with him in his death, resurrection and glorification.

For centuries, this kind of community meant a locality, a small area in which a group of people lived and did nearly everything together. Our Catholic traditions and laws concerning parishes developed in such situations.

In today's more mobile society, however, except in small towns, it is hardly more than a legal fiction to say that members of a parish are "neighbors." A person's "community" is far less likely to be based on where he lives than on his work, education, recreation, social life — and even on his religious and apostolic activities, including the liturgy.

Thus, the church recognizes national origin, for instance, as a consideration in establishing national parishes (Irish, German, Italian, Polish, etc) as distinct from parishes based solely on geographical boundaries.

Today especially, the church allows wide varieties in parish liturgies. Not only Masses, but the whole spirit and atmosphere of parishes will differ depending on how both priest and people understand the church and the liturgy, and what they believe a Christian community ought to be.

Current regulations of the church seem to recognize these kinds of factors since they simply ask Catholics, insofar as it is convenient, to participate in divine worship and hear the word of God in their own parish church frequently — obviously, therefore, not to the exclusion of other churches. (Code of Canon Law No. 476)

Your second question is more complicated. In one sense, since most parishes are territorial, one does not normally join a parish any more than he joins a diocese. He is simply in one.

For the reasons mentioned above, policies and attitudes in most parts of the country are much more flexible in this regard than formerly. In his sincere concern for the health of the whole church family, however, it seems to me a Catholic should preserve some sense of responsibility toward the people of the parish in which he lives, even though he may attend and participate in another parish community as well.

Want A "Christian Community"

What advice would you give to parishioners who want very much to have Christian community in the parish, but because of circumstances, it is not available, nor is communication whereby the situation might be reversed.

A living Christian community is obviously not something that is "available" or not, in the same manner as a parish school or boy scout troup might be available. A genuine community is a warm and personal thing, a gradual growth that involves shared and deeply felt faith, goals, experience, loves, hopes and even failures and disappointments.

I presume you mean, therefore, that as you see it the machinery for sharing in this kind of Christian community is simply not present, at least for some significant number of parishioners. In this case several questions might be asked.

Are you sure that what you desire *can* be done, legally, within the present church regulations concerning the liturgy, the parish, or other elements involved?

Are you sure that any significant number of parishioners really want the things you (perhaps very correctly) believe the parish should provide? Chances are good that in any parish many members have only the foggiest notion of what the words "Christian community" mean in the first place, and couldn't care less whether or not any more changes are thrust upon them. Since priests, like everyone else, differ temperamentally in their inclinations as leaders or followers, perhaps your job at the moment is to talk around, test your ideas with other parishioners, and see if you and they might share the same needs and suggestions — and then take them to the parish priest. I know of no priest who is on principle opposed to what might make better Christians and Catholics out of a significant part of his parish, though it is painfully obvious that he and his parishioners may often be poles apart in their view of what constitutes a "good Christian," or a good Christian community.

Finally, you might ask yourself: How far is it to a church that better meets the spiritual needs of my family, as I see them? In all fairness, it must be acknowledged that Catholic Church law is extremely permissive in the leeway it provides individuals as to where they will worship and hear the Word of God — and hence where they will find their "Christian community."

When Does the Pope Speak Infallibly?

According to Catholic teaching, when does the pope speak infallibly? Is it in an encyclical, or what? Could you give an example of such a teaching?

While he was still here on earth with his disciples, Jesus told his followers that he would be with them always, and that the Spirit he would send would keep them always in the truth.

It is our Catholic belief that this promise is fulfilled in part by the fact that, under certain conditions, the Holy Father, as the focal point of Catholic unity and faith, is invested in a special way personally with this promise of Jesus to keep the church free from error.

This unique certitude of truth — infallibility — is present, we believe, when the pope speaks precisely as chief shepherd and teacher of the church on matters of divine faith or morals, and clearly intends to use the full powers of his role in the church in that solemn manner. This, we believe, is the service he is called on to offer his fellow Catholics as chief bishop in the church.

The infallible nature of a teaching depends not on the type of document in which it is included, but on the intention of the Holy Father made clear in the statement itself. Theoretically, it could be on the back of an envelope.

The latest doctrine considered to be taught with such infallibility was that of the Assumption of Mary, declared by Pope Pius XII in 1950.

The last one before that, in 1854, concerned the Immaculate Conception of Our Lady.

Toward the end of a long encyclical, (Munificentissimus Deus), analyzing the long history of the doctrine of the Assumption through the centuries, Pope Pius defined the teaching with these solemn words:

"We have poured forth prayers of supplication again and again to God, and have called upon the Spirit of Truth. Now, for the glory of Almighty God, who has lavished his special affection upon the Virgin Mary; for the honor of her Son, the undying King of the Ages and Victor over sin and death; for the increase of the glory of that revered mother; and for the joy and exultation of the entire church:

"By the authority of our Lord Jesus Christ, of the Blessed Apostles Peter and Paul, and by our own authority, we pronounce, declare, and define it to be a divinely revealed dogma that the Immaculate Mother of God, the ever Virgin Mary, having completed the course of her earthly life, was taken body and soul into heavenly glory."

Infallible Teachings

In a discussion on Catholic beliefs, we tried to think of some "infallible" teachings by the Holy Father, but couldn't think of any except the one you mentioned. Could you help?

I'm afraid not — at least not very much. With all the talk and controversy about papal infallibility, one would expect to be dealing with a long list. In fact, it is generally agreed that the defined Catholic doctrines that are such because of a properly "infallible" papal statement total — believe it or not — *two!* They both deal with the Mother of Jesus: the definition of Mary's Immaculate Conception by Pope Pius IX in 1854, and of her Assumption into heaven after her life on this earth, by Pius XII in 1950. (It is possible that another statement of Pius XII concerning the matter and form of the sacrament of holy orders would also fall into this category.)

Both of these truths were, of course, celebrated and accepted in Christianity as much as 1,000 years before these dates.

John the Baptist and Original Sin

In your answer about papal infallibility, you mentioned that the doctrine most recently considered taught with such infallibility was the Assumption of Mary in 1950.

When making a retreat about a year ago, the retreat master told us that the pope had defined the doctrine that John the Baptist was born without original sin. This happened about six or seven years ago, and it was all kept low-key by Rome. Is this true?

No, it is not true. I am sure you misunderstood the retreat master somewhere along the line.

My mail indicates a huge misconception by many Catholics of the teaching role of the pope and of the bishops, something which we shall probably have to come back to.

Speaking directly to the point you make, there would be no reason whatsoever for an important doctrine of the church to be kept low-key. The very purpose of proclaiming any belief, whether with the character of infallibility or not, is to make it known to the world, and especially to all Catholics.

In the Gospel of Luke (1,44) we read that at the presence of Mary, the baby (John the Baptist) in the womb of Elizabeth "leaped with joy." Based on this passage, it has long been a pious belief among many Christians that John received the gift of sanctifying grace before he was born. This is not, however, and never has been, an official teaching of the church.

Anti-Popes?

A magazine article I read referred to someone as a possible "anti-pope," and implied that he would not be the first one in history. Were there really anti-popes? I thought there could only be one pope at a time.

It has happened more than once that strong political or religious factions in the church have not liked the man chosen as pope — or perhaps thought he was chosen unlawfully — and so picked their own man and called him pope.

These are complicated messes usually, and difficult to untangle. While there is technically only one pope at a time, historians sometimes have a hard assignment sorting out which is which.

A classic example was during a considerably hairy time for the church in the third century, when Pope Callixtus and a very popular anti-pope, Hippolytus, spent a good deal of their adult lives condemning each other. Yet today both of them are honored as martyrs and saints.

There hasn't been an anti-pope, by the way, for over 500 years.

Predictions about Popes

Does the Catholic Church believe in sayings of soothsayers or prophets concerning who will be elected pope, and how long the popes will live?

An article in our paper pertaining to the prophets who foretold about the popes said one pope would die very soon after being elected (Pope John Paul I), and the next pope's name would have a "V" in

it. (In Polish, the present pope's name is pronounced with a "V.")

One prophet said we would have three popes after John Paul I, and the other said four popes. How true are these prophecies?

The so-called prophecies of Nostradamus and St. Malachy have long been discredited. At least they were written long after some popes they claimed to foretell. Early "predictions" are relatively plain. But later ones get fuzzy.

Like the daily newspaper horoscopes, we can read almost anything into them if we want to.

A Woman Pope?

A friend of mine was raised a Catholic but no longer attends Mass or any church service. He told me that a woman was declared pope sometime in the church's past. Her name was Katherine.

I know that a woman cannot become a priest, much less a pope, at least not legally. But could a woman be named pope incorrectly? Did this happen?

The legend of Popess Joan (not Katherine) pops up regularly, especially in certain anti-Catholic tracts which usually speak as if they have discovered something new. Perhaps your friend has encountered one of these.

The story of Popess Joan is a weird tale which first appeared in the 13th century, nearly 300 or 400 years after she was supposed to have lived. She disguised herself, so the story goes, so effectively that she became a priest, a cardinal in the Roman Curia, and finally pope. She reportedly reigned for two-and-one-half years as Pope John Angelicus, sometime between the years 800 and 1100.

Her sex was discovered when she gave birth to a child during a papal procession near the Colosseum. The legend is given no credibility whatsoever by historians.

Any Married Popes?

A book we are discussing refers to the fact that some popes have been married, but doesn't go into detail. Is this true? Have we had married popes?

Of course we have had married popes, beginning with St. Peter, though we don't hear anything about his wife after the references to her mother in the Gospels. (See, for example, Mark 1,30)

The same is true with certain other popes. Records are sparse, so we know little about their married life before or after they became head of the church. We do know that one married pope, St. Hormisdas (514-523), was the father of another pope who was a saint, St. Silverius (536-538).

To my knowledge, the last married pope was Adrian II (867-872). At least for a while after being named pope he apparently lived with his wife and family at the Lateran Palace in Rome, even though an unmarried clergy was, by this time, rather common in the Western church.

Maybe this was just part of his "liberalism," which he demonstrated in other significant ways during his brief pontificate. For example, against great opposition from those Catholics who wanted to preserve the Latin language and customs, he approved the new Slavonic translation of the liturgy which Saints Cyril and Methodius had just composed for use in some of the Slavic nations.

Franciscan Orders

I am acquainted with a number of nuns, and they all seem to be Franciscans, even though they belong to different "orders." We have several groups that I know of here in our own city. How many different kinds are there, and why are there so many? Can you tell them apart?

It is said that one of the three things even God doesn't know is how many congregations of religious women there are in the church. I suspect he doesn't even know how many groups of Franciscans there are. There must be a few hundred in the world, and dozens of them right here in the United States.

All Franciscan congregations of Religious have in common that they profess the vows of poverty, chastity, and obedience, and follow basically the same rule of life founded on the Gospel as taught and lived by St. Francis of Assisi. Most separate congregations, however, were begun some time during the 700 years since St. Francis died. Each is intended to fill a particular apostolic need — teaching, nursing, contemplative prayer, and so on. Some are very old, others have died out, and some are relatively new. Membership may total anywhere from a few dozen to several thousand.

Considering the number of groups, it's nearly impossible for most of us to distinguish one congregation from another, especially with the recent modifications of dress among the Sisters. Most religious communities, however, still preserve some dress or insignia that identifies them as members of their religious "family." Most Franciscans are identified by the initials O.S.F. — Order of St. Francis.

Just for the record, there are, of course, hundreds of religious communities that are not Franciscan. Some, like the Franciscans, are identified with one of the major "schools" of Christian spirituality, such as the Benedictines (Order of St. Benedict, O.S.B.), or the Dominicans (whose identifying initials are O.P. for the Order of Preachers, the name given by St. Dominic to his followers). Others have roots which are more independent, as, for example, the Maryknoll Missionary Sisters (M.M.) and the Sisters of the Holy Cross, (C.S.C.)

Which Convent to Enter

The priest in our parish asks us often to pray for vocations to the
Religious life. I believe my daughter may be interested in entering a
convent, but I'm at a loss about which ones I might suggest.

What would be a good traditional convent for her to write to?
Restoring sensible habits that distinguish Sisters would be a great
incentive for young women, I'm positive.

Let's not get into a discussion of nuns' habits at this late juncture.
My only question might be: Does your daughter have the same
attitude about Sisters' habits and lifestyles as you have? What kind of
Religious community might she herself be interested in investigating?

One thing is sure. There is enough variety in congregations of men
and women today to suit anyone who is serious about dedicating his or
her life to Our Lord through Religious vows and service. Please suggest that your daughter write to the vocations director, in care of the
chancery office of your diocese, express her thoughts and hopes as
clearly as possible, and ask for advice. I'm certain she'll receive all the
assistance she needs.

"Stuck" in Religious Life

I am 19 years old, have had one year of college, and am interested
in finding out about entering the Religious life. But I don't want to
"get stuck," if you know what I mean. Where could I write without
committing myself to that particular community?

I'm happy you are thinking along these lines, and that you seriously
intend to follow through with some investigation. You honestly don't
have to worry about committing yourself before you are thoroughly
prepared to do so. Nearly every Religious community today is deeply
concerned to give an inquiry like yours the sincerest help without
attempting any undue influence.

Religious congregations or orders do "their own thing" much more
now than in the past. You must have some tentative ideas about what
kind of work you might be interested in doing as a Sister — nursing the
sick, teaching, caring for the aged or the young, etc., or perhaps a more
formally prayer-centered life in a contemplative order.

I suggest you write to a specific group that attracts you for this or
other reasons and get their information. Chances are they can give you
assistance with information about other communities as well, if you
wish.

Why Don't Sisters Wear Habits?

The nuns in our parish, as most nuns today, no longer wear their veils and habits. But I have seen some Sisters recently who have and wear the full religious garb. Why is this? A Protestant friend asked me and I don't know the answer.

Within rather broad regulations supplied by the church concerning the dress worn by Religious men and women, each order or community has the responsibility of setting its own policies on the matter.

Some groups of Sisters still adhere to the traditional style habit, or something quite close to it. Others provide for considerable flexibility for their members as to color, style, and so forth. Without getting involved in the wisdom or propriety of the presence or lack of changes, this is at least the reason for the differences you note in the types of dress worn by women in Religious orders.

Of course, rules concerning dress, no matter how carefully and prudently drawn up, are not always respected by all Sisters — or Brothers or priests for that matter. So it may not be fair to blame everything you see on the whole church, or on the community to which an individual belongs.

Will There Be Sisters Much Longer?

With all the changes and confusion in the Religious life, do you think the Sisters will be around much longer?

Yes, I think Sisters will be around for a long time. There has been, and will always be, an important place in the church for the witness of the celibate life for men and women, and of those with life commitments of Christian obedience and poverty. They help us to carry (as good husbands and wives do in their vocations) important and unique messages of God's love and fidelity that men will always need.

Forms and structures will change drastically, as they have in the past. But while many still seem under the illusion that a change of rules can somehow make a community or an individual more Christian, there are many other truly dedicated Sisters in many different communities working hard also at personal and interior renewal of life, which Pope John XXIII said is the beginning and heart of any valid, worthwhile reform in the church. First of all, of course, this includes a loving, unselfish concern for their own Religious community, and for the needs of the families where they serve.

Ever since Abraham, God's will has been worked out through man's humble, prayerful, and patient willingness to change. There's no reason it should be different for Sisters.

Handicaps to Vocations?

Must a person have a personal reference or sponsor to enter a Religious order? My brother tells me that if someone has a physical

illness this is a sign that the individual doesn't have a vocation. What about handicapped men and women who are otherwise healthy?

Religious orders of men and women vary greatly in the types of work they do in the church. Mental and physical qualifications would vary accordingly. A foreign missionary needs certain different abilities than a high school teacher, and both of these would differ from a more contemplative order which demands its own physical and mental qualities.

Some illnesses or handicaps would naturally make life in a Religious community difficult or impossible. But orders exercise such a variety of service today, that it is entirely possible yours would not rule out the Religious life.

My suggestion is that you write to a priest, Brother, or Sister whom you know — perhaps in the Religious order that you are considering — and ask their advice. You don't lose anything by trying, and with some asking around, and with some prayers, you may find just what you're looking for.

What Are Theologians Trying To Do?

Maybe you can tell me what the theologians are trying to do, destroy the church? As far as I can see, all they are doing is undermining the faith of good people.

This considerably abbreviated query was preceded by several other obviously rhetorical questions concerning current developments in the church. Perhaps this final comment wasn't really meant to be answered either. But its spirit is evident often in letters that cross my desk.

Theology is a highly specialized and intricate science, and theologians are nothing but specialists in that field. Through the centuries, the church has depended heavily on the research and writings of trained experts in this science — theologians like St. Jerome, St. Thomas Aquinas, St. Augustine, St. Alphonsus Liguori, and thousands of other great and lesser lights. Most of them, incidentally, were "prophets without honor" through much of their own lifetime.

When I say the church has depended on them, I include bishops and popes. While they are the official teaching body in the family of Christ, bishops are rarely theologians with highly advanced training, particularly in the critically important fields of scriptural and doctrinal theology, or in specialized technical areas of ethics.

Of its nature, theology is a speculative, open-end science. Part of its business is to be at the cutting edge of Catholic thought as the church's understanding of Jesus and his message develop through the ages. As with mothers, fathers, or priests, there are capable and less capable ones. A theologian may be right or wrong, or in between. His expertise may be in one field rather than another. Above all, his theories and opinions are only as good or as bad as his reasons for them.

When anyone condemns or ridicules "the theologians," therefore, I can't avoid the suspicion that he has never seriously studied what specific theologians have to say on a subject, or he is seeking someone to blame for things he doesn't understand or approve of. Or possibly both of these.

Blanket blaming of parents, teen-agers, intellectuals — or theologians — for our discomforts and crises is a cop-out, and rarely contributes anything toward our understanding or the search for truth.

Denying Services to Non-Contributors?

Do parish priests have the right to deny parish privileges such as baptism, marriage and funerals to parishioners they feel are not contributing enough money to the parish?

Every Catholic has an obligation — and it is an obligation — to contribute his fair share, to the best of his ability, toward the financial responsibilities of his particular parish community. Parish priests almost always give every benefit of the doubt in making allowances for families and individuals who cannot give as much as they would like to give. To arbitrarily cut people off from the services of the church would unquestionably be wrong.

However, this is not the whole story at all. People who continually ignore their financial responsibility to the church, who place a very low priority on carrying their fair share of the burden with other members of their parish, not infrequently manifest some poverty of faith in other ways as well.

As we discussed before, certain basic requirements of commitment to the Catholic faith, including some assurance that the parents intend to raise their children as Christians and Catholics, is absolutely required before baptism can take place. Similarly, couples may come to be married and demonstrate such immaturity and ignorance of their religion and of the meaning of the sacrament of marriage, that the priest may seriously question whether this boy or girl should (or even could) enter a valid marriage in the church.

In other words, a priest has no right to baptize or marry people simply because they present themselves for these sacraments. If any requirements are lacking, he has a responsibility to refuse, or at least delay the ceremony until the situation is changed. In such instances, the individuals involved may protest that they are being discriminated against for financial reasons, when both they and the priest know the facts are otherwise.

Do I Give Enough?

I am deeply hurt by some people in our church who think I don't give enough money in the collection. I almost died three years ago and cannot work as hard as I used to. I do try to give what I can to poor people. I know some people laugh at me when I give 25 cents a week in the collection, and 25 cents in the poor box.

I am old, and spend a lot for medicine, but I feel I spend more money on poor people in a month than those who laugh at me spend in a year. What can I do?

If 25 cents is all you honestly feel you can place in the collection basket each Sunday, please don't be embarrassed. Many other parishioners, especially older ones, are in the same position you are. I really doubt that anyone is laughing at you for what you are doing, but if anyone ever says anything to you, ask them to read Mark 12,41.

If it is any consolation to you, I know other pastors agree with me that the ones who disturb us most (because they are grossly unfair to the rest of their parish) are those who totally ignore their responsibility to share in accepting the financial responsibilities of the parish by giving absolutely nothing. Others, of course, are in nearly the same category, giving only a token of what they could and should give. Obviously you are in neither of these categories.

Incidentally, please don't let yourself into the same trap you dislike in others. There's no way you can possibly know how much these other people give to the poor in one way or another. Do what you can, and leave them and their responsibilities for God to judge.

Does It Cost Money?

Doesn't the Catholic Church want converts? My daughter-in-law had been married before. She decided on her own to take instructions to become a member of the Catholic faith. They informed her there would be a charge for the paper work, but isn't a total of about $200 just a little steep? I was a convert 27 years ago, and if they had charged like that, I would have said "forget it."

There is no charge at all for anyone entering the Catholic faith. Any minor expenses for some books or other materials are usually absorbed by the priest himself, or the parish.

The figures you gave indicate to me that your daughter-in-law had asked for an annulment of her first marriage so she could marry your son. The normal offering requested for such a case is $70 or $80 for the work performed by the diocesan tribunal, and $120 for the final stages of the case which are handled in Rome.

Admittedly this may sound steep but even most Catholics have little idea of the average amount of hours and days, including usually professional consultation with psychiatrists or medical doctors or others competent in the fields involved in a particular case, that are required at all levels to complete an annulment procedure. In other words, whatever money is given is by no means a gift to one or another priest who works on the case. It simply pays basic expenses of the offices and personnel whose services are needed before the final decisions are made, sometimes a year or more after the original petition.

Furthermore, no one is denied these services simply because they cannot pay for them. Provisions are made in every diocese and in Rome for the waiving of these charges when necessary. In some cases, as in our own diocese, the bishop authorizes that these be paid out of parish funds if the individuals are too poor to give the stipend.

Coming Back to the Faith

How does a person who has been away from the church for years redeem himself and get back to the faith? Or is that even possible? It would be like starting all over again — relearning prayers, how to act at Mass, and all that.

How does one make a confession after all these years? I could never remember all the sins since my last confession.

Believe me, it is not nearly as complicated or as difficult as it appears to you now. In fact, if you have decided that you wish to return to full practice of your faith, the hardest part is already over.

Make an appointment with a priest you have confidence in, perhaps one that you have had occasion to see is considerate and thoughtful, and ask his help. It isn't at all necessary that you even known him now. He will guide you. If you are ready and have made all the decisions necessary, it may all be done in one visit with him — except for catching up, as you say, on a lot that you may have missed through the years. But with your good will, that will come. The important thing is to take the first step.

Active Married Priests?

Because of some actions that have taken place in our area recently, a number of us Catholics wonder about the rule that forbids priests to marry. Can priests now marry and still be active priests? Has there been any change in the church on this matter?

No, there has been no change. The church's policy and practice that its priests be unmarried is the same now as it was before Vatican Council II.

Through a process called laicization, a process handled directly by the pope and his administration in Rome, priests may ask that they return to the lay state — in other words they become again, in effect, laymen in the church. For awhile during the past 15 years or so, this process was simpler and faster than it had been. Pope John Paul II temporarily halted it, however, pending study on how such cases should be dealt with in the future.

Just as a baptized man always remains baptized even if he later ceases to call himself Christian, a man is always an ordained priest even after he is laicized. For several reasons, the church does not allow him to serve as a priest (celebrate Mass, hear confessions, etc.) except in the most serious emergencies, such as if a dying person needs the sacraments.

While a celibate priesthood remains the rule in the Latin Rite, certain other rites of Catholics had, and still have, married priests. Generally these rites are smaller and in other parts of the world, so the ordinary American Catholic would never encounter them.

Was Mary A "Priest?"

Why do women want to say Mass when Christ's mother didn't? Our Blessed Lord chose 12 men, and not one woman, to be his apostles. Are they in their right minds?

I've heard a lot of arguments for or against ordination of women to the priesthood. But yours is a new one to me. My first reaction is: How do you know Mary never presided at the celebration of the Eucharist — or "said Mass" — with the early followers of Christ? My guess also would be that she did not. But the Bible tells us not a word about what she did or didn't do after Pentecost. The clergy structure of the church developed slowly after Jesus' death and resurrection, and if any women were considered as possible leaders in the celebration of the Eucharist, Mary could have been high on the list.

As for the apostles, Jesus excluded not only women but all non-Jews from that core group of leaders. In the Jewish, male-oriented culture in which he lived and worked, it would have been socially unthinkable for him to have named either a woman or a Gentile as an apostle. Yet, when the time and cultural situation allowed — which was very soon after his death — Gentiles were allowed into the priestly function of the church. Who is to say the same could not, or should not, happen with women as the social and religious equality of the sexes becomes more accepted in human society.

Good arguments exist on both sides of the women's ordination question, and I'm not at all sure which position is more convincing at the present time. I'm afraid, however, that those opposed must have better arguments than these to carry the day.

Ordination of Women

In a response about ordination of women, you mistakenly said that there are good arguments on both sides, and that you are not at all sure which side is more convincing at the present time. This is a strange thing for a priest to say since our Holy Father has ruled against it. If you are a Catholic, that settles it, and you should say so!

You are right. Pope Paul VI — and now Pope John Paul II — have stated quite clearly that there will be no ordination of women to the priesthood.

But this is not a reason for or against. It is simply a statement of traditional theology which the Holy Father intends to follow. A good Catholic will follow that teaching; a bishop has no right, for example, to go around ordaining women simply because he disagrees with that rule. The matter is much too serious in its implications for the spiritual health and reasonable order within the whole church.

One can, however, disagree with the pope's assessment and conclusions from a set of arguments, and still be a perfectly "good Catholic." In fact, expressions of such disagreement, along with reasons involved, are precisely the kind of input people in responsible positions like the Holy Father must have to make wise and fair decisions.

An Angry Pope

A friend who is kind of liberal about the church most of the time anyway, told me the other day that a long time ago one of the popes got angry at his cardinals and had them all killed. That's hard to believe. Did it really happen?

I confess I cannot grasp what this might have to do with being liberal — but unfortunately your friend is right, or at least she's more right than wrong.

It happened in the time of Pope Urban VI, who died in 1389, and who was involved in an unbelievable complication of ecclesiastical and political intrigues. When he was elected pope in 1378, he set about "reforming" the church, which had for a long time been heavily under the influence of the French kings. His idea of reform was to make the church more Roman, especially in the persons of his relatives and cronies.

In answer, France's King Charles V and the French cardinals elected their own "pope," which helped set Urban off on a frenzy of harsh and imprudent moves that finally turned his own cardinals against him. When they tried to put him under "guardianship," he had them captured, tortured and put to death.

The whole story is confused, and it's hard to know where to parcel out the blame. But it wasn't the happiest point in the church's history. It did much to set the stage for Martin Luther and the Protestant Reformation, which already waited in the wings.

Why Pope Lives in Italy

Why is it that the Catholic Church has a pope who lives in Italy? Couldn't we just as easily have a leader who lived in the U.S.A. or in China?

There's nothing to prevent a non-Italian from being pope, nor is there anything that says the pope has to live in Italy. As you must know, there have been popes of other nationalities. And during one period of nearly 100 years, all the popes lived in France.

However, no matter who he is or where he lives, the pope holds that position because he is the Bishop of Rome.

To discuss fully why this is so would take many books. Briefly, the Bishop of Rome has held the position of pre-eminence among other bishops in the church from its earliest years, since this is where St. Peter (whom we consider the "first pope") spent the last part of his life, and where he died.

We possess letters and other indications that, even before the last of the twelve apostles died, the Bishop of Rome was recognized as the authority over all other areas of the church. Probably the most significant and famous of these is the letter of St. Clement, the third pope after Peter, to the Church of Corinth, Greece, in the year 95.

Of course, other more specific ruling and teaching prerogatives that we attach to the Holy Father's position developed in Catholic doctrine and practice in later centuries.

Is the Liturgy Movement Over?

My husband and I have been interested in and involved in the liturgy for a long time, long before a lot of the present changes began. We don't necessarily like or agree with everything that's happened in the last 20 years, but we're still working in our parish with the music, and like it very much.

After our long experience with what we always called the "liturgical movement," I was surprised to read an article quoting a Vatican official as saying that this liturgical movement is over. Can you tell us what was meant by this? Certainly it cannot mean that the church intends to move "back" to the past in the liturgy.

I believe you are referring to a statement by Archbishop A. Bugnini, one of the experts in the church's liturgical renewal, and secretary to the Sacred Congregation for Divine Worship. The remark, made in an international liturgy journal called Notitiae, was that the liturgical movement now "belongs to history." His meaning, however, was quite the opposite of the one you suggest.

Far from intending that the church would go back to the past, he meant that what was once a sort of "sideline" movement without official status has now become part of the essential activity of the church. This movement, he says, "has now become *the* pastoral action of the church which aims at making the faithful participate in, and live fully, the paschal mystery of Christ which the liturgy celebrates."

He does indicate that the hardest part of the whole liturgical renewal is still ahead of us — to implement and adapt the renewed liturgical rites to each country and parish.

Parish Pro-life Coordinators

Is it mandatory for each parish to have some type of pro-life organization or coordinator? My parish is the only one I've heard of that doesn't have anything like this. I would assign myself the task only my parish priest seems negative towards the idea.

There exists no church law that would demand a pro-life unit or representative in each parish, though individual bishops could certainly recommend it or require it in their own diocese. And many do.

The importance of such activity on the parish level is indeed urgent, more urgent, in fact, than most Catholics realize. Parish-level responsibilities will become increasingly critical during the next few years in the national effort to pass a Human Life Amendment, to which American bishops have given highest priority in the area of respect for human life. So I applaud your interest, and wish there were more like you.

Malachy's Prophecy

What is the Prophecy of St. Malachy? Supposedly it foretells a terrible time for the church during the rest of this century. Is it supposed to be true?

One is tempted to say that anyone could foretell a "terrible time" for the church almost any time, and he'd probably be right. Sorry to disappoint you, however. The famous Prophecy of St. Malachy can hardly be said to have even that in its favor.

The prophecy that bears his name was supposedly written by Bishop St. Malachy of Ireland, who died in 1148. It pretends to designate 111 successors of Pope Celestine II, who lived about the same time as St. Malachy. These successors are not mentioned by name but by short "verses" said to characterize the man or his time as pope. The first 60 or so are quite clear, and bear a remarkable resemblance to the popes they refer to. After that, however, the prophetic verses become so general many of them could refer to almost anyone at any time.

With a brief Latin phrase that professed to characterize each pope or his reign, the prophecies presumably extended to the end of the world. The phrases are extremely cryptic; it takes a good deal of imagination to pull some meaning out of them for most of the popes.

According to the alleged predictions, only two popes remain after the present one, ending with Petrus Romanus (Peter of Rome) who is to preside over the destruction of Rome and the end of the present age.

The whole "prophecy" is, in fact, an elaborate and imaginative forgery. St. Malachy, who was bishop of Armagh, Ireland, truly did live and had an illustrious career. He died, however, more than 400 years before his supposed prophecy first appeared in Europe.

Interestingly, the phrases for each pope are quite explicit up to about 1590, when the document was obviously written. After that they become impossibly obscure.

The author must have had a bit of fun composing this interesting historical and literary curiosity. But it is a fake.

Forgery or not, however, it seems to be "rediscovered" about every 10 or 20 years.

The Baltimore Catechism

The Baltimore Catechism we hear so much about — where did it come from? And why isn't it used as much in religion classes as it used to be?

The Baltimore Catechism was the result of the desire of the American bishops in the last century to have a concise summary of Catholic doctrine. It was written at their request in 1885, after the Third Plenary Council of Baltimore, from which it receives its name.

One of the many so-called "national catechisms" having the same purpose, it followed basically the tradition and format of the famous Roman Catechism written by three Dominican theologians after the Council of Trent, around the year 1565. This Roman Catechism, by the way, was not meant for general use by the faithful, but only as reference material for "pastors and others who hold the office of teaching."

For several centuries after that, such catechisms largely replaced Holy Scripture and a living liturgy as a primary means of transmitting the faith. Biblical research, and its practical application in the understanding of Christian life and belief, was minimal in the church for various reasons. Official rites, the Mass and sacraments especially, also became less meaningful and useful as a help to teaching a living faith.

More recently, as a result of the unprecedented expansion of knowledge about Holy Scripture, and of the liturgical renewal of this century, many varieties of catechetical books are based more on the Bible and on a re-vitalized liturgy. For this reason, these books are increasingly relied on for catechism courses and other types of religious formation of young people and adults.

Why No Catechisms?

Why does there seem to be a general rejection of "catechisms" today? We learned our religion from catechisms, but you can hardly find one anywhere these days, at least any that satisfy me now.

Your questions concern many others than yourself, though perhaps not so much now as a few years ago. There are at least two quite important reasons that religious educators, priests, and others, rely less on the old-style catechisms than they once did. First, the simple, often one-sentence responses to the great questions about God, man, life and eternity, often implied that these few words wrapped up all that the church knows, or could know, about the questions. Human language is always limited and very incomplete when it comes to topics or questions like these.

Second, and this is closely related to what I've said already, most answers to man's religious searching are open-ended; they're always subject to new insights, further enrichment and adjustment, even to the point that the emphasis in former answers may be found not nearly as accurate as ones later arrived at. This is true even — perhaps, especially — of our Christian faith. As it lives out its life on earth through the ups and downs of history, the church will be expanding and growing in its understanding of Jesus and his teachings until the end of time.

Who Wrote the Baltimore Catechism?

I am a CCD teacher, and we still often use the Baltimore Catechism in our parish. A magazine article we were given spoke of "the theologian who wrote the Baltimore Catechism." This is very misleading. The Baltimore Catechism was written and approved by the American bishops, who said it should be used in all religion classes.

Actually, the American bishops said the doctrine in the catechism should be the foundation of religion teaching; they never suggested even at that time the book be used in all religion classes.

The theologian you speak of was Father John McCaffrey, a highly respected expert in theology, who served as personal theologian for several bishops at the various Councils of Baltimore in the latter part of the last century. Apparently, at the bishops' request, Father McCaffrey drew up the catechism. After some revisions, it was eventually adopted as the "Baltimore Catechism."

Catholic Church and the UN

Has the Catholic Church ever condemned the United Nations? How can so many priests and bishops defend it?

Catholic leaders, especially those who speak officially for the whole church, have consistently promoted the existence and growth of the United Nations (UN) and urged that its international authority be strengthened.

Since the UN was founded, Popes Pius XII, John XXIII, Paul VI, and now John Paul II, have recognized its limitations and weaknesses, but insisted it is still the best hope for world peace and order. This position is confirmed by the encouragement and support the church has offered in all the major agencies of the UN since World War II.

American Pope?

Do you think there will ever be an American pope? I think we should strive for this.

No one knows, of course, if or when there will be an American pope. But my guess is as good as anyone else's, and my guess is that it will be a long time before an American is elected to that office.

The church in the New World, especially in North America, is still relatively young. We were officially a "mission country" until just a few decades ago. In the eyes of Europeans, particularly those in leadership positions of state or church, we are still somewhat of an upstart in relation to their part of the world where Christianity has been present and operating (well or ill) for 1,500 to 2,000 years.

That kind of long tradition, or lack of it, inevitably weighs heavily in the feelings and minds of those who do the choosing.

A second reason is more subtle, but in some manner tied to the first. Many attitudes toward authority, law, and even religion itself, that are typically American, or at least are considered so in other countries, are still somewhat "maverick" positions in Catholic tradition. Some of these are more liberal or permissive than older Catholic countries are used to. By general admission, for example, our bishops and our experience in the United States relative to other Christian churches contributed heavily to the more open and accepting stance toward those churches at Vatican Council II.

Some American traditions are more conservative or strict, as, for example, our understanding of the function of law and regulations and how they are to be made and observed. Anyone familiar with European attitudes in these areas of life realizes the significant differences between here and there.

Don't hold your breath. Even if we want an American pope, and I'm not sure we do, we'll probably have to live through a few more Italians — and maybe Spaniards, French, or Germans, not to speak of Poles — before we get one.

Archbishop Lefebvre

Why all the furor about Archbishop Lefebvre, the traditionalist prelate who wants to use Latin, when the funeral Mass for Pope Paul was in Latin? Why wasn't it in Italian?

The announcer on at least one television network answered your question during the late pope's funeral liturgy. While Pope Paul did carry through the reforms by which the Mass would be normally offered in the language of the country, Latin remains the international language of the church.

Attending the funeral were representatives from numerous nations, with numerous languages. It was certainly appropriate, therefore, that the language of any one country not be used, but that the ceremonies be in Latin, as they often are in similar international circumstances.

Your comment about Archbishop Lefebvre seems to reflect a misconception held by a number of Catholics. His problem with the church is not simply that he wants Latin Masses. He does not want to follow the new order of the Mass based on Vatican II decisions, which provide in certain instances for Masses in Latin. Far more serious and critical is his rejection of the authority of the popes and of the ecumenical councils to establish directions and statements of belief and worship that bind all Catholic people.

He argues, of course, that the pope and the other bishops are all wrong, and that he and his followers are the only "real" Catholics — an argument, by the way, that is used by other smaller and lesser known groups today. By now, as you probably know, in major defiance of the pope, he has ordained his own priests and established his own seminaries.

It is well known that the sad situation was a cause of great anguish to Pope Paul, who, until the very day he died, attempted (as has our present Holy Father) by every means possible to keep the archbishop's break from the church from becoming total and final.

How Many Masses?

At our parish, there are five Masses on Sundays, and three priests in the parish. How many Masses is a priest allowed to say in one day?

Also, isn't it a rule that a priest must say Mass every day?

According to general church law, priests are allowed to offer no more than one Mass each day, though bishops can permit them to offer two Masses on special feasts and Sundays when necessary.

The basic principle in all such matters is that the reasonable needs of the people must be met, especially where Mass and the sacraments are concerned. Thus, it is not at all uncommon for priests to offer two Masses on weekdays — for example, when a funeral Mass must be added to the daily Mass schedule.

Many priests also must frequently offer three Masses on Sundays to fulfill a minimum schedule of Masses in a parish church. Priests properly avoid this as much as possible, but sometimes, in light of the disproportionately small number of priests available in a given parish, it must be done if the priests wish to give appropriate service to the people.

The church has no specific regulations on when a priest is required to offer Mass. The law says rather quaintly that priests should celebrate the Eucharist "several times a year, but the bishop or religious superior should try to see that they celebrate the liturgy at least on Sundays and holy days of obligation." Bear in mind, this is not the ideal or recommendation offered by the church; it is the minimum a priest is expected to do from the nature of his role in the church. Obviously, any priest in a parish will celebrate the Eucharist almost every day, under normal circumstances.

Anglican and Roman Priests

We have many friends in our community who are members of the Anglican Church. While we go to each others' churches sometimes, we realize we are not supposed to receive communion in these other churches, since there is a problem about the recognition of Anglican priests.

With all the changes in the church, has there been, or will there be, any change in this matter?

The story of the Roman Catholic Church's concern about Anglican orders (which is the center of your concern) is a long and complicated one. But these are at least the highlights.

The primary official document of the Roman Catholic Church on the subject is a decree, "Apostolicae Curae," of Sept. 18, 1896, in which Pope Leo XIII declared that the defects in the ordination of Anglican bishops and priests are so critical that Anglican orders must be judged invalid.

Very simply, the Holy Father gave two reasons for this judgment. The first was a presumed disagreement about the nature of the Eucharist, especially the relationship of the sacrifice of the Mass to the sacrifice of Christ on Calvary.

The second was an apparent difference of belief about the origin of the order of bishops and priests. Pope Leo had concluded that there was a serious divergence between the Anglican belief and the Roman Catholic position — which is that the commission of bishops and priests derives from the same commission which Jesus gave to his apostles.

Since Vatican Council II, Roman Catholic and Anglican scholars have devoted years to a restudy of these differences, and have found that these differences are perhaps not nearly as great as they seemed at the time of Pope Leo. The Anglican-Roman Catholic International Commission, appointed by Pope Paul VI and the Archbishop of Canterbury, concluded a few years ago that the judgment of Pope Leo XIII should be put "in a new context" for the church today.

It is impossible here to enter into more details about these agreements, but they are expressed in two documents which you can obtain, each treating one of the major differences that I mentioned above. They are titled, "The Agreed Statement on Ministry and Ordination," and "The Agreed Statement on Eucharistic Doctrine." (USCC Publications, 1312 Massachusetts Avenue, N.W, Washington, D.C, 20005.)

Officially the matter is still being weighed. There is no change at this time in the position of the Roman Catholic Church regarding Anglican orders.

Theology or Dogma?

Our study club had a disagreement over something in the book we are discussing — a reference to the "theology of St. Paul." Some of us found no problem with the words, but others claim the phrase is misleading. There is, after all, only one theology that is true, isn't there — at least only one that we as Catholics can accept?

I think you are getting theology mixed up with dogma. They're two very different things.

Theology can mean any development or discourse on ideas relating to God. More specifically, however, it is an organized *system* of thought which tries to synthesize the truths we have about God from reason or from revelation. It is simply some individual's, or group's, insights on how the various doctrines of Christianity, for example, hang together, how they fit in with other aspects of human life and knowledge, and so on.

In that sense, there are many "theologies" which are perfectly respectable and acceptable in Catholic tradition, even though they may profoundly disagree with each other. St. Augustine, for instance, developed a theological system which St. Thomas Aquinas often radically disagreed with in his own theology 800 years later. Today, nearly 800 years after St. Thomas, theological systems frequently take basically different avenues toward explaining the meaning of Christian truths than he did.

St. Paul was a man of incredible faith and insight who developed his own theology, putting together the teachings he received from Christ, and enriching his and our understanding of them.

At different times in Christian history, other "schools" of theology placed their emphases quite differently than he did. A good example is the place Paul gives to the Resurrection as the central event establishing Jesus as the Son of God with the power of the Savior. During perhaps most of the centuries since Paul, the theological tendency has been to identify this key event as the Incarnation itself, rather than the Resurrection.

Such differences may appear academic, but they have significant implications in the direction of Christian spirituality and belief. Many "difficulties" with modern theology, for example, result from the fact that it leans heavily toward the Resurrection emphases of St. Paul — which, however, vastly enriches our understanding of the real meaning of the Incarnation of the Son of God.

Priests' Wills

I would like to know why priests, monsignors and bishops do not leave their bank accounts, etc., to the church. Please don't tell me they do. Maybe a few, but many very wealthy ones have passed away in my time and not even a tenth of it went to charity. I fully intend to leave my God more than any relative. I am just a lay person and can't understand our leaders' attitude. I can give three very good examples with clippings.

I can agree with you on one thing: Priests and bishops do have at least as great a responsibility as anyone else to provide for a just and charitable use of whatever they leave behind at death — just as they should during their lives.

I believe I'm fairly well acquainted with a significant number of priests, and in general with what they do with their money before and after they die. With almost no exceptions, I'd have to say my experience doesn't jibe with your interpretation.

Maybe our difference is partly in your remark about three "good examples with clippings." You surely are aware that for a variety of reasons many individuals, clergy or laity, arrange for the disposal of their money after death in ways that are nearly totally private, and for this reason never show up in "clippings." I know personally of at least two recent instances, one involving a priest of extremely modest means, and another where the priest had a good amount of money from his family, in which these priests left generous gifts to parishes, Catholic education programs, or missionary work, but did it in ways that do not show up on wills or other public documents. Few knew about it except the individuals or institutions involved.

When we start judging other people, chances are better than even that we'll arrive at some unbalanced or unjust conclusions, not to speak of usurping a prerogative God has wisely reserved for himself.

We priests probably should be more aware than we often are that such things are publicized more now than formerly, and that our leadership in this matter should be more visible than it is.

Are Catholics a Denomination?

We Catholics are often asked: "What denomination are you?" Our answer has been: "We have no denomination. We are Catholics."

Is this the correct answer? We define denomination as "a sect which has broken away from an established church."

The root meaning of the word "denomination" is simply the name you go by. If you're hung up on your definition, recall that we Christians did, after all, break away from the Jewish faith, which is about as established a religion as you can get.

Endorsing Candidates

Is it permissible or proper for a Catholic priest to endorse by name a candidate for public office from the pulpit? To me this is inconsistent with the statement on political responsibility of the U.S. Catholic bishops in 1976.

I presume you're referring to the bishops' plea that all citizens "become informed on relevant issues" and vote freely according to their conscience. Nothing any priest says, of course, can deprive you of that right or obligation.

Promoting (or attacking) specific candidates by name is dangerous, in my opinion, if for no other reason than that it violates the legal prohibition of such electioneering by tax exempt institutions, which includes our churches.

Such siding with one candidate or another from the pulpit is usually (maybe always) counter-productive and can alienate as many as it converts. Catholic people want and deserve to have their churches free of this kind of political activity.

Just as certainly, however, neither the church nor its pastors can allow themselves to be above, or ignore, the political scene. It is their duty to assist their people — from the pulpit or otherwise — in understanding the Christian and Catholic teachings involved in current issues, and to remind their congregations that they are individually reponsible for the moral and social consequences of their political decisions. And that includes the votes they cast.

The bishops themselves teach and operate in this fashion on everything from the death penalty and abortion, to human rights and arms sales to foreign countries. As they affirmed during the 1976 presidential campaign, "We are not supporting religious bloc voting, nor are we instructing people for whom to vote. Rather we urge that citizens make this decision for themselves in an informed and conscientious manner, in light of candidates' positions on the issues, as well as their personal qualifications...We shall continue to address the issues facing our nation by all appropriate means at our disposal."

It seems to me that's excellent political procedure for all of us to follow.

Physical Handicaps in the Priesthood?

A friend of mine was told that the Catholic Church would not ordain a man if he did not have all five fingers on his right hand. Two other priests said they had never heard of the situation.

I know of one priest ordained when he was paralyzed and in a wheelchair. Why should having all one's fingers determine whether you are allowed to serve God as a priest?

According to church regulations, a physical defect such as you mention could be an impediment to ordination. The reason for this, insofar as it applies at all today, seems to be simply to assure that a priest be capable of performing his liturgical and other duties in a proper and seemly manner.

As long as a man is able to perform duties to which the bishop might assign him, dispensations related to physical defects are regularly given. There are, after all, far more important qualifications for the priesthood than the number of one's fingers.

Former Priest Receives Sacraments

About five years ago, a young man near our small town was ordained a priest; there was a big celebration with all the trimmings.

Now this priest is married and can receive the sacraments.

Our daughter married a divorced man about a year ago. He is a wonderful man and they have a child. When he was in his teens, he got a girl pregnant. Her mother said he had to marry her or pay for an abortion. So he married her, and they lived together for three or four months before they were divorced.

I would like to know how that fallen-away priest can receive the sacraments and our daughter cannot. This hurts very much.

She is too shy to talk to a priest. When she was little, the priest always scolded the children, and she has been afraid ever since.

First, let's talk about your daughter. If you have related all the basic facts accurately, this case should unquestionably be presented to your diocesan tribunal with a petition for annulment of the first marriage, and the sooner the better. Regardless of her shyness, urge her to speak with a priest she can feel reasonably comfortable with.

If she cannot do that, at least help her write to the diocesan tribunal (I'm sending you the address privately) and ask them for help. The priests there will be happy to help all they can, I'm sure, and will advise your daughter concerning further steps that should be taken.

Considering your concern for your daughter, I understand your feelings about the priest. Remember, however, that the rule that a priest may not marry, as serious and as significant as it is, is made by the church. The church can, therefore, dispense from that rule, as it does when it "laicizes" an ordained priest. The permanence of marriage, however, is outside the power of the church to change.

Hence, while he has failed to follow through on his commitment to the priestly ministry, the man you refer to should not be labelled a "fallen away priest." That implies a judgment which none of us has the knowledge or the right to make. Apparently, he followed all the procedures the church requires in changing to his present state of life.

Why No More Monsignors?

Why is it that priests no longer seem to be named monsignors? Is there a new ruling on this?

The rank and title of monsignor is probably best described as a remnant of the times when much more importance was placed on honorary titles in the church.

Today, when the church is trying to simplify its life in many ways, it seems to be attempting at several levels to de-emphasize positions which are purely honorary in the sense that they have no necessary relationship to the individual's official ministry in the church.

The word "monsignor," incidentally, which means "my lord," is still in some countries the title given to bishops.

As the saying goes, some of my best friends are monsignors, but I suspect that even though some monsignors are still being named, they will be an increasingly lonely breed in the church, at least in the foreseeable future.

History of Celibacy

In light of the present controversies concerning celibacy in the priesthood, I have two questions. Do we have any examples of a celibate life in the Old Testament? And when was celibacy for the priesthood made mandatory in our church?

To my knowledge, the only major Old Testament figure who was celibate was the prophet Jeremiah, who lived around the beginning of the destruction of Jerusalem and the Babylonian exile (sixth century B.C). He was told by the Lord (Jer. 16:1-4) not to marry as a sign to the people that children then being born would die in the tragedies to come.

The very idea of a celibate life for men or women was generally repugnant to the Hebrew culture as it was to most cultures at that time. For a woman to be unmarried and childless was shameful. For men and women, marriage and a house filled with children was seen as a mark of God's blessing.

The first general law in the Western church obliging the clergy to a celibate life did not appear until the later part of the fourth century. This occurred through the decrees of several popes, beginning with Pope Damasus (366-384), and numerous local councils in Africa and Europe.

During the next 700 years the marriage of priests, deacons and bishops was unlawful in the Western church. The movement toward a clerical celibacy finally culminated for the universal church in the 12th century at the First and Second Lateran Councils, when such marriages were considered not only illicit but also invalid.

Much later, at the Council of Trent in 1563, the law of clerical celibacy was reaffirmed. However, against enormous opposition, the council firmly declared that priestly celibacy was a matter of church law, not divine law. This means that the church could change its legislation concerning celibacy, and priests would no longer be obliged to observe it. The church did this for deacons at Vatican Council II when it instituted a married permanent diaconate.

The road of clerical celibacy has been rocky through the centuries, particularly in the early Middle Ages and again in the period before the Protestant Reformation. Rocky or not, it seems clear that the church is not prepared to alter easily a practice which has been so intimate a part of its life for the past 17 centuries.

Duties of Permanent Deacons

Since 1971, a number of men have been ordained permanent deacons in our archdiocese. Please enumerate the duties they perform as permanent deacons. This point is not clear to many Catholics. Do the deacons receive remuneration for acting in this capacity?

It is not only in your archdiocese that Catholics are confused about the proper functions of permanent deacons.

Before I answer your question directly, it should be noted that liturgical functions of the deacons, especially at the celebration of the Eucharist, are intended to be a climax and a symbol of the other services they render to the community outside of the liturgy. This important point is made constantly by those who work in the training and supervision of the deacon programs.

The following liturgical functions are assigned to deacons by the church:

1. to function as deacon at celebrations of the Eucharist,

2. to function as celebrant of the sacrament of baptism (anyone may administer the sacrament of baptism in emergencies; deacons are officially appointed ministers of that sacrament by the church),

3. to take Holy Communion to the sick in their homes, hospitals and other health care facilities,

4. to serve as celebrant of Benediction of the Blessed Sacrament (this includes wearing the proper vestments, exposing the Blessed Sacrament, and giving the blessing with the sacred vessels containing the Eucharist),

5. to serve as celebrant at wake services for the dead and at graveside burial services,

6. to officiate at marriages,

7. to administer the sacramentals of the church according to the rite indicated by the church (this does not include blessing religious articles, or the blessing of throats on the Feast of St. Blase), and

8. to assist in the distribution of ashes on Ash Wednesday. (In January, 1975, the Vatican notified the American bishops that laymen and women who are special ministers of the Eucharist may assist the celebrant in distributing ashes on Ash Wednesday. In fact, if there is no priest, and the ashes are already blessed, the lay ministers may impose the ashes by themselves. The Bishop's Committee on the Liturgy then judged that if special eucharistic ministers may do so, certainly certain deacons may also.)

Deacons may also preach at celebrations of the Eucharist and other ceremonies. However, this function, as well as the faculty to officiate at marriages, must be explicitly granted to them by the bishop of the diocese.

Many, perhaps most, of the permanent deacons receive no regular pay for the services that they give. Policies concerning remuneration are established by the diocese and the institution in which the deacon serves.

Did Early Christians Have Priests?

In a Bible discussion group recently, we talked about the priesthood. Someone said she thought the Bible said nothing about priests — meaning priests as we know them in our church.
Is this true? Didn't the early Christians have priests?

The New Testament speaks of three main ministries in the church: bishops, deacons and presbyters (elders). The exact function of these ministers, especially of the presbyters, is not perfectly clear, although the bishops clearly have the predominant supervisory responsibility.

The Greek word for priest, "hiereus," is not used in the New Testament at all to designate an official of the church. It is applied to Jesus himself in the Letter to the Hebrews. In a couple of other places it refers to Christians in general to describe their special character as the people of God.

There is some likelihood that the presbyters performed certain functions which we relate to priests, although their ministerial relation to the church is far less clear than that of the bishops and deacons.

The word "hiereus," priest, only came into use in the Christian Church about 150 years after Jesus' death and resurrection as the Eucharist came to be more and more recognized as a renewal of the sacrifice of Calvary as well as a meal. In the religious traditions of that time, a sacrifice was offered by a priest. Thus Christians began to refer that title to their minister who presided at the Eucharist.

Ecumenism

Are Only Catholics Saved?

I am 14 years old, not Catholic, but I have two questions.

First, I attend a Catholic church often, although my mother does not recommend it. I desperately want to receive Holy Communion. Is this possible?

Second, I read somewhere that you have to be Catholic to be saved. Is this true?

My response to your second question is easy. No, you do not have to be Catholic to be saved. Your first question is more difficult and I can't possibly give you a final answer.

I don't want to encourage you to go against your mother's wishes or commands. She is, after all, primarily responsible for you and, I assume, cares for you very much. Her concerns undoubtedly reflect what she feels is best for you.

On the other hand, you are not an infant or a small child. You are approaching adulthood, and are gradually assuming full responsibility for your life and your decisions. If, then, you feel honestly attracted to something in the beliefs and worship of the Catholic Church, I feel you should at least do a little inquiring about it.

The details you give in your note are nowhere near enough for me to be more explicit than that. Perhaps you can talk with an adult Catholic friend, or arrange through one of your Catholic school friends to discuss your thinking with a priest.

You want to follow the leads of your own thoughts and conscience. But you don't want to hurt your parents. I am sure a kind friend or clergyman will be helpful in meeting both of those responsibilities.

I'll say a prayer that everything goes well for you.

Protests Name "Roman Catholic"

Whenever I speak of the Catholic Church, a Protestant friend

insists that I should identify myself as a **"Roman Catholic,"** since there are other Catholic churches besides ours. Could you comment on why they should want to be identified as **"Catholic?"**

The use of the word "catholic" ("universal") to identify the Church of Jesus goes back to biblical times. Even today, Protestant communities use the Apostles' Creed in their worship, including the words: "I believe in...the holy catholic church." They obviously do not mean the Roman Catholic Church.

Regular attachment of the word "Roman" to the name began around the time of the Reformation, when many reform leaders resented the implication that they were not part of the "catholic" church. Even at that time, however, many Catholics — English Catholics in particular — who remained in union with Rome, didn't like the name "Roman" since it implied that they were somehow on the fringes, or coattails, of the "real" Catholic Church.

There is nothing derogatory, of course, as far as we are concerned, about the name Roman Catholic, for several reasons. Obviously, the main reason is the fact that, while it may be only an accident of history, up to now the pope as spiritual head of the church has been identified as the man who is chosen as Bishop of Rome.

Non-Catholic Label

Several times I have been told that people of other faiths don't like to be called non-Catholics — and shouldn't be. What can you call them, then? Sometimes it's hard to know.

It does present a sticky situation occasionally (as it might if we were referred to as non-Protestants), and there's no easy answer.

Technically, in Catholic documents, the term non-Catholic usually refers to baptized Christians who are not Roman Catholics, though often the name is used for anyone not of our faith, including Hindus and Moslems.

The title "Protestant" would cover most of the Christians in our country who are not Roman Catholic. Large numbers of Anglican or Episcopalian communities, however, consider themselves more Catholic than Protestant, and do not wish to be called Protestant.

In general, I feel the title "non-Catholic" might have an unintentional disparaging ring to it today, but often a substitute isn't always easy to find.

Are Protestants Heretics?

Why don't we hear the word "heretic" any more? With so many crazy teachings today, I think it's a sign of how far we've come in

not knowing what we believe. Our catechism called Protestants heretics. Aren't they any more — or what is the reason?

Also, why all the Protestant hymns at Mass? I asked a priest one time, years go, why we couldn't sing "A Mighty Fortress Is Our God." He said it was because it was written by a heretic.

First, let's clear up that word "heretic." With all respect to your memory, I don't believe any catechism ever called Protestants heretics. A heretic, by traditional definition of the church, is one who knowingly and obstinately denies some doctrine that he knows is revealed by God, and which is proposed as an article of Catholic faith by the church. Obviously, if you consider that definition carefully, it does not apply to sincere Protestants. In fact, there might be serious question whether, at least today, it applies to anybody.

You ask why the word isn't used anymore. Beyond the reason just given, I believe the church (which means all of us) realizes these days that this kind of labeling and name-calling accomplishes little toward the cause of truth or charity. In the earliest years of the Protestant revolt from the Catholic faith, there may have been some justification for this either-or drawing of lines. The situation then was different from now in numerous ways.

Protestants and Catholics clearly still differ on certain significant beliefs, generally dealing with the Eucharist and the structure of the church as an institution. These differences may not be ignored or shrugged off. However, both of these groups of Christians finally seem more ready to acknowledge that substantial points of doctrinal agreement between them are more numerous, and just as significant, as points of disagreement. The feeling seems to be, among the leaders and members of the churches involved, that when our larger "enemies" are the common enemies of all Christians, it is of small value to attempt to pinpoint heretics.

As for your other question, what makes a hymn Protestant anyway? If the words are doctrinally and spiritually suitable, and if its music is of appropriate quality (which may be debatable), a song may be used in our worship no matter who wrote it or who used it first.

Heretics?

I would like to ask prayers for people who call us Protestants heretics. I was born, baptized and raised by strict Methodist parents. We lived by the Ten Commandments and were taught when we got married it was for better or worse until death.

If we hurt or did wrong to someone, we had to go to that person and say we were sorry and make amends.

Six years ago I married into a Catholic family; there are now six grown children. My husband goes to Mass every Sunday and makes his tithe, which he never did before. I go right along with them.

Every time I just about have my mind made up to convert, something like this — hearing that some people consider Protestants heretics — comes up, and it makes my heart sick to think there are such narrow-minded people.

You said it better than I could. Some of us Christians still carry a remnant of the days when a large part of a Protestant's religious identity (at least in my experience) was that he was not Catholic.

Happily, we've come to have much more positive ways of identifying ourselves as Christians, Catholic or Protestant. And so we've come to acknowledge openly, and often with some surprise, how much faith we do have in common.

Don't let such remarks keep you from doing what you think you should. Often questions or statements such as you have heard are just as much a search for an answer, as they are a statement of position.

Anglican-Catholic Communion?

My elderly Episcopalian friend has not been to church in years. She would like to come to Mass with me if she could receive Communion. I feel this would be perfectly marvelous. Could she do that?

The Catholic Church's policy on interfaith Communion indicates that there may be situations of "urgent necessity" in which a Christian of another faith cannot approach his or her own clergyman for Communion without considerable trouble or expense. It is the bishop's role to decide whether he or she might receive the Eucharist in a Catholic church.

Perhaps you could encourage your friend to go to her own church, and even offer to go with her. If you discover that she finds it personally extremely difficult or impossible to take that route, there is nothing wrong with taking the matter to the bishop and asking his approval. That is precisely what the church urges you to do, if you think you can be helpful to another's spiritual life this way.

It would be wise not to make any, even tentative, commitments until you know for sure.

Catholic Organist in Protestant Church?

May a Catholic be an organist in a Protestant church without violating Catholic laws? The priest at our parish believes it is a sin, but if so, how serious a sin is it? Several people I know believe that there is nothing wrong in playing for Protestant services, but I'd like to know for sure myself.

Much depends on the circumstances. To play on a special occasion, perhaps with a Catholic choir, as a gesture of friendship or ecumenical prayer, or even to help out in time of need, could usually easily be acceptable.

Some thoughtful questions should be raised, however, if the playing is intended as a regular practice. Even many organists (and choirs) do not sufficiently realize they are liturgical ministers — at least as Catholics and many other churches understand their function. They are not merely detached professionals providing a paid service; even less are they merely performers putting on a show.

Insofar as this is true, they are directly participating in the worship of that church and, to some degree at least, implicitly professing the faith of that particular congregation.

I'm not sure I'd be as categorical about it as your priest, but it deserves conscientious consideration, and perhaps some more advice locally.

Ecumenism and Women's Ordination

Some years ago the Anglican Church Board approved the ordination of women to the priesthood. This surprised me. I have been interested for a long time in the ecumenical movement and this should set it back a hundred years. Why did they decide to allow this now? Do you think it ends hope for the reunion of the Anglican and Roman Catholic Churches?

No, I certainly do not think it ends the hope of reunion between our two churches. But a couple of assumptions behind your question are, perhaps, more important than the questions themselves.

First, while the reunion of Christians should be a fervent prayer and goal of us all, our first responsibility, in whatever church we are, is to be as faithful as we can be to the traditions and inspirations of the Holy Spirit as we find them in our own particular community. Christian unity, in whatever form it gradually comes about, will be the work of the Spirit, not of our human ingenuity and compromise.

Those most deeply involved and experienced in ecumenical labors have long since learned this truth. Fidelity to what we believe, along with an open charity and humility toward what other Christians have to say to us and with us — these are the tools the Spirit uses to do his work of bringing us together.

Thus, if our Anglican brothers and sisters (or even a significant group of them) honestly feel this is the way for them to go, all things considered, then decide they must — regardless of possible ecumenical repercussions.

As for ending hopes for reunion of our two churches, this would presume that we know what a "united" Christianity will look like. But do we?

Judging from recent papal statements, it appears quite unlikely that the Roman Catholic Church will allow the ordination of women, at least in the near future. But even the statements of our bishops indicate that the strongest argument against such ordinations is our tradition of ordaining only men. From past experience we know that, while tradition is a significant theological argument, it is not always a final argument. Traditions can be changed by the church.

Might not the Roman Catholic Church, for instance, preserve its present policy, and still be able to live with a united Christendom in which one branch allows women priests — much as it has for centuries lived with other branches which allow married priests — while it continues to require that its own priests be celibate?

Unthinkable? I'm not so sure. The Holy Spirit has already brought us far along the way to healing the shameful division in the family of Christ, a long way that 20 years ago would have been called ridiculous and impossible.

So let's keep moving, and give him the benefit of the doubt. He just might have something big going that will astound us even more.

World Council of Churches

I was told recently that the Catholic Church is about ready to join the World Council of Churches. This puzzles me greatly. How could our church become a member of a Protestant organization like this? Is this where ecumenism is leading us?

The World Council of Churches, founded in 1949, is a partnership "of churches which accept our Lord Jesus Christ as God and Savior." Its purpose is to promote Christian unity, and to aid cooperation among the churches in doctrinal research, relief and welfare programs, missionary activities and other common projects.

From the beginning, even though it numbered some Orthodox and Anglican groups among its members, the WCC was primarily Protestant-oriented, dealing mainly with problems that were considered to concern Protestant churches. During the 1960s, however, Pope Paul VI and WCC officials began a close working relationship, especially in areas involving social justice and peace.

Consultants and observers from both groups work together, and agree there is no theoretical reason the Roman Catholic Church should not join. The problem with Catholic membership is practical. Membership in the Catholic Church totals more than the entire membership of the churches presently part of the WCC. (In fact, more than half of all the Christians in the world are Catholics.)

A serious question is, therefore: How can a church of this size and scope share membership with the WCC without, in effect, dominating the whole organization? This is why Pope Paul said in 1969, during his visit to WCC headquarters in Geneva, that the time is not ready for a decision on the matter.

WCC leaders generally agree. Dr. Eugene Carson Blake, then secretary general of the organization, said at the time, "How does a church of approximately the size of the total fellowship of the World Council best cooperate with or have relationships with the World Council, which consists of 240 churches in 80 or 90 countries?"

By now, the WCC consists of nearly 300 churches, with 450 million members, in 100 countries.

Eventually it will be the Catholic Church's decision to ask to join. Until an answer to these practical questions is found, however, we'll have to be satisfied with continued informal, but close, collaboration.

Hanukkah and Christmas

During the past few years around Christmas time, there's been a lot in the papers and on television about the Feast of Hanukkah. Is there any connection between the two feasts?

The eight-day festival of Hanukkah (often called the Festival of Lights) is a commemoration of a joyous event in Jewish history, the rededication of the temple in Jerusalem about 165 B.C. This rededication, described in the Book of Maccabees, followed a period of religious repression and is therefore a particular celebration of religious freedom.

Hanukkah, unlike other major Jewish feasts, is a family affair, celebrated for the most part in the homes rather than in the temples or synagogues. An additional candle is lit on each of the eight days, symbolizing the growth of holiness that should occur during the feast, and gifts are usually exchanged — in some homes on each of the eight days, which, I suppose, gives the Jewish children some kind of an edge over Christians.

The theme and use of light is also very prominent, of course, in the customs and liturgy of Advent and Christmas. Apart from the religious symbolism, however, and the fact that they both occur about the same time of the year, there seems to be no connection between the two celebrations.

Latin-Ukrainian Rite Marriage

I am a devoted Roman Catholic going with a girl who belongs to a Ukrainian Catholic Church.

I need to know whether this is a Catholic church. If we are married, will this be accepted by our church without any changes on the girl's part?

The Ukrainian Rite is one of the Eastern churches which are under the pastoral authority of the Bishop of Rome.

As many Eastern-Rite churches, however, this rite has undergone a tumultuous history, including current severe pressures and persecution under the Russian Communists in the countries of Eastern Europe. As a result of these centuries-old conflicts and divisions, there are today both Catholic and Orthodox groups using the Ukrainian Rite.

Ukrainian-Rite Catholics are as much a part of our church as are Latin-Rite Catholics, though certain permissions and delegations are normally required before a marriage can take place between Catholics of these different rites.

It happens that the church you mentioned (in Pennsylvania) is one of the Catholic churches of the Ukrainian Rite. Your question, however, is a wise one, and should be asked by anyone contemplating marriage with a person who belongs to a different rite. If a Latin-Rite Catholic wishes to marry someone from an Orthodox church, long and complicated preparations might be required before the marriage can take place.

Happy Interfaith Marriages?

I recently broke an engagement because of religious differences. My parents were of two different faiths and we children were raised in both churches. I remember the confusion of it all. After I grew up, I chose to go only to the Catholic church. Shortly before we were to be married, my fiance began pressuring me to drop my formal religion and indicated that he would like to return to his former teachings of the Baptist Church. I refused.

After the break, his brother said they were both taught that all Catholics went to hell. He also said his brother wasn't very stable in his religion and was frightened by the possibility of loving someone who may never be "saved."

I guess I want to know if Protestants, especially Baptists, could ever make it in a marriage to a Catholic. Are there differences that would make a miserable marriage?

As you probably do also, I have dozens of friends and co-workers who are in happy interfaith marriages. To my knowledge, however, not one of them would deny that differences in religion place tensions and strains in a marriage that are normally not present when both partners are of the same religion. It is not unusual for these strains to be more than the husband and wife can handle.

Obviously, much depends on the nature and extent of the difference of faith, and the degree of conviction with which each party adheres to that faith. It is not possible to draw general conclusions beyond stressing the absolute necessity for the prospective husband and wife to discuss thoroughly and honestly all the aspects of differences in faith that will affect their marriage and their role as parents, and to do this before making any solid plans or commitment to a marriage.

Younger or inexperienced people tend to underestimate the influence of their spiritual backgrounds on their deepest (often unrecognized) desires for themselves, their spouses and their families. If their parents have passed on to them any kind of religious culture at all, then their understanding of God and how he relates to us and we to him, the ways we encounter Jesus and commit ourselves to him and to his people, the place of the church and its caring love for us in our lives, and even whether any of these elements of faith are seriously important or not — all these determine what a prospective spouse expects to give and to receive during the marriage. To ignore these realities and these expectations can be disastrous whatever the difference in religious faith.

Obviously, these differences may occur just as significantly between Protestants of different faiths as between a Catholic and a Protestant. One must admit, particularly today, that even two baptized Catholics may be so at variance in their understanding and practice of their faith that their union might also need to be approached, for all practical purposes, as an interfaith marriage.

To answer your question then, people of differing faiths can have a successful marriage, but only on the condition that their convictions are strong, that the demands of their consciences are clearly known to each other, and that they have each assured themselves that they will be able to pursue a good normal married life without either of them betraying their hopes or their beliefs.

This may sound like a fairly heavy task, but today more than ever such prayerful reflection and honesty is essential to a rich married life.

If you meet someone else, and marriage appears as even a remote possibility, please don't wait until you're engaged to begin this kind of discussion. Good luck.

Marrying Non-Catholics

I am confused about the church's rule regarding a Catholic marrying a divorced non-Catholic.

I can understand a rule against a Catholic marrying a divorced Catholic. But most other religions do not forbid divorce. Therefore, a divorced non-Catholic is acting completely within the laws of his own religion.

Why then should marriage with such a divorced person be against the Catholic Church's regulations?

On many matters, each religious denomination has, of course, the right to make its own rules.

When it comes to marriage, however, the rights of all religions (and that includes the Catholic Church) to make their own rules is severely limited. The reason is very simple.

The institution and covenant of marriage was not made by any individual religion. It was established by God himself, the creator of our human nature.

Certain basic things concerning marriage are, therefore, outside the jurisdiction of any religious group. Any religion, for example, which would presume to declare homosexual marriages to be real marriage covenants, subject to all the graces of a sacramental marriage, would be acting far beyond its powers.

Similarly, no religious denomination has any power to set a time limit on marriage. It could not, for instance, inaugurate a form of so-called marriage which would last for five years, or until one of the partners developed gray hair, or until the couple just could not get along together any more.

In a word, the belief of the Catholic Church is that no religion has any power to grant or approve of divorces in the way they prevail in our society.

Thus, when it comes to divorce, the position of the Catholic Church is the same for all people as it is for its own members. God is the creator of the community of life that we call marriage. Its basic structure and characteristics come from him, not from human lawmakers.

The Catholic Church, along with most other Christian churches, believes that special characteristics of sacredness and permanence arise from a Christian marriage, that is, a marriage between two baptized persons. This does not, however, change what is said above about its belief in the essential permanence of all true marriages.

Mass at Interfaith Marriage?

My fiance and I will be married in November. I am Catholic, and he has no denomination but he attends Mass with me regularly and loves the Catholic Church. We have begun our pre-nuptial instructions. The priest told us that since my fiance is not Catholic, we could not have a Mass.

We are both disappointed about this, but will accept it. However, several people, including a nun, told me that it simply isn't that way anymore, that it had changed with Vatican II. What is the rule now?

Some things obviously have changed since Vatican II, and nuptial Masses are now sometimes allowed at the wedding of a Catholic and non-Catholic.

By no means, however, is a Mass automatically possible at every interfaith marriage. Two major conditions are required. First the non-Catholic should be a baptized Christian. Normally only a Christian would understand and believe in the religious significance of the Lord's Supper, and therefore appreciate in some proper way its reenactment in our Eucharistic Celebration.

Second, both partners must desire and freely request that their marriage be celebrated within the Mass. The intent here, of course, is to be sure that the sensibilities of the non-Catholic and his family are honored, and that both partners see the ceremony as a commitment to God and each other in the sacrament of marriage.

Both requirements also aim at eliminating any use of the Mass as simply a social adornment making the marriage ceremony more ostentatious.

Decisions on this matter should be reached in consultation with the priest performing the wedding, who ultimately is responsible for assuring that all requirements are fulfilled.

Non-Catholic Marriage Recognized?

I am a convert to the Catholic Church and am engaged to marry a non-Catholic in about a year. He was married before (not in the Catholic Church) and is now divorced.

Because he was not married in the church, does the Catholic Church recognize his first marriage? Will I still be able to participate in the sacraments?

We plan to be married in the Catholic Church. Even though he has no plans to become a Catholic at this time, he enjoys going to Mass with me.

Contrary to what many apparently believe, the Catholic Church always has recognized the marriage of non-Catholics. Catholic regulations require only that, without a dispensation, all members of the Catholic Church be married before a priest in order that their marriage be valid.

As long as two non-Catholics are free to marry (in other words, if they have not married before and are not otherwise impeded from entering into marriage together), the Catholic Church looks on that union as a perfectly valid and real marriage.

Too many facts are missing from your letter for me to give you any more than one very critical piece of advice. Please go to your parish priest or to another priest you know and explain the situation to him immediately. A marriage between you and your fiance may be possible in the Catholic Church; it is also possible that such preparations would require a good deal of time, perhaps even as much as a year if formal action would be required through your diocesan marriage tribunal.

I wish you good luck. But please don't set any dates at least until after you have talked to your priest.

Can I Receive Communion?

I had a great loss in my life last May. My son, who was in college in Los Angeles, was killed playing basketball.

I am a Baptist, but I attend Mass regularly at the parish church near us. All of my young children are Catholics, as was my son who died. He tried so hard to get an education and to serve God; he also tried to help as many children in our family as possible to attend church and school.

My husband has started to go to Mass with me every Sunday and I'm grateful to God he has made up his mind to do that. My question is: To take Communion at Mass, do you have to be of the Catholic faith? I would really like to go. My heart is heavy and even though I read the Bible, I still don't understand everything.

I am deeply sorry for the hurt you are suffering because of the death of your son. From your letter, it seems that his death was an unusual loss to all your family.

Through your frequent participation at Mass with your husband and children, you have obviously come to recognize to some degree why Communion holds such an important place in the hearts of Catholics. It is the main way in which we, in our worship, unite ourselves to the death and resurrection of Our Lord, which we offer again to the Heavenly Father in every celebration of the Eucharist.

It is true that, except for emergency situations, only people of the Catholic faith should receive Communion at Mass. I have already discussed these reasons in previous pages.

For now, I would suggest you go to one of the priests you know and honestly talk your situation over with him, if you have not done so already. I am sure you would like to participate and share in the Mass as intimately as possible; he will help you do that.

Non-Catholics Receive Communion?

I realize it is possible for people who are not Catholic to receive Communion in our church. But it seems different priests have different rules. What exactly is required for a person of another faith to participate in the Eucharist at a Catholic Mass? A Methodist

couple I know received Communion at the marriage of their son at a Catholic Mass.

Catholic regulations require that five conditions be fulfilled for the administration of the sacraments of the Eucharist, penance, and the anointing of the sick to non-Catholic Christians. The person involved must:

1. be in danger of death, or in urgent need (examples: during persecution or imprisonment),

2. be unable to have access to a minister of his own faith,

3. ask for these sacraments on his own initiative,

4. have faith in these sacraments in accord with the belief of the Catholic Church, and

5. be properly disposed — that is, he or she must be aware of no serious offense against God which would be contradictory to that union with him professed in the Eucharist. (Instruction of the Vatican Secretariat for Promoting Christian Unity, June 1, 1972.)

However, the bishop of a diocese (or a national conference of bishops) may allow Communion by non-Catholics in certain other "urgent necessities." I know of instances in which bishops have, for example, allowed non-Catholic parents to receive Communion at the marriage of their Catholic son or daughter, non-Catholic spouses to receive at the funeral of the Catholic husbands or wives, non-Catholic graduates to receive with their classmates at a baccalaureate Mass, and so on.

In all such cases, however, only the bishop has the right and reponsibility to judge whether inter-Communion should take place. Of course, the conditions concerning faith in the sacraments and proper disposition must always be present.

You ask about Methodist parents receiving Communion at the marriage Mass of their son. From what I've already said, you can see that if the proper conditions were fulfilled, and if permission of the bishop was obtained, neither the priest nor the couple did anything wrong. One would assume that the priest would have explained the situation to those parents and the family in order to avoid, as far as possible, any misunderstanding.

Behind the regulation allowing Communion under certain conditions is the recognition that, while full Christian unity is not present under these conditions, there is still present enough basic communion of faith in Jesus and in the Eucharist to justify sharing Communion when these requirements are fulfilled.

Eucharist and "One Faith"

I cannot understand how Holy Communion can be given to Prot-

estants, even in the special cases when the church says this is permitted. Isn't Communion supposed to be a sign of unity? If we are not united, isn't it a sin to act as if we are?

This question particularly involves one of the conditions required before Protestants may receive Communion in the Catholic Church: that they "have a faith in the sacrament in conformity with that of the church."

There are many different levels and degrees of Christian unity. I'm sure, for example, that you disagree on some very important religious attitudes with many people you are at the Communion table with each week. Yet, you would probably say that you agree on the "basics."

What are these basic Christian beliefs? Certainly the most fundamental are a belief in God the Creator and in his redeeming love for mankind; in Jesus, the incarnate Son of God, as our Savior and Lord; that by his death, resurrection, and glorification with the Heavenly Father, Jesus has united us with himself and with each other in a way that transcends all hope and power without him; that we are reborn into this eternal life with him through baptism; that we celebrate and keep alive this redemptive act of Jesus by offering and eating the Eucharist as he commanded at the Last Supper; that in this Eucharist it is truly himself — his body and blood — that is our offering and our food; and that we are destined through faith, hope, and mutual love to be together with Christ, our brother, in eternal life.

All Protestants hold most of these truths as sacredly as we do, and many Protestants believe *all* of them as explicitly and as sincerely as we do. Surely it is quite an array of awesome doctrines to be united about.

There are other considerable beliefs which divide us, mainly in the area of church structure: the nature of the ministerial order, the role of the spiritual head of the church in the person of the Roman Pontiff, other sacraments, and so on. While acknowledging these differences, the Vatican Council and the Holy Father have insisted that it is equally important to acknowledge in word and action, wherever possible, the much greater elements which unite us as all truly "brothers and sisters in Christ."

We must keep in mind that the Eucharist relates in a special way to the Mystery of the Church, and is the sacramental sign par excellence of visible unity. Even here the church says we must acknowledge our common faith, especially if that faith includes similar beliefs concerning the Eucharist, and if the other prescribed conditions for inter-Communion are present.

Priests Differ On Communion?

Two years ago my daughter married a non-Catholic in the church.

She did not want to receive Communion because her husband-to-be wasn't Catholic, and most of the wedding party was Protestant. The priest told her they were all Christians, so they could all receive Communion.

How can this be? One priest says it is wrong, and another priest says it is all right. How can two duly ordained priests differ so much on such an important rite?

I must say honestly, I don't know. If you have reflected accurately what happened, and have not left out some important detail which might be unknown even to you, the priest who told them to receive Communion had no right to do so.

Whatever a priest's individual opinions may be, I believe Catholic people have a right to be guided by the official practices of the church. A priest may disagree with those regulations, and in important issues there is certainly ample room for dissent and protest. In a matter such as you experienced, however, it seems to me that lay people have a legitimate expectation that priests will direct them according to the teachings and rules of the church, not according to their own personal dissenting views — at least unless they make clear that the position they present is their own and not the church's.

Communion in a Protestant Church?

Your answers concerning the conditions under which a Protestant may receive Communion in a Catholic church are helpful.

How about the other way around? May Catholics now receive Communion during a worship service in a Protestant church? If so, do you think they should?

You may recall that one of the requirements for a Protestant to receive Communion with Catholics, even in the most urgent situations, is that his faith in the Eucharist (regarding the true presence of Jesus) must be in harmony with that of our church. This is because the Eucharistic Sacrifice and sacrament celebrate and signify the oneness of faith of those who share it.

This same principle answers your new question. Naturally, every ceremony commemorating the Lord's Supper, even in a Protestant church, has some similarities to our own Eucharist. All Christian churches at least believe that eating the bread and drinking the wine is a special way of recalling the death of Jesus and uniting us to him in faith.

It is our belief as Catholics, however, that the fullest Eucharistic Celebration — that is, one in which there is the true transformation of the wine and bread into the body and blood of Christ — is possible only when that liturgy is presided over by one who is a validly ordained priest. This (along with other differences in faith and doctrine which are relevant here) means that there will be significant variations of belief between Catholics and the official positions of most Protestant churches about what is happening at a Eucharistic Liturgy, and what the Eucharist is.

For these reasons, the Catholic church has specific guidelines about receiving Communion in non-Catholic Christian Churches.

"Catholic" in Apostles' Creed

During a funeral I attended in a Protestant church, the whole congregation prayed the Apostles' Creed just as we say it — including "I believe in the Holy Catholic Church." This surprised me very much. They're not Catholics, so why do they say that?

The word "catholic"(Greek: catholikos) means universal or general. At least by about the year 100, the Christian community was already sometimes referred to as the Catholic Church, meaning that it was for all men, not just for certain classes or certain places.

The Apostles' Creed did not, as was once believed, derive from the apostles themselves. It went through a few minor changes even after its first use in about the form we have it around the year 200. So it's not strange that it should include the phrase "Catholic church."

When Protestants use this creed, they mean the words in their stricter original meaning, not in reference to the Roman Catholic Church.

Refuse to Give Communion?

Our son, 18, has a girl friend who was baptized in another (Protestant) church. She attends Mass with him occasionally, and I hear that she receives Holy Communion. I have since sought the advice of priests, and among their reactions was: "We cannot refuse to give her Communion unless her receiving would create some scandal." I feel that until a person is officially received into the Catholic Church he should not receive Holy Communion. What is the correct attitude?

You are correct. The Catholic Church is not alone in its position that Holy Communion is more than a merely friendly act, or something nice to do at Mass. The Eucharist is the sign of community and oneness of faith with those who are with us around the altar, and normally should not be received by anyone who at the present time does not share that membership in the community.

Many Protestant denominations, though not all, have the same belief and policy. Persons of other faiths are asked not to receive Communion at their worship, and their own members are asked not to do so elsewhere. In a sense, receiving Communion in a church where one does not share beliefs and membership with that church demonstrates at least a fuzzy faith, and perhaps even a certain dishonesty; something is said in action that is not, in fact, true.

On the other hand, what the priests told you is also true. It is impossible for a priest to check on such things when an individual presents himself for Communion at Mass. As I explained in a previous question, there are certain, though very limited, conditions under which a Christian of another faith could receive Communion in the Catholic Church. For this and other reasons, the priest gives everyone the benefit of the doubt at the time.

However, if he suspects that the individual involved should not be receiving the Eucharist, he should check with that person later to make sure there is no misunderstanding.

Catholics and Masons

I like reading your column in our paper which I get at church on Sunday. Two years ago, I joined the Masons. I know this has helped me to be a better man in many ways. There is a man in our lodge who belongs to the Knights of Columbus, which I think is great. I would like to know the church's view on a Catholic being a Mason, and also, being a Mason, can I join the Knights of Columbus?

The prohibition against Catholics belonging to the Masonic Order arose out of a tradition of strong anti-Catholic and anti-religious policies of Masonry in the past. In many parts of the world, that spirit no longer exists.

The church has said, therefore, that where there is no hostility or enmity toward the church — which still endures in certain parts of the world — Catholic laymen may belong to the Masons. Many Catholic men in our country now, as yourself, are Masons.

As a fraternity that is strongly Catholic, the Knights of Columbus have traditionally followed the laws of the church in such matters. I know of no regulation that would prevent a Mason, who is a member of the Catholic Church in good standing, from being a Knight of Columbus as well.

Mass Intention for Non-Catholic?

During the last few years I have seen Mass intentions in our parish bulletin for people who are not Catholilc. It was my understanding in the past that such Masses were not allowed. Has there

been a change in this regulation? Could I have Masses offered for the intention of friends of other faiths who have died?

The church's Code of Canon Law has always allowed the private celebration of Mass for a non-Catholic Christian. "Private" in this context was generally interpreted to mean a Mass that was not announced, for example, in the bulletin.

In June, 1976, the Vatican Congregation for the Doctrine of the Faith liberalized that regulation a good deal. Recognizing that many Protestants hold the Catholic religion and its liturgy in considerable honor, and that many non-Catholics who hold public office have served everyone in that community regardless of their religious beliefs, public celebrations of the Mass for Christian Protestants who have died are permitted on two conditions:

1. The request for the celebration of Mass must be made explicitly by the friends or relatives of the person who has died, and this request must come from a genuine religious motive.

2. There should be no scandal involved for either Catholics or those of other faiths.

Assuming these two requirements are met, the practice you have noticed in your parish is entirely proper.

Joining Non-Catholic Ceremonies

We know that the church has changed a lot in matters pertaining to Catholics and Protestants. What are the rules about the extent we can participate as Catholics in ceremonies of other faiths?

Prayer services involving Catholics and Protestants are fortunately more and more frequent today. These services focus on common interests such as peace, Christian unity, social problems, and similar concerns. In this type of ceremony, Catholics are not only permitted but encouraged to share, whether in a Catholic or Protestant church or other location.

Catholics may also attend official liturgical ceremonies of another faith, on occasion, for any good reason — friendship or relationship with a member of that congregation, duties of public office, or even out of a simple desire to be better informed. "Official" ceremonies are those carried out, according to the proper books and rites, by the minister — such as the usual Sunday worship, the rite of the Lord's Supper and so on.

However, participation in (receiving) the sacraments of another church, such as baptism or the Eucharist, is generally not permitted. Theologians of most other churches agree with the Catholic position on this matter since Vatican II: "Celebration of the sacraments is an action of the celebrating community, carried out within that community, signifying the oneness of faith, worship and life of the community." (Directory of the Secretariat for Promoting Christian Unity, 1967)

Using Catholic Churches

Is it permissible for a priest to allow non-Catholics to use a Catholic church for religious services? A parish church was used in our city for several months by Protestants while they were building a new church. I think it's a good idea, but I'm sure surprised and wonder if this is officially allowable.

Normally Catholic churches are definitely reserved for Catholic worship for reasons which should be obvious. It is a building consecrated to the celebration of the sacraments and other most sacred rites of our faith. In addition, the exclusive use of the church for these ceremonies has a teaching purpose: It reminds us of the holiness and special character of what we do and profess there.

However, under certain circumstances, it is and always has been allowed to use the church for other appropriate purposes, sometimes even artistic performances. More recently the use of such buildings for other religious ceremonies has been approved much more than in the past.

Present regulations specifically provide that bishops may allow the use of a Catholic church or other building by Protestants if they have no place in which to carry out their religious rites properly. The practice now is quite common. (See the "Directory of the Application of the Decisions of the Second Vatican Council Concerning Ecumenism," 1961.)

Traditional Catholics Barred?

Why is it bishops may allow the use of a Catholic church or other building by Protestants, if they have no place in which to carry out their religious rites properly, but they do not allow traditional Catholics the use of their church? There are many hundreds of traditional Catholics who have to travel many miles to a motel or some other non-Catholic building in order to have their religious rites.

If by "traditional Catholics" you mean Catholics who insist on using a former Mass ritual that is now revoked by the church, the answer to your question is simply that a bishop has no authority to allow ceremonies by supposed Catholics that are in direct violation of church law. If a sufficient number of people wish a Mass in Latin according to the new rite of the Mass, they should talk to the priest of the local parish and ask him about the possibility of such a Mass. Most Catholics, however, even those who yearn for a Latin Mass, would probably not be able to follow the Latin Mass in the currently approved rite.

It should be obvious to anyone who stops to think that if a bishop were to give approval to a dissident group which calls itself Catholic, but which insists on acting contrary to the liturgical laws of the church, to have its services in a Catholic church, the result would be enormous confusion for Catholic people. In fact, most bishops would understandably be reluctant to offer Catholic facilities to a group of Protestant dissidents who wished to take advantage of these facilities to symbolize their rejection of what their own church teaches and stands for.

Thus, in terms of scandal, confusion, and misunderstanding, the situation is wholly different between permitting a Catholic church to be used by an openly and honestly Protestant congregation, and by a group which claims to be Catholic but which has, in effect, set up its own church and its laws.

Protestant Monks and Sisters?

Are there any Protestant groups of Sisters or monks in existence today? I have heard there are, and that they are getting along better than Catholic Sisters. Is this true?

Around the time of the Reformation, monasteries and convents were outlawed in most Protestant areas, especially in England. A few, however, lasted up to the present, though their membership is small.

During the last century, a major revival of the religious life developed in England, with many Anglican-Episcopalian orders of men and women being formed in Europe and the United States. Numerous such communities still flourish.

Since World War II, a remarkable increase of interest and reappraisal of the importance of religious community life for both men and women has occurred in Europe and, on a smaller scale, in this country. Dozens of orders and brotherhoods have been founded by the Lutheran and Reformed churches alone. Nearly all place heavy emphasis on spiritual renewal and the contemplative life. Many have contributed enormously to the ecumenical and liturgical renewals of the past generation.

Catholic officials, including the pope and monastic scholars, acknowledge often how much Catholic spirituality today owes to some of these Protestant orders, especially in understanding the role of religious communities.

Since most Protestant communities are newer and smaller, they frequently can avoid much of the turmoil from which larger, well-known

Catholic orders are suffering. All communities, however, both Catholic and Protestant, feel the pinch of the times, admit they have much to learn from each other, and agree that arguments about which is "getting along better" are presumptuous and futile.

Joining the YMCA

Is it permissible for a Catholic to join the YMCA? I am nearing retirement and am considering taking out a membership, mainly for use of the swimming pool. I remember some opposition to the YMCA many years ago. What is the present position?

Membership in the YMCA was formerly discouraged for Catholics because such membership was much more closely identified with the religious aspects of that organization than it is today. The organization was, of course, founded by a group of Protestant men for religious as well as recreational purposes. Members are encouraged, and sometimes expected, to share in the Protestant religious activities and worship provided by the YMCA.

Nowhere in our country, to my knowledge, is this still true of YMCA centers. Under these conditions, many Catholics, including many priests, hold membership in the YMCA.

Lambeth Quadrilateral

Can you tell us what — or who? — is the Lambeth Quadrilateral? Our group is interested in ecumenism. This name appeared in an article we read, and we're all stuck. None of us ever heard of it before.

Maybe you never before encountered the name, but if you've followed ecumenical activities for very long, I'm sure its ideas are not new.

The Lambeth Quadrilateral lists the four minimal requirements offered by the Anglican Church as conditions for eventual possible reunion with other Christian churches. The points were outlined at the 1920 Lambeth Conference, an assembly of Anglican bishops held every ten years at Lambeth Palace in London. Hence the name.

The four articles involve acceptance of Scripture; acceptance of the Nicene Creed (the one we usually use at Sunday Mass); the sacraments of baptism and the Eucharist, and the "historic episcopate," dealing with the need of bishops and recognition of Anglican Orders.

The Quadrilateral was more officially titled an "Appeal to All Christian Peoples." Its provisions naturally must be seen in the light of the significant ecumenical statements and activities during the years since it was written.

Marriage Before A Priest

I understand that now a Catholic girl can be married in a Protestant church by the boy's minister. I thought it had always been necessary for a Catholic to be married by a priest to be validly and truly married in the eyes of the church.

The rule you mention was the one most of us grew up with, but your feeling is a good example of how easily we believe something has "always" been simply because it's the only way we've known. This danger applies particularly to disciplinary laws of the church, which is what is involved here.

Although Christians were urged from early days to be married in their religious (Christian) family before a priest, no rule said all Catholics *had* to to be (for validity) until 1563. For technical reasons, even that rule didn't apply to most of the United States or to some other parts of the world. Thus, a marriage involving a Catholic could be performed by a minister or judge and be recognized by the church.

In the U.S., only since 1908 have all Catholics been bound by the requirement to be married before a priest, a law which the church is relaxing in some instances now, as you indicate in your question. However, even today, a dispensation is always necessary from the bishop in order for that marriage to be valid according to Catholic Church law.

Death and Burial

A Fear of Eternity

Sometimes it seems that I am the only one who worries and is depressed by eternity and life hereafter. It frightens this man of 73 that we will go on and on after death. My choice would be to just be reunited with our departed family and call it a day. My weary bones say I have been around long enough. Almost every month one of my former schoolmates takes his leave. I'm ready to join them except for the specter of eternity.

Believe me, you are not alone. Something of your experience is shared by everyone, especially as she or he advances in years. Your question is simply your way of expressing one of the major elements in the age-old experience of the human family, the fear of death. It is not so much death itself, but the wonder of what is on the other side that can give one the shivers.

Even Jesus could not explain that fear away, and he did not try. However, one of his favorite expressions was, "Don't be afraid." And there is nothing about which he was more emphatic in that statement than about the fear of death.

I believe his entire attitude can be summarized like this: "I can't begin to explain to you what is on the other side of death. I can only tell you, as I have tried to prove, that the heavenly Father loves you and that where you are going will be your home just as it will be mine. Just try to do as I have told you, and then trust me."

That may sound extremely simple, but it really is what we well might call the last will and testament of Jesus. I urge you to read the Gospel of St. John, chapters 13,17, where Jesus attempts, among other things, to prepare the disciples (and us) not only for his death but also for our own. Everything revolves around his promise that he is going before us to prepare a place for us, that where he is, we also will be, and that the joy that is his will be ours to the full.

As I have said before, Jesus really does not tell us too much about life after death, probably because he knows we could not understand if he tried.

Only a few great saints have found the experience of death a total joy, and to be honest, sometimes I wonder about them. For the rest of us, what God asks is a calm, grateful acceptance of his will, and trust that the Father will surely answer the moving prayer of Jesus that all his family, all his friends, will be in his company in the glory of eternity. (John 17:24)

That may not be all we would like to know about eternity, but it far surpasses what mankind once dreamed it would ever know.

Church's Position on Cremation?

I am a senior citizen and would like to know about cremation. How can it be permitted now if the church once did not allow it? What happens to the ashes? I've been thinking about being cremated, but some of my family is against it.

You're not the only one wondering about this. I receive more letters and questions now about cremation than any other subject.

Cremation was formerly forbidden by the church because it was promoted years ago, especially in Europe, by groups who used cremation as an argument against belief in the resurrection. How could God possibly collect all those ashes and smoke together to make us rise again?

It's been a long time since that argument was raised seriously by anyone. So cremation is no longer forbidden, provided that the individual involved and his family intend no disrespect or contempt for the body or for our faith. In fact, the funeral rite of the church explicity provides for cremation ceremonies.

The ashes need not be buried, as long as they are disposed of in a manner appropriate to the dignity of the human body.

I strongly suggest a few considerations, however, before you or anyone else decides on cremation. When it speaks of cremation, the church points out its "preference for the custom of burying the dead in a grave or tomb, as the Lord himself willed to be buried." There are good reasons for this reminder, at least in our Western culture.

Fifteen centuries ago, St. Augustine noted that our Christian funeral rites are more for the living than for the dead. The deceased individual may be unaffected by cremation as distinct from usual burial, but his friends and relatives still have many lessons to learn about life and death, the shortness of our time on earth, and the priorities in our life that can become extremely confused in the business of daily living. As Augustine said, our confrontation with death can put things back into proper focus.

The point being made by the holy bishop was that we need the reminders that come to us in the presence of the body of a friend, in the Eucharist we offer, and in the placing of the body in the grave. All our funeral liturgy, from wake to burial, beautifully spells out those reminders in the context of Jesus' own death and resurrection.

Even though cremation is now lawful, we should think of what we can do for those left behind. At very least, when family is involved, I believe one should discuss the matter thoroughly with them and make sure they are psychologically and spiritually comfortable with the arrangements. Should we ever lose contact with those large spiritual realities that confront us in death and in the liturgies of burial, we would lose something very precious in our Christian lives.

Anatomical Gifts

In your answer about cremation you said, "Even though cremation is now lawful, we should think of what we can do for those left behind."

This remark prompted a question that has been on my mind for some time. Is it permissible for a practicing Catholic to will his or her body to science? I would like my body used for the betterment of humanity in any way, after I am finished with it. I am also concerned about the effect on my grieving relatives.

It is certainly lawful, and can be a great act of charity, for one to donate his or her body, or a needed organ, at the time of death. The use of organs and bodies for transplants, education and research is still significant, even though medical schools themselves rely heavily today on models which simulate most major physical structure and functions.

If the decision is made for such a donation, record is kept by the individual or the family, and the body is removed for that purpose immediately after death.

In my opinion, you are wise and thoughtful to consider not only your own feelings but those of your relatives as well. The funeral and burial rite can help them deal with the grief resulting from death, and also help them accept the reality of death — their own as well as yours. I agree that you should discuss your thoughts with them, and learn their feelings before you make a decision.

If you're interested, there are several excellent sources of information. Perhaps the most comprehensive is the Continental Association of Funeral and Memorial Societies, Inc. (CAFMS) (Suite 1100, 1828 L St. N.W., Washington, D.C. 20036). Their "Manual of Death Education and Simple Burial" includes addresses for groups arranging specific organ transplants (kidneys, knee joints, glands, corneas, etc.)

along with addresses of medical schools and other agencies which may need bodies for education and research.

(Unfortunately, I must point out that, in addition to the above and some other helpful information on death and burial, the manual includes a number of rather bizarre ideas and suggestions, among them a chapter entitled "Ground Rules for Self-Termination," a nice-sounding phrase heading a series of suggestions on when and why to commit suicide!)

A Uniform Donor Card, providing for a gift of part or all of one's body to a living person who needs it, or for education-research, may be obtained from Medic Alert, Turlock, California, 95380. Many states now have donor forms on the back of, or attached to, drivers' licenses.

Sisters Donate Bodies?

As archivist for our religious community, I have on record that several Sisters wish to donate their eyes to research, and others wish to donate their bodies to science.

I can accept the giving of an organ, and I can understand if there is death resulting from a rare disease. I find it hard to reconcile the exposure of that body and depriving it of Christian burial in the interest of science after a run-of-the-mill death. It seems to me there are, or will be, enough cadavers for that purpose.

There seems to be a significant difference in the need for bodies for scientific purposes from one part of the country to another. I would suggest you contact a medical school in your part of the country and ask if they need such gifts.

Assuming that the institutions provide as much respect as possible for the body (a fact which should be investigated also), the gift of the whole or part of one's body with the hope that it will advance medical knowledge and perhaps allow another person to live, can be, as I have pointed out in a previous question, a thoughtful and loving act.

The body should be given a decent burial later on when the time is appropriate.

Limbo

I was speaking with a recent convert to the Catholic faith about Limbo, and she said she had never heard of it. Don't they teach that any more? Don't we believe that that is where children go who are not baptized?

One objection to older approaches to teaching Christian doctrine (which the church is trying to correct today), is that all teachings were often presented as of equal importance and certainty. Thus, some

Catholics suspected that the entire doctrinal structure of the church was collapsing when meat was allowed on Friday.

The teaching about a "Limbo" for infants is a good example. It revolves around a question about which we still know very little: What happens to an infant who dies without baptism?

For centuries there apparently was not much concern on the subject. It was simply assumed that God took care of these children in his own way. Some theologians held that such unbaptized infants suffered some pain of sense, but by the 12th or 13th centuries that idea was widely rejected.

A few centuries later, Limbo was a subject of some heated debate. The heretical sect called Jansenists taught that, according to God's revealed doctrine, all infants dying without baptism are condemned to the fires of hell. In 1794, Pope Pius VI condemned this teaching. One may believe in a Limbo — a place of happiness that is not heaven, and which has no suffering — and still be a Catholic, he said. This is the only mention of Limbo in all the major official documents of the church.

God's plan for infants who die without baptism is one of many subjects he has not told us much about. They certainly do not suffer the painful separation from God that is the result of serious personal sin. Does God, as some theologians hold, give a dying infant a moment of awareness in which he or she can make a decision for God? Or does God in some way accept the faith of the child's parents — or the faith of Jesus in his church — as the faith of that child, sufficient for salvation?

We simply don't know. We are certain only that God, in his clear love and desire for the salvation of all mankind, has arranged some plan for fulfilling that desire through the merits of Jesus our Savior.

A Limbo of natural happiness for infants is, therefore, something Catholics may believe. It is not a necessary part of our faith.

Denied A Catholic Burial?

I read some time ago that one could no longer be denied a Catholic burial regardless of his standing in the church, if that was his request. This was to include persons married out of the church, those who didn't go to Mass for other reasons but still supported the church, and so on. But this isn't happening in some places. Why?

The general rules on Catholic burial have not basically changed anywhere in the United States, though bishops and parish priests normally tend to go as far as possible in giving individuals every opportunity for a Catholic burial if it is clear that this is what the deceased man or woman would want.

You may be referring to some reported practices in several European dioceses, particularly in France. Not long ago it was announced that full Catholic burial would not be automatically denied to divorced and remarried Catholics if they have kept their attachment to the Catholic faith during their lifetime and at the time of their death. Evidence of this attachment would include the religious training of their children, attendance at Mass, etc.

In these instances, bishops have pointed out that this policy has no relation to the permanence of marriage, or to the right to receive the sacraments. It simply expresses the link the church keeps with those who are baptized.

Funeral Services for Non-Catholic

Can the funeral of a non-Catholic ever be held in a Catholic church?

Under certain circumstances it is possible for funeral services to be conducted for a non-Catholic in a Catholic church.

Priests often officiate at funerals of those not of our faith, especially when the person is a relative or is otherwise close to a member of the Catholic parish, and when the family requests it. Usually these ceremonies are conducted in the funeral home, but there is nothing in general church law that would forbid holding such a service in church. Naturally, the ceremony would rarely, if ever, include the offering of the Eucharist, but it could include any other appropriate Scripture readings and prayers.

The decision on each case would be subject to the discretion of the pastor, or perhaps the local bishop.

Burial After Cremation?

If I were cremated, could I be buried in a Catholic cemetery? I talked to a priest who told me I would need permission from the bishop for cremation and that only under certain circumstances would that permission be given.

Cremation is no longer forbidden by the Catholic Church. The practice was for a long time considered wrong for Catholics and numerous other Christians because opponents of Christianity promoted cremation as a protest against the belief in the resurrection.

Supposedly, if the ashes were scattered, God would not be able easily to gather all the pieces together.

Except possibly in a few corners of the earth, this anti-Christian mentality no longer has anything to do with cremation. Thus the church's prohibition has been rescinded. As long as there is no such anti-religious motive, cremation is perfectly permissible for Catholics.

A funeral Mass may be offered with the body present before the cremation, or a memorial Mass for the deceased may take place later. The ashes may be buried in a Catholic cemetery; in fact, it would be appropriate to do so.

No special permission from the bishop or other church authority is required for cremation. The only condition necessary is the one I mention above, although, as I've stressed before, one should thoughtfully consult the wishes and feelings of one's family before making such a decision.

History on Cremation

I still get arguments from fellow Catholics, including a couple of priests, that cremation is not allowed by the church even yet.

Could you be more specific about when the church allows cremation, and how it happened to put such emphasis on ordinary burial in the first place?

It seems generally agreed that the Christian Church adopted the practice of inhumation (burial in a grave as we have traditionally known it) from the ancient Romans, who adopted the custom in order to have more elaborate and demonstrative funerals.

Whenever feasible, this form of burial became common for nearly all Christians, even in those parts of the world such as the Far East where significantly different funeral customs prevailed.

Burial of the dead was so common in Western society that no laws prohibiting cremation were proposed until the late Middle Ages. The most stringent regulations appeared only about 100 years ago, when cremation became rather suddenly more popular in Europe.

The first general legislation banning the burning of bodies as a funeral rite came from the Vatican's Holy Office in May, 1886, noting the anti-religious and Masonic motivation behind the movement. The Code of Canon Law of 1918 continued the ban because cremation was still considered a flagrant rejection of the Christian belief in immortality and the resurrection. That code forbade Christian burial to anyone who ordered that his body be cremated. (Exceptions were always made for times of urgent public crisis, such as epidemics, war, etc.)

Less than 60 years ago, in 1926, the church was forced to repeat the warning, noting that, because of the virulent anti-religious motivation of most cremation proponents, its promoters were "enemies of Christianity."

With the decline of the anti-Christian symbolism of cremation, however, regulations have become far less strict. An instruction of the

Holy Office in 1963 recognized that there may be many personal reasons for desiring cremation — financial, emotional, hygienic, and others. While it indicates the church's continued preference for inhumation as more traditionally respectful of the human body, it presumes that people who request cremation are doing so in good faith, not out of some irreligious motive. Laws forbidding cremation now apply only when it is clear that cremation "was chosen through a denial of Christian doctrines, or results from a sectarian spirit, or from hatred of the Catholic religion and the church."

The official Rite of Funerals (which took effect June 1, 1970, by decree of Pope Paul VI) says "Christian funeral rites are permitted for those who choose to have their bodies cremated unless it is shown that they have acted for reasons contrary to Christian principles." In other words, cremation with all ordinary Catholic funeral ceremonies is permissible, unless someone desires it in order to deny his belief in the resurrection or other Christian truths.

When a body is to be cremated, the funeral Mass may take place with the body present before cremation, or the funeral ceremonies including the Eucharist could be celebrated after the cremation and burial.

The church has no regulations whatsoever about a casket. Religious customs on this matter differ from country to country.

No state in our country has an actual requirement for a casket if the body will be cremated. A few states do require that the body be shipped to the crematory in a "casket or other suitable container."

These are the facts. However, I must repeat what I said previously: Before deciding on cremation (or giving one's body to science or any other out of the ordinary plans for one's funeral), I believe the psychological and religious needs and desires of your family and friends deserve careful consideration. One of your last beautiful gifts to them can be the way you allow your death and burial to help them remember you well, and support them in their own lives.

Funeral Mass

A friend of mine, a former Catholic, died recently. I say "former Catholic" because for years she did not go to Mass. She requested that she not be brought into church after her death. In spite of this there was a funeral Mass for her.

Is this usual practice? Would a person like this always have a funeral Mass?

When a person dies after years of neglect in the practice of his or her faith, every benefit of doubt is given in determining the type of funeral rite that is provided. Often the children of such individuals are aware of situations in the family that color the attitude of the dead person quite differently than the person appeared to outsiders, possibly even to the parish priest.

On the other hand, the church does not feel it has a right to impose religious ceremonies on people who have explicity and with full consciousness rejected them. It does not presume to judge how that person stands before God, but the position of the church is that it must respect the clear intent and will of the individual as expressed when that person was alive.

It is impossible to evaluate the circumstances of the individual and family you mention. In fact, I would guess that many elements of that person's religious and family life are unknown even to you as a close friend. I assume, as I suggest you do also, that the parish priest on the scene acted with as great a concern as possible for the woman who died and for her family and friends.

Why Buried Without Mass?

A Catholic friend of mine was buried during the past few days, but there was no Mass. She was taken from the funeral home to the cemetery for something called a committal service, which lasted about 10 minutes.

In our city, Catholics are always taken to church for Mass before burial. Why wasn't she? Is this something new?

In our country, as in most of the rest of the world, the celebration of the Eucharist is nearly always a part (in fact, the central part) of the funeral rite for Catholics. For one reason or another, it occasionally happens that Mass is omitted at that time, and that the funeral proceeds from the mortuary directly to the cemetery. Such a plan is explicitly provided for in the official "Rite of Funerals."

However, whenever the Mass is not part of the burial rite itself, the Eucharistic Celebration for the deceased person should take place without the body, either before or after the funeral.

You are aware, of course, that someone who is known as a Catholic might not have a Catholic burial at all if he has, in some significant way, rejected the church and his membership in it during his lifetime.

Communion at Funeral

A dear friend and I attended the funeral of another friend in the Catholic Church. My friend is a Lutheran and is very devoted to her church.

At Communion time, this lady went up to receive and the priest gave her Holy Communion. How could she receive in our Catholic

Church if she is not a Catholic? I didn't want to question her about it for fear of hurting her feelings.

According to our Catholic teaching and understanding of the meaning of the Eucharist, unless the special conditions already described were present she should not, of course, have received Communion. In fact, many Lutherans are equally strong in their restrictions about their members' reception of Communion in other churches, or about people of other faiths receiving Communion in the Lutheran Church.

Your friend surely did what she did in a true spirit of friendship, reverence and Christian faith. Since the situation is not likely to be repeated, and since there seems little chance of misunderstanding by others, I believe you acted prudently in not attempting to correct her.

The priest, of course, had no way of knowing she is not a Catholic. Priests usually must assume that anyone who approaches for Holy Communion is a practicing Catholic.

In Which Cemetery?

Is it permissible for a parent baptized in another Christian church to be buried in the Catholic cemetery where her Catholic child is buried?

This is certainly permissible, unless there is a particular local problem. If you have any specific questions about it, please talk to the priest or funeral director and he will help you.

Distasteful Funeral Cards

Why can't something be done about the cards given out at certain funeral homes? I received one recently that prayed for "a drop of the precious blood on the devouring flames" of purgatory.

Our non-Catholic friends may be shocked at the idea of a merciful God consigning their kind and charitable friend or neighbor to "devouring flames."

You don't have to be a non-Catholic to be shocked, not to say angered, by that kind of prayer.

Such expressions go far beyond the teachings of the church concerning purgatory and life after death, and it certainly is embarrassing to be placed in a position where one feels he should explain or defend them — which is, of course, impossible.

I'm sure the writer of the prayers meant them to profess our faith in the power of the cross and of Jesus' saving death. But the good intention got lost somewhere in the purple prose and an over-fertile imagination.

Your experience, incidentally, is one reason the church insists that all prayers intended for public use be approved before they are printed. This rule isn't always followed, unfortunately. Even when it is, bizarre and easily misunderstood expressions of the kind you question occasionally slip through.

Can Catholics Avoid Wakes?

My husband and I oppose wakes for the dead. When we die we'd like our caskets closed, with no wake, and a service at the funeral home by a priest.

Sometime after the funeral, our loved ones would go to Mass and offer it for the one who has died. Would such a funeral arrangement be permitted by the church?

I realize you are simply exploring the idea. Remember, however, that the funeral ceremony is not primarily for the dead but for those who are left behind. Prayers for the deceased individual and for all the dead are included in the funeral rite. But much more significant is the aid that the funeral liturgy gives to those who are still alive to evaluate their own lives, confront again the priorities of which death reminds us, and allow our grief over the loss of a loved one to be worked out in a Christian context.

All this may not be important to you after you have died. It may be extremely significant to your children, grandchildren, and friends who will be reminded of some important truths by their encounter with the death of one of their loved ones.

I urge you not to make any such preparations without consulting your family. The ritual you wish to avoid may (excuse the expression) leave you cold. It may also be the richest and most valuable final gift you leave to your family.

Funeral Mass Passe?

Many Catholics in our area just have a funeral service at a funeral home but do have a priest present. Is there a reason for this? Is there a trend against bringing the deceased person to the church for a funeral Mass?

There surely is no trend in that direction to my knowledge. As pointed out in a previous question, the celebration of the Eucharist in church, with the body of the dead person present, remains the ideal and normal ceremony before burial. It is a profoundly significant act of prayer for the one who has died, and of faith and hope by those who are left behind.

The official rite of burial does provide for a funeral service outside of Mass. I have officiated at such ceremonies on occasion when the desires of the family or other special circumstances seemed to make that form of funeral rite more appropriate. This is surely the explanation for those occasions you have encountered.

Donate Organs After Death?

What is the position of the Catholic Church on donating vital organs after death?

One may donate one's organs for use by another person after death, provided he or she properly respects the needs and rights of friends and family who are left behind.

Several larger questions over which the individual usually has little control, but which are urgent concerns in this matter, are continually under study and evaluation by scientists and moral theologians. Such questions center on the exact time of death, in other words, at precisely what point a doctor may remove an organ for transplant to another; the proper treatment of the corpse of the human being so that it is not unnaturally dealt with as simply a thing or an animal; and even social concerns such as the not unheard-of willingness of some institutions and individuals to sell organs of a deceased person for profit.

I point out these factors only to emphasize that the question is a lot more complicated than you may realize. If you wish to do so, and your family has no reasonable objections, giving part of your body to someone who needs it is permissible and charitable.

Dead Fetuses

What does the Catholic Church teach should be done with dead fetuses? Some of those who are in favor of liberal abortion also say that, even in Catholic hospitals, such fetuses are simply thrown away, which proves that Catholics don't really think fetuses are human after all.

Those who think that proper Catholic practice is to discard the fetus are totally wrong. According to the directives followed in Catholic hospitals (and to large degree in many other hospitals), a dead fetus normally is given proper burial regardless of how mature that fetus is, as is "consonant with the dignity of a human body."

I say "normally" because in some instances there may be serious reason against it (for example, the need to use the fetus for laboratory study and observation) or it may even be impossible. Since the fetus is less than an inch long even after four or five weeks, it is entirely possible, for example, for a spontaneous abortion (miscarriage) to have occurred several days before the mother or doctor would be aware of it.

Prayer and Devotions

Do Prayers Affect God?

Could you explain how our prayers affect God's activity in the world? We ask for recovery from illness, help in safe traveling, and to be protected from rainstorms. Are these things in which God meddles — or do we really think we will change his mind? Aren't we asking for a miracle when we pray, if it doesn't happen to be "God's will?"

It isn't so much a matter of changing God's mind as of recognizing that his providence and care for us include his awareness of our prayers, our desires and our longings. We are dealing here with at least two great mysteries. One is the mystery of God's knowledge of all things, which means that nothing ever takes him by surprise or makes him realize something that somehow "slipped his mind."

The other is the mystery of man's free will, which means there is some way men and women work together with God in shaping their individual lives and destinies. Ours is a genuine personal freedom, not just a game of "let's pretend," a freedom which involves above all a personal relationship with God. It includes sharing with him our joys and sorrows, our hopes and disappointments, our wonders and our regrets — all of which is nothing else but prayer.

This is, of course, why Jesus urges us so often to pray fervently, and why he prayed so frequently himself. What the heavenly Father plans, and what he does, depends very much on what we show is important to us, in our prayers.

Doubting the Existence of God

I am 14 years old and have recently been having doubts as to the existence of God and Jesus and all the other characters of the Bible.

I used to be so devoted to God, said my prayers every night and every morning and participated fully at all the Masses. I know that

faith is believing in something you cannot see, but I am finding it very hard.

It started one day at Mass when I got to thinking: What if we're all worshiping something that doesn't exist? I started feeling very silly, like I was taking part in something that had no meaning.

Here are some questions I hope you can answer for me. If there is a God, why is there so much bad in the world? Is everything in the Bible true? How do we know ours is the right religion?

Why doesn't Jesus appear on earth every once in a while just to visit? What exactly is the Holy Spirit?

What was Jesus' job on earth? Wouldn't everything still be the same if he would not have come? Couldn't God allow reincarnation?

I will be anxiously awaiting your answer to all my questions.

First, let me tell you that few of the thousands of letters I have received through this column have pleased me nearly as much as yours. You are a prayerful person; you have a lot more faith than at this moment you give yourself credit for, and you are thinking and probing. That's a perfect combination for a potentially full and real Christian life.

Most of the questions you ask (the ones I have listed here are only about a third of them) reflect searches that have intrigued intelligent men and women as long as the human race has existed. It's impossible to respond to all of them, but I do have a few thoughts that may be helpful.

First, anyone who has not seriously asked these questions has not yet begun to live a deliberate adult life. The fact that you are asking them should in itself be kind of thrilling for you.

Second, you are at an age where you begin to question many significant things in life, most of them involved with the numerous emotional, physical and social changes you are experiencing. You are probably either a freshman or sophomore in high school, which means a lot of adjustment there also. So don't be disturbed at finding yourself confronting these large concerns about God and the meaning of life openly and squarely. It is a sign of your developing maturity that you are doing so.

Finally, in this as in other facets of your life, have a lot of confidence and trust in the people who love you, especially your family, close friends who may be a little older, your parish priest and so on. You are smart enough to know that the big questions of life do not have easy one-paragraph (or even one-book) answers. A good bit of study, prayer and the kind of wisdom that comes from thoughtful living help us toward finding those answers and, maybe even more importantly, help us to accept the relationships with God and those around us which make it possible to integrate those answers into our lives.

You may also be consoled by knowing that millions of good faith-filled Catholic men and women have lived through the same process of doubting and wondering that you now are experiencing.

In other words, for one reason or several, you must have enough insight to know that the kind of answers you are looking for are beyond you right now, but you are beginning to find them far more than a lot of other people your age. It is valuable that you keep your inquisitiveness without losing sight of your own very real faith as you go along, and the faith of those others whose lives reflect to you one solid truth: God and his love really do exist.

I realize this doesn't respond to each of your questions. But as one who still enjoys enormously finding fuller and better answers to them, I believe you are on the right track. At this point for you, that's far more important than knowing all the answers.

Praying for Good Health

I am up in years and in very poor health. No one seems to be able to help much or relieve the pain. I am getting worse every day and pray for the one thing that is very precious to me, my general health.

Someone told me that it is wrong to pray for this; it is simply meant to be that way by God. Is it a sin to ask someone to pray for your health and to pray for that intention yourself?

By no means is it a sin to pray for anything that is good. Certainly one's health is among the most valuable goods of life and it is natural that one should ask one's friends to pray for that health when it is endangered.

Frequently in the Gospels, in fact, God strongly urges us to put pressure on him with our prayers, not because he is reluctant to help us, but because perseverance and urgency in our prayers helps us to realize our dependence upon his help and increases our openness to the good gifts he can give.

Jesus tells us about the man who was asked in the middle of the night for bread. The lady at the door kept knocking so long he finally got up to give her what she wanted. He tells us that that's the way we should deal with our heavenly Father in our own prayers.

I know you can count on the prayers of many of our readers for your good health, and for courage to carry with grace and love whatever crosses may be yours.

Pray for Someone's Love

My boy friend and I will graduate from college next year. I love

him and want to marry him, but he wants his freedom to date other girls, which he is doing now.

My question is: Can I pray for help from God in this matter? I know God will not allow a relationship to continue if it is not in my best interests. I do want to marry this boy, but only if he wants to. I just think he needs inspiration.

If your boy friend still wants to date other girls, for heaven's sake don't push. If there is something good between you that might result in marriage, it can only be helped by his (and your) having the experience of knowing and relating to many other friends, male and female, until you're both comfortable and sure about settling down.

Certainly you should pray about it for God's guidance, that things work out best for both of you, and even that your friend eventually decides to marry you. But don't be surprised if each of you does a lot of changing in the meantime. The entire situation may look a lot different a year or two from now.

Infant of Prague

We have a picture of the Infant Jesus of Prague in our church. I've seen the picture or statue numerous times in homes and churches but no one seems to have any idea where the picture originated. Can you help us out?

The statue of the Infant of Prague has held a special place in the devotion of Catholics in Eastern Europe and elsewhere for nearly 300 years.

Brought to Czechoslovakia from Spain in the 1500s, it represents Jesus as an infant clothed in apparently royal robes and holding a globe with a cross on top in one hand. The other hand is held up in blessing. The original statue of wood and wax is in the Church of Our Lady of Victory in Prague, which is under the care of Carmelite priests and Brothers.

Particularly through their auspices, devotion to the Infant Jesus of Prague has spread throughout the world and many special favors have been attributed to prayers made to Jesus under that title. Since about 1650, the church has attached many special privileges and indulgences to this particular devotion to Our Lord.

Pentecostals-Charismatics

What do you think of the Pentecostal movement? Is it all right for a Catholic to belong to one of these groups and attend the prayer meetings?

The increasing interest in and growth of the Pentecostal movement (more commonly called "Charismatic renewal") seems to have paralleled the growing interest of the church and of theology about the work of the Holy Spirit in the church. Certainly at this point there is no evidence that the movement holds any threat to Catholic doctrine or spirituality. In fact, many Catholics and other Christians have found participation a help to their prayer and to their whole religious life.

The convictions on which the Pentecostal movement is based are that there is a great new outpouring of the gift of the Holy Spirit in this time; that the Holy Spirit shows these gifts and powers in some ways that resemble his activity among the early Christians, and that this outpouring of grace can help a person to a new and holier way of "living in the Spirit." There appears to be nothing in this in any way contrary to Catholic teaching.

Rapture in Prayer

Some Protestant friends of mine tell me about a "rapture" that takes place in their church. I've heard this mentioned a few times by other people also. What is this rapture?

Rapture is simply another word for a condition that Christian mysticism more generally refers to as ecstasy. In certain stages of prayer, it is not uncommon that the individual becomes so absorbed in God and things of heaven that he goes into a form of trance and is quite literally out of touch with the senses of hearing, sight, and so on.

The situation is expressed very well by the word itself. "Ecstasy" comes from a combination of Greek words that literally means "standing outside of" one's self.

While real mystical ecstasy may accompany higher forms of contemplation, some degree of this experience is not at all uncommon in Christian prayer life. When it does accompany or result from genuine prayer, it is always the work of the Holy Spirit leading the soul to a greater union with God.

The experience of people who have written about this, however, proves that it is not always a pleasant one. In fact, the word rapture more commonly identifies the forms of ecstasy that are more violent or painful.

Obviously the church has enormous respect for this kind of manifestation of the work of the Holy Spirit in our movement toward God. It is also aware that the externals of genuine ecstasy can and do often result from purely psychological causes and not necessarily from any religious experience.

As in any area of our prayer life where what is purely emotional or temperamental might be confused with genuine devotion, the church is cautious, and asks us to be aware that it is easy to confuse one with the other. As I said, these experiences are not uncommon. We should thank God for them when we recognize them, see them as a gift to increase our faith, and not use them as a criterion for how advanced we may be in the spiritual life. Such experiences may be evidence of an advanced level of prayer, or they may be more a nudge from God telling us that we are spiritually dragging our feet and that it's time to get moving. *(See next question.)*

Another Rapture

I believe you misinterpreted the meaning of rapture. To most "born again" Christians, rapture means only one thing, and that is the "great snatch" when Christ comes to take us who live, and his church, out of this world "to meet the Lord in the air."

The subject of the rapture is discussed at length today because they feel the signs of the Great Tribulation Period (Seventieth Week of Daniel) are close at hand. I am sure this is the rapture to which your writer referred.

Rapture in our Christian tradition does also embrace the meaning you indicate: the final coming of Christ to take the world to himself and unite mankind together with him to the Heavenly Father. The Catholic Church obviously considers the final coming of Christ the climax and completion of all human history. To be honest, however, it learned centuries ago not to take too seriously the dire predictions that the heavens are about ready to drop, and that the end of the world is just around the corner. It has lived through hundreds of such predictions that have come and gone.

Whether the end of the world comes one year or a hundred thousand years from now doesn't really make that much difference. The more critical concern is whether we individually are prepared for the "end," for the close of our personal pilgrimage on this earth. Our life as Christians must always be guided by faith in the supreme Lordship of Jesus which will come to its perfection when he comes again. How soon that coming will be isn't at all important.

Rosary and Marian Devotion

Is the rosary a thing of the past? This past October, no one had a rosary in his hand at church. Don't you think people are losing their devotion to Our Blessed Mother when they don't say the rosary?

I agree with you; people are saying the rosary a lot less now than they did 20 years ago. However, I'm not at all sure that indicates any less love of Mary, or of Our Lord.

We must remember a few things. One is that the rosary as a popular devotion developed over about 400 years (the 12th to the 16th century) when Catholics were almost completely cut off from any meaningful participation in the liturgy. In fact, the period was one of the low points in seeing the Mass as a community celebration.

Because of this, and because most persons couldn't read anyway, many devotions arose as a substitute for taking a more direct part in the liturgy, especially the Eucharist. The 150 Our Fathers (later 150 Hail Marys) were sometimes called the "poor man's breviary" — they matched the 150 psalms said by clerics or by others who could read.

Interestingly, saying the rosary together was one of the first ways, in modern times, that Catholics began to do anything together aloud at Mass, and to see the Mass as something more than just another private prayer, which is about the way some spiritual books described it before the present liturgical renewal.

As the Mass and other sacramental ceremonies become more significant liturgical events in our lives, it is understandable that certain devotions which partially substituted for them will decline in use.

I really don't believe there is a relatively great loss of honor and love for Mary. She will inevitably hold a high place in any religion that believes her son is God. The rosary has been and still can be a tremendous help to Christian growth. But I wouldn't identify Our Lady's position in the church with how many rosaries are said every day.

Merit for Self-Denial?

Does a Catholic who follows the old rule of Friday abstinence gain more merit than those who do not?

When anyone uses words like these, I suspect he or she still has something of a "cash register" understanding of grace. Our friendship with God, and his sharing of his love and life with us — which is what we mean by the words grace and merit — doesn't come in neat packages. It grows in mysterious, deeply personal ways, just as our other loves, by living and acting under its influence.

Anyone who follows Jesus' command to deny ourselves, take up our cross and follow him, whether by not eating meat on Friday or by other practices of self denial, "grows" in friendship with God according to the love and desire for union with Christ that lie behind it.

Personal Spiritual Growth

What advice would you give to a person who sincerely desires to grow spiritually? Would making a private retreat be a good start?

Our spiritual life, and our growth in it, is a many-faceted reality. It involves our knowledge and trust in God; our increasing realization of the presence of God in the events of our daily lives, and especially in ourselves and in those around us; our spirit of hope and faith in what is offered to us in the Gospel as essential elements of our Christian commitment, and many other things. Growth comes through prayer and reflection and action, and depends greatly on the circumstances of our personal life — about which, incidentally, you mention nothing.

The best step for you at the moment would not necessarily be a retreat, but some thoughtful reflection and consultation with someone in whom you have confidence, possibly a priest you feel you can talk to about your ideals and concerns. He will assist you in evaluating where you are, the expectations you have of yourself, and what expectations others around you may have. Much depends on whether or not you are married, have children, and their ages. Your own age and experiences of life are important factors.

Please think it over in these terms, and ask a priest, if you wish, for an appointment so you can talk with him in some leisure and allow him to offer some thoughts and options for you to follow through on.

Sacramental Holy Water

Why does the church use holy water, and what are the effects of its use for those of us who believe it combats evil?

I saw a pamphlet which says that the "devil hates holy water" and that we can sprinkle holy water for a blessing to our loved ones who live far away from us. What do you think of these beliefs?

The pamphlet from which you quote contains some questionable comments about the use of holy water, making it sound almost like a spiritual rabbit's foot.

In all uses of sacramentals, including holy water, we must keep straight exactly what a sacramental is in the church's tradition. A blessed medal, picture, or holy water, is simply a material item over which the church has prayed, asking God to accept the prayers of the church for those who reverently use it.

In a sacramental such as holy water, therefore, the devotion, faith and charity of the person using it is augmented and supported by the prayers of the church. There is no magic-like power in the water itself.

Use of holy water in the proper manner can be of great spiritual benefit. It can be a striking reminder of our baptism and of the commitment to Jesus which we made in receiving that sacrament. It can symbolize and strengthen our faith in the forgiving love of God and therefore assist us in a spirit of conversion that brings with it the forgiveness of sins.

Again, all this can be strengthened and enriched immeasurably by the blessing of the church, which carries with it the assurance of the prayers of all our fellow Catholics and Christians. Properly used with these intentions, there is nothing superstitious about holy water or any other sacramental. Unfortunately some over-zealous devotees of certain sacramentals occasionally come close to stepping over the line.

Religious candles

Where did our use of candles at Mass come from, and are they still required? There seems to be no consistency about the number of them, or even whether there should be any at all?

Christian use of candles was taken over from the Romans, who used them for various civic and religious occasions. It goes back to the earliest Christian liturgical practice.

Perhaps some idea of the symbolism can be understood from the fact that the lighted ceremonial candle for evening prayer developed into our paschal candle. These lights were also used in funeral ceremonies, before the tombs of deceased Christians, and in front of images of the martyrs and other saints. In other words, they signified then what they do for us now: light (Christ), life, hope, resurrection, and faith.

Candles should still be used at Mass, though regulations concerning them — composition, number for various kinds of Masses, etc. — are not nearly as detailed as they once were. The new Order of Mass, in effect in the United States since November, 1971, stipulates the following concerning candles at Mass:

"Candles are required during liturgical services to express devotion or the degree of festivity. They should be placed either on the altar or around it, in harmony with the construction of the altar and the sanctuary. The candles should not block the view of what is happening at the altar or what is laid on it."

Praying for One to Die

Is it wrong to hope and pray that someone will die? I know it sounds bad, but I think there are times when it is the right thing to do, for all concerned?

It is always wrong to wish evil to another. If one desires that another person die from a motive of hatred, so that death is seen as a punishment or suffering, it is obviously wrong and a gross violation of charity.

Death may often be seen, however, from every prudent and Christian viewpoint, as a blessing not only for others but for the individual himself. One common example is that of an individual with a terminal illness, whose condition is cause of enormous pain and suffering not only to the sick person but to his or her loved ones as well.

Another situation (and this appears to be what your letter is speaking of) is that of an elderly person whose senility causes immense suffering and much needless tragedy for others. This may be because of close family relationships, positions of responsibility held by the older individual, or other ties. Often — perhaps most of the time — such a condition is as painful to the individual himself as to those around him, and death may once again be seen, from the human and Christian viewpoint, as a true good for all concerned.

After all, we do believe that death is not the ultimate evil or final destruction, but the necessary passage to eternal life. Also, there is always for us Christians the realization that life and death are in God's hands, and our thoughts and prayers in these matters imply recognition of his Divine wisdom and providence.

Someone once said it is wrong to wish another to die, but one may rightly wish him to go quickly to his eternal reward. The remark may sound frivolous, but there is more than a kernel of good theology in it.

Rosary

Is it necessary to say all five decades of the rosary at the same time?

I sometimes say only a decade each day. Is that all right?

There is no required way to say the rosary. In fact, different countries, different Catholic cultures, sometimes vary a good deal in the sequence and number of prayers — though all are based on 150 Hail Marys and reflections on the chief events in the life of Christ.

Regular praying of the rosary, all of it or any part of it, was and still is a powerful prayer and a marvelous way to express one's love for Our Lord and his mother.

Nine First Fridays

I am still one who likes to make the nine First Fridays, but I don't know anything about where and when these promises were made. What did Christ promise about this devotion?

The practice of the nine First Fridays resulted from certain revelations apparently made by Jesus to St. Margaret Mary Alocoque about 300 years ago. St. Margaret Mary was a French Visitation nun who had a remarkable devotion to the Heart of Jesus as a symbol of God's love for us. At her urging, after these revelations, the great devotion to the Sacred Heart of Jesus was established in the church, including the Feast of the Sacred Heart which we celebrate in June.

According to St. Margaret Mary, Jesus made 12 "promises" to those who honor his Sacred Heart. The last of these was this: "I promise you, in the exceeding mercy of My Heart, that Its all-powerful love will grant to all those who go to Communion on nine First Fridays of the month the final grace of repentance; they shall not die in Its disfavor nor without receiving the Sacraments, My Divine Heart becoming their assured refuge at that last moment."

The practice is, in other words, a sort of novena — a nine-time prayer which Christians have used for centuries as one of the ways of emphasizing the importance of perseverance and trust in our prayer to God.

One must remember that, at the time of these revelations, Holy Communion was rarely received by many Catholics, especially in France, where the severe Jansenist heresy was strongest. Neglect was such that once a year was often considered enough, even for the "most worthy." The weekly, even daily, Communion so common among practicing Catholics today was all but unheard of.

As a private revelation, of course, these promises in no way constitute an obligatory part of Catholic belief or practice. However, devotion to the Heart of Jesus, as the sign of Our Lord's love, is now an important and special part of Catholic tradition. In approving and promoting it, the church indicates that it contains nothing contrary to our faith, and that it may be devoutly believed and practiced.

Novena Devotions

When I was younger, about 30 years ago, my parish had novena devotions one night a week. Other churches had similar devotions on other nights.

Do any churches hold novenas like that anymore? If not, why were they discontinued? I used to enjoy them and looked forward to these ceremonies.

I'm not sure anyone knows the answer to that one. Perhaps it's something like asking why, for no apparent reason and with no change in the teaching of the church about sin or the sacrament, people stopped going to confession with anything like the former frequency. No one has the answer to that either.

My opinion is that a major explanation of the decline in extra-liturgical devotions such as these lies in the greatly increased emphasis on Eucharistic Liturgy since Vatican II. Before the liturgical changes of the past two decades, the Mass was viewed, far more than it is today, as the priest's personal action, and Masses were generally limited to early morning, particularly on weekdays.

Today peoples' devotional lives are far more Eucharist-centered. Many who in former days might have attended novena devotions now participate in evening Masses. The Eucharistic Sacrifice often constitutes an integral part of important afternoon and evening religious gatherings, which was of course impossible before Vatican Council II.

Add to this the emphasis on Scripture as the primary inspiration of Catholic spirituality, and several significant social developments (change in parish structure, reluctance of people to go out at night, and so on) and you probably have most of the explanation why the kinds of devotion you speak of have declined in American Catholic life.

Can We Bless God?

During the Stations of the Cross and other prayers, we say, "We adore Thee, O Christ, and we bless Thee." I can't understand what talent or ability I have to bless Christ. Isn't it wrong to say we bless Christ or God?

In a way it is wrong. The Latin word "benedicere" usually means to bless in the commonly understood sense to communicate life or some other good to another. It also, however, may mean to thank someone, or to acknowledge another's power and goodness. The phrase "Blessed be God," for example, which we find often in the psalms and in the New Testament is a prayer of praise and recognition of the goodness of God, and of the benefits he has bestowed on us. The phrase carries the same meaning in your prayers.

Stations of the Cross

Do the stations of the cross, as we have them in our churches, actually describe happenings during the passion of Christ? Someone has said they do not, but I heard from a neighbor who recently visited Jerusalem that the 14 stations are marked along the way of the cross there.

The devotion which we know as the Way of the Cross developed during the very late Middle Ages, perhaps the 1200s and the 1300s, both as a form of prayer and as a sort of catechism about the sufferings of Our Lord.

Various Franciscan communities, which already had charge of the holy places in Jerusalem for Latin-Rite Catholics, helped popularize the devotion, which went through many forms. Once they included seven falls under the cross. Another variety totalled 43 separate stations. Eventually, the 14 stations as we know them, concluding with the burial of Jesus, became most common.

We may, in fact, be experiencing right now another transition in this devotion. Many, if not most, of the books of stations include a sort of 15th station which in one way or another calls to mind Christ's resurrection.

At any rate, the markings of the 14 stations along the Via Dolorosa (Sorrowful Way) in old Jerusalem are comparatively recent. The accuracy and even historical validity of some of them are open to considerable question.

Hot Cross Buns

We are converts to the Catholic faith, and some friends gave us hot cross buns during Holy Week. They told us this was a Catholic tradition on Good Friday. If that is true, what does it mean?

The tradition goes back only a few hundred years, beginning in England after the Protestant Reformation. In fact, it seems to have been Protestants who started it.

For some time after the Reformation was underway, many Protestants continued, at least in part, the custom of eating fish on Friday, especially on Good Friday. Probably the hot cross buns idea developed in that same spirit of observing the day Our Lord died.

Sunday Observance

One almost never hears anything about the rules of observance of Sunday — servile work, etc. Does Sunday as a day of rest have any meaning for us Catholics any more, besides the obligation of hearing Mass?

It most certainly does. We have to start with the fact that the importance of Sunday as the Lord's Day never did depend on the "rules" for the day. They depend instead on what the day is: the celebration of the resurrection of Jesus and of our own resurrection with him.

For this reason, not because it is a church law, we Christians have always seen this day as a unique way of worship when we should offer the Eucharist to praise, thank and be glad with God for this central event of our faith, and for all it has meant to the world.

You must be aware that the whole "forbidden" work idea developed in a radically different agricultural-labor society. It is futile and misses the point entirely to discuss (as we used to do) whether crotcheting, gardening or changing the oil in the car are allowed on Sunday.

Our aim is rather to have our home and our activities reflect, on that day above all, the peace, joy, contentment and love that should be ours because of what Jesus has done for us.

While old rules may be de-emphasized, there is no downgrading of Sunday. Just the opposite. This is another example of how much more faith and generosity it takes to think through seriously what it means to

be a Christian, than it does to simply follow a few regulations and feel
we have fulfilled our obligations.

Etcetera

Why Does God Allow Worry?

If God loves us, why does he allow people to suffer mental torment and worry? Why are hospitals filled with people who are sick or who are physical wrecks because of unbearable inhibitions, guilt, lack of self-confidence, loneliness and frustration? This God must be sadistic rather than loving.

In his providence, God has enabled mankind to grow much through the centuries in its capacity to deal with the evils that plague it, including the ones you mention. The advances in sciences of all sorts make possible our management, if not cure, of so many physical and emotional illnesses that once were mysteries and perhaps bearers of certain early death. Our first responsibility, then, is to avail ourselves as much as we can of the care and cure that can help us cope with and heal our hurts.

Your question obviously goes much deeper than that. It is, in fact, among the oldest that has puzzled mankind. The most perceptive people in history have wrestled with what is called the "Problem of Evil" — why is there suffering and evil in the world, and were does it come from? They've never arrived at a satisfying answer.

For example, among the many theological issues addressed in the creation story of Genesis is that of the origin of evil. About the only answer it could give is that suffering and pain certainly do not come from God, from whose hand all things come as good. Evil arises rather in some mysterious way from inside us, from our disobedience and disorientation from the purpose of our creation.

Even Jesus could not remove suffering and death from our human condition, even for himself. For the first time, and for all time, he brought to a pained humanity the promise of meaning, healing and hope in its hurt. But he did not create a new Garden of Eden.

The suffering you abhor would lead us to a sadistic God only if the pain were inflicted by him. It is not. Indeed, God could stop it only by removing our free wills, our opportunity for free choices, which would mean taking away our potential for love. God allows us to hurt ourselves, and does all he can to reduce the hurt and ease the pain (which is what Jesus is all about) because he knows that, in the end, the love that has grown amidst that pain will make it all worthwhile.

Of that Our Lord himself is the supreme proof and assurance.

Jesus: True God and True Man

The other day a priest referred to Jesus as a human being, as you did in one of your columns. I've always been taught that Jesus is one being, one person, the second person of the Blessed Trinity, that he is indeed not a human person, but a divine person. I accept fully and unconditionally the mystery of the Incarnation and all that the church teaches about the two natures and wills.

Years ago, a Sister gave the comparison of a king who fought with his soldiers, himself wearing the uniform of a private. He was a real private without in any way renouncing his royalty. Briefly, he was a soldier like the rank and file, and at the same time a king. This seems an apt comparison, doesn't it?

Only up to a point. The comparison has too many similarities to an ancient heresy called Docetism, which cropped up in the early centuries of the church. Named from the Greek word, "dokesis," meaning an appearance or something imagined, Docetists asserted that Jesus was not really human. He seemed to be a man, through some sort of illusion, but he really was not.

Thus, the king in your comparison was not really a private; he only appeared to be. It seems to imply, therefore, that when God came to earth, he was not really a human being, not really a man; he only appeared to be. And that is absolutely not what we believe about Jesus.

The popularity of that kind of comparison, and the discomfort many Catholics and other Christians still demonstrate when someone insists that Jesus was and is completely, perfectly human, seem to indicate that the Docetists' concern remains quite alive in the church. Isn't it totally beneath God's dignity — almost blasphemous — to believe that God, without ceasing to be God, literally became a human being?

The answer of our Catholic faith is, loud and clear, "No." In some mystery of providence, God found it fitting to his plan of creation — and to his plan of revealing his eternal love for us — that the second person of the Trinity become a member of the human race.

This is precisely what the church means when it says that Jesus is one person, the divine person of the eternal word of God, with both a divine and human nature. He is completely and totally God, and he is completely, totally man.

Gregorian Calendar

A religious tract someone gave me has a lot of insulting things to say about the Catholic Church, especially about the pope. Most of them are ridiculous, and I know the answers. One thing I never heard about, though. It says that several hundred years ago one pope (Gregory XIII) foisted the whole new calendar on the world simply out of spite against the Protestants, and to make a feeble attempt to save the declining prestige of the papacy. What about this?

If your reading of this tract is accurate, the resurrection of this old controversy is almost eerie, somewhat like charging that Columbus' claim that the earth is round was simple religious propaganda.

Back in the first century before Christ, Julius Caesar revised the calendar to correct serious errors in the system. Several centuries later, it became obvious that this Julian calendar also had serious defects. The solar year had been computed at 11 minutes and 14 seconds too long. This perhaps doesn't sound like much, but it means a full day every 128 years. By the time of Pope Gregory XIII (who became pope in 1572), the "legal" calendar lagged 10 or 11 days behind true sun time, and caused considerable confusion and difficulty politically, religiously, and, of course, scientifically.

Numerous efforts at reform stretching back nearly 200-300 years had flopped. So Gregory determined the time had come to act. After long consultation by an international commission with universities and scientists throughout the western world, our present calendar (with leap years, etc.) was developed — including the complete elimination of 10 days in October, 1582. Oct. 5 became Oct. 15.

Most European nations accepted the new calendar at once, but many Protestant governments refused, particularly in Germany and England. Some labeled the new arrangement the work of Satan, claiming the pope was preparing a blood bath of Protestants, and even that the end of the world was imminent because of Gregory's fooling around with Mother Nature.

Only the vigorous defense of the new calendar by such renowned scientists as Tycho Brahe and Johann Kepler gradually brought such opponents to acknowledge that the change was necessary and had nothing to do with religious sectarianism.

Today, no civilized person denies that the Gregorian calendar reform constitutes one of the most praiseworthy and important accomplishments in modern history.

He Descended Into Hell?

In the Apostles' Creed we say, "He descended into hell." Would you please explain why we say this? Jesus was the only perfect person on earth. He never sinned. Why would he have to go to hell?

The word "hell," as it is used in the Apostles' Creed, does not mean the "hell of the damned," which it usually means in current English.

Our word "hell" comes from an old Teutonic word "hela," which means a hidden, or covered place. In earlier English literature, it was used to describe any kind of pit, dungeon or dark hole.

The use of the word in our English translation of the Creed is unfortunate, but has been traditional for so long it will hardly be changed now. The word is a translation from a Latin (also Greek and Hebrew) word which means the "lower regions" — a generic name for the place where people would go after death, without regard to a condition of reward or punishment.

We have a similar word (unfortunately also vastly misunderstood) in our Christian tradition. The name "limbo" has been used to designate a possible place or condition for children who die without baptism — in other words, a place that is neither heaven nor hell, but somehow neutral.

Misunderstandings of what the church has and has not taught about limbo are widespread. Nevertheless, limbo would probably be a more appropriate word than hell for the "place where Jesus went" after his death.

"Privileged" Funerals and Weddings?

I've been to many Catholic funerals and weddings. Frankly, I am mystified often by the differing numbers of priests attending such events. At certain ones many priests are present; at others not even the pastor is there to officiate. How do you explain this different kind of treatment for different people?

As pastor of a fairly large parish, I am sensitive to the concerns you bring up. I know that no matter how simple and often obvious the answer, misunderstandings inevitably arise and rash judgments too often result.

Usually, the answer is quite obvious when one knows the background of the individuals involved. With almost no exceptions, the explanation is simply that the individual has worked (often in a very quiet way) in agencies or institutions that would involve contact with many priests. Or it may be that the family itself includes some priests, or just close friends who are priests.

Many such details would, of course, not be familiar to persons who do not know the family intimately.

As for which priest performs a wedding or funeral, in most parishes I believe that depends simply on which priests are free to do so, and who is able to work best with the family in making arrangements for the wedding or funeral. I have always found people thoroughly understanding and thoughtful in such situations.

Do We Still Believe in Purgatory?

My question concerns purgatory, which we hardly ever hear about any more. I always thought it was a place, and that a certain amount of time was to be spent in purgatory by those who still have punishment due for sin. How can the Catholic doctrine of purgatory be reconciled with the concept that the afterlife is outside of time and space? What, if anything, are we to believe?

Purgatory has certainly not gone by the wayside. It is still very much a part of our faith, as every sacrifice of the Mass and every other prayer for the dead attests.

Perhaps one reason less is said about it today is that we have a lot of collected debris about purgatory to clear out of our minds. The hoary pictures of torture, pain, and a scourging God — which made of purgatory a kind of mini-hell — may literally scare the devil out of someone, but they're totally irrelevant to the doctrine of purgatory.

These gory images grew up around the idea of purgatory through the Middle Ages and later into the Renaissance.

At least two things are clear in the Catholic tradition concerning purgatory. First, the church teaches that there is some condition or circumstance after death by which any temporal punishment remaining for sins committed during life is satisfied, and that by our prayers and good works on earth, we can assist those who are "in purgatory." This is simply an application of our belief in the communion of saints which unites all who are joined in Christ, whether still on earth or in the next world. This much is taught by the church as revealed truth from God. It is, of course, something about which we would know nothing if he did not tell us.

Second, it is equally clear that the official teachings of the councils and other sources of Catholic belief have no intention of answering details about purgatory — whether it is a state or condition on one hand, or a "place" on the other. Or whether "time" is involved or not. Since the world after death would not seem to have hours or days or locations in our sense of those words, it seems quite unlikely that purgatory involves place or time as we usually think of them. It is very possible that, in the burst of awareness of the reality of God and creation that might occur immediately after death, the pain that comes from our knowledge of our sins and shortcomings might be so acute and intense that an entire purgatory — or cleansing, which is what the word purgatory means — could occur in an instant.

While such an explanation seems to square with what we might suspect about the threshold of eternity, we simply don't know for sure. The church hasn't attempted officially to satisfy our curiosity about such questions — and probably couldn't if it tried.

Catholic Press Conservative?

Aren't most Catholic publications conservative?

Apart from the comparatively few which declare almost in so many words that they intend to give one viewpoint — the conservative viewpoint — I believe the more common feeling is that most Catholic publications are *liberal.*

It seems to me that most Catholic magazines and newspapers are, especially on matters of social justice, war and peace, and similar concerns, considerably more liberal than the majority of Catholics. But, for that matter, so are the encyclicals of the modern popes and the official statements of the American bishops during the past generation.

Is Cardinal Mindszenty Still Alive?

We recently saw reference in a news article to Cardinal Mindszenty. Is he still alive, and if so, where does he live?

Cardinal Josef Mindszenty of Hungary died in Vienna in 1975. He left his native country in 1971 on orders from Pope Paul VI, after nearly 30 years of persecution and imprisonment by Communist governments.

Cursillo

What is a Cursillo? How does it differ from a retreat?

Since it is intended to help one to examine and improve his life as a Christian, a Cursillo has some similarities to a retreat, but it also has many important differences.

Started in Spain 25 or so years ago, its full name is "Cursillo de Christianidad" — literally, a short course in Christianity. It is intended to be just that: a basic discovery of one's beliefs and responsibilities to God and man as a Christian. Thus, an individual makes only one Cursillo in his life, though he or she may be part of a team presenting the program many times.

There are also follow-up meetings (reunions), and regular large gatherings (ultreyas) of those who have made a Cursillo, to preserve and develop the spirit of community and mutual support the program is intended to promote.

Another difference is that the 15 talks contained in the three-day program are standard as to subject, but are prepared and written personally by the five priests and 10 laymen or women who give them.

As anything else, of course, details and quality of the Cursillo programs differ from place to place, depending on leadership personnel, general interest, and other factors.

Holy Thursday Mandatum?

Some of us are studying Holy Week as part of our work for Lent. Why is the ceremony of the washing of the feet on Holy Thursday called the "Mandatum?"

Mandatum is a Latin word for command or commandment. After describing how Jesus washed the feet of his apostles at the Last Supper, St. John's Gospel tells us that Jesus then commanded them to follow his example.

As Jesus said, the servant is not above the master. His command — or mandatum — was that their service of each other, symbolized by the washing of the feet, should always be what would characterize them as his true disciples.

Charismatic Movement

How does the Charismatic Movement coincide with the teaching of the Catholic Church and the teaching of Jesus Christ? Many priests and bishops go along with it, while many do not approve of it because it's too emotional. And that it is. I have seen some stand on their toes, exactly as some Protestant sects do.

Jesus said we must become like little children, and little children surely do not become emotional.

I'll pass over your last sentence. You obviously are acquainted with children quite different from the ones I know.

The Charismatic Movement takes its name from the Greek word "charism," which means a free gift, a favor. In the church, it has meant a special talent or power given to certain people by God for the service of the rest of the Christian community, the church.

Some of the charisms are for service in the church (governing, for example), others for teaching or preaching, and others for more spectacular purposes such as healing, speaking in tongues, prediction of the future, and so on.

These gifts of the Holy Spirit were especially necessary in the early days of the church when the Christian people had not yet experienced many of the signs of Christ's presence that intervening history has offered. But such charisms can still be useful even today, and may be a source of faith and hope to those who experience them and use them well.

They are also important to the institution of the church, with which they will nearly always be in tension, as a reminder that the Holy Spirit "blows where he will," and that his actions are not limited to popes, bishops and others.

Already in the New Testament, St. Paul warned against two main dangers in the charismatic activities in the church. An individual may too easily fool himself about the genuineness of his special gifts, especially the more spectacular ones. Also, every gift is suspect if it does not serve the whole community by aiding the spirit of cooperation, love and mutual support. If the Charismatic Movement, or any other movement, becomes divisive or elitist, that's the best proof that there is something seriously wrong with it.

One reason that bishops, priests and others differ on their view of charismatics is that they differ on their basic vision of what the church is. Another reason is that charismatic groups themselves differ enormously in their spirit and in their understanding of where they fit into the rest of the Christian community.

Read First Corinthians, Chapters 12 to 14, for St. Paul's comments on charismatics.

New Gospel Found?

I am reading a book published some years ago ("The Word," by Irving Wallace) that describes the finding of a new Gospel. According to this Gospel, Jesus was supposed to have lived 40 or 50 years on earth after the cruficixion. Could such a Gospel really be found?

The novel you mention does not pretend to be anything more than pure fiction, of course.

You ask: Could it be true? It is not inconceivable that archeologists might someday find a hitherto unknown "Gospel" or other writings by early Christians — perhaps even by an apostle, as is the case in the story you mention. There are, in fact, many such documents, some supposedly about further details in the life of Jesus, which have been known since the earliest centuries of Christianity.

Considering the prominence of the apostles, however, and the eagerness Christian people would have had to preserve their words, it is not likely that anything new from them will turn up.

These other "Gospels" are not, and would never become, part of the Bible. They might be quite uplifting and be in some way inspired by God, as are numerous writings that are not in Scripture. The Bible, however, constitutes that special group of writings the Christian

Church has looked at and said, in effect: These books are inspired in a special way by God. They help identify what we are as Christians; they are for all time a norm and guide to understanding what is essential about Jesus and his teachings.

Any newly discovered works, then, while possibly holy and helpful, would not be included in Holy Scripture.

Hitler a Catholic?

I have just heard the following statement on a national radio religious hour: "Adolph Hitler was a Roman Catholic in good standing."

Is this true?

Hitler's mother was Catholic, and he had some Catholic education in a German Benedictine monastery. He received the sacrament of confirmation when he was 15 years old, but rarely went to church.

Long before he became chancellor of Germany (1933), he had determined to destroy the Christian faith in the German people, and even had visions of wiping out the church entirely. Under the Nazi rule, Catholics and other Christians shared the concentration camps and the gas ovens with the Jews.

I doubt if Hitler himself, let alone the church, considered him a Roman Catholic in good standing.

Were Lenin, Stalin Ordained?

At a recent Knights of Columbus meeting, someone said that Lenin, Joseph Stalin and Adolph Hitler were once ordained Roman Catholic priests. I took issue with this, and we agreed to use you as our authority.

Were any of these men ever ordained priests?

No.

The Black Rubric

A recent article on the statement by Anglican and Roman Catholic theologians concerning the Holy Eucharist referred to a problem about the Anglican "Black Rubric." What is this Black Rubric?

The Black Rubric is a name sometimes given to a sentence that appeared a long time ago in the Anglican Book of Common Prayer. It held that the practice of kneeling to receive Holy Communion indicated simply reverence and humility, not adoration of the consecrated bread and wine.

This "rubric" was included in the Book of Common Prayer in 1551 by the English Council of State (at that time under extreme anti-Roman Protestant influence) over the protest of the Anglican bishops. It seems to have been removed not too long after. Apparently the rubric was an attempt to appease some powerful Puritanical elements in the Church of England at that time.

The Black Rubric contradicts official present belief of the Anglican Church concerning the Eucharist. The joint statement to which you probably refer, and which was agreed upon by the Anglican and Roman Catholic theologians who had been assigned by their churches to study the Eucharist together, declares that this sacrament "presupposes his (Christ's) true presence, effectually signified by the bread and wine which, in this mystery, become his body and blood."

Catholic "Seers"

According to the news media, Jean Dixon, the well-known seeress, is a devout Catholic who attends daily Mass. What is the church's reaction to her prophecies?

I have no knowledge of Jean Dixon's religious practice, so I accept what you say as true.

It is my understanding that, in making her prophecies, Mrs. Dixon claims nothing except an unusually perceptive, able, and sensitive use of purely natural human powers. She is able, she says, to harness and "read" thought waves and other natural phenomena, and to put them together in such a way as to foretell some future events. According to her, no alliance or collusion with supernatural diabolical powers is involved.

This being the case, there's no reason the church should react to her activities at all, and no reason she cannot be a good, practicing Catholic.

Care of Palms

Please explain the proper usage of the palm we received on Palm Sunday. How long should it be kept, in what way, and how should it be disposed of?

Palms distributed on the Sunday before Easter remind us of Our Lord's death and resurrection and of our share in his passage from death to life. Any reverent way of keeping these palms in our homes with this kind of prayerful and devout intention is perfectly fine. Some people place them behind a crucifix; others place them with a picture that is particularly meaningful to us; others merely hang them on the wall or keep them on a desk or table.

As anything that is blessed, palms lose their blessing when they lose their identity. The proper way to dispose of a palm, therefore, is either by burning or breaking it up. The remains may then be thrown away.

When Does Lent End?

We have had some disagreements about the beginning of Lent because of so many changes in the names of the Sundays before Lent, etc. When does Lent officially start, and when does it end?

According to the revised Roman Rite calendar, Lent begins on Ash Wednesday and ends on Holy Thursday, before the Mass celebrating the institution of the Lord's Supper.

The Easter triduum (three days) begins with that Mass. The celebration of the Resurrection at the Easter Vigil ends the triduum and begins the Easter season.

Shalom

We recently received as a gift a plaque for our home with the word "shalom" on it. We've seen if often, even in church; but what does it mean?

"Shalom" is the Hebrew word for peace. At least this is the way it is usually translated, but there really is no English word that carries its rich meaning. The word basically means completeness or wholeness, a situation in which everything is there that should be there, and in proper order and balance. It could refer to an individual or a group.

Shalom is considered one of God's greatest gifts, and the word was (and still is) used commonly among Jews as a greeting or expression of good wishes. It would have been the word Jesus used at the Last Supper: "Shalom (peace) I give to you; my shalom I leave with you." Or when he greeted his apostles on the evening of the Resurrection: "Shalom — peace be with you."

Appearances of Mary at Necedah

Your explanation about private revelations and our attitude toward them was helpful. We get confused by so many conflicting reports on different shrines and apparitions.

Can you tell us about the reported appearances of the Blessed Virgin at Necedah, Wisconsin? Does the church still refuse to approve the visions there?

The story of Necedah and the series of rejections of church authority by Mrs. Mary Van Hoof (who claims that the Blessed Virgin Mary appeared to her in 1950) is unfortunate and sad.

Within five years after the alleged appearances of Mary, officials of the LaCrosse, Wisconsin, diocese investigated the situation and concluded that the visions and revelations were without supernatural basis and were false. In 1969 the bishop of that diocese reached the same conclusion after another investigation. In 1975 he was forced to place leaders of the shrine under personal interdict, which means that they could not receive the sacraments.

In the spring of 1979, the Necedah group seems to have made its final break with the church by inviting someone who claimed to be the "Archbishop and Metropolitan of North America, American National Catholic Church, Roman Catholic Ultrajectine" to bless and consecrate the shrine. The alleged archbishop then left a "priest" at the shrine to care for the pilgrims who might come.

According to the bishop of LaCrosse, this action on the part of the promoters of Necedah "definitely establishes that they are no longer affiliated with the Roman Catholic Church, and acknowledge this separation by this action of approving the celebration of the holy sacrifice of the Mass by an unauthorized person."

Devil Worship

Is it possible for someone to be possessed by the devil? Is there a rite of exorcism performed by the priest in such a case? What about the so-called Black Masses? Have they actually been said, or is it a horrible creation by a fiction writer?

The Black Mass is no fiction. For centuries up to and including the present time, a central liturgical ceremony of many Satanists, or devil worshipers, has been a parody of the Sacrifice of the Mass. Often an attempt is made to obtain and desecrate a consecrated Host from a true Mass in these sacrilegious services.

The question about possession is harder to answer. The belief in angels and demons ("fallen angels") is consistent in Christianity since the time of Christ, and existed before that in the Old Testament. The exact nature of these beings, however, is uncertain; there is very little in official church doctrine about them, though it is common teaching that they are intelligent personal beings.

Partly because of this need for much more theological study about the good and bad angels, many problems remain unanswered about diabolic possession — that is, the physical control of a human being's body by a devil or demon. One thing is certainly true: With the advancement of knowledge about psychological and nervous disorders, many strange happenings once attributed to diabolical possession are known to have other possible, very natural, explanations. In addition, our present awareness of the genuine possibility of mental telepathy (transfer of thoughts from one mind to another) and even telekinesis (mental transfer of physical energy) makes the detection of true possession very difficult.

The rite of exorcism is a series of prayers, blessings and commands used by a priest or bishop to drive out the evil spirit in a case of posses-, sion. This official ceremony is rarely used today, and may be performed only with the permission of the bishop. An effective exorcism is considered by some theologians as perhaps the only absolute proof of true diabolic possession.

Diabolical Obsession

A review of the book, "The Exorcist," mentioned diabolical obsession. Is it the same thing as possession?

No. Possession means control, or near control of a person's body, as it were, from the inside by an evil spirit.

Obsession is the term traditionally used for a phenomenon experienced by many persons through the centuries. The individual is violently molested physically in circumstances that seem to point to evil spirits as the cause. It is, therefore, more of an external than an internal influence, but it is far more than a "temptation" in the ordinary sense of the word.

The Church's Stand on Astrology

Could you clarify the stand of the Catholic Church on belief in and use of astrology? Many of us have become confused about our church's position on it lately.

On this whole subject of astrology, it is helpful to keep a few facts in mind. From ancient times until only about 200 years ago, the study of the influence of stars and planets on human activity was considered a genuine, legitimate science. Many great names in physics and astronomy, like Copernicus and Galileo, believed in it, taught it, and practiced it by casting horoscopes.

Most political and religious leaders, including some popes, governed much of their activity by horoscopes. Pope Julius II set the day of his coronation according to the advice of the astrologers.

All this was possible, of course, because of the simple, very limited knowledge of the heavens. As the science of astronomy developed in modern times — particulary after the invention of the telescope — the discovery of thousands of new planets, stars and other materials in space caused the total collapse of astrology as a true science. The entire supposed "system" fell apart.

During this time, the church officially opposed astrology because of two dangers. If the stars governed all mankind's actions, free will would be meaningless. Also, some claimed that the power of Satan and other evil spirits was behind this heavenly influence and that astrology was therefore the devil's way of infiltrating human life.

These concerns remain at the base of whatever reservations the church has about astrology, and of its warning that it can involve sinful superstition.

In spite of the array of inconsistencies and contradictions contained in astrology, lots of people are getting rich because it still fascinates millions. Maybe they're only curious. Or maybe they're just anxious to discover somewhere "out there" the cause of their problems.

Skull Under Crucifix

Recently we were digging under our new home and discovered a crucifix. The image of Christ is on it, but under this image is a skull and crossbones. The cross looks like it may have come from a rosary; it looks very old.

Do you know anything about this kind of cross?

I'd have no way of knowing how ancient or how valuable your crucifix is.

The design of the cross is, however, not unusual. Particularly in the past, it was not uncommon to place a skull and crossbones, the symbol of death, at the bottom of crucifixes.

The explanation for this symbol seems to be twofold. First, it is a sign of the victory of Jesus over death by his own death and resurrection.

Another explanation results from the tradition, still prevalent in the Middle East, that the cross of Jesus was placed over the burial place of Adam. Thus, the crucifix with the skull and crossbones would echo the remark of St. Paul that, as through the first Adam death entered the world, life comes through the second Adam, Christ.

The Anchor as Symbol

I am a convert and still unfamiliar with many things in the Catholic Church. In three places in our church there is a picture of an anchor. On one of them, in a window, is the letter E. I've seen this in other places as well. Can you explain?

Almost as far back as we go in human history, the anchor (used, of course, by sailors apparently since they began sailing the waters) has been a symbol — a sign — of security and hope. There is evidence that the Jews, even though they were not a seafaring people, also used this symbol even before the time of Christ.

Understandably, the Christian people picked up this sign very early, expressing their own hope and symbolizing the security their faith brings in the ordinary difficulties and trials of life, as well as in special times of persecution. Often the anchor is joined with the fish, the symbol of Christ (and of Christians). This joint symbol expresses, of course, the belief that our faith and hope, our anchor, is ultimately Jesus himself.

The author of the letter to the Hebrews (6:19) uses this symbol explicitly, noting that our hope in Jesus Christ and in his high priesthood are "like a sure and firm anchor."

The letter E which often accompanies the anchor is probably an abbreviation for "elpis," the Greek word for hope.

Eliminate Religion from TV and Radio?

One of our local Catholic organizations has begged us recently to write to the Federal Communications Commission (FCC) asking them not to eliminate religion, Bible reading and prayer from television and radio broadcasting. The request stated that Madalyn Murray O'Hair, who led the successful fight to eliminate prayer from public schools, had gathered thousands of signatures petitioning the FCC to forbid all religious broadcasts.

An article in our local paper a few days later said that there was no such petition by Mrs. O'Hair and that we should forget the whole thing.

Who is right? I would hate to sit and do nothing if my help should be needed.

No one seems to know where the rumor got started. At the present time there is no such petition before the FCC by Mrs. O'Hair or anyone else.

Blessing After Childbirth

What has happened to the "Churching of Women" ceremony? Years ago in my parish, it was given often during the year, but no parish that I know of does it now. Is it still given anywhere?

Part of your answer lies in the history of the ceremony. The Churching of Women, or the Blessing after Childbirth, apparently entered Christian practice as a carryover from the Jewish ceremony of purification. Under Jewish law, a number of actions incurred a certain spiritual contamination or uncleanness. Among these were any actions involving sexual functions, legal or illegal. A woman was unclean after childbirth, for example, seven days if the child were a boy, and 14 days if the child were a girl. (See Leviticus, chapter 12) This uncleanness was formally removed by an appropriate rite of purification. (The purification of Mary after the birth of Jesus is still celebrated by the church as part of the Feast of the Presentation on Feb. 2.)

In its Christian form, the ceremony took more the theme of thanksgiving to God for the safe birth of the child and petition for God's blessings on the mother and child.

One reason the blessing after childbirth is not more widespread among Christians is that many of its features, prayers and blessings are already implied or included in the rite of baptism. The newly revised baptismal rite contains numerous references to the parents, and to what is in their hearts and prayers concerning their new child.

Shroud of Turin

We have seen many references recently to the sacred shroud of Turin. But I've seen no mention of any official church position about it. What does the church say about this relic?

The shroud of Turin is a piece of linen cloth about 14 feet long that reveals the imprint of a human body. Nothing was known of it until the seventh century when the claim was made that it is, in fact, the shroud in which Jesus was wrapped at his burial.

Scientific investigation in this century reveals some intriguing characteristics of the shroud, indicating that it may well be the shroud of Christ. But conclusive proof of that will likely never be possible.

The church has no official position on the subject. There's no reason it should have. The findings, whatever they are, couldn't affect Catholic belief one way or the other.

Woman Makes Her Uncomfortable

I know two people who were Catholics (though they never really practiced their faith), and who changed to a Pentecostal religion. They feel that since they switched, they have become better persons and "got the Lord."

Maybe they are better, but every chance they have they criticize the Catholic Church. One of the women works with me. At first she tried to get me into the Pentecostal bit, but she couldn't. That's made her a little frustrated, I guess, because now she picks on me at work every occasion she has. How do you explain that?

Who can read someone else's heart? Apparently they have found something that satisfies them more than their Catholic faith, which, according to your comments, they never knew too well anyway.

Your concern is more with their present actions, and I must acknowledge that this kind of reaction on the part of those who leave the church leaves me uneasy. On purely psychological grounds, I'm always suspicious of the balance, and even the sincerity, of people's change when they feel they must continually criticize what they decided to leave.

If they were truly comfortable and at peace in their new-found situation, they wouldn't need to continually defend themselves by describing the horrors and evils of their former church and friends.

Her excessive frustration at not being able to change you to her position may be another sign of her insecurity. Her reaction seems to indicate that she needs your conversion to strengthen her own, and to allay any guilt she may feel. This isn't uncommon when people have made uncomfortable religious or moral decisions.

Someone attempting to use us this way always makes us uncomfortable, and even feel a little guilty, which is precisely what the other person is, perhaps unconsciously, aiming at. She has to work out those difficulties herself. So just be yourself, respond to her out of your own convictions, and don't let her turn her problem into your problem.

Are Bishops Divine?

My husband says that when bishops are consecrated that they take on divinity which makes their opinions and decisions the same as those of Christ. Is this true? He says even when bishops are wrong in their decisions according to people, they are still right in God's eyes. Do bishops believe this?

No, Virginia, bishops do not become divine. In fact, God himself is likely happier than anyone that he is not a bishop. He probably couldn't take the hassle.

An Old Altar A Bar?

My husband purchased an old altar from a parish church some time ago. Now he wants to turn it into a bar and the idea upsets me. Isn't that a sacrilege? We're not even supposed to throw away a cruficix or holy pictures. An altar is much more sacred.

An altar should never be put to common use like this. The importance of recognizing the special nature of blessed or consecrated things increases with the closeness they have to the Mass and the Eucharist. Your husband would, I'm sure, agree that it's wrong to take chalices and start using them for beer mugs!

So what to do? When anything is taken apart, melted, or otherwise radically changed, it is no longer considered blessed. Thus, while it would be wrong to use an altar for a bar, it would be perfectly all right to use the materials from an altar for something else, including a bar —

as long as common sense is used and any possible scandal or misunderstanding is avoided. After all, it is the altar that is blessed, not the wood and nails.

The same applies to other blessed items you mention. Unless you own a warehouse, there's a limit to how many blessed candles, cruficixes, statues, rosaries and holy pictures one can accumulate over the years. When they no longer have a use, it is entirely proper to break or tear them so that they lose their identity as a candle or picture, and then discard them. Their purpose is to increase our faith and assist our spirit of prayer and devotion. When they have served that purpose and become worn out or are to be replaced, there is no irreverence in disposing of them appropriately.

"You've Lost Your Soul?"

A very religious friend of mine recently said to me, "You have lost your soul." How does anyone know this? And how do I respond to this sort of statement?

No matter how we have spent our lives, the final bell isn't rung until the moment of our death. Until that time, it is theoretically possible for someone to foul up his or her life very drastically, or, on the other hand, to return to God after some awfully bad falls.

While it is possible for us to say in many instances what is right and wrong, no one has an inside view of another person's soul. Only God, and possibly the individual himself, knows all the weaknesses, fears, pressures, and even ignorance that might considerably lessen the moral evil of what is, in itself, a malice of enormous proportion.

This is why Jesus warns us repeatedly against presuming to judge the state of another person's conscience.

Maybe the best answer to someone who speaks this way is simply, "I'm glad God is my final judge, and not you."

Who Was "Bloody Mary?"

Who is the Catholic queen that the "Bloody Mary" is supposed to be named after? At least this was what I was told a few nights ago by some drinking buddies.

You're thinking of Queen Mary of England, who ruled from 1553 to 1558. Twenty years before she took the throne, her father, King Henry VIII, formally rejected the Catholic faith and took most of the country with him.

When she became queen, Mary tried to reverse the process and as part of her severe program several hundred "heretics" were burned at the stake, most of them peasants. Burning heretics was a popular idea in those days with both Catholic and Protestant governments. History has often referred to this queen as "Bloody Mary," even though her primary mistake in the eyes of most of her countrymen was simply that she burned the wrong people.

The name was given to the modern drink, of course, because of its color, and because of the fact that too much tomato juice can cloud one's mind — as is evident from the kind of discussion you and your drinking buddies get into.

River Brethren and Dunkers

We found a reference recently to a group of Protestant denominations which included the "River Brethren" and the "Dunkers." Are there really churches with these names? If so, why do they have such strange titles?

Both sects you mention were among numerous Mennonite and other Swiss or German groups who settled around Lancaster County in Pennsylvania about 250 years ago. Though primarily of European Baptist or Lutheran background, many of the sects became known almost officially by plain, simple names which distinguished them in some way from the rest.

The Dunkers (German Baptist Brethren) were so named because of their method of baptizing. The present Church of the Brethren is descended from this tradition.

One sizeable group of these early settlers were called the United Brethren. Several of their members broke off and began meeting along the Susquehanna River in Lancaster County, thus becoming known as "the brotherhood down by the river" — or River Brethren.

The River Brethren continued as a loosely connected group of churches until the Civil War, when they changed their name to Brethren in Christ. This is still their official title.

INDEX

on church-Bible link, 2
on family limitation, 221
on Latin liturgy, 85
on purposes of marriage, 220
Venial sin, 118
Viaticum, 131
Vows, marriage, 179

Washing of Feet, 331
Women,
    Anglican ordination of, 281
    counsellors, 240

liturgical ministry by, 57, 61, 88,
    93, 241
ordination after sex change, 242
ordination of, 261
priesthood of Mary? 260
World, end of, 14
World Council of Churches, Catholic membership in, 282
Worry, 325

YMCA
    Catholic membership in, 297